Sacred Play

Soul-journeys
in Contemporary Irish Theatre

Sacred Play

Soul-journeys in Contemporary Irish Theatre

Anne F. O'Reilly

Carysfort Press

A Carysfort Press Book

Sacred Play: Soul-journeys in Contemporary Irish Theatre

Anne F. O'Reilly

First published in Ireland in 2004 as a paperback original by Carysfort Press, 58 Woodfield, Scholarstown Road, Dublin 16, Ireland

© 2004 Copyright remains with the author
Typeset by Carysfort Press
Cover design by Alan Bennis
Printed and bound by eprint Limited
35 Coolmine Industrial Estate, Blanchardstown,
Dublin 15, Ireland

Published with the support of the Research Committee, St. Patrick's College, Drumcondra, and by a grant from the the Arts Council.

To my soul mate, Deirdre
and to my children Sinéad and Brian
who have taught me how to play again.

Table of Contents

Acknowledgements

This book has grown out of my teaching and research over the past thirty years. My interpretive framework has developed from a dialogue with theology, feminist theory and the Irish dramatic tradition. A number of Irish academic environments have nurtured and sustained my own intellectual journey: The Religious Studies faculty at the Mater Dei Institute Dublin; the Theology faculty of St. Patrick's College Maynooth; the Drama Studies faculty of University College Dublin and the Department of English at NUI Galway. I am grateful to all my teachers from these different disciplines, in particular Dr. Eamonn Jordan, who supervised my studies and who saw the possibility of this book long before I did.

I acknowledge the support of friends and colleagues who have read parts of the book in earlier formats. Many conversations have facilitated the development and clarification of my ideas. Gratitude must also go to the Religious Studies Department at St. Patrick's College, Drumcondra, Dublin, who have always supported and enabled my continuing studies.

Behind the book is another journey that has brought me into dialogue with Western and Eastern mysticism, psychotherapy, and many contemporary innovative approaches to the relationship between body and spirit. The work of Dr. Ruth Doherty, (*Annwn Institute*) and Chloe Goodchild (*The Naked Voice*) deserve special mention. My ongoing soul-journey work with Kevin Harnett has been an invaluable source of insight and wisdom.

I am very grateful to all my students both past and present, with whom I have shared many of the ideas in this book. I thank my students in St. Mary's Holy Faith Secondary School (Glasnevin, Dublin), the women from the Creative Writing classes at The Shanty Educational Project (West Tallaght, Dublin), the children and teenagers in Ireland's Centre for Talented Youth (DCU Dublin), and most especially my Religious Studies students in St Patrick's College, who provide me with ongoing opportunities for dialogue, reflection, creativity and play.

Finally, to close friends and family, who have tolerated my absence, tiredness, and preoccupation over the past few years – thanks for your patience and practical support. You kept me grounded. *Anne O'Reilly*

The virtue of play ... is when we do not take ourselves, or our world, or our God, literally. When we learn the humility and humour of participating in a game without emperors. Like a child playing in the sand by the edge of the sea. Not idle play. Sacred play upon which the future of our world reposes.

Richard Kearney

Introduction | Sacred Play

At first there is nothing. Nothing but the empty space. The womb that begets all life – the space of nothingness and possibility, emptiness and potential form. The trajectory of the human journey is from the source into life and back again to the source – from nothingness to separateness and back to nothingness. It is also the trajectory of creativity, of each work of art, of each participation in the play of images.

In the empty space of theatre audiences are invited to participate not simply in the performance of a particular play, but in the play of creation itself. Audiences are invited to recognize that the possibility of anything at all underlies all our attempts to create, to make, shape and invent new worlds. If theatre is one of the sacred spaces wherein we can ritually recreate the world, it can only function as such because it is part of a greater creative energy that underpins and enables everything. Martin Boroson, founder of the *Temenos*[1] project in Ireland (which seeks to bring together the fields of ritual, theatre, creativity and play) talks of theatre as 'a structure or set of rules that facilitate play' (2002:66). Boroson

---

[1] Throughout this work I use this term in ways that are similar to Boroson's threefold use of the term. In ancient Greece the *temenos* denoted the most sacred part of the temple; in medieval alchemy it denoted a vessel which was strong enough to contain a powerful transformation of elements; and Jung used the term to refer to the relationship between therapist and patient, which must be strong and safe enough to allow transformation.

develops his understanding of theatre from Hindu philosophy where creation is understood to have come about because of God's desire to play (*lila*). As Boroson puts it:

> In this view of creation, the universe is an enormous play that is conceived, written, directed, produced and designed by God. It is God in the audience, God working the lights, and God playing every role. The point of this play is to make something so convincingly tangible that it actually appears to be not-God. (66)

Boroson's interest in theatre led to his search to 'find a way to make modern theatre a *temenos* – a strong and sacred container in which people can experience the deepest kinds of play, the play of gods. Play can be fun, of course, but it can also be transcendent. Sometimes, it can be both'. (66)

We may ask who in fact is playing? Behind and beneath all our playing may lie the play of the divine. Our lives may be premised on forgetting or the source may be obscured. The illusion of separation prevents the realization that underneath the many manifestations of forms we are all connected. We breathe the same breath. The mystics east and west always had access to this kind of unified experience of existence. Kilroy's Matt Talbot tries to talk about such an experience:

> There be nuthin' to see when Gawd comes 'cause there's nuthin' other than yerself 'cause yerself is wan with whah ya see so ya see nuthin' 'cause ya can only see what's separate than yerself, ya can only count what's different, not the same, not the wan, the only. (Kilroy: 1997:58)

When he wrote of the empty space of theatre the renowned theatre director Peter Brook had in mind the theatre of the invisible made visible. Theatrical playing can open to moments of epiphany, where the source comes through, and transfigures the ordinary, making it holy. Theatre as sacred play invites a new imagining of the divine human relationship. The human impulse towards transformative play is itself a participation in the play of the divine.

The Clearing or the ritual space of theatre, also invites audiences to play, dance, sing and cry their way towards a new imagining. The theatrical space nurtures a passion for the possible and invites us to have faith in the imagination. In Toni Morrison's novel *Beloved* we encounter the matriarchal lay preacher Baby Suggs, who 'opened her great heart to those who could use it' (1987:87). Regularly she would retire to the Clearing in the forest and lead her people in a healing ritual. She would invite the children, the men and their wives to laugh and dance and weep together before she would share her great embodied wisdom with them. 'She told them that the only grace they could have was the grace they could imagine.' (1987:88) Theatre too can become a place of embodied wisdom.

In the empty space of theatre the body performs, the body watches and the present opens to the eternal. In the now of theatre, in the space of play, the empty space becomes the container for transformation. Just as the body of the person is the container for all that the person is and may become, the space of theatre as concrete physical space, is one of the cultural containers for being and becoming. It too is a container for energies that are both human and divine, a space within which body and spirit can find a home.

Theatre as *temenos*

Theatre as container shares a function like that of the sacred container within traditional alchemy, the crucible within which the raw materials of the alchemists were refined, distilled and transmuted into gold. These women and men shared roles that encompassed magic, mystery, conjuring and philosophy. While allegedly engaged in the transmutation of base metals into gold they were in fact more often philosophers of the human spirit, and the alchemical vessel became a symbol for their own spiritual transformation. Their search for the philosopher's stone often indicated the extent of their own soul journeys as they purified, and distilled the essence from the raw material of their lives. Jung's work in the study and interpretation of traditional alchemical texts led to his interpretation of the alchemical wedding as a metaphor for the integration of different energies within the human psyche. Theatre can work in a similar way as such a sacred container for transformation. Within culture it can become a place that holds the different energies that seek integration. Like the individual human journey these energies whether male or female, conscious or shadow, need to be brought to awareness and integrated in order for wholeness to occur at a cultural level.

One of the central images within the Celtic tradition is 'the cauldron, the vessel of heat, plenty and inspiration' (Matthews, 2001:222). The cauldron was also a central image in the poetic schools, and symbolized sources of inspiration and creativity. In fact in the early Celtic creation stories the cauldron was the source from which all life came, in a manner reminiscent of a cosmic womb. Within the poetic tradition it was believed that within the body there were three cauldrons. The first cauldron was located in the belly and was the vessel of physical health and vitality, the second was located within the heart or solar plexus area and was the vessel of psychic health, the third was located in the head and was the vessel of spiritual health. This model of the interrelation of body, mind and spirit provides a useful way to understand the flow of physical, artistic and spiritual energy. 'The trinity of soul, heart and mind are strong in harmony, yet they can be shattered if not in union. Doubt, distrust and neglected observances are the pathways to madness, heartsickness and soul fragmentation' (302). Soul loss or fragmentation which can be caused by illness, assault or shock manifests itself in 'vitality depletion, mental disorientation and dispiritedness' (304).

Irish theatre can become a similar cauldron for transformation, where the alchemy of spirit can continue. Like the tradition in the great Bardic schools, the theatre can also function as a house of memory and place of dreaming incubation, where new visions are forged. Theatre as container also shares many of the features associated with healing and transformation that we find in the ancient Greek tradition of Asklepios. In contrast to the Hippocratic tradition this model of healing was more holistic, open to the unconscious, and took place in the sacred precincts of the temple. Dreams were integral to this healing, and the person in search of healing spent much time in the dark waiting for a dream that the temple priests could interpret, and which might lead to healing, or transformation in their life's direction. In a similar way theatre can be a place of dreaming, where the audience comes in search of healing and transformation.

Theatre as alternative sacred space

While the traditional sacred space provided by Christian worship has been abandoned by many, others are seeking new ways to access the mystery. Theatre for many playwrights has become an alternative sacred space. The empty space of theatre can function as a rough or holy space. It can enable access to the mystery, it can allow an otherness to emerge. In the fluid shape-shifting space of theatre one can play with what is not yet. One can discover what may be. It is this sense of theatre as the space of possibility that allows identification of theatre as an alternative sacred space.

Where theatre creates the kind of sacred space traditionally reserved for religious ritual it can create a sense of community and enable access to transformation and vision. The ritual aspects of theatre have long been noted from its earliest associations with the Mystery Religions, the medieval attention to the celebration of the Mystery Plays and the contemporary need to access mystery. The participation of the audience can be understood and assessed in different ways. Theatre can be interpreted as an alternative sacred space for the performance of identity.

In this study I am interested in a poetic theatre that functions in a way that is similar to ritual. In the space of theatre an audience finds itself in a space of heightened awareness. A readiness for what is about to transpire is a prerequisite of all ritual. The play as a poetic text can offer images and symbols to the imagination, that can be transforming. When one leaves the theatre it is the image that one carries that has the most effect. Theatrical texts can offer ways of seeing and hearing our cultural story that is healing. Each of the plays in this study has a story to tell, but also forms part of the cultural narrative that is our inheritance as Irish people whether at home or abroad. When the stories are told, the place of memory is important. So too is the journey that the characters undergo in the course of the play. When the playwright does not resist the journey into the dark (whether personal or cultural) the wound can be uncovered and brought to consciousness and language. But there is also the pull of the future. The impulse of drama is towards the future. It is what is possible when the story is told. Where drama forgets its connections with play, the world of *as if*, it remains in the past, determined by the wound, and unable to heal. The truly liberating space is that of play, which can turn the world upside down, and enable a new imagining.

Interpretive Lenses

My approach throughout this work is essentially a hermeneutical one. Hermeneutics allows access to a variety of interpretive lenses, and also draws attention to the cultural lenses and biases that shade and colour all interpretations. Cultural narratives, whether great religious narratives or poetic or theatrical texts, offer horizons of understanding. When an individual life-story comes in contact with these narratives they bring their own life experience into dialogue with them. Understanding occurs where there is a fusion of horizons as the world of the individual is interpreted by the wider horizon of the cultural narrative, and he or she in turn interprets what is received. Texts can disclose possible worlds and possible ways of orienting oneself within them.

The feminist hermeneutic which underpins this work is a dialogue between contemporary philosophy, theology and literary theory. It is inspired mainly by the work of European feminists, using both primary and secondary sources. Contemporary feminist philosophies draw attention to the place of women, language and subjectivity within the cultural symbolic. Many feminist cultural and literary theorists draw attention to the gender ideologies operative within culture and offer different lenses of interpretation that are more interrogative, and that look for the gaps in the text, rather than presuming a seamless narrative of interpretation. Feminist theological sources include both European and American theorists and provide corrective lenses to much patriarchal theology in their attention to critique, retrieval and re-visioning of sources.

As part of this new imagining feminist thought draws attention to the lost history of women. As attempts are made to allow women's experience to surface and be named, narratives are emerging that are genuinely interruptive of the dominant narratives as women refuse the roles ascribed to them in traditional patriarchal discourse, whether these roles have been literal or symbolic. The refusal to be named and represented solely from the perspective of the dominant cultural narratives has led many women to explore ways of writing the female body, and inscribing it in new cultural narratives and forms. The refusal to be defined simply as other to the dominant narratives, and to have all kinds of meaning written on the female body, to be a symbol rather than real, has led many women to espouse a philosophy that stresses particularity, sexuality and the body in contrast to the great universalizing narratives that excluded the reality of women's bodies and women's lives.

The predominance of an almost exclusively male canon in Irish Drama made it all the more important to be explicit in identifying the feminist theoretical framework that underpins this work. A feminist methodology in dialogue with a contemporary understanding of soul and spirit provides a very specific set of lenses for interpreting Irish drama. Choosing this vantage point necessarily means excluding others. This exclusion does not however deny the value and significance of other contributions. In fact awareness of and dialogue with other interpretive horizons is part of my methodology.

Throughout this study I argue for an interpretation that pays attention to the religious or spiritual dimension of human experience. I believe that an openness to this dimension offers a fuller understanding of the human journey, in terms of proposing horizons of possibility within which one can imagine and interpret one's becoming.

Many contemporary approaches to spirituality (in particular feminist and ecological approaches) are interested in stressing its relational aspects. The relational model of the person defines the person in relation to self, others, the cosmos and the sacred. An interconnected and interrelated self seeking integration both inside and outside pushes the parameters of spirituality beyond the confines of traditional religion. It ceases to be narrowly individualistic and is critical of traditional aspirations towards perfection that were dualistic and so other-worldly centred as to be no earthly good. Contemporary approaches to understanding the religious dimension of human experience are aware of the dialogue that must take place between religion and culture.

Increasingly people are looking for spirituality both within and beyond the confines of traditional religions. The search can take many forms, from personal narrative and therapeutic journeys through a retrieval of ancient ways of relating to the world of spirit. For many, a journey that started within a particular religious tradition continues to be enriched by this dialogue. For others the search takes them to new places, with a very different relationship to their religion of origin. Stephen Costello's recent publication (2001) of a series of interviews on the Irish soul presents a very complex picture of what constitutes the Irish soul, and takes us from social action and reflection through philosophy, psychology and the contemplative life. The contemporary interest in rediscovering the roots of a Celtic spirituality (consider the success of John O'Donohue's *Anam Chara*) is further evidence of a similar search to reconnect with something lost and to discover a vital spirituality, that is more in touch with the seasons, cycles and rhythms of nature. The recent publication of *Celtic Threads* (Clancy, 1999) and *Irish Spirit* (Monaghan, 2001) give further evidence of the search for a spirituality that is more earth and body centred, that combines an active and a contemplative dimension and that is more capable of sustaining a new imagining for the present and the future.

Soul-journeys

It is my understanding that Irish theatre addresses a loss of soul. Over the past thirty years many Irish dramatists have attempted to reconnect with, to retrieve or to rediscover soul. My working understanding of soul is influenced by Christian and Buddhist sources, humanistic integrative psychology, and the dialogue between East and West found in contemporary approaches to the relationship between mind, body and spirit. Throughout this study I consider soul as the impulse towards the embodiment of spirit. Where spirit soars, soul descends. If the impulse of spirit is towards flight and being uncontained, the impulse of soul is towards the earth and the body (Moore, 2002:86-87). Where spirit aspires towards light, soul grapples with the dark. If spirit transcends, soul remains rooted to earth, in the messy place of birth and embodiment. Where spirit seeks non-engagement and the ultimate liberation in death, soul calls us back towards life and to the daily realities of relationship, love and commitment. 'Classically, the understanding of life, the unfolding of identity and creativity, the notion of growth and discovery were articulated through the metaphor of journey' (O'Donohue, 2003:25). Whether we recall Virgil's *Aeneid*, Homer's *Odyssey* or Dante's *Divine Comedy* the 'journey is the drama of the heart's voyage into the tide of possibilities which open before it' (25). The theme of journey runs through this book, whether that journey is the hero journey, the vision quest, the shamanic journey or the mystical journey towards illumination and enlightenment. The traditional pattern in the great hero journeys or quest narratives always involves a separation from the world, a penetration to some source of power and a life-enhancing return. But while the 'passage of the mythological hero may be overground,' 'fundamentally it is inward – into depths where obscure resistances are overcome, and long lost forgotten powers are revivified, to be made available for the transfiguration of the world' (Campbell, 1993:29). Many of the plays selected for this study deal with quests that involve crossings and thresholds, that move between worlds, and search for a language that narrates the divided and split self, that sense a hidden presence, and an emptiness which can become a source for transformation and vision (Gilsenan Nordin: 2001). Each play selected exhibits aspects of the journey theme, some achieving more complete resolution than others. In this study I offer an interdisciplinary interpretation of journey that takes inspiration from anthropological, psychological, shamanistic and mystical sources.

When we come to consider how the soul journeys towards the Self, towards deeper or higher levels of integration it is important to be aware of the relation between body and spirit. The aspiration to bring the body to consciousness and spirit must be matched by a corresponding journey which brings spirit into the body. This journey towards embodiment has often been neglected in favour of the move towards spirit. However it is vital that one completes the journey. In the great quest narratives the hero/heroine faced all kinds of challenges both on the journey out into the world and on the journey back home. Bringing home the treasure is the task of the hero. Similarly the shamanic quest required that the shaman journey to an *illud tempus*, to find what was needed and to bring it back for the healing of the individual and the community.

While some playwrights might feel a certain resistance to having their plays labelled 'spiritual' or interpreted as 'soul journeys', I would hope that my working definitions of spirit and soul would be seen as sufficiently expansive to allow their inclusion in my study. As my reflections on the nature of soul and the journey of spirit towards embodiment have led me into dialogue with both classical religious and contemporary sources, I feel that the plays I have included are genuine narratives of soul-journeys and each has earned its place.

Thematic Overview of Chapters

One of the difficulties of working thematically is that of delineating boundaries. My study of soul journeys in contemporary Irish drama includes twenty-eight plays by fifteen playwrights and spans almost three decades. Plays were selected that reflected different aspects of the soul-journey, whether that was the journey through memory, and ritual, or the journey into the dark, or journeys of transformation and vision. While many plays exhibit aspects of each of these themes, it was necessary to group them in order to study and interpret them. Plays were grouped according to their major focus. Some plays were much more obviously dealing with memory, others with ritual, others with the dark, transformation etc. And yet memory plays also had ritual moments, grappled with the dark and offered moments of epiphany, or plays dealing with vision also dealt with grief, ritual, and transformation. Hence the theoretical focus that I develop in each chapter has significance for each of the other chapters. Each of the lenses can be superimposed on the other to enhance the reading or reception of a particular play.

Chapter One explores soul journeys through the lens of memory and storytelling. The memories which surface are painful and dissociated arising out of trauma, fragmentation and a wounding that is the legacy of an exclusively patriarchal imagining and ordering of history. The six plays selected journey into the labyrinth of Irish cultural memory and find themselves facing the way culture has dealt with its own strangeness and otherness.

Through an exploration of three plays by men and three plays by women a patchwork of memory emerges which draws attention to the place of the body in Irish identity (and in wider culture when we consider *La Corbière*), and to how woman has been the site for projections of the male unconscious. As traumatic memory moves towards narrative memory these plays map a significant part in the Irish soul's journey towards wholeness as their stories become integrated into the culture's consciousness.

The journey through memory also features in many other plays in this study. Later chapters depict soul journeys which also reconnect with lost parts of the Irish soul but they reflect higher levels of integration and resolution. Traumatic memory continues to haunt and wound the characters in many of the selected plays and brings to awareness years of repressed grief and suffering that have inhibited the characters from returning home to themselves. Marina Carr's protagonists find themselves trapped in spaces where memory obsesses (*Portia Coughlan*), is fragmented (*By the Bog of Cats*), determined by fate (*Ariel*), or doomed to endless repetition (*The Mai, On Raftery's Hill*). But memory seeks instances of restoration through ritual and storytelling (note the plays in Chapter Two), or through a descent into the dark that enables different levels of integration, transformation and vision (Chapters Four and Five).

From his study of ritual patterns the anthropologist Victor Turner has developed the concept of the liminal or threshold space. In liminal space people inhabit an in-between state, they are neither here nor there and there is a certain fluidity and ambiguity around identity, whether personal, sexual or cultural. The language of the liminal space is that of symbol, myth and ritual. Another important feature that Turner identifies relates to the sense of community and solidarity that develops among people who share this liminal space. He gives the Latin term *Communitas* to this state, and sees it as essentially juxtaposed with the more structural understanding of society (Turner, 1995:96).

Pilgrimage which is part of many religious traditions is a physical manifestation of the centrality of the metaphor of journey to life. In pilgrimage the pilgrims also experience themselves in liminal spaces where the normal boundaries that separate people

are not as significant as they are in ordinary day to day life. As
Turner has identified, the stripping away of distinctions of rank,
wealth, clothing etc. can facilitate the experience of *communitas*.
Religious traditions have always used ritual to enable access to
journey and transformation, through connecting one's story with
the larger mythic story of a tradition. In the plays in the second
chapter the characters find that they need one another, that this
need is often only highlighted when they find themselves in liminal
spaces. And where they experience breakthrough moments of
transformation they find themselves searching for symbols, myths
and rituals that will enable them to really mark or own what has
taken place. Chapter Two, which pays particular attention to ritual
as part of the human or soul journey, finds characters in
borderland or liminal spaces, whether that space is the
womb/tomb space of the church in *The Sanctuary Lamp* and
Misogynist, or the space of prison in *Cell* and *Someone Who'll Watch
Over Me*, or shared pilgrimage in *Wonderful Tennessee*.

But this desire to find appropriate rituals is also a feature of
many other plays in this study: McGuinness's Baglady's ritual cairn
of objects associated with her defilement; Mommo's mythic
narrative in Murphy's *Bailegangaire*; the Mundy sisters' desperate,
defiant dance in Friel's *Dancing at Lughnasa*, Christina Reid's
women's rituals of *Tea in a China Cup*, Le Marquand Hartigan's
ritualizing of the drowned women in *La Corbière*; the rituals of play
itself in Burke Brogan's *Eclipsed* and in much of McGuinness's
work. The ritual reversals of McGuinness's *Innocence* and the
ritualizing of grief in McGuinness's *Carthaginians* occur alongside
rituals of play which have the effect of turning the world upside
down or inside out. Caravaggio's role as a Holy Fool who leads a
Carnival of the Animals in *Innocence*, or Dido's interruptive status
(as homosexual female playwright in *Carthaginians*) question all
symbol systems and their power over human beings.

Every human journey must enter the dark. All the traditional
journey narratives represent the dark in different ways: Orpheus or
Demeter's underworld, Aeneas's hell, Dante's dark forest, John of
the Cross's dark night of the Soul, the Shadow for Carl Jung. The
journey whether for the hero or the soul journeyer today always
involves a descent into the darkness of the self, where the way

seems totally lost, where one faces one's deepest fears. The journey towards wholeness involves entering the world of one's own vulnerability. The threshold space of vulnerability is a liminal space in which anything can happen. This space has been described as the zero point, the edge of oneself, the perimeter of one's being. This point of self-emptying is the zero point of humanity, and represents the very last skin between the human and the abyss of nothingness beyond which is the absolute otherness of the divine (Hederman, 2000:102-103). All the great mystics knew the darkness. In the Western tradition the mystical journey includes the stages of awakening, purification and illumination. On this journey one may pass through an agonizing dark night of the soul, 'going down to hell alive' as John of the Cross has described it.

How one negotiates this territory of the dark is also a concern of many of the plays in this study. Chapter Three represents how one contemporary female writer, namely Marina Carr, attempts to move in this territory. The liminal spaces of Carr's plays are invitations into the dark. They represent the crisis of soul loss, characteristic of a people who have lost their connections to origins. The depth and scope of Carr's imagination demanded to be treated on its own and allowed an opportunity to dialogue with contemporary feminist philosophers and theorists in developing a framework appropriate to the task of interpreting these extraordinary plays. Chapter Four also deals with the descent into the dark in particular for characters like Kilroy's Matt Talbot, Murphy's JPW, and McGuinness's Caravaggio. The contrast between the two chapters is best explained in terms of their ability to negotiate their way through the dark and towards some kind of hopeful transformation. Carr's plays certainly know the dark and manage to negotiate the descent. But in Carr's plays transformation is interpreted in terms of dissolution rather than resolution. The only way out of this debilitating darkness is through suicide. The plays in Chapter Four attempt to move through the darkness towards some type of transformation, albeit achieved and imagined in different ways. They succeed in opening to a transcendent dimension. Costello in his introduction to *The Irish Soul* writes about how contact with the transcendent 'can alleviate suffering, can provide an overwhelming sense of reality, can soothe the spirit' (Costello:xii). He also speaks of despair and suicide and suggests that 'it is a choice, ultimately of closure (chaos) or of a rediscovery of the spiritual order of existence (cosmos). Closure of soul is the suffering of one cut off from all contact with transcendent reality. It is to elect the darkness of disorder over the divine Ground of being' (xii). The soul-journey can lead to depths of darkness, which are similar to the darkest depths of depression. Where soul open towards a horizon of possibility rather than foreclosing reality through the choice of suicide, it negotiates the darkness in a different way.

In ancient communities the shaman was one of those who undertook a journey on behalf of a community, to heal either an individual or the community itself. Contemporary interest in shamanism makes many aspects of the traditional shamanic journey available and accessible to ordinary human beings, who use the techniques of drumming, trance, journeying and power animals to enter into the shaman's world and to access new levels of consciousness and new awareness. Many of the plays studied here fulfill a similar shamanic function for the community. At times the playwright may consciously choose the shamanic (or appropriate a priestly) way in order to access new levels of awareness. Friel and Murphy are often conscious of their artistic work as providing this function in general terms. Specifically in a play like *Faith Healer* Friel develops the shamanic hero in the character of Frank Hardy. Whereas Murphy or McGuinness may not name any one character as shaman, nonetheless their protagonists often fulfil shamanic functions, particularly in terms of how they journey into the dark. Mommo's brooding narrative of the laughing competition (*Bailegangaire*) shows her capacity to journey as shaman to the source of her grief. JPW in *Gigli* or Caravaggio in *Innocence* negotiate the territory of the dark and their own unconscious in a shamanic way that has repercussions for the society as a whole. Tom Kilroy's Matt Talbot shares a similar outsider status to the shaman in his journey as a working-class Dublin mystic. A playwright like Michael Harding is also a shamanic figure in that he is not afraid to allow his characters journey into their unconscious worlds, thus opening up these very same worlds for the audience and for culture as a whole. The Man in *Misogynist* and the Pooka Man in *Una Pooka* give audiences glimpses of the destructive power of a patriarchal Irish unconscious. Women playwrights are also exploring the territory of the female unconscious, and naming it in new and exciting ways. The shamanic function of Marina Carr relates to the significance for her of the quest or journey itself. Tom Mac Intyre in a programme note to *Portia Coughlan* (Mac Intyre, 2003) notes 'the *search* energy in her, the quest compulsion and its attendant verities' and suggests that when 'a body goes looking for that which is lost, Marina Carr wisely tells us, everything becomes a sign'(82). The drivenness of Carr's female characters to reconnect with what is lost shares the classic features of the shaman's journey towards soul retrieval. Anne Devlin's quest play *After Easter* portrays Greta as a madwoman who also journeys like the classic shaman in search of her soul. Liz Sweeney's urge to transform the suffocating bleakness and darkness of her own community's life sees her organizing an elaborate fancy dress where the women transform themselves like shamans into exotic feathered birds (*Mrs. Sweeney*).

The outcome of the journey towards transformation must lead to some kind of vision for the future. The ability to bring back the treasure, to come home is an important part of the journey. The great quest narratives, whether we remember Orpheus searching for Eurydice, Demeter searching for her daughter Persephone, Jason in search of the Golden Fleece or the medieval Percival in search of the Grail, all demand that the journey be completed – that the one who searches returns home. The treasure or whatever has been sought is vital for the future health and well-being of the community. Coming home suggests a level of integration which is vital both for the one who searches and for the community. This is often represented in fairy tales in terms of a sacred marriage where the different aspects male and female (or even animus and anima) are integrated into the healthy psyche. Transformation that achieves high levels of integration has value not just in personal terms. A transformation in consciousness can happen over time for whole communities, when individual members are willing to undertake a personal journey of transformation. Transformation itself is a process, a long slow journey towards living with awareness and mindfulness. It does not, however, suggest the elimination of all human problems, the end of greed or selfishness, bigotry, resentment or vengeance, as the traditional fairytale might suggest.

The journey towards transformation needs the sustenance of vision, ways of seeing and dreaming that break open old ways of behaving and suggest new ways of being. This openness to possibility is what distinguishes the plays in Chapter Five. In the grip of old imagining one can feel that nothing new is possible. When a character like Greta (*After Easter*) listens to the voices that haunt her unconscious and attempts to integrate them into living embodied awareness, a new space of possibility opens for the spectator too. Stewart Parker's vision of wholeness also imagines the possibility of any future at all (*Pentecost*) as he invites audiences into a dialogue with some of the ghosts which haunt the cultural unconscious and inhibit genuine community. As Irish audiences find themselves trapped between old and new ways of seeing (whether religious or political), Sebastian Barry's *Prayers of Sherkin* offers a poetic and evocative imagining of how to move into newness and Michael Harding's *Una Pooka* enters into an imaginative dialogue with the repressive energies of the Irish cultural unconscious. Where McGuinness's graveyard characters (*Carthaginians*) can move beyond numbness and grief into feeling, connection and relationship, the space of play opens before them. Something similar can happen to an audience when grief gives way to newness. The specificity of place and time, and the gendered identity of the protagonists is important. It gives their stories sufficient particularity for embodiment. It should not however limit their efficacy if performed in other cultural situations.

Irish theatre as reflected in the plays studied in this work attempts to negotiate the labyrinth of the Irish soul and in so doing contributes to a poetics of Irish culture that enables a new imagining. The soul-journeys of the protagonists invite similar journeys for audiences and readers. The plays and their different journeys become, in turn, part of the weave of the fabric of Irish identity. They become part of how Irish people can imagine themselves and in turn reshape their world. But the effectiveness of the plays is not limited to Irish audiences. While the journeys may bear witness to the specificity of Irish identity in terms of time, place, language and cultural concerns, they also have something to say to people in other times and places. Just as the heartbreaking moments of a Chekovian drama can find resonances with audiences anywhere who have known the grief that accompanies the irrevocable loss of old orders or worlds, so too, these plays contribute to a deeper understanding of the human condition. They can enable one to make contact with the longing and quest for transformation that is so integral to the human journey.

1 | Journeys Through Memory

In essence, the soul is the force of remembrance within us.
(John O'Donohue)

We inherit memory like a family quilt – a patchwork of squares that tell us who we are and where we are going. Irish theatre can be imagined as sharing in this quilt-making function in its particular weave of narratives. Memory which is so important to identity, whether personal or cultural, is a complex weave of many strands, textures and colours. When intact it can give a sense of home, a sense of belonging. When fractured and interrupted it can lead to dislocation and abandonment. Whether one talks in terms of the personal journey towards integration or the great quest narratives or shamanic journeys, the destination is always home.

Many contemporary Irish plays are concerned with the journey home. Whether the sense of home is real or metaphorical many Irish dramatists depict characters searching for home. One strain of story is the journey through memory. The journey home may be possible once the story is told. This desire to tell stories, to find coherence and meaning in the disparate moments and events that make up a human life, finds a resonance with audiences, who seek similar integration in their own journeys. While the stories unfold in the present, memory tries to make sense of the past in order for one to move into the future with awareness and insight. In the narratives of personal therapy where memory encounters abuse and trauma, fragmentation and dissociation occur. The telling of the story becomes a remembering, as split-off parts become reconnected and feeling replaces numbness. As the narrative becomes more conscious and embodied, further descent into the repressed or shadow side is enabled. The confrontation with one's shadow, or otherness – one's strangeness to oneself and bringing it to conscious embodiment is the challenge of awareness or even the journey to enlightenment. It is a pattern evident in all journeys whether inward or outward. Each individual must learn to strengthen the container that they are, in order not to be overwhelmed by negative memories.

What is the place of the wound in Irish drama? Is it true that there has been a tendency to overemphasize the wound whether it is the wound of the colonized, the wound of a lost language, the wound of a territorial border? Has the endless lamenting in Irish drama enabled the wound to heal? It seems important that we hold the memory of wounds but that we also remember that there are other memories. To hold the tension between the wound and the promise, between a type of death and a hope of resurrection is a theme that we can identify in many of the plays selected for this study. It seems that however we identify it there is a trauma or a wounding at the heart of Irish identity. But there is also a defiance, an ability to enter the dark and find a voice that soars, a dance that liberates. In poetic drama we find the images and symbols that allow for a new kind of imagining. Theatre functions as an alternative sacred space wherein contemporary audiences can experience a type of secular ritual where what is enacted works on the imagination proposing alternative ways of seeing the world and inspiring what Paul Ricoeur called a passion for the possible.

The way one tells the story, the way one remembers is vital. Where there is traumatic memory it remains somehow frozen in time. Until it becomes narrative memory there is no opportunity for the individual to integrate the traumatic experience into consciousness. Something similar can also happen culturally. Where traumatic or deeply wounding experiences have occurred, the experiences become split off from consciousness, and continue to haunt the psyche through nightmare, hallucination or flashback images. Until the unspeakable becomes understood and integrated into consciousness it will continue to haunt the psyche.

In the Irish psyche the trauma has not been integrated, because of one significant factor which relates to the place of the body within Irish identity. The body is the missing link in Irish identity. There has been a significant mind/body dualism running through Irish experience and literature. The neglect of the body is essentially the legacy of a patriarchal imagining where mind, and spirit are valued over body and flesh. In the dualistic and hierarchical paradigm of domination that emerges from such imagining we find a similar valuing of male over female. The tendency to associate the male with the higher realms of culture and spirit and women with the lower realms of nature and body have deepened the split. The fact that men predominantly have been the meaning-makers and women have had meaning attributed to them has meant that women have not been allowed the same kind of access to the spiritual and metaphysical levels of culture. Until this wounding is brought to consciousness and integrated no healing can occur. But a significant part of bringing this to consciousness is to allow it to come to awareness in the body.

In Irish theatre over the past thirty years many stories have been told, many journeys have been made through memory to reconnect with the lost, abandoned parts of the individual or Irish psyche. That many of these stories reconnect with the female part of the Irish psyche is not surprising. That most of them are also written by men should not be surprising either. In this chapter I examine three plays written by Irish men foregrounding the voices of Irish women (as they imagine them) with specific attention to the relationship between journey and memory. I will also consider three non-canonical plays written by Irish women that address the same theme. I am interested in whether there is a difference in the representation of women for both sets of writers, with reference to particularity, voice and embodiment. Each individual play tries to be a container for the feelings and thoughts that it explores. Similarly theatre functions as a container. Theatre can be interpreted as a *temenos* – a sacred space and/or container which can hold together the energies that it explores in order to enable transformation both for the audience and culture as a whole.

In *Drawing on the Right Side of the Brain*, Betty Edwards (2001) highlights five basic perceptual skills for the student who is learning to draw: the perception of edges, spaces, relationships, of light and shadow, and the perception of the whole or gestalt (96).

These skills which draw on the right side of the brain could also be helpful tools of interpretation, in relation to individual plays and Irish theatre as a whole. They are particularly useful when considering plays from a feminist perspective. Looking for the gaps in the text, looking for what is consciously or unconsciously repressed (the shadow), looking at the spaces between the characters and the various spaces they occupy, are also aspects of feminist perception and interpretation. It is important to consider how each play sees itself as a whole and to evaluate its relation to the overall gestalt of what constitutes Irish theatre. In this context one should not try to force connections between the plays. Perhaps there is no universalizing narrative. What we find instead are disparate moments, snatches of memory which are fractured and splintered. If we focus on particularity, the narrative of each play is a moment in a larger cultural narrative. Where cultures are asking for attention to the narratives of those on the margins written out in the grand narratives of history, Irish theatre has responded by telling the stories of women. To try to force all the stories into one coherent narrative of identity is to miss something of the complexity. Discordant sounds, patterns of dissonance, are what we find. Women are both contained and constrained within Irish drama which is largely located within patriarchal narratives and ideologies of family, religion, sexuality and sacrifice.

A number of the plays in this section allow women's voices to surface. Women are often found occupying different spaces to the traditional spaces associated with them. *Baglady* is homeless and walks the streets, and her narrative is traumatic. Mommo as shanachie recounts a long personal narrative of the laughing competition that gave the town of *Bailegangaire* its name. The Mundy sisters in *Dancing at Lughnasa* face the collapse of their known world. And as women playwrights tell their stories we find a narrative of lament and grieving for women prostitutes who drowned during the Second World War (Anne Le Marquand Hartigan's *La Corbière*), a reflection on war and the Troubles through an exploration of mother/daughter relationships (Christina Reid's *Tea in a China Cup*) and young women punished for the sin of becoming pregnant outside of marriage who live in the harsh environment of a Magdalen laundry (Patricia Burke

Brogan's *Eclipsed*). The sense of loss is huge in each of these plays. It is more akin to trauma. Woman is what has been sacrificed within the patriarchal symbolic. The particularity of women's embodied subjectivity interrupts the ways we have known, and what we have known. Allowing the unspeakable to come to consciousness and be told is part of this journey.

Caruth writing on trauma notes how the traumatized carry an impossible history within them or become the symptoms of a history that they cannot actively possess (1995:5). Where the traumatized tries to access memory he/she encounters a void – an inability to fully witness the event as it occurs, or the ability to witness the event fully only at the cost of witnessing oneself (7). The dissociation characteristic of trauma causes large parts of identity to be disowned. The failure to locate the traumatic experience in time inhibits its integration into a coherent narrative. For the individual the traumatic event is in fact constituted by its lack of integration into consciousness (152). Traumatic memory must become narrative memory in order to become integrated into consciousness. The strange combination of detailed flashback and recall along with amnesia alerts us to the difficulty of such integration:

> The history that a flashback tells – as psychiatry, psychoanalysis, and neurobiology equally suggest – is, therefore, a history that literally *has no place*, neither in the past in which it was not fully experienced, nor in the present, in which its precise images and enactments are not fully understood. (153) (Emphasis in original.)

It might be interesting to use this understanding of trauma as a way of reading and interpreting these plays which essentially make journeys through memory to reconnect with lost or fragmented parts of the self. Many of the plays deal directly with trauma – and the story they tell is particular. We can read these plays as narratives of the Irish cultural self and its traumatic dissociation from a gendered embodied subjectivity. We can also read them as narratives of soul loss, narratives of fragmented and disembodied spirits that cry out for remembering, reconnection and embodiment.

Baglady, Frank McGuinness (1985)

Frank McGuinness's monologue *Baglady* (McGuinness, 1996:383-399) introduces many of the themes that will feature in his later work. A woman barely distinguishable as a woman (other than a grey scarf protecting her head) attempts to tell the story that is written on her body. It is a harrowing story of incest, rape and abuse by her own father which culminates in the birth and drowning of her baby boy in the river leaving the Baglady to wander homeless but carrying a grey woollen sack on her back as reminder.

Annie Rogers, a developmental psychologist and clinician, identifies dissociation and repression in women's narratives of trauma (Rogers, 1995). In working with these 'exiled voices' she notes how the outcome of

> repeated exposure to cultural denials or lies creates a vulnerability to repression, which often begins as psychic splitting, or a doubling of voice. (5)

Rogers also noted that whereas repressed memories once triggered can surface and be narrated often as whole sequences, 'memories that have been dissociated are recalled with great difficulty, leaving gaps in the narrative, fragments of a memory sequence' (6). Often physical or sexual assault leads to dissociation which Rogers interprets as 'a brilliantly creative solution to living through trauma and coming to terms with traumatic memories'. Dissociation was identified by passages of forgetting, blankness, contradictions, and confusion about time.

Dissociation is a major feature of the Baglady's narrative. Through layers of denial, repression, lying, pretence, the Baglady's awful story surfaces and must be told. Jordan says that McGuinness dramatizes the process of 'recognition' rather than the process of 'withholding' which we find in a play like *Baile-gangaire* (Jordan, 1997:14). The play highlights what can happen when one colludes with authority (patriarchal and priestly) in one's own negation. 'The refusal of a society to confirm an assault provokes the victim to question the validity of her own memory, integrity and innocence.' (15)

Baglady's painful narrative of dissociation and trauma is part of the culture's memory. To locate the play culturally within the Ireland of its time is to enter the territory of the tragedy of Ann Lovett (Jan. 1984) when a young teenager who became pregnant outside marriage died giving birth next to a grotto in Granard, Co. Longford and that of the Kerry babies case (Apr.1984) where a dead baby was found on the White Strand beach in Cahirciveen Co. Kerry and twenty-five year old Joanne Hayes was wrongly accused of having murdered the child. Nell Mc Cafferty's book *A Woman to Blame: The Kerry Babies Case* which was published just after the official enquiry closed relates how 'in contrast to the protected privacies for men involved in the case, this investigation displayed for public scrutiny a woman's most intimate sexual history and inflicted a public humiliation on her family' (quoted in Mikami, 2002:132). The following year (1985) was the year of the moving statues which occurred in a climate of a changing Ireland where public debates were taking place around female sexuality specifically in the areas of divorce and abortion.

However one interprets the phenomena of the moving statues, the symbol of the Virgin says much about the collective unconscious of the time. There is no denying that the Virgin is a powerful female symbol, with roots in a collective unconscious that predates Christianity. While recourse to the symbol could be liberating and transforming for women who find themselves undefined and un-represented within a patriarchal religious symbol system it can also be interpreted in a more conservative way. The desexualized Virgin of Catholic iconography may indeed weep at the fate of Irish women in Ireland of the nineteen eighties but she remains ultimately powerless as we see in Paula Meehan's poem 'The Statue of the Virgin at Granard Speaks' (Meehan, 1991). While the poem looks at small town hypocrisies and intolerance it also looks critically at religious symbols which have become remote, alien and disembodied and have no connection with the lived experiences of people. The virgin who speaks in the poem laments her demise as the ancient mother goddess, and harks back to a more ancient earth-centred religion which celebrated and gloried in fertility and coupling. In the bitter cold remoteness of the winter night, the virgin remains aloof and remote from the suffering of the young woman – unable to intervene. The traditional Catholic symbol system has failed to offer a sustaining or healing vision. A similar failure underlies the narrative of the Baglady, where priests and religious cannot offer healing but actually deepen the sense of wounding and violation.

Baglady echoes many of the themes noted by Annie Rogers, psychic splitting, doubling of voice, disavowal of the self, and most importantly, dissociation characteristic of the trauma of violent sexual abuse. As a victim she carries her abuser's sins. Consequent on the abuse her body is destroyed, her voice silenced. This play explores how brutality silences and deforms the psyche (Jordan, 1997:15). The fluid feminine space of the theatrical space is very significant as the Baglady

> speaks (writes) through the body. It is a body which has been violated sexually, has been possessed by her father and it has been possessed by masculine values, repressions, secrets and solutions. (15)

More recent events in Irish culture (through the 1990s) bear witness to the truth of McGuinness's work. The level of physical and sexual abuse disclosed through many reported cases of incest has highlighted the culture of silence that has surrounded and enabled the abuse to continue. Denial or the necessity for collusion in order to survive, are indicators of the unhealthy state of Irish sexuality and the persistent triumph of a patriarchal imagination that controls through domination, silencing and abuse.

McGuinness's play involves a search for symbols that will help interpret or reinterpret what has happened. The traditional religious authority has failed to hear the pain of the wounded child. Fintan O'Toole quoting from the *American Irish Catholic Reporter* (*The Irish Times* Weekend Supplement 19 Oct. 2002) drew attention to how often the institution was more concerned with preserving its public image than having compassion for the victims. Many people abused as children find themselves scarred and psychologically wounded for life. Sister Stanislaus Kennedy's report on Homeless Women in Dublin (quoted in Mikami, 2002:133) cites a variety of events that can precede homelessness: namely family death, family disruption or desertion, violence, rape and incest.

The Baglady finds herself homeless. In place of woman as symbol of the home, McGuinness presents us with a woman wandering the streets. There is no place of safety for the wounded child/woman, who haunts the streets, and stands at the river's edge seeking resolution with the painful truths of her childhood.

Through a language that is fluid and shifting and accompanied by the use of water and mirror imagery, McGuinness takes the audience on an extraordinary journey into the Baglady's past and unconsciousness, layering the text in so many ways. The all-seeing, all-knowing patriarchal father hears everything. This play questions all abusive patriarchies whether domestic, churchly or divine. The priest is central to the Baglady's disavowal of her experience as he 'implicates' her 'in her own violation, forcing her to return again and again to the act of sexual defilement' (Jordan, 1997:15).

The colours of McGuinness's narrative – white, red and black – are stark, evoking purity, violation and death. Original innocence has been lost, the child is bloodied and lacerated. Something dies. The sense of violation that runs through this play makes it hard even to read the text. An amateur production of the play in St. Patrick's College, Drumcondra, Dublin (directed by Pat Burke, Oct. 2001), made it almost impossible to miss the connection between the body and the text. The text, written on the female body, is foregrounded in performance. The challenge to the female actor to embody a narrative such as the Baglady's allows for no disconnection. The depth of the damage that this violation has done to the young child is almost unspeakable and yet must be spoken. The hands will tell the story: 'It doesn't have a name for it's written on my hand, and your fingers can't talk' (*Baglady* 386). Later she will ask her hands to clap if they want to tell the story.

The way the Baglady carries all her life experiences with her is reminiscent of McGuinness's Caravaggio in *Innocence*. She too carries her father and her mother within her and that memory destroys her and renders her homeless. Her denial of the past in her assertions of how good and respectable her father was are similar to Caravaggio's denial of any connection with home. Her recollection of two homeless tramps from her childhood who slept in their barn, prefigures her own homeless fate. She recalls looking at her house from different angles and vantage points. The windows in the house suggest an endless hall of mirrors, reflecting, and distorting as the child learns to identify with being the mother because of the abuse. 'The imagery of a window, which is to recur frequently in her monologue, somehow mediates, refracts, contains the relation between the Baglady, the observer, and what she observes' (Mikami, 139). Throughout the play marriage functions as the 'central symbol governing cleanliness, virginity, purity and expectation. Her father broke the contract between child and parent, yet she is the one who bears the burden' (Jordan, 18). The Baglady carries an old wedding dress with her, a symbol of what has been taken from her and destroyed.

The Baglady only eats white bread and drinks red lemonade, the bread becoming a symbol of the rupture. The Baglady also does not want to be left in the 'black room' (*Baglady* 389): 'Don't leave me in the black room. If I can't see, I can't talk, and if I can't talk I can't tell'. The father/abuser becomes in her imagination a black dog, menacing and attacking her, going for her throat. The Baglady says: 'When things are torn, you can't put them back again. When something's taken from you, you can't get it back.' (391). The trauma tears her body and soul apart:

> She got such a shock she jumped that hard from her chain that she tore her head away from the rest of her and all that was left behind was her skin and bones. (394)

'He set the dog on his daughter's body and it ate all that was left of her.' (394) The violation goes very deep and the language to get hold of the experience shifts and changes between literal and symbolic.

> Did you hear that falling? Was it a crack? It could have been your heart, it could have been your mind. Still, the sound was breaking, like a glass on the ground. (391)

Jordan suggests that the shattered glass 'is associated with violation and with the fragmentation of a consciousness which needs to be pieced back together' (Jordan 16) but also says that while the Baglady pieces together the fragments of her narrative into a coherent tale she succeeds in addressing but not solving her own fragmentation. (17)

In the course of her narrative the Baglady will turn to reading the cards in an attempt to uncover an old/new way of seeing and interpreting her experience. The fractured sequencing of her narrative, the loss of chronology, and the childish rhymes, explanations and sensory memories alert us to the traumatic nature of her story. The narrative appears to be frozen in time, as if it has no place. Equally it leaves the Baglady without a sense of place, homeless and wandering. In a way all her knowing (remembered, repressed or disavowed) is in the cards. She begins her story with a card that is the sign of water. The symbol of water carries both creative and destructive connotations. It can cleanse, purify and renew or drown and destroy. Her sense of her own defilement is something that can never be washed away, as she feels unclean and dirty because of her father's abuse. As she selects the five of clubs she identifies the wounds of sorrow that she carries on her body and notes that they are beginning to heal because they are black. The sense of being healed through her wounds is reminiscent of Christian theology and spirituality that stresses the healing power for all future generations of Christians through the wounds of Christ. The symbolism of the cards is mutli-layered as is the child's memory. The queen of hearts may be her own heart, her mother or the Divine Mother. This queen has lost a son and has disguised herself in the clothes of a beggar to search the earth for him. The queen of spades, the quiet card that keeps her own counsel, may be the aspect of the child that had to keep silent, became angry although no one understood its source and now wonders whether she is a woman at all. The Baglady wears all her father's clothes, suggesting an internalization of her abuse as she in turn becomes her own abuser, continuing to erode all traces of her female sexual body. The child/woman has received a blow which has left her scarred. 'It could be the track of a fist. This woman's received a blow that will shut her up forever, and she's with you through all your life' (393). The themes of death and marriage which have been haunting her narrative begin to come together. As she turns up the seven of diamonds it is a card associated with luck and marriage – an irony that one cannot ignore. The knave of clubs she associates with the priest, and also with his presence at weddings and funerals which do not seem all that different. When she turns up the ace of spades she sees death and she has to name it. 'What I see I have to tell. I have to say it.' This card tells her that she will be attending a funeral, of either a young woman or a child. The ritual with the cards opens a new space for the Baglady where she can start to piece together the fragments of her trauma into narrative memory.

Her perception shifts and changes throughout the play: 'When I stood beside the river, our house looked a long way away. That's where I lived then, in our house, and my son lived in the river.' (388) From another perspective it is as if her mother and father are magic shape-shifters:

> Sometimes my mother is my father and my father is my father too. Sometimes they turn me into each other when they think I don't know what they're doing but I do. (395)

This loss of identity and loss of security of home continues as the sexualized child realizes that she has 'jumped through the window' and it has cut her in two (396). What she now knows cannot be spoken. Her father threatened her with drowning and then bribed her with a ring. In her dreams her father gives her a necklace:

> But if she breathed a word of their secrets, the necklace grew black, blacker and blacker, and it tightened about her throat, tighter and tighter, twisting her face up, so she hardly had a face and she couldn't breathe again until she said she was sorry. (397)

The Baglady performs an important ritual. Ritual transferred to the sacred space of theatre may allow for a new imagining. In an attempt to bury her past she makes a ritual pile (like a cairn) of all the objects. Starting with the chain (her bondage), the cards that help interpret the past, the red lemonade, the wedding dress, she piles them one on top of the other and finally the ring her father gave her. Her narrative moves from third person to first person as the reconciliation takes place within her. She has felt dirty all her life. She tried calling on God but his answer in the 'man in black' was to call her a liar and offer her forgiveness. Similarly the sisters, 'women in black', offer no consolation. Their washing her clean was like being washed with fire. 'They nailed her son to a river.' Baglady appropriates the imagery of the sorrowing mother Mary who has also lost her son. Her son was not the only one who died.

Life for the Baglady has been a living death. The burial ritual becomes her marriage, as she piles her wedding dress and ring on the pile. The concluding words from the Anglican marriage ceremony close the play, followed by the word 'Drown'.

This harrowing story has been brought to consciousness and narrated. In its movement from traumatic to narrative memory it now becomes part of the cultural memory. The theatre has been the container, the sacred place for the holding and transformation of the story both for the Baglady and for the audience. While *Baglady* tells a story of personal trauma it is nonetheless a trauma that is part of the cultural fabric. The culture must now try to integrate and appropriate this memory, in order to create a new future. A similar invitation to integrate dangerous memories is found in Tom Murphy's *Bailegangaire*.

Bailegangaire, Tom Murphy (1985)

In the symphony of soul-making that has taken place in contemporary Irish theatre Tom Murphy's *Bailegangaire* (Murphy, *After Tragedy*, 1988: 41-77) deserves special attention. Third in a trilogy of plays that includes the Television drama *Brigid*, and *A Thief of a Christmas* it is a particular journey through memory. Noteworthy too for its all female cast, it gave veteran actress Siobhán McKenna her last opportunity to perform for Irish audiences. In a stunning performance in the Druid Company production of the play (1985), McKenna played the part of Mommo, a senile, crotchety, incontinent grandmother, to her two grand-daughters Mary and Dolly, in a play set in a kitchen in the west of Ireland in 1984. While Murphy may have been adamant at the beginning of his career as a playwright that he would never set a play in a kitchen, it is to this very space he returns in this powerful play. The play tells the story of *Baileganagaire* and how it came by its appellation. It pivots on Mommo's account of a laughing competition, which had taken place some thirty years earlier, and one that had traumatic and catastrophic implications for Mommo and her family.

Murphy's *Bailegangaire* is one of the most amazing pieces of writing to surface in Irish theatre. It lingers somewhere between pure poetry and music. At times it could almost be a musical score, as Mommo's narrative soars and swoops, in cadences and trills, in crescendo and diminuendo. But it is also poetic theatre at its best, exploiting the full potential of language with its haunting, evocative, rhythmic, lyrical, humorous and heart-breaking registers. As Mommo's narrative broods over what is remembered, and compulsively and repetitively revisits the original experience, audiences are drawn into the story, until it becomes their story too. Levels of dissociation consequent on trauma are much in evidence and the subsequent fragmentation of identity and soul loss are harrowing to behold. Mommo's inability to fully own the experience is reflected in a third person narrative that only gradually moves to a first person one. In the course of the play Mommo will finally finish the story that she has been telling for years, parts of which both grand-daughters know by heart. But if it is a memory play it is dysfunctional memory – a memory that has broken down (Grene, 2002:76). The family may be bound together in the 'inextricable knots of family dynamics but 'the play enacts a sort of family therapy that expresses the trauma of a nation for all of us who share in it' (81).

All her life Mommo has stood at a distance from the narrative of her life, leading to fragmentation and disembodiment. Her inability to come home to the truth of her life also leaves her grand-daughters in similar places of exile or alienation. The play presents us with three fractured female subjectivities, three women who are trying to come home to themselves. As is so often the case within a patriarchal society, these women have found them-selves in violent or loveless relationships, where lies, secrets, fear and denial, are part of the fabric of their lives. Murphy 'resists easy resolutions to the desperate situation of the women in *Bailegangaire*, a situation that is all the more desperate because it is one they share but can apparently only experience alone' (78).

There is a particular wounding in the area of female sexuality, which while acknowledged superficially is never brought fully into awareness throughout the course of the play. Further recon-ciliation to the painful truths of Mommo's narrative is needed, and a deeper level of integration than what is achieved in the play. A language of female embodied subjectivity is missing from the play, but Mommo's narrative of the laughing competition does share many of the features of what Kristeva has called women's time, as it interrupts, backtracks, slides and weaves in its telling. The registers of language move between English and Gaelic, and the many animal and human sounds, including various types of laughter, that Mommo has recourse to mimicking in the telling of her story, bring us closer to the semiotic. Her granddaughter Mary's insistence that she finish the story ensures that Mary is a co-author of the story that has become integral to her existence. Her need to be author of her own story can only be facilitated by Mommo's telling of the story in full. Generations of Irish women have lived stories that have been authored by men. It matters little whether the authors have been their fathers or their husbands or the cultural fathers (priests, artists and historians). In addressing soul-fragmentation it is important that women come to tell their own stories. The female quest for self has so often been overshadowed or rendered silent and invisible within a patriarchal culture. Mommo as shanachie holds the strands of memory that she must weave into a new story. That Mommo might journey shaman-like to the depths of her own soul and meet the demons that have long denied her access to her self may facilitate a similar homecoming for other women.

Mommo is a monstrous character – rude, dirty, incontinent, bed-ridden, cruel, somewhat senile and constantly re-telling the story of this incident from her life. All her children have either died, or left her and her endless lamentations make it impossible not to interpret her as some kind of Mother Ireland figure or a cliché of the Irish Mother, within a patriarchal imagining, of both history and home. The story of the laughing competition which resulted in the deaths of her husband and young grandson Tom, within a few days of each other, and her guilt about her own participation in it, also create a sense of the inadequate mother (or grandmother in this case) or woman as victim. And yet it is part of the achievement of this play that Murphy succeeds in taking his audience beyond cliché and stereotype, towards a level of new imagining. The story of the laughing competition shares the features of fable or myth as the strangers to the town (Mommo and her husband Seamus) challenge the local (giant) Costello to a laughing competition, in the village pub, on their way home from a bad day's trading at the fair. When the village hero falls down dead, wheezing and laughing, the local people attack the stranger and try to force off his shoes, to ascertain whether he is not in fact the Great Adversary himself, come among them in human form. This is mythic territory, the space of folklore and legend, where good and evil are not always so easy to identify, where scapegoats are needed, or at least satisfactory explanations to hold the energies of the community in balance.

Who owns the story? While much of the play attests to the reality of women being violated, ignored or abused in cold, or violent relationships, their subsequent reactive states of being are defiant, desperate, angry, cruel. Mommo tells us that women were actively discouraged from voicing opinions in a man's world. Genuine communication between men and women seems impossible and there is a hopelessness and hate at the heart of these relationships. Dolly hates her husband Stephen so much that she is making plans to have him 'fixed' and she engages in casual sex with strangers more out of hatred than a need for money. Mary has also been in a relationship with Dolly's husband but what this means for the relationship between the two women is not discussed. It is deep seething anger and disappointment that motivates Mommo to prolong the laughing competition that would ensure that the contestants kept on laughing and that she would not return in time to save her young grandson Tom from the paraffin explosion that would eventually lead to his death. Mommo recalls the night, realizing that they could have gone home:

> But what about the things that had been vexin' her for years? No, a woman isn't stick or stone. The forty years an' more in the one bed together an' he to rise in the mornin' and not to give her a glance. An' so long it had been he had called her by first name, she'd near forgot it herself...Brigit...Hah? ... An' so she thought he hated her...An' maybe he did. Like everything else. (*Bailegangaire* 65)

As Mary searches for a sense of home in both physical and metaphysical terms, Dolly hates her 'own new liquorice-all-sorts-coloured-house' (69) and the violent contradictions that it hides. There is a terror and desperation at the heart of her life and secrecy, betrayal and a deep sense of failure at the heart of Mary's. Trauma and wounding are at the heart of the narrative that Mommo withholds. An inability to feel the pain of one's life and to come to a genuine state of grieving contributes to the freezing and paralysis that is so often characteristic of women's lives within patriarchal narratives of history. Trapped within a naming which excludes their experience it is almost as if their stories have no place, no history. The play searches for a vantage point from which to re-tell the story of the laughing competition, in a manner that is true to how Mommo has experienced it in her life, both past and present. Such a re-telling of the story in its fullness allows the traumatic experience to be experienced once and for all, so that it can now be integrated into the lived history of the women's lives.

There is an ambivalence around Mommo's story. The night with the most tragic consequences was also the 'nicest night ever'. Mommo recalls how her husband's eyes met hers, and 'the moment was for them alone' (73), how she felt included and laughed along with the men, and had no desire to go home. She would eventually provide the topic of 'misfortunes' that would ensure that the laughing competition would continue. As her narrative twists and turns in its brooding, hypnotic recall, the story of the event makes it present once again. But now it is filtered through the paralysis and grief of Mommo's life. She recalls the failure of the potato crop, and moves into a great litany of the dead which includes her own children. But now *'[t]he hih-hih-hih which punctuate her story sounds more like tears – in-grown sobs – rather than laughter'* (Stage directions *Bailegangaire* 75). Mommo confesses that 'nothin' was sacred an' nothing a secret. The unbaptized an' still-born in shoeboxes planted at the dead hour of night' (74) and every memory an invitation into the liminal space of laughter:

> The nicest night they ever had, that's what I'm sayin'. The stories kept on comin' an' the volleys and cheers. All of them present, their heads threwn back abandoned in festivities of guffaws; the wretched and neglected dilapidated an' forlorn, the forgotten an' tormented, the lonely an' despairing, ragged an' dirty, impoverished, hungry, emaciated and unhealthy, eyes big as saucers

ridiculing an' defying of their lot on earth below – glintin' their defiance. (75)

Even in the telling of the story it is not so easy to distinguish between laughter and pain. Mommo tells us 'The ache was in the laughter' and Costello's laughing lines on his face were more like 'lines of pain' (75). As Mommo's story comes to an end Mary takes up her part and tells about the three waiting grandchildren, the paraffin explosion, and the deaths of both Tom and Grandad. Interspersed with Mommo's recital of the *Salve Regina*, the story in the present becomes an invitation to grieve. Mommo and Mary share the final moments of the soul-symphony. The space of tears becomes the site for transformation and Dolly's unborn child a symbol of possibility and new life.

Dancing at Lughnasa, Brian Friel (1990)

Brian Friel's *Dancing at Lughnasa* (Friel, 1990) is set in the home of the five Mundy sisters who live outside the imaginary village of Ballybeg, in Co. Donegal in the late nineteen thirties. It is narrated by a young man, Michael, who was seven years of age at the time of the play's events. It is *Michael's memory* of the events of the summer of 1936 that we find in the play. *His* narrative frames and punctuates the play from the opening to the closing tableaux. Memory is unreliable, sketchy, selective, partisan. Memory is not simply recollection but how events were experienced. In adult life, the intervening years, the awareness of social history, the awareness of later outcomes will colour the remembering, shade the events in ways that make remembering at times indistinguishable from imagining.

Michael as a young man narrates the play and Michael as a young boy occupies a space in the play, which the audience must imagine, as he does not appear on stage as a child. His introductory narrative has the fluidity of poetry, the completeness of reflection, the brush strokes of the work of art as he shades the key images from the summer of 1936 into a coherent narrative. 'When I cast my mind back to that summer of 1936 different kinds of memories offer themselves to me' (*DL* 1). The memories include the family's first wireless set, his aunts dancing to Irish music and the return home after twenty-five years, of his mother's brother Father Jack, from a leper colony in Ryanga, Uganda. (2).

The audience is introduced to the shifting, changing world of a seven-year-old boy who has had an opportunity to meet and observe his father (Gerry Evans) for the first time, and whose day to day life is interrupted by the presence of the lost, shuffling Father Jack, who is not the hero he had expected. And even those kind, sensible aunts become strange and other as he talks about them in the abandon of the dance – an abandonment that must have held terror for a young child, as it hinted at adult ritual excess and areas of life beyond his experience. And yet when it comes to the dance sequence within the play Michael does not in fact observe it.

Behind this play lies an otherness, a strangeness associated with more ancient ways of knowing, that presents itself in both positive and negative ways throughout the play: the otherness of the pagan world represented by Lughnasa and by the festivals of Ryanga and presented to us in the manic nature of the sisters' wild dance (21-22). As memory searches and scans, looking for words as if misplaced, the gaps are filled with snatches of music, and song, and the rhythms of the dance which move from the shuffle, to strictly ballroom, to wild abandon.

The world of the child is also the world of the women, largely domestic, restricted socially and economically, and subject to interruption and disruption by outside forces that are beyond their immediate control. It is largely a female world but one that the men in the play shape and define. Jack returns home, in disgrace, as he has abandoned the rituals and practices of Catholicism in favour of the communal and tribal rituals of the Ryangan people. The disgrace that this brings on the family is best expressed by the off-stage power of the parish priest who decides not to re-employ Kate as a schoolteacher after the holidays, thus removing the only wage earner from the family. The two visits during the summer of 1936 of Michael's father affect the interconnected lives of all the women. The social reality of the women's lives makes them economically dependent either on Kate's salary or on piece knitting, which they do from home. With increased industrialization on the horizon, (a knitting factory to open in Donegal town), cottage

industries flounder and women and children suffer. With very few
eligible men, a woman not married by her mid-thirties would have
had little chance of improving her social or economic status. With
mass emigration of young men (and also of women) the prospects
appeared dimmer.

The summer of 1936 would have been the last remembered
idyllic summer of Michael's childhood. Michael's narratives shift
the time scale of the play. He occupies a time-space – which is
many years later (but is not the present) – and while narrating
events of that fateful summer of 1936 he can give the audience
information about the outcome of events before they happen. The
shadow cast is cold, ominous, as we learn that two of the sisters
died poor and destitute in London, that his father was injured in
the war and had a second family in Wales, that the factory came to
the town, that Kate lost her job, and that Jack was dead within the
year. The events that unfold give a corporeal reality to Michael's
narration, but also a ghostly type of presence, almost like voices
from the grave, similar to *Faith Healer*, where the actors embody
the space of the narrative for the benefit of the audience. Michael's
last speech draws attention to the kind of memory operative in the
play:

> But there is one memory of that Lughnasa time that visits me most
> often; and what fascinates me about that memory is that it owes
> nothing to fact. In that memory atmosphere is more real than
> incident and everything is simultaneously actual and illusory. In that
> memory, too, the air is nostalgic with the music of the thirties. It
> drifts in from somewhere far away – a mirage of sound – a dream
> music that is both heard and imagined. (*DL.* 71)

Where memory owes nothing to fact, and atmosphere is more real
than incident, and everything is simultaneously actual and illusory
– one could be talking here of theatre, the performance space of
such enacted memory, the physical fore-grounding of what is
remembered, however 'real'. Locating this memory securely within
the realist parameters of a Donegal kitchen in 1936, with minute
attention to the furnishings etc., stresses the particularity of the
incidents. What emerges and unfolds is something else. It is where
the real defies representation, where the fissures in the text

disclose unprecedented worlds. And in this play the most unreliable element is memory itself.

Does the unreliability of memory imply that there is no truth in
the events? Or is the truth of events what they become in the
individual's life story as it unfolds over time? The lines between
objective and subjective become blurred, interpretation colours
everything, and all experience becomes interpreted experience. The
individual constantly revisits the memories that make up his or her
life, gleaning all that can be gleaned, fashioning and refashioning
memories. Imagination is what gathers memory into coherence in
order for it to become a story out of which one can live. Similar to
what an audience can say after a night at the theatre: something
happened, a story was told, and we were witnesses.

Michael's memory drifts nostalgically back to the music of the
thirties, which is also both heard and imagined. The Marconi
wireless, beaming music into the farmhouse kitchen, from somewhere far away, was both a marvel and a miracle. That it also
disclosed another world is apparent. The music of the thirties – the
dance music of the ballrooms, was a different world to that of a
small rural community controlled and policed by the twin orthodoxies of church and state. It hinted at forbidden pleasures –
bodies close, moving in harmony, stirring passions long repressed.
The music that Michael remembers is bewitching, haunting,
mesmeric. Elsewhere he talks of Marconi's voodoo. This kind of
music creates moods, shapes worlds, offers different vantage
points. Throughout the play, dance becomes the language to hint
at these other worlds, other ways of being. It becomes the language of the repressed, the language of the possible, the language
of ritual, the language that over and over creates sacred spaces
within which anything might happen.

The talk of the town is the forthcoming harvest dance:
'Ballybeg's off its head. I'm telling you. Everywhere you go –
everyone you meet – it's the one topic: Are you going to the
harvest dance?' (10-11). It's 'like a fever in the place' (11). Kate is
critical of one young woman's description of the upcoming dance
as 'supreme.' The thoughts of the dance can grip people like a
fever, offering a promise of transportation, release from the
crushing mediocrity of their lives. The sisters, almost gripped by

the fever, imagine that they too could go to the dance. It is almost decided when Kate refuses to allow it. The clash of worlds is best captured in the exchange between Agnes and Kate. Agnes asks:

> How many years has it been since we were at the harvest dance? – at any dance? And I don't care how young they are, how drunk and dirty and sweaty they are. I want to dance Kate. It's the festival of Lughnasa. I'm only thirty-five. I want to dance.

But Kate panics and refuses permission:

> Do you want the whole countryside to be laughing at us? – women of our years? – mature women, *dancing*? What's come over you all? And this is Father Jack's home – we must never forget that – ever. No, no, we're going to no harvest dance. (13)

The promise of the dance is one of pleasure, gaiety, levity, shedding of responsibility. It is a liminal space where barriers are removed, where the excess of celebration facilitates encounter with an otherness that is usually veiled, hidden or repressed. The clash of worlds – between the closed, cold, sober world of Irish Catholicism and the wild abandon of the harvest dance with its pagan overtones is too much for Kate's sense of propriety and responsibility.

A short incident follows this exchange where Maggie (who has been off-stage) approaches the child Michael who is making kites. She appears to have something fragile cupped in her hands. When she opens them, she follows the imaginary flight of something up to the sky and out of sight. Encouraging the child to share her fantasy – so that he too believes he has seen something she says:

> **Maggie:** Wasn't it wonderful?
> **Boy:** Was it a bird?
> **Maggie:** The colours are so beautiful. (*She gets to her feet*) Trouble is – just one quick glimpse – that's all you'll ever get. And if you miss that. (14-15)

This short encounter mirrors the scene that has just occurred indoors. It is about the power of imagination to create worlds, where anything is possible. The fractional glimpse however is all that we may get. The sisters' imagined glimpse of their going to the harvest dance was only that – it didn't last. The space opened by that momentary imagining is now closed. Or in the space of memory and theatre it is always open.

But while the reality of their going to the dance has receded something continues to circulate in the air. Stories of Okawa, Father Jack's house-boy, and hints of a homosexual relationship evoke a strange and different world. Kate has a story of the young Sweeney boy who was anointed following a prank in the back hills. Rose fills out the details, much to Kate's disgust and disapproval.

> **Rose:** First they light a bonfire beside a spring well. Then they dance round it. Then they drive their cattle through the flames to banish the devil out of them.
> **Kate:** Banish the – ! You don't know the first thing about what –
> **Rose:** And this year there was an extra big crowd of boys and girls. And they were off their heads with drink. And young Sweeney's trousers caught fire and he went up like a torch. That's what happened. (16)

Kate's vehement denials of what Rosie is saying lead her to identify the perpetrators of these atrocities as 'savages' from the back hills, engaging in pagan practices, that she doesn't want discussed in a Catholic home. Later we will learn that she does know what happened, even more than Rose does and is trying to protect them from it. The young lad's trousers didn't catch fire, rather 'They were doing some devilish thing with a goat – some sort of sacrifice for the Lughnasa Festival: and Sweeney was so drunk he toppled into the middle of the bonfire' (35).

Kate tries hard to keep things together both for herself and her family. But hair cracks are appearing everywhere, things are slipping away and everything is ready to collapse around her:

> You work hard at your job. You try to keep the home together. You perform your duties as best you can – because you believe in responsibilities and obligation and good order. And then suddenly you realise that hair cracks are appearing everywhere; that control is slipping away; that the whole thing is slipping away; that the whole thing is so fragile it can't be held together much longer. It's about to collapse, Maggie. (35)

Where there is huge social upheaval and new ideas pushing aside old certainties there is often a similar return of the repressed. Whatever has been culturally denied, repressed or relegated to the margins can resurface and exert power and influence on the imagination. Older ways of behaving (ancient rituals and tribal ceremonies) may appear to be more grounded and connected than much of what happens in the contemporary world. Where traditional religious rituals have atrophied, and are no longer life-giving, the older, nature-based religions may offer consolation. There is also a certain nostalgia here – and a belief that one can simply re-create these rituals and inhabit them easily.

The possible ritual space of the harvest dance has been denied to the women. Maggie, lost in a reverie about an old childhood friend, suddenly turns to face her sisters. The radio has just been turned on and about ten seconds of Irish dance music ('The Mason's Apron') have played. Stage directions here are very important (especially if one has not seen a performance of the play). Maggie's features

> *become animated by a look of defiance, of aggression; a crude mask of happiness.[...] Now she spreads her fingers, (which are covered with flour), pushes her hair back from her face, pulls her hands down her cheeks and patterns her face with an instant mask. At the same time she opens her mouth and emits a wild raucous 'Yaaah!' – and immediately begins to dance, arms, legs, hair, boot-laces flying ...* (21)

Maggie, *a white-faced frantic dervish*, enters the ritual space of the dance, her face masked with white flour – she could be in Ryanga or the back hills. A space is opened with her face painting and her shriek. Before she enters the dance she absorbs the rhythm into her body. It energizes her, makes her defiant, enables her to find a language to express the inexpressible. Her school-friend Bernie O'Donnell has escaped and made her way successfully in the world outside. So often in the Irish psyche the state of exile enables and even sets a precedent for self-realization and expression. The confinement of a poor farmhouse, full of maiden aunts, with insufficient food is stifling, confining. Maggie's defiance in the dance is all that she has. She calls the others to join her, the ritual needing more than one. Each participates in her own way '*Rose's wellingtons pounding out their own erratic rhythm,*' as she had danced earlier defying the rhythm of the song. And Agnes, of all the sisters, '*moves most gracefully, most sensuously,*' her movements indicating a dormant sexual energy that is quietly consuming her. Then Chris '*who has been folding Jack's surplice, tosses it quickly over her head and joins in the dance*' (21). The appropriation of the priestly vestment implies a ritual reversal or parody. The sacred garment transposed to this 'profane' space assumes a new significance and transgresses all received notions of holiness? Kate's protest is drowned out as the sisters join in the rhythm of the dance.

Stage directions indicate that their movements are caricatured, too loud, too fast, grotesque (21). These are not the words of celebration, but of desperation. The combined pent-up energy and life force of the sisters bursts its bounds and like a river in flood is chaotic, out of control. Carried by the rhythm and the remembered pattern (*all doing a dance that is almost recognizable*) they move into the liminal space. The grotesque suggests carnival, the space of ritual excess where the old order is overturned, at least for the duration of the festival. There is a collapse into a formlessness where new beginnings could be possible, where hopes might be rekindled and things could be different. As the music stops abruptly mid-phrase none of the sisters notice and continue dancing for a few seconds. Gradually they emerge from the trance of the dance, each in her own time until only Rose is '*dancing her graceless dance by herself*'. When everyone stops, the only sounds are their '*gasping for breath*' and static from the radio. Stage directions indicate that '*They look at each other obliquely; avoid looking at each other; half smile in embarrassment; feel and look slightly ashamed and slightly defiant*' (22). How can such energy and abandon be faced within the confines of a 1930s kitchen in Donegal? Its momentary release has allowed the inside to be on the outside. The frustrated longings, buried desires, stifling confinements that have been internalized in their bodies have been released. The space has been changed irrevocably. However no further liberation is possible. When the sisters attempt to return to normal, it is noticed that Michael has been missing for at least ten minutes. If he has not in fact seen the dance, how can we interpret this memory?

The conversation that follows the dance is irritable, and somewhat uncontrolled. The dance has disturbed the underlying harmony of the household. Buried resentments surface. The tension is finally broken by Maggie's sighting of Gerry Evans

(Michael's father) at the bend in the lane. The turmoil that this introduces in the household highlights the absence of men in their lives. They dash about in confusion, weave around the immobile Chris and talk over one another, excitedly – another crazy dance? The travelling salesman who gives dancing lessons (strictly ballroom) is a chancer, a charmer, a liar, a foreigner – a man. He makes Chris laugh. When Kate suggests that he is a tinker, a loafer, a wastrel, Maggie replies that Chris knows that too. Gerry is to go away to Spain, joining up as a soldier with the International Brigade. The stage of international politics affects the lives of the women, whether they like it or not. 'Dancing in the Dark' begins to play softly on the radio. Outside, Gerry takes Chris in his arms and they dance. From inside the sisters watch, each in her own way. Agnes refuses to look 'I'm busy! For God's sake can't you see I'm busy!' and Kate looks on uncomprehending. Yet even she can see how beautiful a dancer Evans is and how Chris' face 'alters when she's happy. They dance so well together. They're such a beautiful couple' (33).

Since Jack has returned from Africa he is having trouble finding the words for what was once familiar. Without language he has no container for his experiences. The gap between memory and language is highlighted first in relation to his Irish past and then in relation to his Ryangan experiences. Language seems inadequate and unable to bridge the gap. How can Jack find a way to speak of ancestral spirits and medicine men, of sacrifices to appease the spirits, of ritual dancing and incantations? How can one express such otherness?

'Ceremony! That's the word! How could I have forgotten that? Such a simple word.' As Jack begins to remember he recalls how when he was on the boat home 'there were days when I couldn't remember even the simplest words'.

Jack: And you can always point, Margaret, can't you?
Maggie: Or make signs.
Jack: Or make signs.
Maggie: Or dance. (40)

Signs and dance – the language that allows the otherness to surface. Listening to Jack's experience the illegitimate child becomes the love-child that every Ryangan woman is anxious to have. As adult Michael intervenes in the play he confirms Kate's forebodings. She does in fact lose her job and the two sisters Rose and Agnes leave the home forever. Jack takes the child's pieces of wood and:

> begins to beat out a structured beat whose rhythm gives him pleasure. And as Michael continues his speech, Jack begins to shuffle-dance in time to his own tattoo – his body slightly bent over, his eyes on the ground, his feet moving rhythmically. And as he dances – shuffles, he mutters – sings – makes occasional sounds that are incomprehensible and almost inaudible. (Stage directions *DL*: 41-42)

Even in the midst of chaos there may be an older language of connection through the ritual movement of the dance. Michael's speech anticipates the next visit of his father which occurs in Act Two, which is set three weeks later. He speaks of another dance between his mother and Gerry Evans, a dance with no 'singing, no melody, no words' which he interprets as a kind of marriage:

> And this time it was a dance without music, just there, in ritual circles round and round that square and then down the lane and back up again; slowly, formally, with easy deliberation. (42)

In the second Act there is no further reference to this dance.

The worlds of old Celtic Ireland and Ryanga begin to come closer as Jack shifts from remembering his mother's bilberry jam, to festivals in Ryanga, when a few hundred people would gather to offer sacrifices to Obi the Goddess of the earth (47). The gap between Ryanga and traditional Catholic Ireland widens as Kate allows herself to realize that Jack will never celebrate Mass again, that he has changed completely, and has become someone they don't know. His description of the two Ryangan harvest festivals associated with the New Yam and the Sweet Casava shows an intrinsic connection between ritual and life and also such a different world that it both fascinates and repels the listeners. As the formal ritual celebration ends:

> it grows naturally into a secular celebration; so that almost imperceptibly the religious ceremony ends and the community celebration takes over. And that part of the ceremony is a real

spectacle. We light fires round the periphery of the circle; and we paint our faces with coloured powders; and we sing local songs; and we drink palm wine. And then we dance – and dance – and dance – children, men, women, most of them lepers, many of them with misshapen limbs, with missing limbs – dancing, believe it or not, for days on end! (47-48)

The surfacing of the forgotten or repressed can happen either diabolically or symbolically. The practices in the back-hills are of a more negative nature, with the ritual functioning to sunder and sever rather than to join together and unite (diabolic rather than symbolic). In contrast Jack's account of the Ryangan rituals shows them taking place within the context of a community, in touch with the rhythms of nature and the cycles of the year. The world of the Ryangan can contain the excesses of the ritual. The dancing and drinking in the context of ritual festivity is what makes them a people. The Ryangans are what Eliade would term 'religious man'. Their world is one in which the divine has manifested itself and continues to do so. Their openness to repeated manifestations of the sacred (Eliade names them hierophanies) in the context of ritual celebration and festivity is the only way they know how to be in the world. In contrast the barren liturgical celebrations that would have characterized Ireland in the thirties where Catholic ritual was overly cerebral, priestly and hierarchical, and certainly out of touch with the body and nature, would leave a people hungry and longing. The underside of this world-view is to be found in the practices in the back-hills. Jack's accounts allow us to see a more harmonious, integrated spirituality where there is less of a duality between body and soul, spirit and flesh, male and female, heaven and earth. But there is a danger in idealizing or romanticizing this.

Gerry Evans makes a second appearance. Having signed up to go to Spain as a dispatch rider for the International Brigade we learn that this 'ritual' took place in a Catholic Church. Does this indicate its redundancy as a place of religious ritual or simply the tacit validation of the Spanish Civil War by Catholic authorities? Gerry's conversation with Chris suggests that the cause he is supporting is the right thing for him to do:

And there's bound to be something right about the cause, isn't
there? And it's somewhere to go – isn't it? Maybe that's the
important thing for a man: a *named* destination – democracy,
Ballybeg, heaven. Women's illusions aren't so easily satisfied – they
make better drifters. (*Laughs*). (51)

While the truth of this remark for men's lives ultimately validates
their worthy causes, as they simply need to name where they're
going (however illusory the naming may be), women's inability to
name or satisfy their longings (within a patriarchal imagining) may
lead to the kind of drifting that will characterize the poverty-
stricken existence of Agnes and Rose when they become destitute
on the streets of London. Gerry brings news of a changing political order and Chris returns with news that Vera McLaughlin, the
knitting agent will no longer be able to buy any more hand-knit
gloves from Agnes and Rose, as there is a new factory starting up
in Donegal town.

The sexual tension underlying this act continues, with Rose's
account of her meeting with Danny Bradley, who took her to the
back-hills. The frisson created by the second visit of Gerry adds to
the tension. Maggie jokingly declares that if she had to choose
between a Wild Woodbine and a plump widower of fifty-two, that
she would choose the man. Time is running out. The possibility of
alternative ways of being in the world, while present, is not really
entertained. Agnes will not take up the position of dressmaker, nor
will the sisters go back to Ryanga with Jack, even if the marriage
arrangements could accommodate them favourably! As Kate rages
against such an invitation, and urges Jack to pay more attention to
Pope Pius XI, the radio plays 'Anything Goes.' Gerry invites
Agnes to dance. While singing the words of the song to her he
dances her out of the house, into the garden and back to the
kitchen. Stage directions indicate that they dance 'with style and
with easy elegance' (64). Gerry kisses Agnes on the forehead
before returning her 'safe and sound' to the kitchen. (Again we
note the contrast. Michael's narrative has intervened and we know
that Agnes ends up anything but safe and sound). When Maggie
offers to dance with Gerry, she asks him to hold her close. Chris
becomes jealous and suddenly turns the radio off. The sexual

frustration is heightened by Kate's information about the engagement of Sofia McLaughlin (fifteen years old) to a sixteen-year-old youth.

Rosie's entrance with the dead rooster which she places on the tablecloth on the ground is like a portent of death. There has been no ritual killing, no space to hold together everything that has been happening. It can no longer hold together. Maggie tries to tell one more riddle, but even the interruptive space of the joke is lost as she cannot remember the answer.

The ritual swapping of the hats that takes place between Jack and Gerry Evans is the final ritual of the play. It enables an exchange that is formally and irrevocably complete (69). Jack has given away his old ceremonial hat from his time as chaplain to the British Army during the Great War. In exchange he receives the straw boater from Gerry. Jack formalizes his leaving of his old life in the ritual space (inspired by his encounter with the Ryangan people). Gerry leaves for the International Brigade. The summer is over – Lughnasa is almost over, and nothing can ever be the same again:

> When I remember it, I think of it as dancing. Dancing with eyes half closed because to open them would break the spell. Dancing as if language had surrendered to movement – as if this ritual, this wordless ceremony, was now the way to speak, to whisper private and sacred things, to be in touch with some otherness … Dancing as if language no longer existed because words were no longer necessary. (71)

Something has shifted irrevocably and can only be recalled through the faculty of memory, where the gaps are filled by the music, dance and ritual. The alternative sacred space of theatre may facilitate an encounter with such otherness.

Tea in a China Cup, Christina Reid (1983)

Christina Reid's 1983 *Tea in a China Cup* (Reid, 1997: 1-65) is a play about the lives of working-class Protestant women in Belfast over three generations. It is essentially Beth's story and her strong narrative voice enables access to her family's past and her own history as she weaves the tapestry of memory. The soul journey that Beth's narrative weaves is a complex and composite one. It is

very much about women's time, in its non-linear, spiralling, fluid
narrating. Shifting time-frames give the audience access to
different kinds of memory, both the stories told and incidents
remembered. As Beth's mother faces her death from terminal
cancer, her daughter remembers and tries to access her own myth
of origins in order to find herself and move forward in hope. In a
prevailing climate of sectarianism and against the changing
historical back-drop of war and the troubles, the women's lives
unfold. Beth's relationship with her family is both a defining and
limiting one as she struggles with love for her mother, whose
staunch Protestant self-definition, is in contrast to her own more
open-minded and tolerant beliefs. The play looks at the whole
question of religious identity. In the context of working-class
Belfast between 1939 and 1972, three generations of a Protestant
family define who they are   – in terms of their difference,
superiority and cleanliness –   in contrast to their Catholic
neighbours. Their tangible personal symbols of pride include sepia
photographs of the sons who went to war, the occasional piece of
linen and the owning of a fine bone china tea set, which set them
apart and give them a sense of identity, in familial and cultural
terms.

The opening line of the play 'I want to buy a grave' (*Tea* 3) is a
stark introduction to the centrality of death to Beth's narrative,
both the imminent death of her mother Sarah, family memories of
death and rituals around dying, deaths from violence and all the
lesser losses that are part of a normal human life. There is a sense
of a decay at the heart of the society. Sarah's illness which was precipitated by the outbreak of 'The Troubles' in Northern Ireland,
began as depression, but grew as an undetected cancer for the
following year. Now in her mid-fifties, Sarah is living in Beth's
house, and spends her last days lying on Beth's red velvet sofa,
listening to the Orange bands practising for the Twelfth of July, an
experience which has an exhausting but visceral effect on her: 'It's
the sound of the flute bands … always gets the oul Protestant
blood going.' (9)

Sarah hopes to live to see one more Twelfth of July and
reminisces about bringing Beth as a baby to the Field at Finaghy.
She asks Beth not to forget; 'You mind it now, you mind all the

old family stories, tell them to your children after I'm gone' (10). As Beth addresses the audience we have a sense of how personal identity is formed. The stories of her family are her stories, they have made her who she is. While Beth cannot literally remember when she was four months old, the narrated story has been formative in her identity as have others about family members who lived and died before she was born. The fusing of personal memory with these remembered narratives gives access to a fuller picture and highlights the complexity of creating a coherent narrative from the perspective of a single coherent subjectivity:

> She carried me to the Field when I was four months old. She was sitting on the grass, her back to a hedge, giving me a bottle, when a gentleman in a clerical collar came up and patted us both on the head. 'I'm proud of you, daughter,' he said to my mother, 'coming all this way with a young baby. Women like you are the backbone of Ulster.' (10)

The notion that women were simply bolstering up the system of patriarchal ideology by providing men to fight for King (or Queen) and country is a theme developed throughout the play. The younger generation questions its assumptions and the constant marginalization of and domestication of women.

Beth's memory of her mother's brother Samuel going off to war before she was born is another event furnished by family narratives rather than Beth's personal recollection. Roche observes that

> Her visionary seeing is related to the act of theatre, especially drama written by a woman since Beth as narrator is 'seeing' what she has never witnessed directly and we the audience are seeing what isn't there. (Roche, 1994:232)

Her later recollection of her own brother Sammy leaving to join the army is almost a reproduction of the original departure, each event colouring the other in Beth's narrative, until they become almost fluid and interchangeable. There is a noted contrast between the women and the men in relation to the ideology of war. Beth's grandmother feels that her son is still only a child, whereas her grandfather feels that he's 'not a wain any more, he's one of the King's men now' (*Tea* 11). The grandmother berates her husband for filling his son's head with 'nonsense about the great times you had with the lads in France during the First World War' (*Tea* 11). While he feels that going to war will make a man of his son, his wife wryly draws attention to the shrapnel in his leg and the effects of gas on his lungs 'from the last great war'. Stage directions indicate that she 'says the word 'great' with contempt'. The reality is that in the eyes of the women war is anything but great. In contrast to her son's desire to return with a string of medals on his chest she says: 'Never mind the medals, Samuel. You just keep your head down, and come home in one piece.' (13) His subsequent wounding and the correspondence from the army that reduced him to a number highlights the loss of individual identity and the countless faceless, nameless casualties of war. Beth *remembers* going to Bradford with her mother and grandmother to visit Samuel:

> I went too, barely formed inside my mother's womb. It was a beautiful day, the day we arrived. The wounded lay on stretchers outside on the grass, their bandages removed. Seemingly, there was some desperate hope that exposure to the sun's rays would stop the spread of gangrene. The smell was indescribable … As soon as we got back to Belfast, my Great Aunt Maisie took my grandmother to consult a fortune-teller. (16)

Both these memories are family ones that Beth has access to through remembered stories. The consultation with the fortune teller will foretell both Samuel's death and Beth's birth. They are familial and cultural layers in the construction of Beth's identity. Remembering them is constitutive of who she is and who she has become. Juxtaposing Beth's birth with her uncle's death pushes the play firmly back into the territory of the women. Roche suggests that

> in this juxtaposition women's experience is asserted against history, against a narrative of absence and death. (Roche, 1994:233)

The grandfather is sent to the pub, while the women hold the space of grieving. His utterance 'He was my son too, you know' (*Tea* 20) is either ignored or not heard. There is a sense that the men are useless, either drinkers or gamblers, and cannot be relied on. The women maintain a sense of pride and respectability, never letting themselves down in front of their neighbours. Letting the side down in any way is unacceptable and encourages comparison with the Catholics, who are not seen to share the Protestant sense of shame.

Beth's memory of her birth is another inherited memory:

> I was born breech on March the eighth, a jaundiced, sickly, under-weight child. My mother was advised to take me home and love me, because I was delicate and probably wouldn't last long. (22)

Her subsequent naming as Beth, after the heir to the throne, is preferable to Mary which has far too many Catholic associations. A scene shift to Beth as a child of eleven with her family and later with friend Theresa shows her attempting to come to terms with the myths that surround her. The perception that Catholics are dirty, with dirty houses allows her family to feel a sense of superiority:

> There's poor and poor. We keep our houses nice, always dress clean and respectable. There's no shame in a neat darn or a patch as long as a body is well washed. (23)

The Protestant sense of privacy and not letting oneself down in front of the neighbours is a mystery to Beth and she questions why she cannot say that her mother made her dress out of an old skirt:

> **Maisie:** Because if you do, you bring yourself down to the level of the Catholics, whining and complainin' and puttin' a poor mouth on yourself.
> **Grandmother:** No matter how poor we are child, we work hard and keep ourselves and our homes clean and respectable, and we always have a bit of fine bone china and good table linen by us. (25)

The significance of cleanliness also allows a sense of moral superiority. The projection onto the other of repressed or shadow areas of the self allows a self-definition to stay in place that needs the dichotomy. In Beth's family their home is considered good enough for the Queen to visit. (Another dichotomy, loyalty to the Queen versus loyalty to the Irish Republic):

> **Maisie:** If the new Queen herself, God bless her, was to call here for tea, we could do her proud. None of your old dirt here. (25)

Beth's revelation that her mother had to sell her china cabinet to her Catholic neighbour in order to pay the rent comes as news to her grandmother and Aunt who see it as a 'fine state of affairs when a God-fearin' hard-working Protestant has to sell her good china to a Fenian to make ends meet' (26). Beth tells them that her mother gave away all the contents of the cabinet except one china cup and saucer:

> She took that out before Mrs Duffy came, and afterwards she made herself a cup of tea in it and cried and she said she'd never forgive my daddy as long as she lived. (25)

The ritual around tea in a china cup is interesting for a variety of reasons. It is associated with the home – a woman's world. The beauty of the china is in contrast to the general poverty of their lives. The ritual space of sharing tea is a moment of grace and beauty in otherwise difficult and harsh lives. It becomes a symbol of aspiration and longing – that all of their lives would be of this quality. Beth will later marry a respectable young man and will be the first one in her family to own her own house. An indication of her success is measured by the quality of the fine bone china that Stephen's aunt owns and Beth's receiving of six bone china tea sets as wedding presents. The fact that she also inherits a Belleek china tea set, finally sets her apart. In the course of the play it will be considered too good to use and will be left in the china cabinet until Beth offers her mother her last cup of tea. However Beth's mother dies before she has the opportunity to drink from this tea set and without Beth ever having shared the disappointments of her life with her. As the play progresses we learn of Beth's increasing sense of disappointment with her unlived life (like unused china). Beth feels she is living a lie with her mother and is unable to let her know that she has repeated many of her mother's mistakes and that her marriage is all but over:

> Because it's all a lie ... and I want to tell *her* about it ... and I can't. My marriage has been the one big success of her life, and I can't spoil it for her, not now. I can't tell her that I faithfully repeated all her mistakes, that if you take away the velvet sofas and the china cabinet ... there's nothing there ...it's all a lie ... (60)

Joanna Luft interprets tea and its rituals as a Brechtian *gestus* which allows for social and political commentary, and offers Reid an opportunity to exemplify and critique the social relationships 'of the women themselves and the traditional values they externalize' (Luft, 1999:214). While the space of tea-drinking is the private and domestic the discourse that surrounds it is social and political. Tea-drinking can mask the ideologies that underpin it. After all it is at home that girls are socially conditioned to be good Protestant citizens. The issues of socialization, the conflict of religious ideologies, the demonization of the other, economic differences, the conditioning of women towards socially acceptable ideals of femininity and sexuality, all occur over the cup of tea. The *gestus* of tea

> exposes the social coercion behind gender formation, and religious strife. The discourse of tea compels girls to fit the mould of decent womanhood, which would be politically expedient in its fashioning of faithful Ulster women. (Luft, 217)

Luft writes about the importance of both Orange Pekoe tea within the house and the Orange Order outside, each being sustained and paralleled by the other. Equally the rituals of tea-drinking betray conventional and even misogynist notions of womanhood (219). China which can stand as a symbol or indicator of female sexuality and anatomy must also be interpreted within religious, economic and political terms and specifically with reference to the commodification of sexuality. Beth on her marriage will receive no less than six tea sets, all attesting to her conformity to tea cup ideology and according to Luft represent how Beth has become objectified into a wife, becoming more china and less Beth. Her friend Theresa on the other hand has become more herself and less china as is evidenced in her life-style in London and her use of non-matching mugs, rather than china cups. Beth's re-appropriation of herself will not occur until much later in the play after her mother's death and the disappearance of her husband.

Complex inherited negative mythologies around women and sexuality were part of Beth's upbringing. Beth recalls Sarah's reaction to her daughter's first menstruation when she told her that 'this is the start of all your troubles' (30). That women's menstruation would be seen as the start of her troubles is juxtaposed with the Troubles later in the play, which precipitate Sarah's illness. Luft suggests that female troubles in fact begin in a culture where womanhood ultimately is not nice (Luft, 1999:219). 'Both "troubles" – social violence and coercive notions of womanhood – work towards securing the trouble-free running of Ulster society' (Luft, 219), where gendered roles are also political ones.

Beth's narrative weaves in and out of significant moments in her own life. She remembers her interview for a job in the Civil Service, her courtship with Stephen, her brother Sammy leaving home to join the British Army, the eve of her wedding. Her friendship with Theresa is woven through her remembering. Throughout her story there is a distinct absence of men, or at least an absence of strong male figures. The world of the women (albeit quite conservative) is nonetheless one where certain spheres of women's wisdom are appreciated. Women have long been associated with rituals around death and dying and the older women have initiated Beth into this knowing. But there is an essential dichotomy between the male and female worlds. Sarah speaking of Beth's deceased father remarks, 'he could have been worse…he never lifted a finger to any of us in his life, he just had a weakness for the drink and the bettin' … he couldn't help it, he was only a man, God help him' (38). The women blame other women for not encouraging their sons or brothers to grow up. The belief is that they are spoilt and need constant minding like children. The men abandon their women, through addiction, business or by going to war. Theresa too has been abandoned by her man and is rearing a three-year-old daughter on her own in London. When Beth finds herself alone on her wedding night with her new husband entertaining business colleagues in the bar, her surprise gift from Theresa of a copy of *The Invisible Man*, is an apt comment on the absence of men.

Women can only escape their family of origin by marrying into another family. Beth feels that she had never made a decision in her life:

I've been my mother's daughter, and now I'm going to be
Stephen's wife...I've never been just me. I've never made a decision in my life (50).

Beth will remain very much her mother's daughter even after her
marriage and will not really be free to find herself until after her
mother dies. She cannot even 'defy' her mother by letting Sammy
know how ill she is, as her mother believes that it would be too
dangerous for him to return home once the Troubles started. Beth
tells Theresa that all her life people have been telling her what to
do and that now she feels scared:

I'm scared, Theresa ... my mother's dying and very soon for the
first time in my life I am going to be alone ... and I'm scared ...
my head is full of other people's memories. I don't know who *I* am
... what *I* am ... (61)

The final phase in Beth's remembering coincides with the start of
the Troubles in Northern Ireland in 1971. As 'the rattle of the bin
lid challenged the supremacy of the Lambeg drum' (59), the
introduction of internment led to rioting and explosions in the
streets. Beth tries to encourage her mother to leave her home and
go with her to safety. Her mother refuses to be intimidated into
abandoning her home despite Beth's warning. Sarah recalls the
stories of the lives that are contained in all the 'contents' of the
house:

Sarah: I remember the day the men came to put it in. She was that
pleased, no more black leadin' ... that was when she started to buy
the brass ornaments, one every nigh and again when she could
afford it ...
Beth: Mum, they're only ... things ...bits and pieces ... they can
all be replaced ...
Sarah: They're my life! (57)

But while Sarah will succeed in holding onto her house and its
lifetime of memories, Beth tells us that 'From that night onwards
my mother began to die' (59). There is a sense of futility in these
final scenes. What has it been about after all? Why did the women
work their fingers to the bone for their families, why did the men
suffer and die in the service of king or queen and country. And if
the answers are no longer clear-cut the question of who the enemy

is poses a serious problem. If they are no longer identifiable in terms of inherited negative stereotyping the question of how a society negotiates its relationship with difference and the other must be faced.

In the closing moments of the play Beth removes a single cup and saucer from her Belleek set, placing them in her handbag, despite devaluing the tea set, which she is selling along with the contents of her house. Luft suggests that in breaking up the china tea-set Beth changes its meaning. It now becomes a symbol of her reclaimed selfhood and sexuality. Beth

> transforms a degrading and restrictive sign into one of empowerment, suggesting her resistance to the ideologies embedded in it (Luft, 220).

The china cup and saucer along with the family portraits of the men who went to war are all that Beth wants to take with her from her old life. She takes the memories of the women and the men to whom she belongs. She will not continue to repeat their notions of sacrifice either in terms of the ideology of war or the false notions of self-sacrifice that traditionally defined and confined women. The ritual of tea in a china cup may still remain part of her self-definition, but its meaning will be very different.

La Corbière, Anne Le Marquand Hartigan (1989)

Anne Le Marquand Hartigan's *La Corbière* (Le Marquand Hartigan, 2001:161-193) is essentially a poetic piece. It offers a grieving ritual for the French women prostitutes, sent to the Nazi soldiers, stationed in Jersey, for their entertainment, who were drowned when their ship went down in a storm during the Second World War. Many of these women's bodies were left floating for days in the indifferent sea, their peroxide hair 'spread on the sea's time'. Cathy Leeney writes:

> Le Marquand Hartigan confronts us with the language of savage insult and obliteration, and uses the healing sea as a metaphor for the redemption of the lost women. Paradoxically, her abstract theatrical vision reaches deep into the tragedy and damage of war, and the will to negate it in honour of remembrance. (Leeney, 2001: viii/ix)

Through language, imagery and sounds the play engages in a
ritual remembering where the stories of these women's lives are
told. Voices are heard and there is an attempt to speak the unspeakable. Theatre in turn becomes the space for a ritual of
grieving and memory where an alternative vision of redemption is
put before the audience. Le Marquand Hartigan's lament offers the
women the burial and anointing refused to them by their religion
and culture. She boldly names these women as *Corpus Christi* (the
Body of Christ), praying that they too will have eternal rest. Her
use of the Latin '*Requiem aeternam dona eis domine*' (Eternal rest grant
unto them, O Lord) is an appropriation for these women of the
traditional language of the church. She will also mourn and offer
the ritual burial they too deserve. Le Marquand Hartigan situates
these nameless women, in the context of a patriarchal culture
where they have been used and abused and discarded. They have
also come to represent everything that the culture has repressed or
denied or cannot own. So often woman as symbol is left in this
ambiguous space, either symbolizing absolute truth, goodness etc.,
or representing the utterly debased and most disowned aspects of
a culture.

In a series of scenes Le Marquand Hartigan takes us from the
wreck and the mourning of Marie-Claire – one of the women who
survived – (Scenes 1 and 2) backwards to the arrival of the women
on the island, and their time there (Scenes 3-6) and returns to
lamentation in the final scenes (Scenes 7-11). This circular structure makes it impossible to forget that the wreck is the centre of
the play, whether the actual shipwreck or the inevitable wrecking
of the women's lives that arose as a result of prostitution. The play
opens in fog which symbolized what many of the women felt
about their lives: 'All my life, in fog just like this. Dumb' (*La
Corbière* 165). The sense of being lost, of not being able to touch or
feel another, and the impossibility of vision (Visibility now nil at
La Corbière) could also be a reflection or metaphor for the
difficulties of their lives. Their inability to swim, their age and the
sense of 'there is nothing to hold' (*LC* 169) further accentuate
their helplessness and powerlessness. The second scene begins the
ritual lamenting that is central to the drama. The words and sounds
echo each other and the juxtaposition of male and female voices

adds its own discordance. As the women are named *Corpus Christi* and eternal rest requested for them, another male voice repeatedly sounds 'Whore' and 'Harlot.' Marie-Claire's voice calls for the women to rise up and her speech is interwoven with sounds of the sea grinding and sucking. 'Rise up ye strong whores. Sisters rise up, strong. Strong sisters. Wronged Sisters. I will weep for thee, mourn for thee, cry for thee. In the strong salt sea will long for thee, sea sister, water sister, we will howl for thee, banshee for thee, weep for thee, as the salt sea seep for thee' (*LC* 170-171). The hope of resurrection may be found in the ritual words. The traditional role of women in keening and lamenting the dead is re-appropriated and their tears become one with the salt water of the sea. There is a sense of language breaking down as the meanings slip and slide into one another. Salt becomes assault (*LC* 172) and dead beat becomes beat dead (172).

Scene Three – The Arrival – draws attention to the obscene brutal reality of war and the particularity of the women's lives. The women are 'at the butt' of a gun, in the hands of people who took their sisters and brothers and who even 'shot the dog' (178). Language continues to exclude the women as their guards 'don't understand French' (175). The reality of their lives, 'I've got my period' and their concern for those left behind, Will I see her again? Will she mind him properly/ Will he be there when I get home? is juxtaposed by their powerful captors who want 'Name, date of birth, nationality?', who tell the women not to speak or show any light whatsoever as they lead them away.

Scene Four which is an account of the women's daily walk on the island continues to juxtapose the particularity of the women's lives with what they symbolize for the men. All of the women are named. This is an important element of ritual. Naming has the power of evoking the particular reality of each woman's life. It is an exercise of memory which reinstates her in history. An extract from the scene gives a sense of how the naming is juxtaposed with what the men see and think:

Kurt: Each day a crocodile of women.
                                    Quietly as
                                  water slopping
Angélique: Angélique Duval   **Kurt:** slop clop slop
Céleste: Celeste Vidal   **Klaus:** slit slut slit
Marie-Claire: Marie-Claire Depret **Kurt:** slop clop slop. (177)

The juxtapositioning of the captors' perception of the women highlights their abhorrence: 'Fuck Cunt Slit. Merde Cochon Putain'. Klaus, one of the German soldiers, watches the crocodile of women out walking under the watchful eye of the Madam. He sees them as 'Docile. Captured' (178) but they also remind him of schoolgirls in a Corpus Christi procession, wearing white veils and throwing petals (179). This echoes the earlier naming of the women who drowned as *Corpus Christi*.

Scene Five brings us the women's dreams. Dreams of marriage and children, of home and safety, of warmth and bread and mothers, dreams which are violently interrupted and juxtaposed by Klaus's rape of Désirée. The separation and tearing apart of the women from their ordinary lives is mirrored and magnified in the rupturing and violation that takes place in the rape. Scene Six which is a Cabaret in the hotel continues to explore sexual abuse where the game of slap and tickle easily slips into the violence of slap, tickle, and punch (184). Marie-Claire's lines again invite the women to rise up. It is an invitation to seize the word (prise de parole), find their voices and to tell their story:

> Rise up from the bottom of the sea. Rise up from the bottom of their minds. Rise. Up pushing down the sea. Rise. Shout out so loud that the world will burst. From the bottom of the sea the world will burst.

When woman speaks her own self, her own particular embodied subjectivity, the whole of western reason begins to crumble and the world as we have had it named and interpreted for us will burst.

The last five scenes explore the wreck and the power of the sea and attempt to give the women the ritual burial they deserve. The sea is both healing and harsh, its sounds alternately soothing and menacing. The rock and swell calls to mind images of mothers swelling with child and nursing babies. But the wreck is the ultimate negative space – the nowhere that the women finally inhabit. The sea closes like a lid on their lives and there is no answer but stone (186). The sea swallows and grinds their bodies and lives to a kind of sand in its final burial. Scene Ten entitled The Drowned Whores' Picnic is stark both in its imagery and naming. The women speak about what they were to the men:

Angélique: Your lovers.
Désirée: Your time-machines. Your nothings. Your holes.
Angélique: Your forgetting.
Céleste: Your guiltholder.
Désirée: Your silences.
Céleste: Your dirt. Your rubbish.
Désirée: Your hate. Your violence. Your punchball.
Angélique: Your face, your Mother ... (190)

The refusal to continue to inhabit the negative space assigned to women, their bodies and their experiences, within the patriarchal symbolic is evident here. To speak with awareness of all that women have been made to carry, of all the meanings that women have had scribbled on their bodies, is to refuse to continue to participate in such naming. But other than exit, the symbolic women have to continue to use the available language to speak. Interspersing this language with multiple meanings, contradictions, and other sibilant and guttural sounds may bring it closer to the semiotic.

The final words of the play echo the reality that these women were left floating for days on the indifferent sea, and that they never received a proper ritual burial:

Marie-Claire: No one is coming with arms to dip. ...No one will lay you out in a quiet room. No one will light a candle at your head and feet. There will be no prayers. No one will push their boat out to take your bodies back to earth. ...No chrism to anoint your brow. No incense around a coffin of wood. No name in the newspaper, no name. Sorrow is a lost word. There are no tears. Can the salt sea weep? Only a harsh gull's cry. (192-193)

And yet in the quiet room of theatre the lives of these women have been remembered. They have been sought out and named. The ritual lamentation has been offered. Their bodies have been brought back to earth. And while the play offers no closure there is a sense of completion. A memory has been restored. The grieving ritual that involves such dangerous memories is an invitation to audiences not to forget. 'Lest we forget' is a phrase associated with memorials of the Second World War. It could be an epigraph for *La Corbière*.

Eclipsed, Patricia Burke Brogan 1992

Another memory play that attempts to deal with the reality of Irish women's lives in the sixties is *Eclipsed*, Patricia Burke Brogan's play about the Magdalen Laundries. This play was 'inspired by the practice – which started in the time of the Famine, and lasted well into the 1960s and later – of forcing pregnant and unwed Irish mothers to work as 'penitents' in church-run laundries' (Burke Brogan, 1994) Burke Brogan, herself a former novice, spent some time working in one of these institutions. This may well be the real hidden Ireland. To tell these stories is to interrupt the master narratives, to give voice to an underside of history, to allow what Foucault called the insurrection of subjugated knowledge to emerge and question dominant cultural narratives of identity.

From a feminist point of view the whole role of Mary Magdalen – traditionally depicted as sinner and prostitute – has been revisited. While traditional patriarchal interpretations of her have tended to stress the quality of her repentance and the forgiveness of her sins, feminist hermeneutics has called attention to her role as apostle in ministry. One of the early ground-breaking works of feminist hermeneutics is Schussler Fiorenza's *In Memory of Her* (1983), which takes the lines from Mark's gospel, that follow Mary Magdalen's anointing of Jesus with precious oil prior to his death, as the epigraph for her book: 'Wherever the gospel is preached in the whole world, what she has done will be told in memory of her' (Mark 14:9). It is how and what we remember that is so important. Burke Brogan dedicated her play 'In Memory of the Magdalens'. She remembers the women who lived and worked in the Magdalen Laundries, as women not as sinners. In a highly theatrical piece she invites us to be on the inside of these women's lives, in their companionship and grief, in their humour, and despair. She opens the theatrical space towards a deeper remembering. Music from plain chant and Handel to Elvis Presley and a host of other songs punctuates the narrative. The props of the laundry become in turn resources for creativity and play while also reminding audiences of the hard physical work that these women actually performed. The women find themselves in a nowhere place from which it is almost impossible to escape. They find themselves carrying a culture's and a religion's negation of the body and of female sexuality. They are scapegoats who embody and carry the sins of the society. They are needed to keep the society and its moral code intact. The conflict between alternative ways of interpreting these women's lives is expressed in the conflict between the women and the nuns who run the laundry (Brigit's experience in particular) and also between Mother Victoria and the novice Sister Virginia. In *Eclipsed* the treatment of this conflict is nuanced and sensitive in contrast to many other portrayals of the same subject.

Act One, Scene One and Act Two, Scene Six take place in 1992, the rest of the play in 1963. It has a cast of seven women. The nuns are dressed in pre-Vatican 2 clothing with full *'veil-coif-domino-guimpe'*, which includes large black rosary beads and long black leather belts. The women are dressed in *'shapeless worn-out overalls with white aprons, black laced-up shoes and thick black stockings'* (*Eclipsed* 3). A series of muslin drapes are pulled back to distinguish the different spaces in the play.

The play opens in the present when Rosa, Brigit's daughter arrives to find out what she can about her mother. In a dusty basement she is shown a large old Laundry Basket which contains many of the props for the play and out of which the story and the memories will emerge. She opens a battered ledger and reads the names and the details of the Penitent women who were signed into St. Paul's Laundry, Killmacha, in 1963 by their parents or employers. She finds her own mother's name Brigit Murphy, along with a baby photograph in a chocolate box. (*E* 6-7). As each of the women is introduced and named, it is almost like a ritual of naming and remembering. The play proceeds to flesh out and embody these lives for the audience and for the culture that has forgotten them. In a similar fluid narrative to Reid and Le Marquand Hartigan we are invited to access the memories of women's lives through shifting time-frames. Rosa's stance in the present allows the audience to participate in her uncovering of the forgotten women's memories. Through a minimum of words and props the time and place is established. Elvis Presley's 'Heartbreak Hotel' is in contrast to the earlier extract from the oratorio of Handel's Messiah. Whether one interprets the women as Christ figures in the way that they too have been despised and rejected, one cannot but feel the poignancy of alluding to their institution as Heartbreak Hotel. The women have been signed into this institution, simply because of pregnancy outside of marriage. Themes of love and sexuality weave through the narratives as the women's lives unfold. Love may indeed be a trick (E 20), but the women still remember and dream. There may be different rules for women and men but they can still imagine relationships with a smasher (E 10), or a pop star like Elvis. The women who work like slaves in the laundry can always pretend, and imagine themselves somewhere else. This element of play pushes the parameters of *Eclipsed* beyond the narrow confines of a realist frame, as the world of *what if* intermittently breaks through the prison of their lives, and questions all received interpretations. The quiet desperation of these women whose children have been taken from them (or who have had still-births) is temporarily alleviated through moments of play but the despair has a darker side, and also emerges in violent outbursts, both verbal and physical, as the women rage against the cruelty and arbitrariness of their condition.

It is imperative that one does not question the *status quo* or try to escape it or change it in any way, whether that applies to the 'penitent' women or to the young novice who is working in the institution. Blind obedience (47), physical beatings and removal of privileges will keep the system in place. The dehumanizing effects of this on the lives of those who keep this system in place are questioned by Sister Virginia, which at least offers an alternative spirituality:

> Are you a God of Love? A God of Justice? – I thought I'd be working for the poor! Am I being brain-washed? Will I become dehumanized too, if I stay here long enough? Locked in Obedience? (32)

Her questioning of her faith is influenced by contemporary feminist theological thinking and provides a believable counterpoint to the authoritarian unquestioning extremes of Mother Victoria. As Sister Virginia wonders how far her own order have deviated from the vision of their founder she questions:

> Was early Christian History rewritten too? Women's witness submerged? – Christ Crucified! Help them! For a woman bore you, carried you for nine months! Mother of Jesus, do something about Cathy, Mandy, Nellie-Nora and the others!

Sister Virginia finds it sad to be working with these women. She feels that the nuns are like jailers, that it is wrong to take the children from the women, and that they need vitamins, medication, fresh air. She disobeys rules and invites the Bishop to visit the Laundry to see the conditions for himself. She chooses not to remain aloof from the women as her superior has advised and endangers her life in the process. She feels that she understands the women's despair and says she would tear down the walls with her nails if her own child was taken from her (46). While she is undergoing her own crisis of faith, the women, and Brigit in particular, see her on the side of the enemy. Brigit wants her to hand over the keys in order to escape but she refuses. Brigit speaks angrily to her:

> Pretending to help! You're just like the rest o' them! You think if you keep us locked up, that we'll forget about living! About being alive? Don't you? That our heads will go soft and mushy from hymns and prayers!

Brigit's rage is palpable, she becomes threatening and menacing:

> You don't know anything! Never had a lover! Never had a baby! So you're white and shining, Sister! Not the same as us, are you? Whose side are you on anyways? Why aren't our lover-boys locked up too? One law for them and another for us! (59)

As she writes Scab on the wall with lipstick she pulls off Sister Virginia's veil and shouts 'I'll daub it on your baldy skull! Scab! Spy! Informer!' (60).

The women's lives have become so despairing that one can identify complete loss of soul, and understand such violent outbursts. We are reminded that one of the women had thrown bleach at another sister in a similar outburst. And in the very opening moments of the play Brigit says how much she hates Mother Victoria:

> That rip Victoria! God how I hate her! Some day I'll put her through the washing machines! Then I'll smather her with red hot irons! Herself and his Lordship with his buckled shoes! (11)

But the soul loss is on both sides whatever Brigit may feel. When one of the women (Cathy) is found dead (from an asthma attack) in a laundry basket after an escape attempt, the women find it hard to believe and they blame themselves. As they are invited to pray for the repose of her soul, Brigit faces Sister Virginia in one final showdown. Brigit asks her for the keys and she unclips them from her belt, allowing her to escape. Brigit leaves, shouting that the nuns are the ones who are dead inside their laundry basket hearts.

The laundry basket is used in an imaginative and resourceful way throughout the play. While it is obviously associated with the kind of work the women do, in being the container for the linens, blankets and clothes that the women launder and repair it also becomes a container for play. In place of the humiliation of laundering other people's undergarments it becomes a space in which they can parody their situation and imagine alternative realities. In turn it will also be used for Cathy's escape attempt and thirty years later will be the last remaining container for the memories of the women's lives. It is almost as if the play emerges from the laundry basket (like the box from which the play emerges in *Talbot's Box* and the basket of vestments in *Belfry*).

While responsible for laundering the Bishop's clothes Brigit puts on his surplice and uses an upside-down mop as a crozier. The parody of Brigit as Bishop allows the women to imagine freedom, in having money for cigarettes and access to a pantry full of rich food. While the reality of their situation doesn't give them access to celebration they can imagine being in Paris or Hollywood, believing that 'It'll be true if you pretend!' (18). The women decide to get Mandy ready to meet Elvis, her idol and urge her into the basket, to pack her off to the USA. They also dress up a mannekin doll in clothes from the laundry to represent Elvis and then plan a mock wedding. Brigit continues to act as Bishop dressed in a crimson soutane and surplice and performs the wedding. All of this takes place accompanied by the women singing a number of popular songs about love and marriage and the poignant playacting ends with the voice-over of an Elvis song. The parody and playacting may give a temporary access to a sense of power and may not render the real power of the church any less significant. However its enactment does allow the performers and the audience to experience some reprieve even if it is temporary and imaginary.

The women find themselves in a world without men, but the issue of sex just doesn't disappear. The women fantasize or remember moments with their men, whether tender or abusive. They create dream lovers and paper babies to remind them of their children. They are very much aware that they are carrying the sins of the society, and that the men can carry on with normal lives while they exist as the scapegoats on whom all the sins are heaped. To refuse to carry such sins demands that the religion and culture look again at their self-definitions. Brigit's outspokenness and anger allows her to name the reality from her perspective. In Act 2 Scene 2 the women are dusting and polishing a floor. When Cathy says that they need a machine for polishing instead of the old wooden blocks that they're using Brigit says: 'We're the machines, Cathy!' (48). As Brigit is emptying the dust into the bin she begins a parody on Purgatory, to which Nellie-Nora chants the catechism answer: 'Purgatory is a place or state of punishment, where some souls suffer for a time before they can enter Heaven!' (50). Brigit throws each of the women (symbolized by their polishing cloths), along with their boyfriends into the bin, which she pretends is the fire of purgatory. She consigns Mother Victoria and her own boyfriend John-Joe to the hotter fires of Hell, and remarks how they are all burning with thirst, which cannot be slaked. Again the elements of play and parody succeed in undermining some of the crushing orthodoxies that define the women's lives.

The women occupy the position of outsiders. Their outsider status can be interpreted in a number of ways. On the margins, they can be rejected, and forgotten. Or they can be accommodated by those who consider themselves carers or do-gooders, but they still remain powerless. If however they are allowed to speak, to have access to tools of transformation including education and money, their status as outsiders can be radically interruptive and empowering as they question assumptions about knowledge and power. All three levels operate in the play. Brigit encourages Mandy to write her return address on her letter to Elvis:

> Saint Paul's Home for Penitent women! Home for the unwanted. The outcasts! Saint Paul's Home for the women nobody wants! (35)

The Catholic Church represented by Mother Victoria argues: 'We give them food, shelter and clothing. We look after their spiritual needs. No one else wants them!' (31)

She feels that they are there to protect these women from their passions, that they are fallen women, and are weak. Such a theology identifies women with nature, bodiliness, sexuality, temptation and evil. Women in this paradigm carry responsibility for the body which is always a source of temptation as it pulls us down to earth rather than allowing us aspire towards spirit. Women who engage in sexual liaisons outside of marriage must also be contained as they threaten the whole social order. They foreground the repressed aspects of a cultural system. Keeping them locked away allows the system to continue uninterrupted. Increasing levels of violence and dehumanization accompany this process. Cathy who tried to escape is beaten around the head when she is brought back. Mother Victoria says she needed to slap her to 'bring her back to reality' (45). Mother Victoria has managed to silence her own conscience: 'When I was nineteen, I had the same thoughts! I wanted to free the penitents' (45). She tells Sister Virginia that she will receive the grace to do God's will and that God's ways are not our ways. When she asks Virginia whether she has been meditating she answers:

> I try Mother! But there are dark – dark clouds – doubts, Mother! The women are drudges, are bond-women! I – I didn't expect this!

Mother Victoria answers:

> We all go through those dark nights! – Dark Nights! Try to remember that We Are Eclipsed! But that deep inside is a Shining

> that is Immortal – a part of us, which is outside Time. Hold on to
> that thought! Do not question the System! You want to change the
> Rule, the Church, the World! You must start with yourself! Change
> yourself first! Get rid of Pride! Obey the Rule, Sister! Remember –
> We are eclipsed. But Blind Obedience will carry you through!
> (46-47)

If we consider the meaning of eclipsed we are in the realms of
what is hidden or overshadowed, what is obscured or darkened. St.
Paul wrote about our human perception of the divine as 'through a
glass darkly.' While this can become in turn the basis for a true
mystical knowing of God (where unknowing and the dark are a
central part) it is dangerous when such a theology is used to
validate spiritual existence over earthly life, and when all human
questioning is to be stifled in a disposition of blind obedience.
When a theology promises eternal life and neglects the quality of
human lives in the here and now, it needs to be questioned. This
would be the starting point for many contemporary theologies of
liberation, where the divine promise of liberation is interpreted as a
call to transformation of unjust social and political structures that
impede human growth and becoming.

The status of the outsider is very important in contemporary
theology. The God of the Hebrew and Christian scriptures is
interpreted as being on the side of the outsider, the marginalized,
those on the outskirts of society whether women, prostitutes,
sinners, tax collectors or despised social classes. This has given rise
to a theology which speaks in terms of a preferential option for the
poor. Theology is urged to find its starting point in terms of the
dispossessed, to ask what might the message of the scriptures be
when interpreted from the point of view of the poorest of the
poor. Sister Virginia's theology begins from the experience of the
women (the outcast or the poor in this situation). Her doubts and
disquiet at the conditions of the women's lives stands as a corrective to the dominant theology represented by Mother Victoria.
Her vantage point and the narratives of the women themselves
foreground the experience of the outsider and cause us to question
many of our received assumptions. The play as a whole presents
the stories of women who were outsiders, and who were almost
written out of history. In so doing it forces reassessment of

narratives of cultural identity that focused exclusively on people of privilege and prestige. The scene between the two sisters ends with a soprano singing of the 'Magnificat', a wonderful biblical female song of praise, of the triumph of the weak over the rich and powerful.

The epilogue of the play continues the story. Brigit escaped and was never heard of again. Mandy who was becoming increasingly unstable in the course of the play was admitted to a Mental Institution the following year and never left it. Cathy had died, Julie returned to the orphanage and Nellie-Nora remained fearful, permanently scarred and institutionalized. In 1992 the bodies of the dead were exhumed and reburied to make room for building development. Hundreds of the women who were exhumed were unnamed.

Conclusion

The plays in this section present six journeys through memory where different voices map the territory of Irish cultural identity within which successive generations are invited to find a standing place for the feet in order to know who they are and where they are going. Attention to gender ideologies alerts us to the fact that men have always found it easier to locate themselves in history, seeing themselves centre stage in the myths and narratives that form one's cultural inheritance. Contemporary feminist thought finds the maps that we have been given as Adrienne Rich says 'out of date/ by years' (Rich, 1984:242). The failure of these same maps to note significant sections of experience and history have left many women without a sense of place or belonging. Many recorded histories have rendered women's experience silent or invisible. Others have marginalized them through a trivialization or negation of their experience. Others have demonized and scapegoated women for all the sins and evil of the world. And yet others have so exalted the place of woman that she simply exists as a symbol (truth, goodness, beauty, justice etc.) that bears little or no resemblance to real women.

Feminist philosophers are interested in a philosophy that thinks differently, rather than one which legitimates what is already known. In this regard they advocate a multifaceted strategy where one listens for silences, notices lacunae, hears sounds from the margins, and pays attention to the relationship between mothers and daughters. Irigaray urges that one engage in 'jamming the theoretical machinery' of the whole cultural system, challenging its claims to truth and meaning that are exclusively univocal. Questioning the symbol systems that underpin a culture involves attention to what is validated or upheld, seeing who has access to power and meaning-making within the culture, and awareness of what is encoded within the symbol system. The mind/body dualism that underpins all of western patriarchal thinking is reflected in a nature/culture divide where men are seen as superior to women, and given the role of meaning-makers within culture. The access to meaning-making at the higher metaphysical levels of culture has always been reserved for men and in turn has been sanctioned and validated by a male deity. Women in turn have been associated with the lower bodily, material, physical and sexual realities. Their place within the cultural symbol system is always 'other'. Culture created out of the male unconscious has privileged male identity and becoming. Male subjectivity is presupposed within the system. It is harder however for women to be subjects. Belsey puts it well:

> To speak is to possess meaning, to have access to the language which defines, delimits and locates power. To speak is to become a subject. But for women to speak is to threaten the system of difference which gives meaning to patriarchy. (Belsey, 1985:191)

Irigaray claims that woman is reduced to unconsciousness or the negative of the masculine unconscious, to the matter which upholds the whole masculine system of representation:

> woman incarnates the oblivion whence flows the forgetting of all matter ... As soon as woman-matter begins to speak, the whole edifice of Western Reason begins to crumble. (Braidotti, 1991:255)

How do we deal with the whole question of the other? If woman has traditionally carried what the male unconscious has repressed or denied, and if that has in turn given rise to a whole symbol system that also denies any specificity to the female unconscious, (Feral, 1980:92) what happens when one tries to inscribe difference into the existing discourse? Essentially to put discourse into question is to reject the existing order (Feral,

1980:91). To inscribe women in all their multiplicity and difference into discourse is to fundamentally question the patriarchal framework within which we think and imagine. Cixous stopped going to the theatre because she felt that it was like going to her own funeral. She believes that the sacrifice of woman is at the heart of all cultural production:

> It is always necessary for a woman to die in order for the play to begin. Only when she has disappeared can the curtain go up; she is relegated to repression, to the grave, the asylum, oblivion and silence. When she does make an appearance, she is doomed, ostracised or in a waiting room. She is loved only when absent or abused, a phantom or a fascinating abyss. (Cixous, 1984:546-48)

Many male playwrights have turned to the creation of strong female characters in order to explore what has been written out of history or to put them in touch with some otherness. In this category we can place *Baglady, Bailegangaire*, and *Dancing at Lughnasa*. In assessing male writing about women one needs to pay attention to whether it is simply a further colonization of the female, a way of giving voice to the cultural crisis for western reason and philosophy, or a method for writing about the male artistic desire for wholeness. Roche questions whether male writers developing strong female characters is not simply another attempt to 'appropriate and colonize the concerns of women in a feat of expert ventriloquism, a pre-emptive creative strike against the increasing number of women writing plays and having them staged' (Roche, 1994:286).

There is no doubting the massive cultural changes that have occurred in Ireland over the past thirty years. Irish politician Gemma Hussey writing in 1993 (*Ireland Today*) noted that

> Irish society has changed more in the two decades leading to the 1990s than in the whole of the previous one hundred years ... An inward-looking, rural, deeply conservative, nearly 100 per cent Roman Catholic and impoverished country has become urbanized, industrialized and Europeanized ... and still the hunger for change is there. (Quoted in Murray 1997:245)

The same basic issues occur again and again in Irish drama, questions about identity, home and a sense of place. All knowledge is historically and culturally conditioned. The social, economic, political and religious reality that is late twentieth-century Ireland foregrounds different questions about identity, home and place. The plays explored in this section span a period from the early eighties to the mid-nineties (1983-1994). Many of them draw attention to the violence, brutality and abuse that is at the heart of Irish culture. So often they are plays of tragedy and loss. The journey home is a long slow process that involves deeper and deeper levels of self-awareness. The painful truths of a culture's history must be brought into consciousness, the shadow faced, the traumatic experience brought into narrative memory before we can imagine a new future.

Baglady's painful narrative has been embodied, within a text, on a stage, played by a flesh and blood woman, and now takes its place within a tradition, which can no longer dissociate itself from this kind of knowing. Mommo's narrative of the laughing competition pivots on misfortunes both personal and cultural that are denied, disowned, and disembodied. Mommo, like Baglady, only succeeds in moving from speaking in the third person to first person in her narrative as she tells the story and stops dissociating from it. The journey from what is known to what is felt and known is the healing journey. The connection with the wounded feeling or generative function is a journey that takes place in the heart. Whether the heart is the individual heart or the cultural heart, the journey is towards feeling and owning the pain. Only then can one imagine newness.

As playwrights search the contours of memory, whether personal or political, they provide vantage points for interpretation which can define, delimit or expand the real. If playwrights create interrogative texts that question all perceived assumptions, they can push drama beyond the limiting confines of a realist frame. *Dancing at Lughnasa* is better considered as a memory rather than a history play. In its foregrounding of five strong female characters, albeit through the memory of Michael, Friel, according to Roche 'puts the Irish stage in touch with the otherness of women' (Roche, 1994:286). While there is no doubting the sheer physical impact of the presence on stage of these five sisters, especially in the famous dance scene, it may be problematic to focus on otherness in the way that Roche does. While his stance is nuanced it may not afford women the same kind of subject position as men, as it expects them to carry and embody an otherness that the culture has disowned. Anna McMullan feels that

> the feminine has frequently provided the missing links of af-
> fectivity, community, corporeality and sexuality, which have
> fertilized the male imagination, enabling it to continue to produce
> authority, phoenix-like, out of the ruins of authority. (McMullan,
> 1999:96)

There is always a problem with creating or painting the other out of the dominant culture's lack. It is equally problematic for the crisis or breakdown in a culture to be expressed through female images and symbols. When this happens attention is drawn away from the broader cultural, social and political realities that have created the worlds that are falling apart. Using women to express the inexpressible, or to figure moments of breakdown or crisis in culture neglects the particularity of real women and their lives within a history and culture that has arisen out of a patriarchal imagining. Woman always remains other within the patriarchal symbolic.

Reid, Le Marquand Hartigan and Burke Brogan have written plays that may be more personal, in their close connection to female embodied particularity but they are no less political because of that. These plays which name the world from the perspective of the other who has been demonized or denied within the dominant culture's symbol system are not as easily categorized. They reflect attempts to come to self-awareness, to speak in voices that are different to how men have spoken and most importantly different to how men have written women. In addressing women's lives in their social and political realities they foreground something that has been lost or unheard. Whether it is Reid's awareness that the politics of tea and the politics of sectarianism operate out of the same warped cultural binarisms, or Le Marquand Hartigan's aware-ness of the negative space occupied by the women whom she remembers, or Burke Brogan's testimony to women who were scapegoated and forced to carry a culture's abhorrence of the body and sexuality, women are refusing the meanings that have been scribbled on their bodies. These playwrights have provided us with the kind of interrogative texts that Belsey has described, texts that interrupt the dominant narratives, unsettle the canon, question its underlying assumptions and its claims to truth. These interrogative texts push beyond the narrow confines of the realist frame. Through the trauma, splintering and fracturing, it may be possible to move towards a particular gendered embodied subjectivity that is not defined by patriarchal madness and amnesia.

2 | Journeys Through Ritual

> Ritual is part of all drama. Drama without ritual is poetry without rhythm. (Friel)

Rituals have always been central to how a culture tells its story, initiates new members, shapes its world. Story and festivity name and frame our human experience, giving us a sense of identity and belonging, in personal, social and cultural or religious terms. Whether we think of primitive people's need to ritually gather and remember and recite their myths of origin, the cult and rituals of Eleusis or Dionysius or the early Christians' awe-inspiring rites of initiation which took place in ornate baptistries amidst elaborate symbols, rites and stories, ritual always takes place in liminal spaces and in times of heightened awareness. This sacred space, and sacred time gave people opportunities for self-understanding and renewal in the heart of their community. In a more secular world, people no longer have access to shared myths of origin, and no longer have the old connections with heightened moments of ritual awareness. In this context theatre, for many, is providing an alternative sacred space. Brian Friel believes that

> ritual is part of all drama. Drama without ritual is poetry without rhythm – hence not poetry, not Drama. Drama is a RITE, and always religious in the purest sense. (Quoted in Pine, 1999:63 Emphasis in original)

Victor Turner writes about the centrality of ritual and theatrical performance in forming and expressing cultural identity:

> Cultures are most fully expressed and made conscious of them-
> selves in their ritual and theatrical performances. [...] We will know
> one another better by entering one another's performances and
> learning their grammars and vocabularies. (Quoted in Schechner,
> 1990:1)

In entering the particular performances of the plays studied in this
chapter, audiences are invited into an alternative sacred space
within which identity is forged.

Victor Turner's concept of liminality in terms of the ritual
process is also a helpful lens for interpretation. He identifies the
characteristics of those in liminal states and discusses liminal
people as threshold people (the Latin *limen* = threshold):

> Liminal entities are neither here nor there; they are betwixt and
> between the positions assigned and arrayed by law, custom,
> convention, and ceremonial. As such, their ambiguous and
> indeterminate attributes are expressed by a rich variety of symbols
> in the many societies that ritualise social and cultural transitions.
> Thus, liminality is frequently likened to death, to being in the
> womb, to invisibility, to darkness, to bisexuality, to the wilderness,
> and to an eclipse of the sun or moon. (1995:95)

While Turner is dealing with rites of passage in more primitive
societies, where these rites fulfil very important social functions in
relation to transition, identity and belonging, his concept of liminality can be applied to all of the plays in this section. *The Sanctuary
Lamp,* and *Misogynist* both take place in the womb/tomb liminal
space of a church. *Someone Who'll Watch Over Me* and *Cell* in the
liminal space of a prison cell, *Wonderful Tennessee* in the liminal
space of shared pilgrimage, where the transitional nature of life is
stressed.

Another important feature that Turner identifies relates to the
sense of community and solidarity that develops among people
who share a liminal space. He gives the Latin term *Communitas* to
this state, and sees it as essentially juxtaposed with the more
structural understanding of society.

Again we will discover many examples of this sense of
communitas in the plays in this section, as the characters find
themselves in liminal spaces where what separates and divides

people is stripped away, to reveal a space of shared identity and the recognition of a shared humanity. (This, of course, should enable those who emerge from the liminal space to live creatively and tolerantly with difference, rather than demonizing or denying it). *Communitas* in the plays in this section is often accompanied by symbolic or ritual behaviour. At the close of *The Sanctuary Lamp* the characters achieve a new level of communion, having told their stories, shared food and wine and moved to forgiveness in the overturned confessional. The prisoners in *Someone Who'll Watch Over Me*, achieve a level of acceptance of the other, beyond stereotypes, having shared their imaginative worlds, through story and imagined celebration. The women prisoners in *Cell* find a level of *communitas* in the shared indignity of their surroundings, but it is very tenuous. A pilgrimage type play like *Wonderful Tennessee* allows characters a glimpse of *communitas* in the liminal space of the pier.

Turner is anxious to stress the relationship between *communitas* and structure. He gives many examples of contemporary expressions of *communitas* from millenarian movements to hippies and communes, from monastic and mendicant religious communities to the power of the weak (symbolic figures like the court jester) and suggests that while

> *communitas* is of the now; structure is rooted in the past and extends into the future through language law and custom. (Turner, 113)

The constant juxtaposition of the two is important. Turner identifies many features of how liminality contrasts with the status system and presents them as a series of binary oppositions which include: *Communitas*/structure, Equality/inequality, Absence of status/status, Disregard for personal appearance/care for personal appearance, Unselfishness/selfishness, Sacredness/secularity, Silence/speech, Continuous reference to mystical powers/ intermittent reference to mystical powers, Foolishness/sagacity (106).

Attention to what he means by the power of the weak and the distinction between foolishness and sagacity may also prove helpful in interpreting the plays in this section (and in fact many of the plays in this study). If *communitas* is the antithesis of structure then there is a sense in which it can be perceived or interpreted as inherently dangerous or anarchical by those whose primary intention is a desire to maintain structure. It is in this context that one can consider the power of the weak or foolish. If we consider the roles of people like court jesters (and holy beggars, simpletons, third sons etc. their function is so often one of stripping away the pretensions of those of higher rank or office and reducing 'them to the level of common humanity and mortality' (110)). Often the people who fill these roles culturally are 'members of despised or outlawed ethnic and cultural groups' whose role, like that of The Good Samaritan in the Christian Gospels, is to be the living embodiment of true human values, when those traditionally assumed to be morally or culturally superior have passed by and failed to respond. This status of the outsider or marginal person is particularly important in societies that are tightly structured and controlled. It is here that the marginal person (the foolish, the poor, the weak, the one on the outside) can call attention to a fuller understanding of what it means to be human. The status of outsiders is a characteristic of much of Murphy's work. The three derelicts in a city church that are the cast of *The Sanctuary Lamp* try to re-discover something about being human in the liminal space of a Catholic Church, where many of their experiences have been excluded. The outsider status of the prisoner can raise questions about identity and belonging in the larger society both at national and international levels (*Someone* and *Cell*).

Communitas also has what Turner calls a subjunctive mood or 'an aspect of potentiality' (1995:127). He identifies many artists and prophets as liminal or marginal people. The work of art (in this case the play) can create *communitas* where a shared experience of what it means to be human can be put before an audience and resonate with their deepest human longings and aspirations. Through the act of imagination they may glimpse the *not yet*. In this regard it can also be interpreted as sacred or holy play because of its ability to imagine in new ways that are not bound by the established structures but open to possibility and transformation:

> *Communitas* breaks in through the interstices of structure, in liminality; at the edges of structure in marginality; and from beneath structure, in inferiority. It is almost everywhere held to be sacred or 'holy', possibly because it transgresses or dissolves the

norms that govern structured and institutionalised relationships and is accompanied by experiences of unprecedented potency. (128)

While the plays in this chapter share many of the characteristics of liminality they do not all succeed in opening to transformation. (Plays that achieve this more completely or successfully will be explored in Chapters 4 and 5 which deal in turn with transformation and vision). Turner writes of the need for the 'regenerative abyss of *communitas*'. It is important to keep the dialectic in mind:

> Wisdom is always to find the appropriate relationship between structure and *communitas* under the given circumstances of time and place, to accept each modality when it is paramount without rejecting the other, and not to cling to one when its present impetus is spent. (139)

Theatrical texts can enable us to enter this regenerative abyss, by providing texts that are moments of concrete historical embodied awareness, where the possibilities of living a fully human life are juxtaposed with the dehumanizing effects of social, political, economic or religious structures. Those who enable the imagining of *communitas* whether prophet or artist are always people who deal with the immediate, the personal and the concrete. Images, symbols and parables are the characteristic language of those who try to nurture this state. This kind of poetic language towards a new imagining is also an openness to a transcendent or mystery dimension of human experience.

In the plays in this Chapter we find characters searching for rituals and symbols that will help them interpret their life journeys. The search for ritual is both private and public. We find characters in the liminal spaces of churches and prisons, or in the liminal spaces of shared pilgrimage. Some plays continue to dialogue with Christian religious symbols, in creative and critical ways. Others are more concerned with finding healing, forgiveness, reconciliation and redemption within a more secular world. While they have moved beyond the confines of traditional religion there is still a sense in which the plays are dealing with what one could call the religious dimension of human experience and are seeking a language to reconnect with mystery. Wherever that experience is located, it often turns out to be 'just so earth shatteringly ordinary' (Paul Mercier, *Pilgrims*, 11). The seeking out of liminal spaces whether in retreat, exile or pilgrimage, the need to reconnect with lost or fragmented aspects of the self, the search for authentic experiences of human mutuality, compassion or forgiveness, experiencing moments of epiphany, represents the trajectory of the Irish soul as it finds itself simultaneously disillusioned and hopeful on its journey home.

The Sanctuary Lamp, Tom Murphy (1975)

The Sanctuary Lamp (in a new version in 1984) locates three derelicts in a city church, towered over and dwarfed by the symbols of Catholicism. It is a play that confronts the grand narratives of a religious tradition with the narratives of the lost and forgotten. It is a play that searches for forgiveness through the telling of each person's story. It is a search for family and community that takes place almost like a Passion Narrative which moves through a night of darkness to the dawn of resurrection. Through a re-appropriation and redistribution of traditional Catholic symbols it searches in the liminal (womb/tomb) space of a church for the kind of language, and ritual that will allow its characters to find reconciliation with their past and to move into the future.

The introductory and bridging music is *The Sleeping Beauty*. One wonders who is sleeping? The Divine? The pre-Vatican 2 church? The Christian community? Harry, an English Jew and an ex strong man from the circus, is sitting hunched in a pew. The Monsignor, a 'disillusioned, but a very humane man' (*SL* 9), is reading Herman Hesse. The Monsignor gives Harry the job of church clerk one of whose duties is to attend to changing the candle in the Sanctuary Lamp, 'signifying the constant Presence', to which Harry replies, 'It's a mystery I suppose' (*SL* 13). As night falls Harry begins his vigil with the lamp, a vigil that facilitates an anguished soul-searching and review of his life. 'My spirit is unwell too. They've been trying to crush my life' (15). He is a paradox both to himself and within the play. He is a Jew tending a sanctuary lamp in a Catholic church. He is also a strongman who has no strength – a performer without an audience. His life experiences have been demoralizing, 'They even had me wrestling with a dwarf – with Sam, y' know? – and he had to win. I don't mind being a clown but I'm not a fool' and his friend Francisco is now living openly with his wife. Harry is also plagued by memories of his little daughter Teresa: 'Help me to forget'. He keeps madness as 'a standby in case all else fails', believing that 'you never feel your soul when you're happy'. His speech is lyrical and full of pathos, communicating the sadness and powerlessness of the strong man who was caught in a situation where 'Nothing could flower' (17). His desire for revenge is strong and he calls on the Lord of Death to strengthen him so that he can 'punish them properly'. (18)

Murphy is concerned with the themes of home and home-coming, and the attendant states of homelessness and exile. His characters are very often orphans. In this play Harry is both literally and metaphorically homeless and Maudie is an abandoned child having left her grandparents' house. They both seek sanctuary in the church. They are driven there by their own stories. Maudie is haunted by images of the dead, and is unable to sleep. Harry is driven to seek sanctuary as he tries to escape his own haunting memories of guilt, death and betrayal.

Maudie, the sixteen-year-old waif, brings Harry's attention back to forgiveness. Harry places a vestment from the vestry around her shoulders – a ritual reversal, the power of the church reduced to a thin frightened female orphan. Once again Harry refers to the 'Presence' – a naming that, spoken in the silence of the night in an old church, might be able to hint at transcendence but is quickly followed by Harry's dismissal of religion:

> Well, it's his spirit actually. They nabbed his spirit, and they've got it here. It's a mystery of course, but that's what religion is. Personally, I think they should let him go, but there you are. (19)

As the conversation continues Maudie speaks about Jesus giving forgiveness. While Harry seems to have respect for the figure of Jesus – 'a veritable giant of a man'- he has no time for what has happened to him within traditional religion. He believes that Jesus' 'sense is gone a little dim. And who would blame him? Locked up in here at night, reclining – y'know? – reflecting his former glory'. Later he will refer to a wheel-chair being more appropriate than a throne for one of the Catholic icons (26). The theme of the domestication of religion is nothing new. Institutions always exist in a creative tension with their origins. The tendency towards sedimentation or innovation is ever present. Genuine prophetic critique of the kind of idolatry that religious symbol systems are prone to has been part of the Judaeo-Christian heritage from the time of the Hebrew prophets. Jesus himself would have been interpreted within this tradition, critical of external religious observance that was not accompanied by a genuine interior religious conversion of the heart.

The theme of family runs through the play. The opening image of the stained glass window of The Holy Family will be juxtaposed with many different images of family. The lives of the characters throw up different experiences of family causing them to dialogue with the traditional image, each one interpreting the other. While Harry and Maudie are speaking, each identifies with a different member of the holy family – Maudie with the infant Jesus and Harry with Joseph.

Maudie's account of her family is anything but holy as she speaks of her mother's death, her father's abandonment, her granddad's violent outbursts and beatings and calling her 'a whore's melt' and her grandmother referring to her as a 'millstone' (22). Her only moments of transcendence in such a life were found in the times when she managed to climb to the top of the lamppost:

> Sometimes I'd climb even higher than the light. I would catch the iron thing on top and pull myself up over the top, and sit there in the night. And sometimes, if I waited up there long enough, everything made – sense. (23)

Harry's jealousy at this experience makes him interrupt with his own story of how he was called Ivan the Terrible when he topped the bill. Maudie's telling however will not be stopped. In her ex-uberance she used to do cartwheels or run home and dance naked on the table, until the older boys would call her outside again. Maudie's moment of epiphany has been sexualized and taken from her.

Act Two is set half an hour later. It is after midnight. We are introduced to Francisco – an Irishman in his thirties who is 'self-destructive' and 'usually considered a blackguard', (stage directions, *SL* 30). He is typical of the angry young man reacting strongly against his strict Catholic upbringing, its authoritarian attitudes and its impossible standards of perfection. His stance is reminiscent of Murphy's own. In a *Hot Press* interview in 1991 Murphy admitted to the overwhelming sense of disenchantment that set in after he experienced the collapse of the old certainties associated with religion:

> When the disenchantment sets in then the person becomes increasingly dangerous as he/she kicks out in agony against the loss of all these certainties...or...of a central certainty. (Jackson, 1991:19)

The scene opens with Francisco's summary of the history of Western Trinitarian theology. Since God made the world he has 'evaporated himself':

> When they painted his toe-nails and turned him into a church he lost his ambition, gave up learning, stagnated for a while, then gave up even that, said fuck it, forget it, and became a vague pain in his own and everybody else's arse. (30)

He believes that Jesus was A-one. And he's inclined to give his vote to 'your man, the Holy Spirit. Alias the Friendly Ghost. He's the coming man' (*SL* 30). Just what this speech really means is never questioned. The male naming of God still remains firmly in place. Francisco's speeches and sermons about the divine and the Catholic Church never take place in a dialogical situation. He is neither challenged nor supported. The imperfection of his theo-logical focus is ignored. His side swipes at Catholicism and its educational institutions use humour or shock tactics to elicit a response. His insights are marred by his anger.

Francisco's refusal to seriously question the patriarchal order is mirrored in his behaviour as he tries to seduce Maudie. Like Harry and Maudie he too 'can't sleep sometimes because I can't stop thinking' (31). As happens also with many characters in McGuinness's plays, the inability to sleep betrays a deep restlessness and anxiety that suggests an existential homelessness.

One possible interpretation of this would be to question how embodied the characters actually are. Many (if not all) of Murphy's characters live out of dualistic paradigms where the bodily experience of being human seems to inhibit the aspiration towards spirit.

When Harry returns he shares a piece of fish with Maudie. He has already shared bread with her in the first act (22). Francisco has opened a bottle of altar wine. This appropriation of the Christian symbol of Eucharist (Bread, Wine and Fish) by the dispossessed may reflect a desire on the author's part to engage in a real way with the traditional symbols. Many liberation theologians have written about the connection between liturgy and justice. One priest sacrificed his right to celebrate Eucharist to work with issues of hunger and poverty in the world, in order to create the conditions that might make the ritual more authentic.

Does Francisco have any vision in this play? His presence in the church is to tell Harry that Olga is dead, having taken an overdose after their last disastrous engagement, subsequent to Harry having walked out on them. He delivers most of this story from the pulpit and believes he is actually being more theologically accurate than the church has ever been. While many would not question the need for a hermeneutics of suspicion in relation to Christian history, Francisco's anger at the institution leaves one more with a sense of demolition than rebuilding. The moves towards the appropriation of a limbo like existence in preference to the heaven promised for the baptized or Harry's theory of the souls as silhouettes merging in a wall are curious rather than genuinely constructive of an alternative spirituality. When the three characters sleep in an overturned confessional, having each told their stories, they find some level of personal reconciliation. They have once again re-appropriated a traditional symbol. Whether Maudie receives the forgiveness she sought is not made explicit. But her role in the play may simply have been one of facilitating the move towards reconciliation for the male characters. Such a role is typical of those ascribed to women in Murphy's earlier plays.

The interspersing of the narrative of the last engagement with Francisco's famous sermon against the Church makes one look for thematic connections between the two. A distinct theme running through this section of the play is the battle for the individual soul. Traditionally within Catholic Religious Education many of the images held up to children were fear-inducing and presented pictures of a very wrathful God. Research into symbol systems and how they operate in the individual psyche suggests that they cannot simply be rejected but must be replaced. Francisco has not succeeded in doing this. As a result his imagination is still locked into imagery of hell-fire and damnation and paying the price for sin. Francisco is anxious to make Harry suffer for his desertion. In his telling of the story he paints a picture of hedonistic consumerism and sexual depravity which turned to violence. Francisco despairs of civilization: 'what a regrettable *volte-face* for civilization, I said to myself a thousand times, and did not God, through his only begotten son, his *only* son – because they had only the one – redeem us from all that kind of thing? (46). Even though he proclaims himself an atheist he still uses the interpretative framework of Christian salvation and redemption to understand what is happening. At the same time he rages against such interpretation and feels now that all Christianity was 'a poxy con' (49). He is especially antagonistic towards clerics, 'like black candles, not giving, but each one drawing a little more light out of the world'.

Franciso's sermon is reminiscent of one of the Old Testament prophets or Jesus' scathing denunciation of the hypocrisy of the Pharisees. The association between religion and violence is stressed with the inherent contradictions between a religion whose founder was a peacemaker and a religious history that has been furthered through conflict, division and war:

> Black on the outside but, underneath, their bodies swathed in bandages – bandages steeped in ointments, preservatives and holy oils! – Half-mummified torsos like great thick bandaged pricks! Founded in blood, continued in blood, crusaded in blood, inquisitioned in blood, divided in blood – And they tell us that Christ lives! Nothing to live for but to die!
>
> [...] They cannot agree among themselves on the first three words of the Our Father Get the police in! – (*He laughs*) Get heavy mounted police in with heavy mounted batons and disperse them, rout them, get them back from the round tables before they start the third and final world war we've all been dreading! (50)

In 1975 this speech must have been quite shocking to Irish audiences and no doubt the spectacular effect of its impact was achieved by having it delivered from a pulpit in the style of a traditional hell fire sermon so characteristic of parish retreats in Ireland in the nineteen forties, and fifties. Francisco ends his sermon with a type of ritual reversal, where he declares his vision in opposition to what has been traditionally taught. (This is developed later in *The Gigli Concert*). His vision of the final judgement will see Jesus call to his side not the sheep but the goats!

> Yea, call to his side all those rakish, dissolute, suicidal, fornicating goats, taken in adultery and what-have-you. And proclaim to the coonics, blush for shame, you blackguards, be off with you, you wretches, depart from me ye accursed complicated affliction! And that, my dear brother and sister, is my dream, my hope, my vision and my belief. (50)

Whether this vision enables one to go beyond the limitations of a traditional Catholic inheritance and whether there would be sufficient to sustain one in this new imagining is difficult to ascertain. O'Toole sees Francisco's sermon articulating a

> vision that is at the heart of Murphy's theatre, the vision of salvation coming only to those who are disaffected with the world as it is. (1994:200)

The vantage point of the disaffected, excluded or foolish may allow insights from the margins to destabilize if not transform the centre.

Murphy's play takes place in the liminal space of church and tries to re-appropriate the meaning of sanctuary. His characters are unable to find their own safety or place of home in the world either existentially or metaphorically. The Christian theme of salvation and redemption runs through the play. Where the old myth could hold and contain the lives and questions of those who lived within it, it is no longer adequate for Murphy's characters. With the collapse of the holding power of the narrative there is no holding space for the complexities of the characters' lives. They still experience guilt, sorrow, betrayal, death. They still find themselves crying out for deliverance. But there is no mythology to contain them. Their experiences of oppression, humiliation, victimization are still there. What was traditionally named sin and was contained within the mythology of salvation and redemption no longer holds meaning. The characters wonder whether the world has been redeemed as the original Narrative told them it was. In their (metaphysical) homelessness they find themselves angry that the old certainties have collapsed and they are left to deal with the conscious realization of the bloody history of western civilization that was founded on the Christian myth. Awareness of the greed, consumerism and exploitation that are integral to modern consciousness brings further realization of the limited definitions of sin that preoccupied the church of their youth. But in this play the characters are simply rebels. They are adolescent but not mature adults. Aware of the limits of their inherited mythology they fail to develop either a new mythology or symbol system to sustain them.

Misogynist, Michael Harding (1990)

Michael Harding's *Misogynist* was originally staged at The Abbey during the 1990 Theatre Festival. Its foreshortened performance and its later re-presentation as a one man show with Tom Hickey draw attention to some of the problems involved in staging such a play which is essentially about the male unconscious. Reviewers (for example Victoria White's Review in *Theatre Ireland* 24: 1990/1991) often missed the point of the play which was not simply to foreground the male Catholic's fear of women (although that is a theme) but a deeper reflection on how integral misogyny is to a patriarchal imagining. Margaret McCurtain in the programme note however acknowledges that 'Misogyny is the unexplored shadow side of the Irish psyche, the unredeemed part of our collective unconscious' (Quoted in V. White).

In an interview with David Grant (*Theatre Ireland* 1991:46-47) Harding summed up his preoccupations as a writer as war, sex and God. Harding makes distinctions between religion and spirituality: 'Public religion is a human activity. Spirituality is a human attribute. Humanity links spirituality and public religion but there is no intrinsic connection between the two. Religion is the way we protect ourselves from God' (Grant: 1991:46). Harding's theatre explores, (often through song, dance and mime), the psycho-spiritual dimensions of the Irish soul, scanning the back-roads of folk memory and ancient festival. In an interview Harding addresses the question of soul:

> In Ireland soul is hidden and suppressed. But we can explore our soul through our imaginations. Theatre can provide a gateway between the worlds of our reality and our imagination. Unspeakable things can thus reach the community. Theatre isn't just packaged nostalgia. (Grant, 47)

In *Misogynist* Harding is dealing with the shadow and the collective unconscious, or more specifically with the cultural unconscious that arises out of the patriarchal symbolic, where woman is always 'other'. This is the hidden or suppressed aspect of Irish soul. If theatre is a gateway for the unspeakable to reach the community, this play certainly plays its part.

The stage space for *Misogynist* is akin to one of the dream where the many levels of the unconscious are foregrounded, and its psychosexual fantasies unmasked. The main character – 'Him', a man in his fifties, costumed '*half-way between Alice in Wonderland and an old bore in slippers and cardigan*' (*Misogynist*, 143) is a type of Everyman – representing the male of western patriarchal culture, whose self-definition is based on a denial of and demonizing of the other, especially when this other is 'She' – woman – whose erasure is at the heart of the culture's production of meaning, and yet whose existence keeps the whole meaning system together. Dressed only in a surplice 'She' becomes the surface onto which is projected all the misogynist ranting of a culture's obsession with the symbols of Catholicism combined with an unhealthy relationship to sexuality. It is essential for the maintenance of the *status quo* that woman occupy the space defined by the projections of the masculine unconscious. Her otherness is essential to perpetuating the paradigm. If she should speak, become articulate, then everything will start to crumble.

Stage directions regarding the set suggest that '*the general impression should be one of props focused in an austere no-man's land*' (*M* 143). The stage space is also cluttered with statues and symbols of Catholic iconography. An oversize and ornate chalice, along with many bells, a space where the actor can stretch himself as if on a cross and a large video screen complete the set.

Robert Ballagh's set for the 1990 Abbey production of the play presented audiences with an amazing bricked belfry constructed on different levels, highlighting the many levels of the un-conscious. The text of the play which is a stream of consciousness has the narrative features of dream or therapy and at many times indicates the multiple splittings of the self at the different levels of consciousness and unconsciousness. The use of a mirror, a curtain and a video screen visually depict the splitting and the use of the attic space with its costumes and 'play' introduces a liminal space where anything can happen. These Brechtian techniques of distancing and alienation contribute to the unsettling of fixed ideas and assumptions. While it can represent access to higher levels of the unconscious it also carries the connotation of 'bats in the belfry', thus foregrounding madness and introducing an area of very dark play and transgression.

The original run of this play was cut short due to protests and dwindling audiences. What was so shocking? That it depicted the male unconscious? That the male unconscious was like this? That it was written by a man? That it was taken literally? The play is still shocking in its naming of the misogyny which is at the heart of a culture's production of meaning. It is still shocking in its attention to the explicit contours of a misogynist imagining that underpins the cultural project. To foreground this misogyny is to speak the unspeakable. If woman has become the non-said of all discourse, Harding's play opens up the space where that can be acknow-ledged. Attention to how core misogyny is to the cultural project also brings attention to the place or absence of woman within that project. The fact that a culture rests so hugely on this kind of un-acknowledged, unnamed misogyny is shocking. To tell the aud-ience this is to ask them to examine their own cultural as-sumptions, to test the validity of such a fundamental criticism, to discover new paradigms. This moves theatre beyond the limi-tations of a realist frame and invites the audience in a more Brechtian type of theatre to consider their role as colluders or innovators of meaning.

The opening pages of the play introduce obsession, denial, paedophilia, temptation, sexual repression and misogyny – a heady mix for an Irish audience in 1990. While the main character may not represent any one male person or priest the constellation of ideas and images that make up his unconscious is in fact representative of the cultural unconscious. (However what has come to light in Ireland – over the past fourteen years since the play was first performed – in relation to sexual abuse of young children by priests and religious has certainly presented a number of very sick individuals who have in fact been quite similar in their sexual dysfunctioning). Harding's main character draws attention to the gender ideologies that underpin a society, those clusters of images and associations that underlie the way we structure society. In this case it is the clustering of images of women, evil, sin, sex, and temptation that have been the legacy of a Catholic imagining. Their clustering and association in the Catholic cultural unconscious is partly the subject of the play. Making such connections explicit and highlighting their basis in misogyny is a daring or even a rebel act. Audiences will however not always like what they see. Certain depictions/portrayals may be rejected as too coarse or crass or untrue – they make Irish people uncomfortable (cf. Murphy's *A Whistle in the Dark*). Socially critical theatre runs the risk of either being prophetic or marginalized, depending on a culture's readiness to engage in critical reflection. With Harding's play, the whole cultural paradigm is under threat. Misogyny as the core of the cultural project with its escalating abhorrence of and violence against woman is indeed a hard pill to swallow.

Harding's central character is frightened to face the depths of his own unconscious. His posturing is a series of denials, evasions and projections. The theme of clothes runs through the play. The male lead engages in transvestism, the plain chant choir of monks throw off their robes, revealing that they are women wearing only their surplices/night-dresses underneath. The changing of women into men and back again with its implied homoeroticism and confusion around gender identity is another theme of the play. But the male lead is unable to deal directly with any of the issues and instead finds himself tumbling further and further into the chaos of his own unconscious.

Within the first few pages of the play there are so many explicitly misogynist remarks about women that they are worth noting. 'Fuck them' (*M* 147), 'Proper little madam', 'cheeky' (148), 'silly little girls' (140), 'fucking bitch' (150), 'my little temptress' how she opened 'a can of worms with one little finger' (151), 'illiterate little bitch' (152), 'the poison really came out of her' (154), 'the creeping rot, the disintegration, the degeneration of history' (158). Woman becomes the carrier of the repressed. Bodily fluids are seen as filthy and contaminating, and she is seen as unclean. As his narrative escalates in misogynist ranting the male lead crucifies himself to a cross while reaching towards a climax. His orgasm/crescendo is reached with the following words:

> She is reeking with venom
> for Christ sake.
> She is poisoned with jealousy.
> She is twisted with jealousy.
> And all she wants to do is to infect the world
> with the bitter little juices of her...
> the bitter little juices of her...(*M* 164)

The denial of the shadow, the demonizing of the other, is continued in a speech where the relationship between women and Jews is highlighted. (The Jews were kind./In ways./What the fuck has that got to do with it? *M* 165). Feminist theorists have written about the relationship between women, witches and Jews and how their treatment as other represents their status as the demonic alien in western culture:

> The late Middle Ages is a world gripped by the image of the devil. The Jew comes to be depicted as a kind of devil incarnate, while the witch is the free-floating anxiety symbol of diabolic femaleness. (Radford-Ruether, 1975:101)

Radford-Ruether refers to the 'peculiar parallelism' between the figure of the witch and that of the Jew in late medieval imagination (105) and to the persecutions and pogroms that they both endured. 'There is a certain interchange of images between Jews and witches whereby each is defined by being associated with the proven demonic character of the other' (106). Radford-Ruether's attempt to understand how such diverse groups of people could be the recipients of 'such similar stereotypes' explains it in terms of unconscious projection on the part of the Christian male leadership groups:

> They saw themselves as the masters of the redemption won by Christ, and regarded Jews, witches and heretics as agents of the devil's plot to subvert their rule. All these groups acquired similar characteristics as devil worshippers, orgiastics, and magicians. (107)

Similarly in this play the male inability to deal with his own darkness and otherness leads to a projection onto woman of everything he has feared or rejected. Her status as demonic alien must be maintained for the cultural paradigm to function. She must be the rot, the disintegration, the venom and the poison. She must carry these meanings for the system to function. He rightly notes that 'it's when she starts talking that the trouble starts' (166). As long as woman is reduced to the negative, the other of the masculine unconscious, the paradigm of western reason is in place. As soon as she begins to speak, the whole edifice of western reason begins to crumble:

> My brothers,
> we have fought many battles,
> many adversaries,
> over the years.
> But this little lizard in the grass is the worst of them all. In the sweet fragrance of the grass with her kind words, gently cloaking the fangs of poison.
> This is the most deadly enemy of all. (167)

Woman speaking and in places where she should not be (on the altar, holding up the chalice) represent a threat to the patriarchal order. Their presence, according to patriarchal myth, is a harbinger of destruction, chaos, everything breaking down. 'The middle cannot stay together' (*M* 158). With part of himself aware of the radical changes taking place he is only partially able to admit that 'If things disimprove any further, we'll be the laughing stock of history' (*M* 163). His hopeful ascent to a place of power has become a decline into grovelling and serving, in a deferential way as he is engaged in the most mundane and meaningless tasks.

A heady mix of religion, sexual fantasy and misogyny propels the play. Naming this constellation of ideas challenges the assumptions on which they are based. Where meaning is made through the sacrifice of woman, a play like Harding's intervenes in the symbol system and disrupts its pretensions to a meaning that is univocal and true for all.

Someone Who'll Watch Over Me, Frank McGuinness (1992)

In the liminal space of a prison cell in the Middle East three hostages share the religious, national and personal narratives of their lives. In the borderland state of confinement three men confront stereotypes both religious and political, explore their wounded masculinities, their sense of fatherhood, and fatherland, their sense of home. Plumbing the depths of personal sanity, under the ever present but offstage watchful eye of the guards they confront their essential powerlessness, as the overarching narratives of identity whether mythic, personal or fictional are played out in their communication, and their shared humanity becomes a gateway to a new-found secular salvation. Brian Keenan whose own experience of captivity in a Beirut prison was part of the inspiration behind the play (cf. *An Evil Cradling*, 1992) wrote about his reaction to the play: '[a]t times I gagged back tears, hoping no one would hear, and then thought about the marvellous theatricality of the play' and its epiphanies, those 'bright sparks of starlight in black sky which was the constant backdrop to the drama and could not have been more exact' (Introduction to McGuinness,1992).

The prologue of the play begins in darkness to the strains of Ella Fitzgerald singing 'Someone To Watch Over Me', evoking images of a watchful eye, a watchful God, a watching guard. The play will end with one of the prisoners dead: 'he's going to save us, he's watching over us' (*Someone* 57) and another being freed and promising, 'For what it's worth, I'm watching over you' (58). In between there are nine scenes where Edward, an Irishman, Michael, an Englishman, and Adam, an American, discover themselves in the limit situation of captivity, facing their demons and their shared humanity. Their shared captivity will see them amidst the many narratives of their lives attempt to discover a language of shared communication beyond stereotype and abuse, through religious faith and beyond to a sense of faith and hope in the power of imagination, friendship and play to sustain a new way of being in the world. The play quickly establishes an intertextual reality as it explores the myriad fictions that structure the prisoners' lives.

The idea of an Irishman, an American and an Englishman immediately evokes the scenario of a joke and in a sense there is something of a joke in the prisoners' captivity. They are pawns in a game of international politics as significant and as insignificant as any Paddy Irishman, Englishman etc. They could be anyone – they could be you or me and that essential interchangeability is put before the audience throughout the play. Their naivety or innocence simply highlights the random nature of their plight and emphasizes their powerlessness.

Edward is a reporter from Northern Ireland. His sense of exile is highlighted early in the play: 'There's some that cannot stay at home' (3). He is also in exile from his own ability to be a proper father, mirroring his relationship with his own father. Adam reminds him that he barely speaks about his kids and he replies: 'I don't know them. Working too hard, playing too hard, me. Like father, like son in that respect. I didn't know him until it was too late. I don't know them. Now I never will' (4)

The use of stereotype in the play is an interesting device. In one sense it enables the characters not to see each other as real persons, at another it enables survival. Hurling insult and abuse at one another because of their inherited stereotypes of the other enables the prisoners to play out the scripts that their respective cultures had given them but also in a way to transcend them by their new appropriation of the stereotype in a transgressive way as a strategy for survival, and resistance in the face of the madness of their situation:

> Whatever else about this place, we're in it together, we have to stick it out together. We'll come out of this alive. One favour – let me be able to do my worst to you, and you be able to do your worst to me. Is that agreed? That way, as you say, they won't break us, for we'll be too used to fighting for our lives. (6)

Throughout the play McGuinness gives his characters opportunities to dialogue with the classic religious texts that have shaped
their lives. In Scene Two a down to earth conversation about sex is
put in dialogue with the biblical Song of Songs. Scene Five opens
with Adam reading the Koran, while humming 'Someone to
Watch Over Me'. The juxtaposition of the jazz song with the text
of the Koran 'In the Name of God, the Merciful, the
Compassionate' (27) is an interesting device. As it connects with
the men's past life experiences and present longings it may open
them to hearing the classic text in new ways. In reality Muslim
Arab guards are watching over these men – the rightness of their
position partly justified by their interpretations of their holy book.
Their faith offers the larger interpretative horizon of God
watching over all. (Over you there are watchers.) But while the
quoted text is full of tolerance and compassion we are aware that
the daily living out of religious beliefs is anything but that. 'To you,
your religion, to me, my religion' (27). Edward is incredulous that
such lines actually exist in the Koran and continues:

> Save us from all who believe they're right. Right, in the name of
> God who is not merciful and compassionate, for he is like them,
> always right. I've seen it at home before. Scared wee shits, panting
> with fear, ready to make the big sacrifice. They must be right, for if
> they're wrong, God help them. And if they're right, God help us.
> (27)

He has allowed the text to dialogue with his own experience of
divisions caused by religious difference and fear and to interpret it
anew. This is reminiscent of the dialectic that must continue to
occur between structure and *communitas*. Later Adam reads a text
from The Koran on power which allows him to move through his
own dissociation and pain, beyond a desire for revenge into a
reconnection with his own difficult childhood and an ability to ask
his enemies for forgiveness. The prisoners and audiences are offered opportunities to reappropriate classic texts where two worlds
collide and offer each other new horizons of understanding.

An intertextual reality is created both by classic religious texts in
dialogue with the prisoners' experience but also through their use
of remembered film, radio, poetry, song and sporting events to

help them pass the time and make sense of their captivity. In Scene Three the hostages use the genre of film to reinterpret their lives. Classic film directors (Hitchcock, Peckinpah and Attenborough) are parodied through three different imagined film versions of events as they unfold in Lebanon or Beirut. Their search for meaning in the random events that have led each of them to this cell are interpreted through suspense, gratuitous violence or sentiment. The genre of film has as much power to interpret their lives as have the classic religious texts. The space opened up by play facilitates a deeper encounter where they are able to name their fears and move through humour to an acknowledgement of the senselessness and perhaps hopelessness of their situation. However '[c]arnival in this instance is not about freedom or a heightened awareness, but about survival and the preservation of consciousness' (Jordan, 186).

Themes of masculinity, sexuality and fatherhood surface throughout the play. Edward raises the question of what makes a man more or less a man:

> They've made themselves less than men, in locking me away like this. No matter what cause they're doing it for they have still made themselves less than men. But I want to say this, I am a better man than any of them, for I would not torture them like this. That is my choice. They do as they're ordered. I do as I choose. Locked in chains, for all to see, but not beaten down to the ground yet. (28)

The theme of manhood and whether external circumstances of oppression can destroy people is mirrored in a subsequent conversation between Michael and Edward. Michael's sense of failed manhood has already been referred to (wife dead, no children). His imaginary letter to his mother, and his references to his pear flan almost seem to imply homosexuality, a theme that Edward develops in an unkind way. The relationship between the English-man and the Irishman develops and plays out the theme of the colonizer and the colonized. The negative definition of the other arising out of one's own disempowerment or oppression is necessary to keep the dynamic alive. The insistence on the part of the powerful oppressor that the natives don't speak their own language, are ignorant or silly or incapable, are familiar colonial tactics. Edward needs a Michael against whom he can define himself. Having pushed each other to limits they succeed in breaking through to a deeper level of communication.

The rituals of play allow the characters access to some level of transformation. As they choose imaginary drinks and pretend that they have invited the guards to a party they ritualize their sense of community with story and song. Ritual behaviour enables them to lay hold of the experience, to deepen it and sustain it. Such ritual replaces traditional religious ritual and stresses the more secular understanding of salvation that McGuinness develops throughout this play. The rattling of the chains after one of the songs celebrates their defiance. Michael retells an old Middle English story based on the myth of Orpheus (37). The medieval mind's profound faith in human happiness to triumph over despair is almost a backdrop for the play. As the characters move into the space of play and celebration, a new energy makes itself known. A compassionate accompanying energy that has wept, that has gone down into the depths of darkness and fear, has entered hell and not been overcome. Orfeo wept for his wife, and knew that he had to follow her into hell 'for he knew whither thou goest, I will go with thee, and whither I go, thou shalt go with me' (37). These lines from the medieval story also resonate with similar lines from the Book of Ruth, the great Hebrew Scripture story of female friendship across cultures and across ages. This openness to the unknown and willingness to embrace the darkness is a true moment of grace. Perhaps it is an energy more traditionally associated with the female. Adam's singing of 'Amazing Grace' appropriately ends the scene.

After Adam's death Edward goes on hunger strike for three days. As Michael and Edward look for meaning in the senseless brutality of Adam's death the theme of salvation and sacrifice surfaces. The question of whether Adam's death might save them from being killed is raised. If they can interpret it in terms of sacrifice perhaps some meaning will be found in it. Michael encourages Edward to let Adam go. In an elegiac ritual of naming and lamenting, Edward gives voice to his grief:

He was gentle. He was kind. He could be cruel, when he was afraid, and while he was often afraid, as we all are afraid, he was not often cruel. He was brave, he could protect himself, and me, and you. [...] Friend. I believe it goes without saying, love, so I never said. He is dead. Bury him. Perpetual light shine upon him. May his soul rest in peace. Amen. (41)

Michael recites Herbert's poem 'Love'. With its strong Christian theological anthropology it could be interpreted as an invitation from the divine at the heart of reality to move beyond guilt and shame and accept forgiveness and sustenance at the table. Edward's experience however refuses to acknowledge any divine intervention. His is a much more human salvation as he begins to eat.

As Edward prepares to leave the cell he promises Michael that just as Adam is watching over them and will save them, that 'For what it's worth, I'm watching over you' (58). In a beautiful ritual moment of farewell Edward and Michael comb each other's hair. Like the Spartan warriors of old (and echoing a story Michael remembers from his own father) they initiate each other into a new definition of bravery and manhood where they are not afraid to show fear, to weep and be compassionate towards each other in a new solidarity that offers the only salvation that either of them can really guarantee.

Throughout the play we have seen and heard (have witnessed) how people in a liminal space, can experience a certain level of *communitas*. Jordan however suggests that the characters 'must translate each other's tales, rather than just tell their own stories before they can find hope in communion' (Jordan, 186). While the play offers audiences glimpses of transformation through the creative play of imagination, it does not quite succeed in offering a sustained vision of transformation which could move beyond mere survival, into a re-imagining of relationship and the possibility of an alternative future.

Cell, Paula Meehan (1999)

Wasted lives, taking life and doing life are phrases that come to mind when considering the difficult territory of Paula Meehan's play *Cell* (*Cell*, 2000). Three Dublin women serving time in prison for drug-related offences are joined by a fourth country woman, accused of murder. This is a play that challenges many assumptions – about women, about mothers, about Irish society, about life itself. It gives voice to experiences that are largely outside the remit of what constitutes the canon of Irish drama, and actually received funding from the Department of Justice and Law Reform because it addressed the issue of women's experience of imprisonment (Merriman, 2000:281). Unlike the men in Frank McGuinness's *Someone Who'll Watch Over Me* these four women have committed crimes. They share one nationality and from the evidence of the play have no real religious convictions worth speaking of. They have no recourse to the transforming moments of play or imagination. There are no memories of classic texts to inspire them. Their only escape is through drugs and alcohol which further embroils them in a system of violence and brutality, which is largely kept in place by Dolores, the cell's longest occupant. But they do await their release – crossing off the days of their sentence. And it is also a woman's world, at least within the cell and the wing. The two acts are set one month apart at the time of the full moon and menstruation too is a monthly reality. It is also a world of drugs and AIDS. They have watched their friends die or commit suicide. The play makes no grand statements, does not romanticize women, does not speak of woman as symbol or carrier of meanings that the culture imposes. Instead we find mothers without their children, women who deal in drugs, addicts, and shoplifters, and women who violate and abuse one another, and women who murder.

In the opening minutes of the play we realize that this is not a sanitized version of life in prison. Dolores (Delo Roche) finds that one of the women has disobeyed her rules and has used the slop bucket while menstruating. She wakes them roughly:

> We had a pact. Right? Don't interrupt! No blood. No faecal matter, or shit as it's known to you scumbags. A copious supply of plastic bags in there. Couldn't be easier. This day and age. The big V. It makes sense. (*Cell* 9)

Confinement, menstruation, shit, disease, drugs – the daily reality of life for Irish women in prison. The journeys that have taken them there are sometimes too painful to own. What they have lost and the grief that they carry is almost beyond endurance. The rituals that sustain them centre around heroin and any other tablet they can get their hands on. The darkness of their lives in the darkening days of the year are only exacerbated by the deaths and suicides of their friends. But the terror can be even more unimaginable as they try to detox, to get clean, to straighten them-selves out, to be free from the tyranny of one of their own who wants to keep them dependent on her and on her supply of heroin. It is very difficult to have vision in such a world. Glimpses are all they are offered. And they are almost impossible to sustain. The haunting dreams of the women stretch the realist parameters of the play, giving us images of dead children and cold restless spirits. Their narratives of what they have done also shift and change, as they try to come to terms with who they are and what they have done. When Martha finds herself on an acid trip her hallucinogenic perspective simply offers another angle of distorted vision. The sense of entombment similar to that in Meehan's earlier play *Mrs Sweeney* (Chapter Four) is heightened here as the confinement and brutality of prison inhibits even the imagination.

Delo controls the activities of the cell in a manner reminiscent of the wicked stepmother. She often refers to herself as mother (*Cell*, 7,10,12) to the other prisoners. She runs a drug racket, keeps them supplied with heroin and in return expects that they will do their share of work both inside and outside the cell. This can involve sexual favours (15) collecting money for orders or cleaning the cell. She believes that they are a family (65) and rules in a tyrannical way that she insists is all for their own good (34). Identifying and naming difference allow the prisoners to set up their own hierarchies and paradigms of superiority. The categories of settled, Dublin, and drug addict are perceived as superior to itinerant, culchie and murderer. Delo is intolerant of any outsider and the other women say that she tortured and tormented Annie (an earlier occupant of the cell), because she was an itinerant. She drove Annie to suicide and after her death succeeds in driving Lila also to take her own life. Her need to define herself against an 'other' continues as she transfers her negativity onto Alice, the new inmate. She lies to Alice about her children, pretending that her girls keep in touch with her. Delo is a woman locked in her own definition of reality which she can only sustain by increasing violence and irrationality. At one stage she tells the women not to think and divides the cell in two with a piece of Alice's crocheting wool. In a final confrontation between her and the other two women she produces a knife. It is her own knife that will be the cause of her death.

Lila is only nineteen years old and is serving a three-year sentence for possession of heroin. Her life in the cell is captured between two moments of 'seeing', when she sits on the top bunk and looks out at the world outside the prison cell. As she looks out the window for the first time she observes the sulky character of the day, the full moon in the daytime, the roofs glittering after the rain, and the cranes on the site of the new prison which they may have moved into by Christmas:

> The weeping willow in the back garden at the other end. Very sad looking. The leaves beginning to fall. Yellow they are now. Annie loved that tree. And I can see the top-half of a lamppost with the election poster with your woman's face on it ...wait a minute ... A New Ireland. Forward to ... something. I can't make it out. I wish I could see more of the garden. The bit of the tree is the only growing thing. No. There's stuff on the wall. Weeds. In the cracks. They had a little blue flower in ... June, was it? Before ...
> (20-21)

The second time she sits on the bunk, she is taking the overdose that will end her life. The limited perspective is heightened by her drug dependency and Delo's increasingly violent behaviour towards her after Annie's death. She is also haunted by dreams of Annie, and feels that she is 'not going to make it' (23):

> Lovely roundy moon, check. Weeping willow, check. Leaves falling, check. Yellow, check. Top of the lamppost, check. Election poster, check. Your woman on it, check. Truck carrying bricks for the new prison, check. One crane, check. The other crane, check. Weeds on the wall. Check. Man hurrying past, check. Glittery black roof, check. Clouds, check. Black clouds away over the canal,

check. Dark blue clouds, too, check. Rain, check. Rain, check. All
the lovely rain … (47)

Neither the promise of a new prison nor the promise of a New
Ireland has any meaning for Lila. Vision does not seem possible in
such a foreshortened life. As Alice remarks:

> All the lost children. There's enough grief in this prison to drown
> the whole city. (69)

Delo ensures that Martha remains stoned out of her mind in
order to get through Lila's death (55) thus ensuring her dependence on Delo herself. Martha in turn begins to be haunted by
dreams of Lila and Annie and other female prisoners:

> And we're all trapped here – the living and the dead alike. Do you
> understand? And I do think I'll be next. They're all waiting for me
> just over there. In a world just beside this one. Like you could put
> out your hand and touch them they're that close. (81)

This haunting is persistent, ancient, almost inescapable. Equally
Martha is haunted by horrific dreams about the loss of her own
child Jasmine. The true story surfaces later in the play but her
grotesque imagining challenges naïve assumptions about motherhood and certainly affords access to the female unconscious.
Martha dreamed that she was in her mother's house and looking
for her child when she noticed a strange smell coming from the
kitchen.

> I went in and there was a pot on the gas boiling away like mad. I
> lifted the lid and there was Jasmine all chopped up. Like a lump of
> meat she was. There was a bit of her face with the eye; and then
> another chunk with her mouth, all rolling around in the boiling
> water. And do you know what I did? I turned the gas down to
> simmer and put the lid back on. (10)

While she initially tells Alice that she simply doesn't want her
child brought to the prison, the truth is that the child has been
taken away from her. As she hallucinates (after taking a tablet that
Delo left for her) she speaks about mothers. There is a sense of
loss and dislocation. As she remembers her own mother, and
childhood fears, she also grieves over the loss of her own daughter, and recalls the event when she fed the child drugs that she was

taking herself, claiming that she never meant to harm her. Delo persists in her role as bad mother, by trying to prevent Martha coming off drugs and Alice who has claimed that she has been wrongly accused of murder has just told another version of her story which if possible is more grisly and horrific than the first account.

Alice's first account of her crime presents us with self-defence in the face of a persistent land-hungry drunken neighbour. She recalls her attempts to contact her political representatives and feels it was wrong that when she was out on bail:

> I had to cycle in to the town every single day to sign on at the Garda Station, like a common criminal. (39)

Her initial account of the murder presents us with Shamy the neighbour who had just kicked her dog leaving him whimpering and bleeding from the mouth:

> Now you have to picture Shamy – the girth of a hay-barn he was and the hands of him like lump hammers. I was standing by the drawer of the table and my hand went in and found the big knife. And … (45)

She claimed that she did not have clear recollection of the events, but that she buried her dog and thought that she would bury Shamy too:

> But there was no moving him and there was blood everywhere. Up the walls even. And I was covered in it. So. I just waited. I washed myself, and put on fresh clothes and I made a cup of tea. I sat out in the garden. (45)

Whether she is deluded or insane it is difficult to ascertain. Perhaps this account gives both audience and Alice access to her unconscious desire to kill Shamy. Later a newspaper report will confirm her second account of the event.

She was putting the hens away for the night in an old byre which also stored a range of old rusted farm implements, when she heard her dog barking and then a silence. Shamy comes into the byre and the cock goes for him. Shamy proceeds to wring its neck:

> He hadn't seen me yet. And I don't know what came over me, or where I got the strength from but I went for him with the sickle. In

the eye I pierced him. The point broke off, it was that rusted. Sticking out of his eye. He was mad. Oh I tell you he was mad. Crazy with the poitín and half-blinded by the sickle, he came at me. And I gave him an unmerciful kick in the testicles. He fell back screaming. And when he was down on his back I took the sock of an old plough from the corner and walloped him three times across the head. And he was dead. (77)

Echoes here of Christy Mahon but there is no marvelling at this woman's violent deed. The story becomes more gruesome as she recalls putting the body in the wheelbarrow and dumping it in a ditch. She planned to use the hay with his blood as compost. She decides to keep his death a secret and a few days later 'dumped a load of lime on him to keep the smell down and I went about my business (78-79). She might not have been discovered had it not been for her new dog:

The cursed lurcher. Up he runs the tail wagging like billio and Shamy's foot in his mouth and the leg trailing after him the length of his body. He was delighted with himself.
Martha: It sounds like something out of a horror movie. (79)

The grotesque details bring us down to the physical reality of the murder, questioning our assumptions about women and violence and upsets cultural expectations that identify women with home and self-sacrifice. Traditionally women were encouraged to identify with and remain at home no matter how brutal, dehumanizing or disfiguring it happened to be. And yet in the closing moments of the play Alice will tell another story. After an incident when Martha stabs Delo with her own knife and she is lying dead on the floor of a cell, Alice tells Martha what their version of events is going to be. Alice is willing to take the blame for Dolores' death, because she believes that she has nothing to lose. She gives her life that Martha may be free. Perhaps it helps her to make sense of her own desperate situation, in offering her another angle of vision from which she can interpret it. Alice looks out the same window that Lila had:

Such a huge moon. Magnificent. There's frost over everything! It's amazing Martha. The whole world is turned to crystal. All the roofs are white. The new prison is like a big ferry sailing across the sky. And Lila's tree has turned pure silver in the moonlight. Glittery and shiny. It's a Christmas tree for sure. Come up and see. Come up Martha. It's so beautiful it would take your breath away. (90-91)

Wonderful Tennessee, Brian Friel (1993)

Three Irish couples in their late thirties / early forties arrive at a remote pier in north-west Donegal. The action takes place in the present. Stage directions for the set indicate that the 'pier was built in 1905 but has not been used since the hinterland became de-populated many decades ago'. It is surrounded on three sides by sea, indicating that the audience too is at sea. Amongst the weather-bleached furnishings lying around there is a 'listing and rotting wooden stand, cruciform in shape, on which hangs the remnant of a life-belt'. (WT Set)

The opening and closing stage directions frame the play:

A very warm day in August. Early afternoon. Silence and complete stillness (11) …The engine starts up. The singing and the engine compete. Both sounds are encompassed by the silence and complete stillness and gradually surrender to it. (90)

The action of the play interrupts and aspires towards this silence and stillness as the characters, lost souls of contemporary Ireland seek ways to witness and attest to the mystery that their culture does everything in its power to keep at bay. Ancient and traditional religions at least kept the question of mystery firmly focused, and its attendant ritual held open the space where the mystery might break through with its possibilities of newness and transformation. Without a shared story or mythology, without shared symbols and rituals how can one access the mystery? Questions about journeys and pilgrimage, about slavery and freedom, about mystery and time, are raised as the characters, through music, storytelling and ritual, attempt to gain access to mystery. 'Friel has explicitly referred to this play as a 'Canterbury Tales' and as a form of pilgrimage, it places the travellers in a liminal situation' (Pine, 1999:280). The liminal space for the characters will become a timeless space, that may facilitate the experience of communitas.

Three couples, Terry and Berna, Trish and George, Angela and Frank embody the crisis of our contemporary world. The play

> depicts through its six 'lost' characters a diagnosis of the spiritual
> illness of contemporary Ireland … It marks a significant expression
> of a rapidly secularizing society still hungering for 'what is beyond
> language. The inexpressible. The ineffable.' (Murray, 1997:228)

and challenges

> Irish audiences on the urgency of finding the means to live with
> some sort of rootedness among the ruins of a collapsed tradition.

Cave writes about Friel pushing beyond the borders of stage realism in 'searching for dramatic structures that will embrace not only the secular but psychological and spiritual intensities' (Cave, 1999:109). The journeys that have brought them to this place show interconnected and interdependent lives. Terry the bookie and concert-promoter has been supporting each of the couples financially. We learn that he has become the owner of Oileán Draíochta, and for his birthday he is to bring his friends there in the hope that they too may experience some of the wonder he found there as a child when on pilgrimage with his father. The planned trip acts as a type of catalyst around which the play unfolds. The journey of the play shares the features of pilgrimage where the journey is also an inner journey, a soul journey. In the liminal space of shared pilgrimage the characters may receive an opportunity to locate themselves in relation to something bigger (mythic) that may help them interpret their journeys. While Terry continues a love affair with Angela (his sister-in-law), his wife Berna, a lawyer, is suffering from severe depression. Trish who remains perpetually a child is married to George who is dying of cancer, has enormous difficulty speaking but becomes the musical or artistic voice of the play with his brilliant accordion playing. Trish and Terry are brother and sister. Both have childless marriages. Angela is a Classics teacher who finds getting through every day is about as much as she can handle. Frank is an academic trying to make his breakthrough with his book on the measurement of time. His head is full of rubbish and panic (58). As the play unfolds we encounter a people spiritually, emotionally, physically and materially bankrupt.

The opening lines of the play introduce us to the characters and to their situation of existential 'lostness' or abandonment.

Angela: You're joking, Terry, aren't you?
Trish: Lost, I'm telling you. This is the back of nowhere.
Terry: This is it – believe me. (12)

The notion that the place where the characters find themselves is the place of revelation seems like a joke. After all it is 'the back of nowhere'. But perhaps Friel is trying to argue for a universality in the particular, the mythic disclosed through the mundane – that the only place to begin from is here.

Friel's Ballybeg at the edge of the world can also be interpreted as the centre of the world. Eliade writes about mythic centres, which are points associated with where the sacred has been made manifest. Whether those spaces are rocks, trees, totem poles or shrines – they designate the centre of the world. Ritually gathering and remembering the original divine manifestation can enable participants to have similar experiences of connecting with the sacred. For the characters in this play the night will give way to the timeless as the space becomes the mythic space of origins, the liminal space where the mystery might be revealed. The gradual movement into the liminal space that occurs throughout the night may open the characters to transformation.

The couples have travelled from Dublin in a mini-bus. Colourful, happy people, educated and successful. Will this journey become a pilgrimage as Terry hopes? They pass the night telling stories, singing songs, sharing food, and waiting edgily for Carlin. Paul Ricoeur writes about myth as the bearer of possible worlds. In this play we find a people with only fragments of story. There is no single myth that unites them. Fragments of Greek mythology, hymns that come from the Christian tradition, heavily tinged with nostalgia, legend and folklore merge into one another. The only language they share is that of old songs about happiness. And so they continue – a poor lost group of children singing happy song after happy song to convince themselves that they are happy and that everything is in place here. However the nearest they can get are times when they are 'about to be happy' (43).

Berna is desperately unhappy, and tells Terry that she doesn't think she can carry on (15). She is an intelligent, sensitive woman trapped in a childless marriage with a man who is having an affair with her sister. Trish who is permanently lost, even geographically, is childish and also barren. Her incessant talk is matched by her husband's lack of voice as he dies of throat cancer. Angela hates her job and seems to exist on a manic edge as she balances the contradictions in her life. Each of the women remains trapped and defined by their relationships with the men in the play. Their access to meaning is similarly confined. Whereas Terry at least has the island (for a period of time), and Frank is writing his book on time (even if he feels a failure) and George (although dying) has an access to meaning through music. The old patriarchal order may be dying but what will replace it? The women can represent another dimension to experience but ultimately don't offer an alternative to the prevailing aesthetic. Berna's rebuttal of the tyranny of reason with her account of the flying house, and her subsequent ritual rebirth in the sea, and discarding of her water-logged watch, offers to redress the imbalance of the prevailing aesthetic rather than replace it. Similarly Angela's recitation of the story behind the Eleusinian mysteries is a reminder of what has been lost or forgotten culturally. Integration of it will stand as a corrective to the dominant discourses rather than radically transforming them.

The underlying search for a mythology that will unite the characters sees them move beyond the Christian tradition (a derelict church without a roof, in the background, WT 32), towards a restoration of an older Celtic mythology, hinted at by the ritual behaviour on the island (in 1932) and a final improvised circling of a mound of stones where each of the characters leaves something of themselves behind. Throughout the play there are references to Greek mythology with emphasis on the Eleusinian mysteries and feasting and ritual associated with Dionysus. Angela's recital of the Eleusinian mysteries, and the harvest festival in honour of Demeter, is an attempt to explain the movement of the play from fasting, through ritual purification, and a ceremony of initiation, accompanied by music, dancing and drinking.

However one cannot simply inhabit the rites of an ancient civilization. Reproducing the rituals will not enable access to the mystery as it may have done. While a demythologizing is necessary in order for a re-mything to occur, the question one must ask is whether Friel goes far enough. His characters attempt to free themselves from the oppressive function of past mythologies and engage in storytelling in order to discover new ones. But the fragmented nature of the storytelling, and the disparate myths that hold characters' attention are not sufficient to give them a common story. Even the play's title reveals the inadequacy of the process.

Angelin A. Kelly, a letter writer to the Irish Times (around the time of the first production in 1993), adverted to the play's title *Wonderful Tennessee*, tracing its origins to the Negro folk song, Nancy Dill, which Friel uses in the play. She wrote of how the black mill-worker in Ohio dreams of Tennessee, his homeland where his ancestors were slaves. Although he is now free, he experiences new kinds of slavery in hard work and poverty. In his song he idealizes the simple lives of his forebears, hoping to find happiness there with his sweetheart Nancy Dill. A people come of age having left behind the old tyrannies of religion are now free, or are they? In its stead we find the tyranny of reason, nostalgia for a simpler past, and the belief that happiness is attainable if we try hard enough and convince ourselves with enthusiasm, frenetic activity and sufficient quantities of alcohol. The space of imagined freedom can become even more oppressive where the deeper questions of life are simply pushed below the surface. Our educated characters may be free from the more oppressive aspects of religion but the questions posed by the religious imagination will not simply go away.

Terry sees himself as the sherpa on this trip (19). Others toast him as host, brother, concert-promoter, showman, turf-accountant, bookie, gambler, eejit, friend, brother-in-law, most generous (23-25). He has been involved in all their lives and now wants to share his experience of the island with them. It is to be their destination. This play is essentially a journey play where the journey to Oileán Draíochta, the island of otherness, island of mystery (28) is more important than the arrival. Terry recites the legend of the island which he knows by heart (29). It has mythic resonances in its associations with the mysterious, the wonderful, the sacred (28-29):

> **Terry:** There is a legend that it was once a spectral, floating island
> that appeared out of the fog every seven years and that fishermen
> who sighted it saw a beautiful country of hills and valleys, with
> sheep browsing on the slopes, and cattle in green pastures, and
> clothes drying on the hedges. And they say they saw leaves of apple
> and oak, and heard a bell and the song of coloured birds. Then, as
> they watched it the fog devoured it and nothing was seen but the
> foam swirling on the billow and the tumbling of the dolphins. (29)

The legend evokes a mythic time of origins – a perfect time to
which one must periodically and ritually return to renew and
celebrate identity. Fishermen who landed on the island during one
of its appearances, lit a fire, which according to legend dispelled
the enchantment and it stopped being spectral. However during
the play the island continues to appear and disappear for the
various characters. 'The imagined place, because it is within each
of them, and because it is shared in a communal fashion during the
night, becomes a sacred space by virtue of the ritual of storytelling
and its consequences' (Pine, 1999:287). Lanters suggests that
through ritual and storytelling they create the island on the pier:

> Unable to reach the island, they nevertheless attempt to get as close
> as possible to their destination, if not in an actual, then in a ritual
> manner. The island they symbolically create on the pier is an amal-
> gamation of Eleusis and the Christian pilgrimage island described
> by Terry. (Lanters, 1996:171)

Through ritual they enter sacred time which is essentially timeless,
and as they perform all of the various rituals associated with
Eleusis or Terry's remembered pilgrimage to Oileán Draíochta,
'the lost souls of the opening scene of the play experience a
temporary homecoming when they create their island of mystery
on the pier' (Lanters, 172).

Terry has been to the island once, as a seven-year-old child,
with his father. Trish his sister, neither recalls the event nor does
she know the story. Terry remembers how they fasted from the
night before, and for the night on the island were given only bread
and water. He recalls a ritual which involved circling beds and
placing stones on a mound (30) and:

I remember a holy well, and my father filling a bottle with holy water and stuffing the neck with grass – you know, to cork it. And I remember a whin bush beside the well […] and there were crutches and walking-sticks hanging on the bush: and bits of cloth – bratóga, my father called them – a handkerchief, a piece of shawl – bleached and turning green form exposure. Votive offerings – isn't that the English word? And there's the ruins of a Middle Age church dedicated to Saint Conall. (31)

Towards the close of the play the characters will mirror this scene as they spontaneously re-enact some of these rituals. A contemporary people trying to understand the behaviour associated with pilgrimage and prayer seek a more universal language and speak in terms of wanting 'to attest to the mystery' (32). The group will wait all night for Carlin, the ferryman, to ferry them to the mystical island. Carlin's family have 'been ferrying people for thousands of years' (35). Carlin is almost a mythical character. He is spoken of as having 'no human feelings' (41), as ancient, filthy and toothless, and smiling all the time (42). This is in contrast to Charlie the minibus driver who has left them on the pier and who is always on time.

The picnic hampers are full of useless exotic food that no one wants. The food of the consumer culture cannot nurture them – and they end up fasting. During the night Frank talks to Terry about the book he is writing on The Measurement of Time and its Effects on European Civilization. His conversation brings him into the realms of monastic fasting, prayer and experiences of 'apparitions – well visions, hallucinations, whatever' (51). He claims that the monks in their witnessing to the mystery made people uncomfortable:

> **Frank:** The mystery offends – so the mystery has to be extracted. (*He points to the island*) They had their own way of dealing with it: they embraced it all – everything. Yes, yes, yes, they said; why bloody not? A rage for the absolute, Terry – that's what they had. And because their acceptance was so comprehensive, so open, so generous, maybe they were put in touch – what do you think? – so intimately in touch that maybe, maybe they actually did see.
> **Terry:** In touch with what? See what?

Frank: Whatever it is we desire but can't express. What is beyond language. The inexpressible. The ineffable. (52)

Ultimately Frank believes that there is no language for this experience: '… language stands baffled before all that and says of what it has attempted to say, "No, no! That's not it at all"' (53). Here we find ourselves in the familiar *via negativa* territory of the Christian mystics. The use of music in the play may be an attempt to move beyond the limitations of language, or as the only possible language to enable access to the transcendent. Perhaps the mistake is to seek a once and for all experience that would enable one to live 'at the still core of it all' (53). Such a teleological emphasis may bypass the now, the changing moments that make up life, each offering the possibility of fullness, but not stasis. In fact Terry will announce later that he does not own the island, which suggests that there is no way to actually possess the mystery, all they can hope to do is to return in pilgrimage and memory.

A similar elusiveness of mystery is explored in Paul Mercier's *Pilgrims* (1993). The search for Paradise, just around the next corner, looking for 'it,' waiting for the epiphany, the revelation, the mystery to manifest itself obsesses all the characters. One character, Tommy, remembers his disappointment on journeying to and climbing Croagh Patrick:

> **Tommy:** And off up the reek I went. It was hard work. Ye know there was more garbage on that summit when I got there. Cans and plastic and…I thought I'd left all that in the garage. I mean, a holy mountain's a holy mountain. If I'm gonna' come this far the least I could expect is…Well, what would you call it Seamas?
> **Seamas:** Mystery.
> **Tommy:** Yes, that too.
> **Mary:** No mystery, Tommy?
> **Tommy:** It was like a tacky yard up there. And they've got PVC doors and windows too. The highest in Ireland, I bet. (*Pilgrims* 79)

Berna's story of the flying house of Loreto stands as a critique of reason and the limitations of the rational cogito. The liminal space she occupies in the play is also a borderland state – between madness and sanity, causing us to question what we perceive to be normal or common sense. The interruptive presence of such borderline characters occurs in much contemporary Irish drama.

Their offering of an alternative discourse can foreground the limitations of perceived ways of knowing and question the hegemony of any one discourse. It is Berna the lawyer, who will jump into the sea in a type of ritual purification and later dispose of her water-logged watch. This desire to experience a time of marvels is often associated with liminal space. The dichotomy between the legal and the marvellous is played out in ways similar to those in *Faith Healer*.

Angela, the sceptic, with access to Greek mythology invents a game involving stones and a bottle. 'It's called: how close can you get without touching it?' (*WT* 66) It is almost like her parody of Frank's discussion of the mystery. She sits apart, doesn't believe that the island is mysterious, and yet begins to get pulled into the space, particularly through her relationship with George. At one point he tells her that if he ever decides to go, that he wants her children to have his accordion (65). When Berna goes to take her scarf off the stand, Angela offers her a different one. She warns the others not to light a fire lest it dispel the mystery and promises to return if only in memory of George.

When Frank returns from his walk and begins to recount his experiences, the three women continue to play their game. They do not seem especially interested in what he has to say. In fact he jokes that 'It left them speechless, didn't it? My Ballybeg epiphany' (70). He has seen the mist clear over Oileán Draíochta, felt that it was 'emerging from behind its veil' and tried to capture it on film. He continues:

> suddenly a dolphin rose up out of the sea. And for thirty seconds, maybe a minute, it danced for me. Like a faun, a satyr; with its manic, leering face. Danced with a deliberate, controlled, exquisite abandon. Leaping, twisting, tumbling, gyrating in wild and intricate contortions. [...]. A performance – that's what it was. A performance so considered, so aware that you knew it knew it was being witnessed, wanted to be witnessed. Thrilling and wonderful; and at the same time – I don't know why – at the same time ... with that manic leering face ... somehow very disturbing.

Frank goes on to describe it as a ceremonial dance, that 'upset me' for some reason. The dance of the dolphins becomes a channel through which the mystery is made manifest. The mystery breaks in on Frank and he cannot capture the moment (he has no film left) – he can only experience it:

> The dolphin, devilish but also symbolic of fertility and salvation, carrier of the souls of the dead to the Island of the Blessed, and symbol of Demeter, Dionysus and Christ, represents the principle of destruction-as-creation at the core of the mystery religions. (Lanters, 175)

It feels unsettling (the mystery offends), and upsetting – this mystery, knows it is being witnessed, wants to be witnessed. The abandonment of the dolphin's dance, the exquisiteness of its form, its sheer theatricality makes him think of a performance. Friel believes that theatre is an alternative sacred space. Can it become the site of such performance – even as remembered and narrated by the characters? Does this remembered performance move the audience to an experience of the mystery? How similar is this telling to Michael's narrative in *Dancing at Lughnasa?* The dolphin with its manic leering face evokes the caricatured and grotesque aspects of the sisters' dance. However perhaps a fuller experience is provided in seeing the sisters dance in wild abandon as words take second place to music and the embodied dance.

It is interesting to note how many of the musical pieces are hymns to Mary in the Christian tradition. For so many, Mary occupies the space vacated by the ancient mother goddess and represents the compassionate, nurturing, feeling side of the divine. It is not however a feminist imaging of the divine, but a gap in the male imaging of the divine that is represented by these songs. Popular piety created this image of Mary, but as it was so often accompanied by oppressive social roles and moral restrictions, it was not in any way a liberating image for women. The nostalgic value of the music (one need only think of the phenomenal success of compilations of Catholic hymns produced in the late nineteen nineties) prevents it having any liberating function in the lives of real women.

Terry has not yet told his story and as he does we realize that the island of otherness has a darker side to it. We learn that, during the Eucharistic Congress in 1932, the island was the site of a brutal murder. A seventeen-year-old young man was ritually killed. Evidence of

> ... burned out fires – empty wine bottles – clothes left behind – blood smeared on rocks. It's thought there was some sort of orgy. Anyhow at some point they dismembered him. That's accurate enough – from the pieces they found. (*WT* 73)

It appeared that a group of young people, high on the fervour of The Eucharistic Congress, had gone over to the island with lots of alcohol, to have a dance and that the young man was sacrificed. All the signs point to an ancient pagan festival – a night of excess and frenzy when the veil between the worlds was thin and the ritual space allowed, demanded transgression. There are echoes here of Faith Healer and the sacrificial death of Frank Hardy at the hands of McGarvey's men. As the underlying or hidden violence surfaces we are also reminded of Lughnasa with bonfires and violence in the back-hills. Confronting the depths of the human condition – tapping into the potential for violence and death that Christian ritual transforms through offering an 'unbloody' sacrifice, the island now represents the otherness that we must confront culturally: the lost parts of ourselves and our cultures, the buried and repressed, the dark, the shadow. The journey to kiss the dark, embrace the shadow is demanded of us personally and culturally. Traditional Christianity has overemphasized the light at the expense of the dark. It becomes part of the culturally repressed inheritance of each generation. It surfaces in the demonic and deadly. It is the underside of civilization – the barbarism and brutality on which our so-called civilization is built. This underside of history must be acknowledged. Can its strangeness become part of our knowing?

Each of the characters leaves something of themselves behind, tying it to the wooden stand. Angela leaves honey cake (for the spirits?) but says it is for Carlin. They are mirroring the scene described earlier by Terry. Frank empties out the alcohol and fills the bottle with water from the well (the holy well) echoing the actions of Terry's father. The other five characters insist that Terry leaves his shirt and wrestle him to the ground, chanting and de-manding that he surrender it. They eventually rip it off him –

echoes of the dismembering of the young man. Lanters believes that the witnessing of the symbolic sacrificial event is what makes it sacred:

> All ritual acts in the play are emphatically witnessed. The revelation of the mystery religions is that death is the source of life; but while a symbolic sacrifice properly witnessed reveals this sacred truth, a bloody killing and the ensuing secrecy evoke nothing but horror. (Lanters, 172)

Angela recites the story of the Eleusinian mysteries and then each of the characters performs a ritual with stones. When they finally take their leave of the place they are like children as they chorus goodbye to the sheep and cattle, the coloured birds, the whin bush, the bell, the clothes on bushes, the low hill, the oak trees, the apple trees, Conall, the dancing dolphin (*WT* 88).

As each of the characters promises to return Angela is the most enthusiastic. She speaks triumphantly, according to stage directions:

> Angela: Yes, we will! Next year – and the year after – and the year after that! Because we want to! Not out of need – out of desire! Not in expectation, but to attest, to affirm, to acknowledge – to shout Yes, Yes, Yes! Damn right we will, Terry! Yes – yes – yes! (87)

Her triple affirmation of the mystery mirrors Frank's triple affirmation in his conversation with Terry. But one cannot always trust Angela's words, given her scepticism and underlying panic. But in the closing moments of the play it is George who asks her to come back. And 'when you do, do it for me. No, no, I don't mean for me – just in memory of me' (90). There are clear resonances here of the invitation of Jesus to his disciples at the Last Supper to 'do this in memory of me.' Impetuously Angela kisses George, and hangs her sun hat on top of the stand, stating defiantly 'For you, George! For both of us!' (90)

Conclusion

In an article about universals of performance in myth, ritual and drama, Turner argues that 'both ritual and theatre crucially involve liminal events and processes and have an important aspect of social metacommentary' (Turner, 1990:8). As already discussed, liminal states in the creation of *communitas* exist in the subjunctive mood, where the potentiality or dimension of 'what if' is heightened. Turner identifies theatre as one inheritor of an ancient complex ritual tradition, and sees it sharing many of the features characteristic of ritual behaviour in liminal space (12)

Unfortunately the massive industrialization of society and the subsequent advances in scale and complexity have pushed many of these theatrical events to the edges of society. In their diluted, amputated and secular forms they are now more associated with leisure and entertainment rather than a central driving force in society. 'The pronounced numinous supernatural character of archaic ritual has been greatly attenuated' (12). However many contemporary theatre practitioners are addressing these very issues, and attempting to restore 'something of the numinosity' that has been lost. We need only remember the ground-breaking experimental work of Grotowski, Schechner and Brook or consider Artaud's theories to be aware of how twentieth century practitioners attempted to create a kind of total or true theatre.

How does contemporary Irish drama attempt to deal with mystery, to open itself to the mysterious? Tóibín writing about Irish drama in the last twenty years notes 'a sense of language as mysterious, a sense of speech moving into prayer, a sense of utterance having at its centre the rhythm and power of song' (Tóibín, 2001:19). He suggests that it is through language itself that the mystery emerges. Poetic language with its attention to symbol and metaphor can expand horizons, open up possible worlds. A poetic theatre can function in a similar way. While one may be critical of Irish theatre's over-dependence on language, a poetic language can affect both how one thinks and how one acts in the world. As Audre Lorde says:

> Poetry is not a luxury. It is a vital necessity of existence. It forms the quality of the light within which we predicate our hopes and dreams toward survival and change, first made into language, then into idea, then into more tangible action. Poetry is the way we help give name to the nameless so it can be thought (Lorde, 1984:37)

Feminist thought pays attention to poetic language as it sees in it a way of bringing together thought and action, where thought is not simply theory but a way of being in the world. Feminist thought values the poetic and visionary as a way of expressing the bodily affective basis of all knowing (Braidotti, 1991:165).

A poetic theatre can similarly express the unity of thinking and being, and the invisible connection between mind and body. Or to expand the idea, it can help express the invisible connection between mind, body and spirit. Brook writes about a Holy Theatre (and he refers quite specifically to Grotowski's Living Theatre) in his classic text *The Empty Space* and discusses theatrical events as 'deliberately constructed social gatherings that seek for an invisibility to interpenetrate and animate the ordinary' (Brook, 1968:64). Brook's holy theatre is holy because of its clearly defined place in the community which he sees as a response to a need once filled by the churches (67). He also calls it The Theatre of the Invisible-made-Visible (47). A certain performance 'performed with beauty and with love fires the spirit and gives then a reminder that daily drabness is not necessarily all' (48). A holy theatre 'not only presents the invisible but also offers the conditions that make its perception possible' (63). The theatrical event of a poetic or holy theatre 'scorches on the memory an outline, a taste, a trace, a smell – a picture. It's the play's central image that remains, its silhouette' (152). Developing Artaud's ideas Brook writes about a holy theatre 'in which the blazing centre speaks through forms closest to it. A theatre working like the plague, by intoxication, by infection, by analogy, by magic; a theatre in which the play, the event itself, stands in place of the text' (55). In many of the plays in this study, particularly those of Murphy and Carr, this theatre of the soul, that scorches and burns in its intoxicating and at times deadly magic, is achieved in performance in the alchemical space of theatre.

As already noted many of the plays in this section have characters searching for language, images and symbols that will help them interpret their lives. This search in turn becomes particularly poignant when we find characters searching for a way to connect (or reconnect) with mystery. Often the search for symbols finds itself re-appropriating older religious symbols and stories in a secular world. The symbol of death and resurrection or its equivalent in self-sacrificing love is found in various guises. The structure of *The Sanctuary Lamp* is similar to that of a Passion Narrative, as it moves through a night of darkness and despair towards the dawn of a new way of relating and being in the world. In *Someone Who'll Watch Over Me*, Edward and Michael attempt to interpret the senselessness of fellow hostage Adam's death? Could his death be interpreted as a sacrifice that might save them? In *Misogynist* we find a perversion of the symbol of death and resurrection as the main character engages in mock crucifixion, as expression of a perverted psycho-spiritual unconscious. In *Cell* Alice offers to take the blame for the murder of fellow prisoner Delo, in order to let Martha go free. It could be interpreted as an act of self-sacrificing love, although she is already in prison for murder.

As they search for symbols and rituals that might help them make sense of their lives, the characters in *The Sanctuary Lamp* re-appropriate traditional Christian symbols of Eucharist and Reconciliation. All religious rituals and symbols in *Misogynist* are suspect when one draws attention to the misogyny that is at the heart of the patriarchal unconscious. In *Someone Who'll Watch Over Me* many religious symbols are re-appropriated in a secular world. Extracts from the Bible and the Koran, are put in dialogue with the characters' lives, and their wisdom experienced anew. An ancient ritual like that of the Spartan warriors combing each other's hair before going to battle becomes a contemporary ritual that allows the characters access to a fuller definition of masculinity, that includes tenderness and compassion. The characters in *Wonderful Tennessee* talk and sing and share food in a night-long vigil that ends with an improvised ritual.

The question of mystery continues to haunt and pursue the characters in these plays. Harry in *The Sanctuary Lamp* senses that the sanctuary lamp can bring him into the presence of mystery. In *Wonderful Tennessee*, mystery haunts and beckons, mystery offends, defies expression. The Ballybeg epiphany of the dancing dolphin cannot be captured on film, but audiences witness it in the telling.

If we are to consider how theatre functions culturally as ritual it is necessary to understand Turner's anthropology of experience in terms of social drama. Turner identifies the stages of Breach, Crisis, Redressive Process and Reintegration. He sees ritual and its contemporary equivalent, theatre, coming from the 'subjunctive, liminal, reflexive, exploratory heart of the social drama, and belonging to the third Redressive phase of the social drama where 'the contents of the group experiences' are 'replicated, dismembered, remembered, refashioned, and mutely or vocally made meaningful' (Turner, 13). Theatre, like ritual creates a state of 'heightened vitality'. Turner speaks of this momentary union or ecstasy as no more than a shiver running down one's back but nonetheless

> a sense of harmony with the universe is made evident and the whole planet is felt to be in *communitas*. This shiver has to be won, achieved, though to be a consummation, after working through a tangle of conflicts and disharmonies [...] Ritual or theatrical transformation can scarcely occur otherwise. (13)

Theatrical texts that exploit the properties of liminal space also facilitate the creation of *communitas*. Through performance they create the same sense of heightened awareness characteristic of great ritual. As audiences participate in the performance there is an invitation to experience that shiver of recognition, that sees the possibility that all human lives might be transformed through moments of grace, healing or forgiveness. Theatrical texts that push beyond limited definitions of the real invite audiences (and readers) to become co-creators of culture, as they enter the regenerative abyss of theatre, and experience its potential for transformation and renewal, whether on or off the stage.

3 | Journeys into the Dark

Who can distinguish darkness from the soul? (Yeats)

To inhabit the territory of a Marina Carr play is to enter a liminal space. It is to find oneself in the dark. It is the darkness of the abyss where there are no familiar maps, roads or bridges. What we thought we knew must be left at the door. And like the descent into Dante's *Inferno* it demands that we also abandon hope. Carr's plays invite us to dwell in a place of disconnection without any promise of redemption. Her territory is that of the soul and her tragedies witness to soul loss, abandonment, desolation and self-destruction. If it is difficult to enter a Carr play, it is even more difficult to find a way out. There is no vision of transformation, no promise of resurrection, not even a secular salvation. The hope-lessness that characterizes her protagonists' lives is harrowing to witness, difficult even to keep in focus. The plays have visceral effects on their audiences, with their capacity to flood or overwhelm, or to splinter all meaning-making into tiny fragments. The pain her characters feel is ancient, deep, unfathomable, pre-verbal. Their loss of connection with their own souls and their loss of connection with their own origins whether maternal or divine haunts her plays. Their search for reconnection is urgent, unstoppable, ending more often in dissolution than resolution:

> For Carr, death in the theatre is not the end, it is a poetic drive to excavate what it means to live. Her plays perform the exorcisms and exhumations necessary to the progression of our souls.
> (Melissa Sihra, Abbey Programme *Ariel* 2002:5)

'All I know is a door into the dark' (Heaney) would be a fitting epigraph to Carr's plays. She is not afraid to inhabit the darkness, the space of ambivalences and uncertainties. She is willing to go to the other side to meet the ghosts that haunt the individual and cultural unconscious, to try to speak the unspeakable, to reconnect with the layers of anger, grief, fear, denial, and repression that characterize our imagining. To stay in the dark without any light, to live in the womb/tomb space of gestation and death is to risk everything. There may be no reason to go on once the story is told. Like the characters, audiences may be unable to see beyond disconnection, fragmentation, and dissolution. The pull towards this uncanny dark re-opens old wounds, presents us with desolate states of disconnection and loss, and questions all our efforts to make meaning, or to identify sources of hope. But most significantly Carr's work calls us both at an individual and cultural level to remember what we have forgotten. As Irigaray notes, our culture is premised on forgetting the scar on the navel, the breath, the cave of the womb. Such forgetting produces many false dualisms between spirit and nature, soul and body, heaven and earth. To re-enter the darkness of the womb is almost like a death wish in Carr's plays, and yet it is the space from which we must begin to re-imagine who we are, if we are to go on. I propose to consider soul loss in Carr's work through the lenses of philosophical and cultural critiques of mother-daughter relationships within patriarchal imagining, to consider what happens when one tries to 'forget our divine origins' (Irigaray), to suggest that the crisis of soul loss is both personal and cultural and that the pull towards the semiotic and abject space of the original pre-verbal maternal bond that is so evident in Carr's plays, needs to be brought into consciousness if our culture is to engage in a new imagining.

While Marina Carr resists the label of a feminist writer, she *is* writing plays about women, their lives, their despair. The plight of her female protagonists indicate the plight of women within the patriarchal symbolic. Irigaray would say that failure to symbolize the mother daughter relationship adequately (within the cultural symbolic) leads to women being unable to symbolize their own connections to origins (and to themselves) resulting in failure within adult sexual relationships. Whitford writing about Irigaray expresses it well:

> By describing this relationship as unsymbolised, Irigaray means that there is an absence of linguistic, social, semiotic, structural, cultural, iconic, theoretical, mythical, religious or any other representation of that relationship. There is no maternal genealogy.
> (Whitford, 1991:76)

Irigaray identifies a state of dereliction which arises in this absence of representation.

Similarly the absence of a female divine image means that women do not have the same horizons of possibility offered to them to sustain them in their becoming. If we identify a connection between becoming and wholeness then:

> Divinity is what we need to become free, autonomous, sovereign. No human subjectivity, no human society has ever been established without the help of the divine. (Irigaray, *Sexes and Genealogies*, 1993:62)

Women need this horizon in order to communicate or share with one another:

> They need, we need, an infinite if they are to share a little, otherwise sharing implies fusion-confusion, division, and dislocation within themselves, among themselves. If I am unable to form a relationship with some horizon of accomplishment for my gender, I am unable to share while protecting my becoming. (Irigaray, 62)

For Irigaray it is important that a 'woman's subjectivity' 'accommodate the dimensions of mother and lover as well as the union between the two'. But as long as a woman

> lacks the divine made in her image she cannot establish her subjectivity or achieve a goal of her own. (63)

Both of these lenses, that of the absence of a maternal genealogy and the need for a divine horizon in the establishment of a healthy female subjectivity are helpful in analysing Carr's work.

As Irigaray's philosophy is primarily an intervention in the cultural symbolic at the level of imagination, requiring its adherents to jam the theoretical machinery itself and its pretensions to univocal meaning, so too with Carr's work. Marina Carr's theatre is a theatre of the imagination. It constantly breaks up the realist frame. It is a place of story and dream. It is mythic and inescapable. 'The plays go beyond realism into a symbolic realm where explanations are not to be found in common sense or psychology, but in mythic reference, poetic language, the presence of ghosts and the telling of stories' (O'Dwyer, 2000:244). Her female protagonists are passionate, driven, obsessed and ultimately trapped. Once unleashed it is impossible to contain their anger or their desire. Her 'incorporation of myth and such uncanny characters as the Catwoman in *By The Bog of Cats* who, like Hester, converses with ghosts, juxtaposes the regulated time space location of realism with other ways of imagining the boundaries of self and world' (McMullan, 2001:83).

Carr's trilogy of plays, *The Mai, Portia Coughlan* and *By the Bog of Cats,* moves in sequence from indoors, to threshold, to outdoors. Carr's plays speak in a powerful voice that captures the rhythms of speech in poetry, dark humour and passion. Each play journeys deep within the divided psyches and murderous longings and desires of its characters, revisiting old myths and re-appropriating them as rich interpretative frameworks for her characters to seek meaning. The confrontation with the real from the depths of their unconscious will see her female protagonists driven again and again to despair. The only possible resolution is in the realm of fantasy, imagination or death.

Carr's female protagonists refuse the labels and naming that patriarchal culture offers them. Their narratives in turn assume mythic proportions as they seek a way of coming home to themselves from heightened states of alienation or dereliction. But while their sense of entrapment drives them to rage against inherited definitions, with their inherent contradictions and dichotomies, their solutions force them to despair rather than a new imagining. The transcendent leap of imagination that moves the plays beyond tragedy is to be found in the writing of them rather than their resolution. Marianne McDonald (2000) suggests that the choice of suicide is similar to the Irish choice of suicide through drink and other forms of self-destruction. But self-destructive behaviour can be provoked by a colonizing culture. Whatever about the political colonization experienced by the Irish, a more fundamental colonization exists in male-female relational dynamics. The discrediting of experience that is different or other to the colonizer leads to cultural disavowal of the self. 'Self hatred and self-mutilation can result from an internalization of the colonizer's negative construction of the colonized. In Carr's play death is a refuge for the mother and daughter, a place where they can be free from patriarchy' (McDonald 2000:22). How often as Adrienne Rich notes, women within colonized cultures find their 'arts of survival turned /to rituals of self hatred' (Rich, 1984:307).

Where Chodorow is interested in exploring the mother-daughter relationship in terms of fusion of identity and inability to individuate, Irigaray is more interested in the woman's ontological status within the culture, her position in the symbolic order. Even in the metaphysical picture women are not individuated, there is only the place of the mother or the maternal function. If we consider that the culture, language, the imaginary, and mythology in which we live at present is built on and underpinned by woman as

> reproducer of the social order, acting as the infrastructure of that order then we may also come to realise that all of western culture 'rests upon the murder of the mother.[...] And if we make the foundation of the social order shift, then everything shifts' (Whitford, 1991:77)

Adrienne Rich's book *Of Woman Born: Motherhood as Experience and Institution* (Rich, 1976), offers many important insights for an exploration of motherhood and the mother-daughter relationship that is so central to Carr's work. Where Irigaray offers an intervention in the cultural symbolic, Rich looks to the historical and cultural creation of the institution of motherhood within patriarchy. As she spoke out of the silences and myths that both surround and in turn construct motherhood within a patriarchal economy Rich was daring in her use of personal experience in dialogue with theoretical sources. Rich locates motherhood within a patriarchal culture that defines and demands that women become mothers as an expression of their sole purpose in life, a culture that also equates motherhood with a definition of femaleness, and she balances this with reflective experiences of women who have tried to be mothers, while also being faithful to a sense of self. Her book captures the anger and tenderness that characterizes many women's relationships with their children, the rage and frustration experienced by women who felt alienated from their own bodies, pregnancies, labour and birth in an increasingly male-defined obstetric environment, the complex, and often ambivalent feelings surrounding mother-daughter relationships, and the matrophobia, infanticide, and violence that often characterize these relationships within a patriarchal culture. It offers a vantage point to interpret the states of despair and entrapment in which Carr's female characters find themselves.

Rich's central chapter on motherhood and daughterhood explores the complexity and ambivalence of these relationships within a patriarchal culture. Her sense of 'the great unwritten story' echoes Irigaray's reflections on the absence of a maternal genealogy. In writing this story into history and culture she offers women new interpretive horizons. Carr's mothers and daughters suffer partly because they have not been allowed access to a new naming of their relationships within patriarchy and are fated to repeat the past.

Rich identifies the highly-charged relationship between mother and daughter as 'the great unwritten story':

> Probably there is nothing in human nature more resonant with charges than the flow of energy between two biologically alike bodies, one of which has lain in amniotic bliss inside the other, one of which had labored to give birth to the other. The materials are here for the deepest mutuality and the most painful estrangement. (Rich, 1976:225-226)

She also acknowledges that 'every mother has known overwhelming, unacceptable anger at her own children'. As she remembers her own mother she remarks on her own ambivalent feelings towards her. She also admits that she no longer has fantasies

> of some infinitely healing conversation with her, in which we could show all our wounds, transcend the pain we have shared as mother and daughter, say everything at last. (224)

Yet she believes that in most women there is

a girl-child still longing for a woman's nurture, tenderness and approval, a woman's power exerted in our defense, a woman's smell and touch and voice, a woman's strong arms around us in moments of fear and pain. (224)

No matter how much women may rationalize their forgiveness, when considering the extenuating circumstances under which motherhood is experienced within patriarchy, the child in us ' still feels at moments, wildly unmothered' (225).

Rich recalls the Eleusinian Mystery traditions (inaugurated somewhere between 1400 and 1100 BC) which centred on the myth of Demeter and Persephone (Kore), and in doing so provides a symbol system that is more woman centred and healing of the mother-daughter bond:

> The role played by the Mysteries of Eleusis in ancient spirituality has been compared to that of the passion and resurrection of Christ. But in the resurrection celebrated by the Mysteries, it is a mother whose wrath catalyses the miracle, a daughter who rises from the underworld. [...] Each daughter, even in the millennia before Christ, must have longed for a mother whose love for her and whose power were so great as to undo rape and bring her back from death. And every mother must have longed for the power of Demeter, the efficacy of her anger, the reconciliation with her lost self. (238-40)

As Rich reflects on daughters who deny their mothers, reject their similarity with their mothers, or find themselves unable to differentiate or thinking of matrophobia she could be writing about Portia Coughlan, Hester Swane or Elaine Fitzgerald. Rich reflects on Emily Dickinson's famous statement that 'I never had a mother' and suggests that she meant in part that she felt herself deviant, set apart, from the kind of life her mother lived; that what most concerned her, her mother could not understand' (229). In relation to Sylvia Plath's relationship with her mother Aurelia, Rich notes the 'psychic osmosis' and 'desperate defenses' that were characteristic of their relationship:

> The power of the bond often denied because it cracks consciousness, threatens at times to lead the daughter back into 'those secret chambers ... becoming like waters poured into one jar, inextricably the same, one with the object one adored. (231)

Rich develops the ambivalent concept of matrophobia which the poet Lynn Sukenick has defined as 'the fear not of one's mother or of motherhood but of 'becoming one's mother' (Rich, 235). She identifies how many daughters reject what they perceive to be their own mother's compromises and accommodations. It is

> easier by far to hate and reject a mother outright than to see beyond her to the forces acting upon her. But where a mother is hated to the point of matrophobia there may also be a deep underlying pull toward her, a dread that if one relaxes one's guard one will identify with her completely. (235)

Matrophobia always involves a splitting of the self, almost a self-mutilation in the daughter's urgency to separate and individuate.

Rich also adverts to the absence of a maternal genealogy and sees the loss of the daughter to the mother, and the mother to the daughter, as the essential female tragedy. While culture has acknowledged the father-daughter split (Lear), or the tragedy of the son and mother rupture (Hamlet, and Oedipus), 'there is no presently enduring recognition of mother-daughter passion and rupture' (237)

The nurture of daughters in patriarchy calls for a strong sense of *self*-nurture in the mother and while the psychic interplay between a mother and a daughter can be destructive, it is not fated to be so:

> A woman who feels pride in being female will not visit her self-depreciation upon her female child. A woman who has used her anger creatively will not seek to suppress anger in her daughter in fear that it would become, merely, suicidal. (245)

Rich looks to cases of individual women scapegoated for crimes of maternal violence. She identifies the scapegoat as one 'around whom the darkness of maternity is allowed to swirl, the invisible violence of the institution of motherhood, the guilt, the powerless responsibility for human lives, the judgments and condemnations, the fear of her own power' (276). However the scapegoat is also an 'escape valve':

through her the passions of the blind raging waters of a suppressed knowledge are permitted to churn their way so that they need not emerge in less extreme situations as lucid rebellion. (277)

Rich suggests that if we could really pay attention to women's experiences as mothers, listen to their fantasies, dreams and imaginings:

> we would see the embodiment of rage, of tragedy, of the overcharged energy of love, of inventive desperation, we would see the machinery of institutional violence wrenching at the experience of motherhood. (279)

Such attention to the institutional violence of patriarchal motherhood offers an interesting starting point for interpreting the murderous and self-destructive behaviours that characterize Marina Carr's female protagonists, and helps to locate them in relation to history rather than to myth.

In a lecture on her writing published in 1998 (Carr, 'Dealing with the Dead', 1998), Carr spoke about the place of soul 'that most unfashionable part of the anatomy, these days' (195) in her work. Like Keats, Carr is also more interested in the creation of soul than the redemption of soul and she believes that our sojourn here is to grow a soul, a process that cannot take place without an amount of suffering:

> Marina Carr is a poet of the theatre. Hers is not the kind of drama that is interested in holding a reflective mirror to reality. It seeks, through the limitless channel of the imagination, the uncertainties, mysteries and doubts of the human condition. If anything, Marina Carr's theatre is an exploration of the journey of the soul, in all its glorious failings and infinite potential. (Melissa Sihra, Abbey Programme *Ariel* 2002:3)

Carr locates herself firmly within the tradition of great artists of the soul. That most of them are men does not seem to bother her unduly. The Greek myths that she explores also come out of a patriarchal imagining, where the nexus of symbols associated with woman cluster around sexuality, the body, evil, chaos and death. She does not appear to question the gender ideologies that influence culture and its meaning-makers whether they are mythmakers, storytellers or poets. And yet her plays feature women as

protagonists, located by voice, syntax and accent in Midlands rural
Ireland. The tragedies of their lives may signal the inability of
women to find a language for what they have lost within the cultural symbolic. Their loss of soul, their fundamental disconnection from their most intimate selves drives them to despair, to
suicide, to self-sacrificing obliteration, to murder. If culture has
failed to adequately symbolize a woman's connections to origins,
this is a fundamental aspect of the soul loss experienced by the
women in Carr's plays.

People experiencing soul loss 'frequently say that they feel
fragmented in some way or that an essential part of themselves is
missing' (Ingerman, 1991:13). The characteristic effects of trauma
(or soul loss) are experienced in gaps in memory, chronic depression, unending grief, physical illness, and coma. Ingerman cites
Jungian analyst Marie Von Franz:

> Soul loss can be observed today as a psychological phenomenon in
> the everyday lives of the human beings around us. Loss of soul
> appears in the form of a sudden onset of apathy and listlessness;
> the joy has gone out of life, initiative is crippled, one feels empty,
> everything seems pointless. (Ingerman, 22)

Achterberg writes of soul loss in terms of 'injury to the inviolate
core that is the essence of the person's being' – which can

> manifest in despair, immunological damage, cancer and a host of
> other very serious disorders. It seems to follow the demise of
> relationship with loved ones, career, or other significant at-
> tachments. (22)

Many traditions of sacred psychology 'tend to map three major
realms of experience' (Houston 1998:34): the factual historical; the
mythic and symbolic; and the unitive or source level. Beyond the
factual historical is the realm of 'symbols, guiding archetypes, and
myths, durative and enduring in an eternal world outside of time
and space, as well as thoroughly transhistorical.' This realm

> functions as the contact point for sacred time and space, the
> container of that which never was but is always happening.

Much of Carr's work happens in this realm, opening to the
depths of the cultural unconscious, in a transhistorical or liminal

space. Carr's characters however seem unable to negotiate the third level. To return to the source, to

> become one with the divine is not to abandon the Self (as archetype of wholeness) but to realize that divine consciousness, who that Self is. (Judith, 1996:414)

Carr's characters do not have access to the mystical or meditative experiences that might enable this journey towards wholeness but remain defined by their attachments to what they have lost and can only imagine a re-connection that involves a dissolution or loss of the Self:

> Letting go of attachment is about how we direct our psychic energy. [...] Attachment fixates our energy outside the self. Rather than focus on the object of attachment – the lost lover, the lost opportunity, the elusive reward – we should redirect our psychic energy to the Self. (Judith, 1996:421)

Carr's work recognizes the impulse of spirit towards liberation but is unable to deal with the soul's need for embodiment.

Carr's characters, sensing their soul loss, seek resolution through the restoration of lost connections. But, unlike the heroes and heroines in the great quest narratives, they are unable to bring the treasure back home. Carr's characters face a paralysis of imagination. Swirling in the chaos of the unconscious, they lash out desperately, in search of home, but find themselves falling into a deeper darkness, unable to imagine a re-connection with the body they have both sought and silenced.

To achieve transcendence is to enter the realm capable of embracing the whole. To bring that divine state of awakened consciousness down into our bodies and act upon it is to experience immanence. As the vehicle that brings the gods back down to earth, immanence is the restoration of the sacred (Judith, 424).

In an article on tragedy and abjection in Marina Carr's plays Wallace (2001) explores the traumatic unstable place of subjectivity in Carr's trilogy. She suggests that Carr's (anti-) heroines seem to be caught in a bind where they are simultaneously compelled and repelled by the abject:

> The abject shadows them throughout the plays and in a sense determines their destinations or destinies. (Wallace, 436)

Sue Vice (1997) discusses Kristeva's abject as a psycho-
analytically inflected development of Bakhtin's grotesque. The
maternal semiotic realm is characterized by bodily rhythms and
pulses that will later form the basis of language and grammar. As
the child enters the symbolic, learns to speak and enters the
paternal arena of language, law and gender difference, she leaves
the semiotic realm. However the semiotic continues to exert
pressure on the symbolic from within in terms of linguistic or
bodily lapses. The mother educates the child in ways of the symbolic through social codes of cleanliness, bodily boundaries, what
to eat etc. The child receives the message that the maternal must
be rejected along with unacceptable practices. Anything that
threatens to send the subject back into the semiotic is accompanied by sensations of dread/disgust/revulsion. Kristeva calls the
abyss which opens when one feels this nausea – abjection. The
subject is thrown down (abjection) towards a boundary its
existence is premised on forgetting. The Kristevan abject includes
margins of the body, the maternal, food, death. The pre-verbal
semiotic space (the primordial matrix of unconsciousness) is a
body without borders. Kristeva argues that devotees of the abject
keep looking for the 'desirable and terrifying, nourishing and
murderous, fascinating and abject inside of the maternal body'
(Kristeva quoted in Vice, 1997:54), whereas abjection dread
protects one from the temptation to return to the maternal
semiotic. Abjection preserves the immemorial violence with which
a body becomes separated from another body in order to be. The
subject must constantly negotiate between its existence in the
symbolic order and the pull to semiotic chaos threatened by
abjection:

> Kristeva argues in *Powers of Horror: An Essay on Abjection* that 'I' am
> simultaneously compelled and repelled by the abject, so that
> perversely, '[...] I abject *myself* within the same motion through
> which 'I' claim to establish *myself.*' (Wallace, 2001:436. Emphasis in
> original)

If Carr's plays are explorations of the struggle to achieve subjectivity and to enter the symbolic they also represent the 'struggle
of a subject with its own insufficiency, its own instability' (Wallace,

437). The constant pull towards the semiotic, towards the undifferentiated space of the womb, haunts the trilogy. Abandonment by the mother constitutes the original abandonment for The Mai, Portia Coughlan and Hester Swane. It is this original abandonment (the loss of this original unity) that is in turn triggered by subsequent abandonments and losses. For The Mai, it is her husband's affair and abandonment, for Portia it is the death of her twin and for Hester it is the rejection and abandonment by her common law husband Carthage, that become the catalysts for the downward spiral of each of the female protagonists. Unconscious forces are unleashed and the pain of the original abandonment becomes unbearable. As the characters are unable to bring the original lost connection sufficiently into consciousness, they remain in turn identified by it and unable to differentiate themselves from it as subjects, and choose dissolution, rather than integration:

> The plays are principally clustered around strategies of repetition and a compulsion to repeat. This compulsion is marked by an obsessional relation to an ever receding 'other'. (Wallace, 438)

The pull is towards forgetfulness and death, rather than a drive towards integration of the shadow and the imagination of newness.

Frank McGuinness in his introduction to *The Dazzling Dark* (1996) writes about Carr's characters and landscapes:

> The landscapes where they conduct their campaigns begin by seeming to be familiar. Yet they, by the perverse logic of love and hatred, grow foreign through their very familiarity. The unhappy unholy family is the only constant in the universe, and it is in the process of tearing itself to pieces. Tragedy is so often the consequence of a fatal lack of self-knowledge. Marina Carr rewrites that rule. Her characters die from a fatal excess of self knowledge. Their truth kills them. And they have always known it would. (McGuinness, 1996: ix/x)

His suggestion that her characters die from a fatal excess of self knowledge tempts one to ask what it is that Carr's characters know or think they know and to wonder whether it is a lack or an excess of self knowledge that leads to their deaths?

> The protagonists derive their sense of self in relation to what they imagine is their destiny. Significantly this is at a remove from knowing. It ties them up in their speculations of this possibility and keeps them at a distance from their actual destiny (or a knowledge of it). (Wallace, 445)

So fantasy, fairytales, remembered stories, and songs feed her characters' imaginations with the sense of an endlessly repeated past. There is no space for possibility or newness. Destiny has already determined what their lives are to be (developed in a most sinister way in *Ariel*). Repetitive patterns of female destruction, the identification of released female emotions as disruptive and chaotic, buy into the enduring definition of women in patriarchy. As Carr's characters cannot imagine any containment of their subjectivity within the patriarchal symbolic, they choose to own their destiny within the same symbolic, choosing death, rather than continuing to live in states of dereliction. If they were able to imagine otherwise than how destiny programmes one to imagine within patriarchy, they might in turn be more open to a future (not yet defined, but probably closely related to the female imaginary) where they could in turn foresee a new morning of the world (Irigaray). The horizon might in turn lean forward offering them space (Maya Angelou) for a new imagining. But Carr's characters remain fearful of a future that is surprising, threatening and other to what they have compulsively and always imagined and re-enacted.

The Mai, Marina Carr (1994)

The Mai, first in a trilogy which also includes *Portia Coughlan* and *By The Bog of Cats* is a play about the lives of women in one family across four generations. It is a play that explores the archetype of the Mother – whether absent, dead, inadequate or without hope. Polarized against the Mother is the archetype of the Lover, which is fed by stories both personal, mythic and fantastic. The fantasy/imagination feeds each generation of women with the same impossible longings and beliefs in an unconditional human love that will not be sullied by contamination with the real. The use of alcohol or drugs can at best offer only a temporary feeling of accommodation. But it is only an escape from the real as it cannot be adequately integrated into consciousness. Music may also offer an opportunity to express and develop soul, but like other beautiful things has been abandoned by The Mai. In the course of the play she will become like the cello, her husband and herself playing her, wildly, discordantly and without rhythm, presenting the audience in Act Two with what D. Morse described as 'one of the play's most unforgettable, violent visual-verbal images' (Morse, 1996:117). As her life slips more and more from her grasp The Mai is trapped in the myth of her own creation and can only find release in suicide.

The Mai opens with the return of her husband Robert (a cello player) after a period of five years. In his absence The Mai has raised their five children alone, continued her work as a principal teacher, worked summers in London to pay for and build the house she now owns, which has a huge bay window, overlooking Owl Lake. The shifting time-frame of the play which gives a sense of cyclical, repetitive time rather than simply chronological time is provided by the narrative of The Mai's daughter Millie who is sixteen and thirty, and onstage throughout the whole play. She recalls: 'When I was eleven The Mai sent me into the butcher's to buy a needle and thread. It was the day Robert left us', and how her mother 'set about looking for that magic thread that would stitch us together again' (*The Mai*, 14). Her mother began a vigil of waiting for and willing her husband to return to her.

The theme of abandonment runs through the play. In each case the woman has been abandoned or deserted by a lover. But this abandonment triggers the deeper wound of abandonment by the mother. This original loss can lead the characters to reject or fear in turn their own capacity as mothers and to over-identify with a self-definition of themselves as lovers. When reality fails to meet with their demands fantasy is on hand to supply the stories that will feed this sense of self as lover either leaving the woman to spend her whole life waiting for the perfect lover or leading to despair. Grandmother Fraochlán named after the island she was born on is one hundred years of age. Cronelike and monstrous, using snuff, smoking opium and sipping mulberry wine, she arrives from Connemara with her oar. In turn her children and grand-children blame her for the way she brought them up or failed to.

Millie tells us that her Grandmother 'was the result of a brief tryst between an aging island spinster and a Spanish or Moroccan sailor.' 'Whoever he was, he left Grandma Fraochlán his dark skin and a yearning for all that was exotic and unattainable' (*The Mai* 18). After a few glasses of mulberry wine 'she began to call up the ghosts' and wrestle them (*The Mai* 21). One of her fundamental beliefs is that people don't change and 'can't help repeatin'.' The 'orchestration may be different but tha tune is allas the same' (*The Mai* 23). In this play the sense of fate and repetition is found in each generation's resort to fantasy or impossible dreams. Richard Kearney has written about repetition as the worst kind of for-getting (Kearney, 2003:194). Repetition, so much a characteristic of Carr's work, would appear to be premised on a type of for-getting that is ancient and deep. It is not simply that the characters do not learn from their experiences, but that each generation passes on the legacy of lost connections in such a way that the characters are fated to repeat the search for what is both lost and forgotten.

While the stage action is set in the summer of 1979 Millie's narrative shifts the time-frame. From a vantage point of fourteen years later it also reminds us of the previous five years and very shortly into the first act informs us of the death of The Mai which occurred in 1980. Her death will not be the climax of the play. It is prefigured for the audience much like Hester's death is prefigured by the Ghostfancier and other portents in the opening moments of *By the Bog of Cats*. Similarly the positioning of Portia Coughlan's death at the beginning of the second act colours the parts of the second act which chronologically preceded it. Time is out of joint. The tragic nature of each of the deaths colours the remembering. Memory is fractured and unreliable. The violence of suicide des-troys the normal sequence of time. It cannot be contained and bursts out of the time-frame demanding a revisiting of events in order to discern some meaning in what seems meaningless. Millie's inability to remember whether she and her father went to town the day after he returned is in sharp contrast to an excursion that she does remember:

> What I do remember, however, is one morning a year and a half later when Robert and I drove into town to buy a blue nightgown and a blue bedjacket for The Mai's waking. (28)

She recalls the neighbours:

> afraid to look yet needing to see, not wanting to move too closely lest they breathed in the damaged air of Owl Lake that hung about us like a wayward halo

as father and daughter stood in the Midland's drapery:

> fingering sky blues, indigo blues, navy blues, lilac blues, night blues, finally settling on a watery blue silk affair. (28)

The cycles of repetition in the women's lives are apparent at a number of levels. The fact that Grandmother Fraochlán's mother (The Duchess) had lived her life under the stigma of being a single parent meant that she was unwilling to let her daughter Ellen suffer the same shame. She forced her to marry someone who was not her intellectual equal, thus consigning her to an impossible life, where her spirit was eventually broken. The Grandmother's own despair and suicidal nature is inherited by The Mai. Her addiction to drugs is passed on to Beck and then to Millie. Her addiction to fantasy as the only way to escape from the harshness of reality is inherited in different ways by each generation. The impossible hopes of what she might have been kill Ellen (40). The Mai is like a child believing in princes and fairytales (46). Millie cannot tell her own child the truth about who his father is (56). 'It's not fair that they should teach us desperation so young or if they do they should never mention hope', (40) muses Julie who at seventy-five years of age feels that she is still not over her childhood. Millie seems to have inherited the sense of despair when she says:

> Sometimes I think I wear Owl Lake like a caul around my chest to protect me from all that is good and hopeful and worth pursuing. (71)

Millie narrates the myth of Owl Lake as Robert enters with the dead body of The Mai in his arms. The juxtaposition of the myth, Millie's vantage point in time, and the presence of the dead body, fracture the realist frame. The myth recounts how Coillte and

Bláth were lovers until Bláth has to spend time with the dark witch of the bog. Bláth must spend the winter in her lair and is unable to communicate with Coillte while he is there. Coillte's grief cries a lake of tears into which the dark witch pushes her. When Bláth returns he cannot find his lover and is told that she has dissolved in a lake of tears. Each member of the family knew the story:

> But we were unaffected by it and in our blindness moved along with it like sleepwalkers along a precipice and all around gods and mortals called out for us to change our course and, not listening, we walked on and on. (42)

Not heeding all the warning signs is a motif that will also open *By The Bog of Cats*.

Early in the second act The Mai talks about her house which is becoming insubstantial:

> It's the kind of house you build to keep out neuroses, stave off nightmares. But they come in anyway with the frost and the draughts and the air bubbles in the radiators. (51)

We learn that Robert has found a new lover, and that The Mai 'can't see a way out' (53). The sense of entrapment features in each of the plays. Here the escape routes are alcohol, drugs or fantasy. As the sisters remember their childhood fantasies of princes coming to spirit them away to happy ever after land, The Mai adds:

> She filled us with hope – too much hope maybe – in things to come. And her stories made us long for something extraordinary to happen in our lives. (55)

One wonders whether the stories were a source of hope or a contributor to despair. The inability to replace childhood fantasy with adult dreams means that the characters remain trapped in an impossible world that is less and less in contact with the real.

Grandmother Fraochlán articulates one of the central themes of the play – the conflict between woman as mother and woman as lover. O'Dwyer notes a similar pattern in the two other plays in the trilogy. 'In each case motherhood as a female role is deconstructed: by neglect in *The Mai* (1994), by rejection in *Portia Coughlan* (1996) and by tragic transformation in *By the Bog of Cats* (1998). When the traditional mother's role is not performed, the children are neglected and the family falls apart. The events which lead to this catastrophe are traumatic and apparently inevitable in each play, in a manner reminiscent of Greek tragedy' (O'Dwyer, 2000:243-244). For Grandmother Fraochlán these two roles appear to be mutually exclusive:

> There's two types of people in this worlt from whah I can gather, thim as puts their childer first an' thim as puts their lover first an' for whah it's worth, tha nine-fingered fisherman an' meself belongs ta tha laher a these. I would gladly a hurlt all seven a ye down tha slopes a hell for wan nigh' more wud tha nine-fingered fisherman an' may I roh eternally for such unmotherly feelin'. (70)

The same complete belonging to the lover preoccupies The Mai. 'No one will ever understand how completely and utterly Robert is mine and I am his' (*The Mai* 72). She is unable to imagine herself without him and cannot think of 'one reason for going on without him.' (72)

The play reflects the inability that woman faces in emerging as subject in her own right. With the loss of the original mother-daughter bond there is a constant disavowal of the self, a denial of connection and yet a sense of something lost irretrievably. Intimacy with the lover may appear to heal the original wound, but if this connection is lost then the original wound resurfaces.

Portia Coughlan, Marina Carr (1996)

Portia Coughlan, the second play in the trilogy is set in the midlands. This sense of place is firmly established through details of the topography being inscribed in the play but more significantly through the language and dialect which in earlier versions of the play is written as it is spoken. All references throughout this section are taken from an edition of the play published in 1996, in a collection entitled *The Dazzling Dark: New Irish Plays* which are selected and introduced by Frank McGuinness. It is important to note at the outset that this original version of the play differs substantially from later written and performed versions.

The territory of any Marina Carr is not an easy one to inhabit. This play is no exception. Portia Coughlan's story is about a woman in search of her soul. It is a violent, haunting narrative that stretches language and syntax to its limits. It is a woman's story, weaving and spiralling backwards and forwards in a non-linear way. It is like a narrative trying to get another angle on the truth of events. Frank McGuinness in his introduction to *The Dazzling Dark* writes about Marina Carr as a

> writer haunted by memories she could not possibly possess, but they seem determined to possess her. This haunting is a violent one, intensified by the physical attack on the conventions of syntax, spelling and sounds of Standard English in the language of *Portia Coughlan*. It is a violence that avoids resolution to its conflict. (ix)

Portia Coughlan's world is a cold one, haunted and possessed by death. It is a world where love seems almost impossible and hatred, rivalry, bitterness and violence underline all relationships. Portia's fated journey back to a state of original unity is the journey of the play. This internal journey must be interpreted in the context of midlands rural Ireland where the issues of land owner-ship and status, the hidden and denied shameful reality of incest, and the perception of difference or otherness haunt the cultural conscious and unconscious. Portia, haunted and possessed by the memory of her twin brother Gabriel, dead for fifteen years, seeks reconnection and release from the state of abandonment, derelict-ion and suffocation in which she finds herself. The full horror of the play unfolds as Portia, suffering increased feelings of isolation and displacement, moves towards disintegration and death. Her in-ability to find a language to represent or symbolize herself leads her to invent and create her own myth of origins. Portia Coughlan's story is a rich illustration of the status of woman within the cultural symbolic and a testament to the state of dereliction described by Irigaray. Portia's feelings of abandonment may relate more to the loss of the mother than the loss of her twin. And both these losses may push further back to a loss of connection with one's essence or core which may be the unacknowledged pain of the play.

As the play opens, stage directions indicate that Portia is dishevelled and barefoot and holding a drink. As the lights come up simultaneously on her dead twin Gabriel who stands at the bank of the Belmont river singing, 'they mirror one another's movements in an odd way, unconsciously' (*Portia Coughlan*, 239). The unconscious connection with Gabriel haunts and frames the play. *Portia Coughlan* has been referred to as a threshold play. In many senses this is true. The threshold is a liminal space – a place between worlds – that is neither here nor there. In this liminal space the boundaries between the worlds are more fluid. Portia is caught between this world and anywhere that is not here. She is poised between life and death. She is torn between the conscious and the unconscious, between inside and outside. While this play explores one female unconscious and gives it both a language and specificity one must question whether it ultimately validates the patriarchal aesthetic, in the way it portrays the female unconscious as violent, disturbed, eccentric, demonic, destructive and generally wreaking havoc – a theme that will be further developed in *By The Bog of Cats*. As *The Mai* failed to lead to any kind of new imagining, *Portia Coughlan* similarly only offers release through suicide. Adrienne Rich remarked at her funeral oration for Anne Sexton (following her suicide) that we need to move beyond seeing suicide as the only possible creative act of resistance for women.

Portia Coughlan is trapped in marriage, motherhood and middle-class mediocrity. Drinking brandy at ten in the morning, still in nightclothes, unable to care for her children and her home, is a fairly typical portrait of alcoholism or depression, which is endemic to Irish society. Raphael, her husband whom she married because he had an angel's name, is a rich factory owner and father of her three sons. She despises him for his wealth, his calculating ways, his calm undemanding nature and for the fact that he wooed her and trapped her into motherhood. Unable to love her children, she fears what harm she might do to them and wants them to be kept away from her. She quickly discards the five thousand pound bracelet that he has given her for her birthday, directing her attention to an old musty box she pulled out of the river the previous night. She felt that Gabriel was clutching at her leg and struggling with her as she tried to retrieve it.

The contents of the box bring the childhood of the twins into her living room. Photos, music, a jar of money, clothes pegs, crayons – 'in this box we puh everthin' for whin we'd be free an' big…we war goin' ta travel tha whole worldt me an' him' (247). The poignancy of the childish preparations for the adult world are set against Portia's increasing inability to survive in the same world. We later learn that the twins had earlier tried to escape the reality in which they found themselves. Their first attempt was on a school tour when they stole a small boat and were found rowing five miles out to sea, trying to get to anywhere that's not here. The sadness of their mother throughout their childhood caused a huge amount of bitterness in the two children. They hated her weakness and their memories of her crying, while banished to the bedroom with the twins in the early years of her marriage, led to their elaborate plans to murder her or to do away with themselves.

Their desire to leave or to die went very deep and Portia remembers not just wishing that she had never been born but wishing that she had never been. 'We wished never ta have been, which be a different thing. Ta never have bin born, manes yar alreada here. Never ta have been, manes ya chompletla an'uteerla never war' (303). In conversation with Fintan, the local barman, Portia talks about both of them needing 'ta be pounded inta dust an'med all over again' (295). This desire to be unmade or remade feeds a longing for dissolution which Portia eventually chooses. Her journey is a regression towards a state of undifferentiated unconscious unity rather than forward through adult conscious-ness and awareness to integration. Unable to integrate the shadow into consciousness she seeks resolution through escape. Impatient with ambiguity and unable to deal with aspects of the shadow in herself or others, she opts for death as the only possible means of self-definition and soul- retrieval.

Portia is haunted by her own death and imagines what she will be like as a ghost:

> 'ah'll lie here whin ah'm a ghos' an' smoche ghos' cigarehs an' observe ye earthlin's goin abouh yeer pintless days …' (251)

This sense of the dead still present through the elements and nature taps into an older cosmology and more ancient spirituality than Christianity. Her memories of Gabriel are similar:

> There's noh a stone, a fince, a corner of ana' your forty fields thah don't resemble Gabriel. Hees name is in tha mouths a' tha starlin's

thah swoops over Belmont hill, tha cows bellows for him from tha
barn an frosty winter nights. Thah vera river tells me thah wance he
war here an' now he is gone. (261)

Paradoxically his presence everywhere highlights his physical
absence and feeds her despair.

Portia is aware of her difference from those around her.
Sometimes she simply feels superior and more intelligent. She says
to Damus, 'An mebbe yar as thick as tha rest a' thim. Though ah'd
tache y'ouha that slime buh ud's still drippin' offa ya' (251). She is
not interested in the local men and their opinions don't count. She
has used them for sex in the past but is no longer interested. She
speaks of Fintan as 'a fuchin' clodhopper liche yar people afore ya
an' liche those ya'll spawn ater ya in a weh ditch an a weh nigh' in a
drunken stupour' (268). At other times she feels that she is in the
grip of fate, her destiny is mapped out and she has seen it. As
surely as the salmon knows its way from the river to the sea she
knows where she is bound and has always been (266). She
appropriates the myth of the Belmont river because she believes
that she was a river in a former life. The story features a woman
who could see the future and was feared by the locals because they
thought she was *causing* events to happen. They eventually impaled
her on a stake in the place where the river now is until her cries
were heard by Bel who carried her from there to the ocean. Portia
recounts how Bel, the valley god, 'could noh unnerstan' how her
people could treah her so far she war wan a' thim, on'y a little
different' (267). Similarly Portia's difference sets her apart, a
difference she shares with her dead twin who is still clutching her.
Her life is monstrous and mythic and driven by forces larger than
her. She imagines that if she had her eye gouged out like her friend
Stacia that she wouldn't wear any eye patch (253). She feels that
she is in a place that 'mus' surela be tha dungeon a' tha fallen
worldt' (267). Her cries too are ancient and part of the landscape.
People believed that the girl's cries could be heard when the river
was low. Gabriel had heard the song which he described as 'liche
an aria from a chave, sayed there war no soun' i'this worldt ta
match ud; sayed if God tooche ta singin', be tha soun' he'd mache'
(267-68). Portia has not yet heard the song. It is almost as if she is

listening for the sounds of a more ancient spirituality, which is found beneath the myth in the landscape.

Portia's sense of suffocation grows throughout the play. She feels that she and Raphael might as well be dead for all the joy they get from each other. Her house feels like a coffin, and 'sometimes ah chan't brathe anamore' (255). She is however unable to leave the place – like both The Mai and Hester Swane. She cannot imagine surviving even a night away from the Belmont river. Her thoughts would keep returning to the river:

> Ah'd be wonderin' war ud flowin rough or smooth. Was ud's banks mucky nor dry, was tha salmon beginnin' their awful rowin' ta tha sae, was tha frogs spawnin' tha waher lilies, had tha heron returned, be wonderin' all a these an' a thousan' other wonderin's tha river washes over me. In a former life ah'm sure ah war a river. (256)

Portia's hatred of her mother (and her rejection of her own capacity as mother) puts her in an impossible situation. She needs her mother to validate her stories about Gabriel and yet she blames her for his death. She knows and understands how her mother's mind works. She is both the same and different to her mother. She disowns the similarities which in turn destroys her and prevents any kind of new imagining of the mother-daughter relationship. She accuses her mother of putting a death wish on her sons, simply because she couldn't save her own son Gabriel. This seems to be a projection of the shadow on Portia's part. She is unable to come to terms with her own violent impulses towards her children and imagines that if she keeps away from them she won't harm or mark them. Portia's logic (which she says is the only one she knows) will lead her to imagine that abandoning her children through suicide will not harm them. Marianne accuses Portia of being dark, to which she replies:

> Ah rades subtext mother, words dropt be accident, phrases covered over, sintinces unfinished, an' ah' knows ever' inch an' ditch an' drain a' Belmont farm. So don't you bluster in here an' puh a death wish an my sons jus' acause ya couldn' save yar own. My sons'll be fine for if ah does natin' else ah laves thim alone an' no marche be behher than a blache wan. (258)

Portia feels that the better part of her went into the Belmont River with Gabriel. The story she had inherited says that they came out of the womb holding hands. This sense of an original unity of male and female identity haunts Portia. Her search constantly drags her backwards. She believes that they

> Cem ouha the womb howldin' hands …whin God war handin' ouh souls, he musta goh mine an' Gabriel's mixed up, aither thah or he gev us jus' tha wan atwane us an' ud wint inta tha Belmont river wud him…Oh Gabriel ya had no righ' ta discard me so, ta floah me an tha worldt as if ah war a ball a' flotsam, ya had no righ'. (259)

As Portia cries hysterically her mother tells her to control herself, reminding her that if she behaved like any normal woman, there'd be none of this. Portia's inability or refusal to accommodate herself to what is perceived as normal for a woman increases her sense of isolation. Rather than question (as Adrienne Rich does) the cultural assumptions that underline definitions of what is normal for women, Portia seeks answers in the undifferentiated space of the womb. Portia's threshold status may in fact allow her access to the cultural unconscious, where she is aware of the lies and the shame that underlie her particular community. However her reading of subtext, both in the people and its inscription in the land will eventually overwhelm her.

Blaize Scully, Portia's grandmother on her father's side is another monstrous character. Like Grandmother Fraochlán in status but much more bitter and vindictive, she is an example of how a woman might survive in the culture (Maggie May an elderly aunt of Portia's also offers a model of survival in becoming a prostitute. Her status, regarded negatively during Portia's child-hood, is almost preferable now to that of Portia who wishes she could at least have chosen this way of survival. The status of prostitute within patriarchal culture feeds into the myth of the sexual availability of women, and one must question what kind of freedom it really affords, and what kind of survival it enables). Blaize Scully curses and abuses those around her. She does not behave like a woman should behave. Linguistically she has a greater register than other women, which may enable her to speak her mind. She tells us that she spent the first eighty years of her life

> howldin' me tongue, fuchin' an' blindin' inta that pilla. An' Jaysus, if God sees fih ta gimme another eigh'y, th'll be spint spachin' me mine foul nor fair. (259)

There is a sense that she sees and knows in a way similar to Portia. She loves the music of Count John McCormack 'a midlander liche me, born on'y up tha road...on'y he goh away' (276). During her childhood it was the only record they had. The sense of freedom and longing for something more contained in the music was in sharp contrast to the barrenness and hardship of their lives. In one of her conversations after Portia's death she talks about the discovery of ancient coins from Afghanistan in the region of the Belmont valley. This becomes an invitation to her to imagine a whole different ancestry for herself, one that is exotic and foreign, romantic and poetic. Even the word Afghanistan would be one to say into the pillow at night (One cannot read this text naively now in the light of contemporary awareness of the Taliban regime in Afghanistan, and the atrocious conditions for women living under its rule.) She feels different and superior to those around her, believing that none of them have any imagination:

> No yees paple 'roun' here chan't imagine anathin' beyant nex' Frida i' tha pub an' a bag a' chips an tha way home.' In contrast she believes that Portia would have understood. Portia now, she'd imagine ud. In a sourta way Portia war an Afghanastanish. (277)

Blaize Scully's self-definition also has its darker side. Aware of the history of incest within her own family, knowing that her husband was also the father of other children including Marianne, a victim of domestic violence, and aware of the importance of land in defining who you were in midlands Ireland, her definition of self as pure and superior is sustained by needing an other who will carry the negated, repressed or demonic aspects of herself. Her perception of Marianne's family – the Joyces, is that of tinkers or a black-eyed gypsy tribe:

We don' know where ye cem from, tha histories a' yeer blood. Ah warnt ya Sly! D'ya thinche ya'd fuchin' listen! There's a divil in that Jiyce blood, was in Gabriel, an ud's in Portia too. God protec' us from thah blache-eyed gypsa tribe wud their blache blood an' their blache souls. (262-63)

Marianne will accuse her of having no right to look down on her for thirty years, and speaks of Blaize's family as 'inbred, ingrown scurvied McGoverns! Tha say yar father war yar brother!' (263). Blaize accuses Marianne of killing her son by the way she looked at him:

...tha whole worldt knows ya can kill a body jus' be loochin' ah thim if ya looche long enough an' ya looche wrong enough! Ah know yar darche aul fuchin' Jiyce strake an' whah ud does to a person! Looche ah Sly! Y'ave turnt him into a lump a' jelly afore me eyes. Tha's tha Jiyce power Sly, gets hoult a somethin' beauhiful an' pure, liche Gabriel, an' crushes ud till there be natin' left buh tha shell. (264)

The reality of incest is not acknowledged but goes underground to emerge as vindictive thwarting and blaming behaviour towards the other.

Blaize's perception of Gabriel is also as other or different. She alternately refers to him as demonic or angelic. Sly refers to him as 'thah unnatural childt thah shamed me an' yar mother so' (261). He shares his mother's view of 'thah wild Jiyce strake an yar mother's side' (262) which made Gabriel and Portia unpredictable so that he could never know what they were thinking. He is equally torn between attributing demonic or angelic features to Gabriel. At times he would look at him in the rear view mirror as he drove him to his singing lessons and he would think:

this be no human childt buh some little outchaste from hell. An then he'd sing tha long drive home an' ah knew ah war listenin' ta somethin' beauhiful an' rare. (280)

After Portia's death Blaize drinks a toast to her:

i' tha murchy clay a' Belmont graveyard where she war headin' from tha day she war born, cause whin ya brade animals wud humans ya chan on'y brin' forth poor haunted monsters wh've no sinse a' God or man. Portia an' Gabriel. Changelin's. (279-80)

While Blaize knows that Sly and Marianne are half sister and brother she still projects her anger onto the Joyces with their 'waxy blood an' wanin' souls.' Their otherness allows her to preserve her own sense of self and to hide or lie about the shameful realities of incest and marital infidelity.

As Portia's increasing sense of isolation and dislocation grows she becomes fearful around what she might do to her children. She also becomes increasingly dismissive and brutal in her relationships with men, in particular with Raphael. She feels that she cannot love her children. When she looks at her children she sees

> knives an' accidents an' terrible mutilations. Their toys becomes weapons for me ta hurt thim wud, givin' thim a bath is a place where ah could drown thim. An' ah have ta run from thim. Lock thim ouha tha room, for fear ah cause these awful things ta happen. (284-85)

Her unconscious world begins to blur the boundaries of her conscious world. As the inside becomes more manifest on the outside she fears the power of the unleashed forces and projects them outwards in her fears for her children or in her hatred of Raphael. As she vehemently denies that Gabriel is in any way responsible for her mental state she tells Raphael:

> Tha problem's you! Ah fuchin' hate ya! Moochin' up ta me wud yar sliche theories an wha's wrong a' me! Ya haven't a fuchin' clue y'igorant fuchin' cripple ya! A chan't bear tha sigh' a' ya hobblin' 'roun' me wud yar bad fooh an' yar custom med cowbiy boots.'

She tells him that when he touches her at night he's lucky that 'ah don't rip ya ta pieces or plunge a breadknife through yar lily heart! She continues 'A chompletla an uhherla despise you for whah y'are in yarself, buh more for who ya will never be! (270)

This is one of the last speeches that Portia makes before she drowns herself in the Belmont river. The second act opens with Portia's body being hoisted wet and dripping from the river. Its shifting time-frame will see it move from her death to her funeral and back to the last day of her life. It is shocking and disorienting. Portia has already imagined herself as a ghost, now she becomes one for the audience. The shadow of death which has haunted the play becomes a reality in the second act. It is almost as if Portia is saying I told you but you didn't listen or you couldn't hear me. In conversation with Maggie May she remembers the childhood connection with her twin:

> everthin's synchronized, tha way ya thinche, tha way ya move, tha way ya speache, tha blinkin' a' yar eyes, tha blood in yar veins moves be unison. Thah time tha cemetery gates fell an Gabriel, tha migh as well've fallen an me too, amimber ah war found unconscious aside of him, wud noh a marche an me, five feeh from where tha gahe fell. Tha's on'y a small example of how we ware. Ah'm dead Maggie May, dead an' whah ya seen this long time gone be a ghost who chan't fin' her restin' place, is all. (293)

Portia traces her present dissatisfaction and longing back to a state of remembered unity with her twin. Irrespective of whether one had a twin or not, the path to personal integration often involves a sense of loss of an original unity, whether with the mother or with the divine. Portia feels this loss acutely. Her guilt around their original suicide attempt where she lost her nerve, along with her guilt around her emerging adult sexuality continue to haunt her. An inability to separate or differentiate combined with an inability to integrate adult sexual desire leaves her fractured and searching. She talks about her original rupture with Gabriel. He had overseen her making love with a local boy when she was fifteen. Prior to this they had spent much of their time together making love by the banks of the Belmont river. The original incestuous relationship mirrors the incestuous relationship between her parents. Perhaps this is the subtext that Portia Coughlan inadvertently picked up. Maggie May suggests that the inbreeding could have caused the instability in Gabriel or that his antennae were too finely tuned to cope with the asphyxiation in the household (298). The original loss of connection with her mother, the death of her twin and the subsequent disappointment of marriage and family, contribute to her loss of soul. The growing realization that she is living without soul is eventually what drives Portia Coughlan to suicide. Whether she is correct in where she identifies this loss of soul or in the steps she takes to retrieve it, one cannot doubt her sincerity.

Portia Coughlan felt that she was fated to die in this way. Her last attempts to try to achieve some kind of normality or success in domesticity cannot work the miracle for her. She tries to get the children ready for bed, to read a story to the little one, to cook a dinner with wine for Raphael but it is hopeless and too late. She has moved from history into the mythic. She is fated to act the way she does. As she becomes less and less defined by her human ties, she becomes increasingly monstrous, and larger than life. She tries to hold onto normality but fails. She is in the grip of something larger than herself. Call it fate but it is a vision of life that scoffs at puny human responsibility. The canvas is much larger and there is no escape. Portia has seen it all prefigured in Gabriel's song, similar to the people in the story of Bel, the river god, and the woman.

As Portia is dancing with Senchil she asks him, 'How'd ya geh ta stay so unsiled Senchil?' (298). She goes on to describe him as clean as snow falling on snow. The notion of clean/unclean or pure/impure draws attention to Portia's sense of loss of an original innocence through the death of Gabriel. Life has contaminated her, both personally and culturally. She cannot remain unsoiled. Her inability to accept her reality along with her desire to unmake herself find expression in a row with her mother where she, Portia, physically attacks her. She has told Maggie May that she wants to rape her mother, (although later editions of the play have changed this). This desire to punish her mother is retaliation for having been born and having been separated from Gabriel. During her childhood her mother would interrupt them in their games and their love-making. Portia's resentment of this, along with blaming her mother for Gabriel's subsequent death leads to her desire for revenge. As rape is such a violation of woman and expresses such hatred of woman on the part of the perpetrator, it is all the more horrifying that one woman should want to rape another. Portia's desire to violate her mother in this way is a further expression of her desire to wipe out her own existence and to deny any feelings of maternal identification. The severing of the mother-daughter bond through aggression and denial leaves her in a state of dereliction. Her mother's response is to attribute demonic characteristics to both Gabriel and Portia; 'Yar crazier than yar twin an' he war a demon' (303). She returns Portia's physical and verbal violence, and ends by telling her that Gabriel was the one she loved and that Portia was only his shadow, that he had all the gifts and Portia none, that he was the fire and she only the charred remains.

Sly tries to undo Marianne's cruelty by reminding Portia that she was the first girl to come into the Scully household for over a hundred years, and that she was very precious because of that.

Portia's growing alienation from those around her sees her more and more immersed in her story of origins. She believes that Gabriel and she were lovers before they were born:

> Times ah close me eyes an' ah fale a rush a' waher 'roun' me, an' above we hare tha thumpin' a' me mother's heart, in front of us tha soft blubber of her belly, an' we're atwined, hees fooh an me head, mine an hees foetal arm, an' we don' know which of us be th'other an' we don't want ta, an' tha waher swells 'roun' our ears an' all tha world be Portia an' Gabriel packed for ever in a tigh' hoh womb, where's there no brathin', no thinkin', no seein', on'y darcheness an' heart drums an' touch ... (307)

She does not want to be left alone in this place of longing for dissolution but no one could have stopped her. She recalls Gabriel singing in the Belmont chapel, fifteen years earlier, where both his and her death were prefigured. They both experience a stabbing pain in their side and as she listens to his song:

> we seen him walchin' inta tha Belmont river; seen me wud you an our weddin' day; seen me sons, this barn of a house; seen tha lane ta tha river an a darche nigh'; grake darche aspite tha pile up a' stars; an' me walchin' along tha lane carryin' an aul box, older an' wiser than ah've ever bin; we seen ud all Raphael down ta tha las' detail. (308)

By The Bog of Cats, Marina Carr (1998)

By the Bog of Cats (the third play in Carr's trilogy) is an appropriation and reworking at one level of the myth of *Medea*. Hester Swane, a woman abandoned by her own mother and now rejected and discarded by her common law husband, plots revenge as she roams and paces the bog waiting for her own mother's return. The woman scorned – Hester Swane – could still be the classical *Medea*. Her anger unleashed is powerful enough to destroy the whole community. Woman's emotions within patriarchal culture can be interpreted in terms of what are acceptable and what are not. Women are certainly permitted to express emotions relating to compassion, tenderness, nurturing but not so readily allowed to express anger, discontent, frustration and rage. When women express these emotions they have been interpreted as inappropriate or having the potential to cause chaos within or destruction of the patriarchal order. The question a feminist reader of this play must ask is whether the character of Hester Swane validates or questions the patriarchal aesthetic. She doesn't keep the rules (unlike her mother in law) but questions them (*By the Bog of Cats* 55). Agreements written down can always be changed. Hester needs to tell her part of the story, retrieve the lost parts, and believes that she belongs on the bog and can never be made to leave it.

The classical drama would have seen Medea's part played by a man in drag. Carr's play foregrounds a woman in the role. And not just woman in general but a specific, particular woman, identified by accent and voice as being an Irish midlands woman, who began life as an itinerant, living in a caravan on the bog. A particular gendered subjectivity is in question here. When the play opens Hester has a daughter Josie who is seven years old, the age Hester was when abandoned by her own mother Josie. The mother-daughter relationship is a vital key to interpreting the play. It is this original abandonment that is triggered by her husband's abandonment and that unleashes such violence and destruction. The character of Hester Swane is not the fictional woman of traditional patriarchal myth. She is a motherless woman, searching for a myth of origins that will help her to interpret and make sense of this awful present in which she finds herself.

The 1998 Abbey production with a wonderfully atmospheric set design by Monica Frawley, and Olwen Fouéré playing Hester provided an exquisite realization of the text in performance. Hearing the cadences and rhythms of the midlands speech and dialect, and seeing the desolate stretches of a bog in winter are integral to receiving the story of the play. Sihra suggests that the

> conceptualizing of space and property in *By the Bog of Cats* is unstable and indicative of the nature of identity. Hester crosses spatial boundaries more radically than in Carr's previous work. (The Mai remains indoors, while Portia flirts with the threshold.) Her representation in contrasting spaces such as the indeterminate bog 'always shiftin' and changin' and coddin' the eye', a caravan

and a fixed house lead to the representation of the self with which they are entwined. (Sihra, 2000:261)

Frank McGuinness in the programme note for the same production says that in this play Marina Carr writes in Greek:

> She knows what the Greeks know. Death is a big country. And hers is a big imagination, crossing the border always between the living and the dead. She speaks in a strange language, but has no truck with the gift of tongues. In her plays words are like boiling water. They scald you if they so choose.

The play opens at dawn on The Bog of Cats. Hester's death is prefigured three times, through the death of the swan, through the Ghostfancier's mistaking dawn for dusk and through the advice of the blind Catwoman who tells Hester that if she doesn't leave the bog today she never will. The stage is set as in the classic Greek theatre. We are in the realm of the mythic, the stories that never happened yet always happen. We know the contours, the inescapable fate of the protagonists. It is the particularity that we await:

> Listen to me, Caroline, there's two Hester Swanes, one that is decent and very fond of ya despite your callow treatment of me. And the other Hester, well, she could slide a knife down your face, carve ya up and not bat an eyelid. (30)

This play is more concerned with the second Hester, the woman who can recognize another's darkness for she knows it in herself. A woman who can slit the throat of her only brother because he had lived with the mother who abandoned her, in another life that excluded her. A woman who thinks that love is 'for fools and children', and describes her relationship with Carthage thus: 'Our bond is harder, like two rocks we are, grindin' off wan another and maybe all the closer for that' (16). She believes that her ' life doesn't hang together without him'. This second abandonment exacerbates the original wound. Her unresolved grief, her feelings of anger, vengeance and inability to forgive her own mother surface as she faces the prospects of leaving the bog and leaving her relationship with Carthage. She feels discarded, thrown on the ash pit while she is still alive. The echoes of Indian suttee suggest the community's collaboration (or at least tacit approval) in her fate. It is easier and more appropriate for the community to celebrate the marriage of Caroline and Carthage, who are both settled people and deemed respectable than to validate the union of Carthage and Hester, an itinerant woman, despite their being partners for fourteen years and having a seven year old child. Elsie Kilbride, Carthage's mother, is particularly antagonistic towards Hester whom she regards as a tinker, despite the fact that her family too were tinsmiths. Monica, a neighbour, refers to these same tinsmiths as nothing but tinkers with notions. The perceived otherness of Hester and her mother is alluded to in terms of their itinerant status. In fact it masks a deeper kind of rejection, a rejection of difference, and a denial of darkness within the characters themselves. Hester knows this darkness:

> I can tell the darkness in you, ya know how? Because it mirrors me own. And that's why ya want me out of here. And maybe you're right. I can't tell anymore. (70)

Hester's two selves, split apart when she lost her original innocence at seven years of age, had found some level of healing and integration through her relationship with Carthage and in her relationship with her daughter. Hester's splitting apart has resonances with Portia Coughlan's sense of splitting and soul loss when her twin brother Gabriel died. In this new abandonment the dissociated parts of the lost self scream for attention, demand to be heard, because the pain of the original wound has become unbearable. Hester Swane is not simply fighting for her life, she too is searching for her soul, in a passionate, embodied searching that cannot be silenced or easily dismissed.

The territory of the mythic is similar to the unconscious territory of the dream. It is outside morality and history and the ordinary 'rules' of civilized behaviour do not apply. As Carr reappropriates an older myth, she explores a space where one can imagine access to passion and behaviour that is not constrained or contained in any way. Is this play simply a rewriting of the Medea myth? That the patriarchal imaginary cannot contain Hester's searching, that it does not recognize her voice or acknowledge her pain is not surprising. That her position appears mad or hysterical or morally inappropriate may question the underlying aesthetic that demands that women live and behave in prescribed ways. Mrs Kilbride informs Hester that she has never overstepped herself and that she has lived by the rules. Hester asks 'What rules are they? Teach them to me and I'll live by them' (55). Hester does not live according to these rules, which are about status and respectability, and more specifically about the place of woman. If her common law husband chooses to discard her after fourteen years she should accept her fate and leave quietly without causing a fuss. That she refuses to do so, that she turns up at the wedding also dressed as a bride, that she allows the full range of her emotions to find expression has no place within the patriarchal aesthetic. It certainly could be the cause of a jamming of the theoretical machinery, giving voice to an otherness that is rejected and debased within the dominant culture. Or it could simply be a validation of the patriarchal myth that sees the unbridled expression of woman's emotions as destructive of the social order. Either way, whatever Carr's intention, as the play moves deeper into the territory of the female unconscious, its unleashed forces will prove to be destructive, both of the individual and the community.

Catwoman, a woman in her late fifties, who lives in a turf house on the bog and wears a full length coat of cat fur, which is studded with cat's eyes and cat paws, is a friend of Hester's and believes herself to be the guardian of the Bog. Blind, but with the gift of a deeper seeing, she eats mice and occupies a liminal space in the play. Like a shaman or priestess she negotiates the territory between worlds. In contrast to the Catholic priest in the play she has access to another knowing (The failure of the priest to access any depth of spiritual knowing, because, as one of the characters remarks, he has 'lost the run of himself', suggests a failure of the Christian vision. Father Willow wears his pyjamas under his vestments, drools over Catwoman and remembers the lost love of his own youth. Like Father Jack in *Lughnasa* and Father Welsh in *The Lonesome West*, the priest has lost the capacity to access and interpret the sacred in any kind of healing or transformative way for his community). Catwoman in contrast has the capacity to inhabit both the spirit and the human world. She prepares potions of herbs for healing, and can often see the future. She indicates that Hester has similar abilities to see but refuses to acknowledge them. She will be invited to a wedding in the local community because it would be considered bad luck not to invite her. Her flaunting of the accepted social values of cleanliness and her blurring of the line between animal and human and her particular friendship with the local priest causes offence to Mrs Kilbride whose desire is to 'fling her in onto the milkin' parlour floor, turn the water on full blast and hose her down to her kidneys' (50). Catwoman knew Hester's mother and was responsible for ensuring that Hester survived as a baby by rescuing her each night from the nest of the black swan, where she had been placed by her mother. Catwoman survives by occupying an eccentric place – in standing away from the centre she can allow her intuitive nature to be recognized and tolerated if not actually accepted. On the margins of the culture her intuition is less feared than if she remained in the centre.

Hester in contrast is viewed as practising some kind of black art when she turns up at the wedding in a wedding gown and later burns down the house and barns. Hester scoffs at this idea, knowing that she does not have any demonic powers:

> And yes, there's things about me yees never understood and makes yees afraid and yees are right for other things goes through my veins besides blood that I've fought so hard to keep wraps on. (66)

Hester is acknowledging her own shadow, the darkness within her, which when unleashed is violent, mean and destructive. Speaking to the ghost of her dead brother she shows no remorse and says that she would slit his throat again if he was to stand in front of her. She vows that if her mother were to show up that she'd

> spit in her face, I'd box the jaws off of her, I'd go after her with a knife, I'd make her squeal like a cornered badger. (60)

The anger and vengeance expressed in Hester's conversation with her dead brother where she believes that someone has to pay the price is the kind of thinking that is also behind her eventual destruction of the animals and the farm. Bringing this level of unconscious anger to consciousness and unleashing it in violent destructive behaviour is not at all acceptable to the *status quo*, especially when it is performed by a woman. The wanton violence and destruction of war is not similarly questioned as it has its place within a patriarchal economy of sacrifice. It is woman's violence and refusal to play her proper role that is more threatening. Xavier Cassidy whom Hester knows to have murdered his son James, through strychnine poisoning, and who has also been guilty of abusing his daughter, is particularly vehement towards Hester:

> **Xavier:** A hundred years ago we'd strap ya to a stake and roast ya till your guts exploded.
> **Carthage:** That's it! I'm takin' Josie off ya! I don't care if I've to drag ya through the courts. I'll have ya put away! I'll tell all about your brother! I don't care.
> **Hester:** Tell them! And tell them your own part in it too while you're at it! Don't you threaten me with Josie! This pervert has been gropin' me with his gun and you want Josie roun' him –

Xavier suggests that Hester is beyond 'reasonin' with' and admits that, 'if she was mine I'd cut that tinker tongue from her mouth, I'd brand her lips, I'd – ' (72). Culture has always found ways of silencing women, preventing them from speaking their truth or naming things as they see them. Identifying their behaviour as mad, demonic or heretical and eliminating their voice has allowed the patriarchal world view to remain in place. Whether this is achieved through exile, death or marginalization, cutting out a woman's tongue, whether physically or metaphorically, certainly silences any critical or dissenting voice.

Hester has waited over thirty-three years for her mother to return. At points in the play she feels that she is finding it harder to remember her:

> Every day I forget more and more till I'm startin' to think I made her up out of the air. If it wasn't for this auld caravan I'd swear I only dreamt her. What was she like? (*Bog* 62)

This sense that she is losing contact with the memory of her mother increases her sense of desolation. Her fractured memory along with other people's reminiscences is all that Hester has to reconstruct her mother. She cannot leave the bog. 'I watched her walk away from me across the Bog of Cats. And across the Bog of

Cats I'll watch her return' (43). Catwoman recalls Hester's mother chaining her like a rabid pup to the caravan when she left her there on her own. Hester remembers her mother 'pausing' (22) as she smoked her cigar, and wonders now if she ever found what she was waiting for. Catwoman remembers Josie Swane as a great song stitcher, but 'somewhere along the way she stopped weavin' them songs and became small and bitter and mean' (22). Xavier Cassidy says that her mother would go off for days with anyone that would buy her a drink, and that she was renowned for getting into fights and 'wance she bit the nose off a woman who dared to look at her man' (40). The shadow of Josie Swane dominates Hester's consciousness. When she meets the ghost of her brother she asks him if he has met her mother since he died and is anxious to know why she left her:

> Was it somethin' I done on her? I was seven, same age as me daughter Josie, seven, and there isn't anythin' in this wide world Josie could do that'd make me walk away from her. (60)

A large part of Hester remains an abandoned child and she has never been able to integrate this into her adult consciousness. Unlike The Mai and Portia Coughlan she has a very good relationship with her own daughter and this will ultimately lead to the choice she makes to kill her too rather than have her waiting all her life for her to return. Hester's anger at her own mother's abandonment is still palpable. In her conversation with her dead brother's ghost she is still angry that her mother called her brother Joseph after herself and named her Hester after no one. She scavenges for bits of information about her mother and whether she ever talked about her in her life with Joseph and his father. Even though he tells her that he was also abandoned by his mother she is jealous of the fact that he had her until he was ten. Joseph recalls her as 'fierce silent', gentle even, whereas Hester recalls her with 'a vicious whiskey temper on her and a whiplash tongue and fists that'd land on ya like lightning'. He tells her that she told his father that Hester had died, because she had a bad heart. Her reasons for killing Joseph are very clear to Hester.

Hester: She stole my life from me.
Joseph: So you stole mine.

Hester: Well somewan had to pay. (62-3)

Monica recalls Hester's mother as 'a harsh auld yoke...came and went like the moon' (64). She describes her larger than life physical appearance:

> She'd be sittin' on the step just like you are, with her big head of black hair and eyes glamin' like a cat and long arms and a powerful neck all knotted that she'd stretch like a swan in a yawn...But I was never comfortable with her...There was lots spent evenin's tryin' to figure Josie Swane, somethin' cold and dead about her except when she sang and then I declare ya'd fall in love with her. (64-5)

While she and Hester recall her mother being invited to many celebrations to sing the songs she had composed, Monica insists that Hester's waiting for her mother is a refusal to grow up and face reality. 'You up on forty, Hester and still dreamin' of story-book endin's, still whingin' for your Mam' (65). Sihra interprets the figure of Big Josie Swane as 'an alternative to the romanticized literary Mother Ireland figure' (Sihra, 2000:260) and suggests that the 'nation as female is now depicted as an overweight, erotic, foul-mouthed transgressive energy' (260).

When the Cassidy family try to force her to leave the bog, Hester insists that her mother said she would return:

> I can't lave till me mother comes. I'd hoped she'd have come before now and it wouldn't come to this. Don't make me lave this place or somethin' terrible'll happen. Don't. (57)

She feels that she belongs on the bog:

> I know every barrow and rivulet and bog hole of its nine square mile. I know where the best bog rosemary grows and the sweetest wild bog rue. I could lead yees around the Bog of Cats in me sleep.

Hester's identification with place is similar to Portia Coughlan's. Where she knows every inch of the bog, Portia knows the moods and changing seasons of the Belmont river. The Mai feels her connection with Owl Lake. Aspects of the landscape match an inner landscape for each of the protagonists. The loss of the outer would somehow imply a loss of the inner:

> If the lake, river and bog are understood in terms of indeterminacy and fluidity of signification then they are also antithetical to the subjects' desire to anticipate the future. (Wallace, 2001:449)

It is impossible therefore to imagine removing any of these women from the place or landscape within which they have come to know themselves. 'I was born on the Bog of Cats and on the Bog of Cats I'll end me days. I've as much right to this place as any of yees, more, for it holds me to it in ways it has never held yees' (35). Each of the places – the bog, the river, the lake – is also associated with abandonment for each of the women. The landscape provides access for each of the women to a myth of origins. It operates on a soul level, promising the possibility of access to a state of original innocence or wholeness. The water or the bog almost reclaims the women. Hester talks about the ritual of burning; 'only an auld house, it should never have been built in he first place. Let the bog have it back. In a year or so, it'll be covered in gorse and furze, a tree'll grow out through the roof, maybe a big bog oak' (*Bog* 63). In the face of loss or abandonment the protagonists choose suicide as a way of remaining connected to the landscape. Dissolution in a lake or a river or dying on the bog having burnt down everything connected with one's life may however indicate the impossibility of access to the state of original innocence.

Hester interprets Carthage's leaving her in relation to his guilt over his involvement in the murder of her brother. She claims that he 'rose in the world on his ashes' and that he needs to forget that Hester ever existed. When Carthage reminds Hester of her drinking and nightly roaming of the bog she responds:

> **Hester:** The drinkin' came after, long after you put it into your mind to lave me. If I had somewan to talk to I mightn't have drunk so hard, somewan to roam the bog with me, somewan to take away a tiny piece of this guilt I carry with me, but ya never would. (73-4)

Hester's feelings are quite complex. On the one hand she seems to carry some guilt around her brother's death (even though she has told us that she would murder him again). Her drinking and roaming the bog seem to have been precipitated by Carthage's decision to leave her. Yet she also indicates that she never thought much of their relationship, never having found there what she needed. If her guilt is more correctly located in relation to her mother, then her dissatisfaction with Carthage and her roaming the bog make more sense. Her behaviour is a conscious or unconscious search for reconnection with the mother. Nothing else can answer this longing. When Caroline describing the fiasco of the wedding says, 'None of it was how it was meant to be, none of it', Hester responds:

> Nothin' ever is, Caroline. Nothin'. I've been a long time wishin' over me mother too. For too long now I've imagined her comin' towards me across the Bog of Cats and she would find me here standin' strong. She would see me life was complete, that I had Carthage and Josie and me own house. I so much wanted her to see that I had flourished without her, and maybe then I could forgive her ... (76)

The stories of Owl Lake and the Belmont river provide a mythology for the female protagonists in *The Mai* and in *Portia Coughlan*. 'In each of the three plays the 'fictions' metonymically echo anxieties concerning identity and the threat of annihilation and indicate a desire to make sense of tragedy' (Wallace, 2001:444). In this play the songs of Josie Swane have a similar function. The song, 'By the Bog of Cats', is a love song of abandonment and loss which Hester believes was written specially for her. As the stories of the lake and the river indicate the enduring presence of the characters in the landscape, so too with the last verse of this song. Hester's last words to Carthage are:

> Ya won't forget me now, Carthage, and when all of this is over or half remembered and ya think ya've almost forgotten me again, take a walk along the Bog of Cats and wait for a purlin' wind through your hair or a soft breath be your ear or a rustle behind ya. That'll be me and Josie ghostin' ya. (80)

In the second song, 'The Black Swan', the singer tells her troubles to a black swan and wishes for wings to fly away. Hester's life has been closely connected to the life cycle of the swan Black Wing. As she trails the corpse of the black swan in the opening moments of the play, we know she is fated to die. The reputed fidelity of swans to their mates is reflected in Hester's fidelity to the memory of her mother, for whom she waits like an abandoned lover until her final, almost erotic, death dance with the Ghost-fancier, brings her home.

On Raftery's Hill, Marina Carr (2000)

In the nineteen-sixties when Tom Murphy wrote his first play he was adamant that it would not be set in a kitchen. Anxious to move away from stereotypical depictions of life in rural Ireland he wanted to represent the real struggles of Irish men and women searching for soul in stringent economic circumstances in modern Ireland. Marina Carr, whose work is also in the area of soul-searching and soul-making, sets her play, *On Raftery's Hill*, in the present, in the kitchen of the Raftery household, in the Irish Midlands. If any play tries to confront an audience with the reality of Irish life in the new millennium, by confronting myths and stereotypes about the family and exposing the lies and the sickness that are endemic to this society, this play by Carr manages to achieve it. The reality is almost too real for theatre. At times this play is like a documentary exploring one family's experience of incest and violence, and the tacit approval that allows such a reality to remain unquestioned. The brutal loss of innocence that is at the heart of this play is set against a community's acceptance of a patriarchal madness that is out of control, yet still powerful and dominant.

The play opens with Sorrel, the youngest daughter, listening to fiddle music coming from the yard. The musician Ded, a man in his mid-thirties, is the eldest son. He is bearded and filthy, speaks incoherently like someone deranged, lives like an animal in the cowshed and is in mortal terror of his father. He is afraid to come inside the house in case his father has slid 'back in like a genie' (*On Raftery's Hill* 13). His horror at being forced as a young boy to help deliver the child of his sister Dinah, as a result of his father's incestuous relationship with her, along with the secrecy demanded has caused his mental breakdown. Ded's marginal vantage point can offer some critique of what is going on but his fear and incoherence renders it almost useless. The grandmother Shalome occupies a similar position, also according to stage notes '*a bit gone in her mind, but with flashes of accidental lucidity*' (15). Neither of them can offer any kind of sustained critique of the reality and yet their presence to the audience is a reminder of the sickness and madness that are the shadow side of patriarchal reality.

The play is full of references to the decay and stench of the land. Dead sheep and cattle are rotting (19) and the farm is described as becoming like an abattoir. Raftery's belief in the superiority of those who live on the hill in contrast to the scrubbers and skulduggery in the valley is juxtaposed with images of his own farm as a river of slurry and rotten animals (31). There is a sense of everything being out of joint. The family should be out working the farm (46) and perhaps the inner decay would not be as it is. The sickness of the land and the sickness of the king have long gone hand in hand in the folk imagination. The brutal tyrannical Raftery is described as 'butcherin all' (18), hunting out and unnecessarily killing the leverets (19) after he had shot the hares and also of cutting the udders off a cow before he shot it and dragged it into the river with a rope (33). Whatever rage has surfaced is never brought properly into consciousness. Throughout the play it will continue to be displaced onto the innocent and vulnerable. When Raftery overhears a conversation that highlights his brutality he responds by raping his young daughter Sorrel. The parallel imagery of teaching her how to gut a hare as he cuts open her clothes before the rape is harrowing for an audience to watch.

The play questions what it means to be human. It explores the relationship between an instinctive animal nature and the civilizing effects of culture. It foregrounds a brutal destructive sexuality that is beyond the reach of morality or legislation. In affirming it as more basic and instinctive it allows the characters to justify their behaviour, seeing nothing wrong in what they are doing, and accusing anyone who questions their truth as spreading lies.

Incest within the Raftery family and outside it are treated in the same way. When Sorrel's boyfriend Dara blames the neighbour Brophy for having a child with his daughter, Red says he is wrong to do so, that 'it is your word against our beliefs' (23). Red also asks Sorrel if she is now going to start spreading lies about this family (46) after her rape. Dinah her sister encourages her not to tell Dara lies, that whatever happened was an accident, that the family love one another and would never harm each other. When

Sorrel says that she can't live with Dara and tell him a pack of lies
Dinah says:

> Ud's not lyin, ud's just noh telling him things. Ud's just sayin the
> opposite of whah you're thinking. Most goes through their whole
> life sayin' the opposite a whah they think. What's so different about
> you? (56)

The whole culture is based on this lie. Sorrel's attempt to speak
the truth of her life experience highlights the lie. Her truth becomes the lie – because she is uncovering the secret, she is giving
voice to what is hidden, denied, repressed. This kind of truth
cannot be heard. Sorrel feels that she cannot tell lies to Dara (i.e.
she cannot withhold her truth). But she is being invited to collude
with the culture's lie to say the opposite of what she is thinking.
The wedding doesn't happen. The grandmother Shalome's noc-
turnal wanderings based on her desire to return to Kinnegad to her
own father (when there are more indications of an incestuous
relationship), now dead for many years, sees her dressed up in
Sorrel's wedding dress, which she has dirtied and torn. The closing
image of the play with Red Raftery cleaning the barrel of a gun
with a strip from the wedding dress is preceded by the following
conversation:

> *Enter Red with Shalome on his arm, muddied wedding dress.*
>
> **Red:** Would you look ah the stahe a Sorrel's dress!
> **Shalome:** (*To Red*) Do you think will Daddy recognise me after all
> these years?
> **Red:** I tould ya a hundred times he's dead. Dead, Mother! Dead.
> **Shalome:** No…you must be thinking of someone else.
> **Red:** Don't ya remember hees funeral? Ya took me, I must a been
> whah? Twelve, thirteen, the army out blowin their bugles. A
> woman came up to me and said, God but you're the spih a him.
> (*Laughs*)
> **Shalome:** Daddy dead? What a lark. Daddies never die, they just
> fake rigor mortis, and all the time they're throwing tantrums in the
> coffin, claw marks on the lid. (57)

Throughout the play there is a huge gulf between the world of
the women and that of the men. The women find themselves in
relationships with brutal, angry, taciturn men. The men are abusive

towards their women both verbally and physically (20). Old Raftery (Shalome's husband) is described as rough and ignorant (28) and Dara Mood has been reared by his mother, his father being prone to stingy silences. Sorrel's father has a tendency to fly into perverted rages. Red cannot remember ever talking to his father (41).

The women are the ones who are left to carry the more refined, gentler aspects of a cultured civilization. Dinah's mother is remembered as a lady (16). Shalome is full of grandiose notions. However the reality of their lives is a source of great disappointment and they gradually lose all hope. They also treat their men cruelly. Shalome boasts that she never touched her husband for thirty years:

> I was cruel to him, Red, crueller than necessary to keep him at bay. And the crueller I was, the bigger and sadder his eyes. In the end he just stood in ditches and stared, died in a ditch, staring at God knows what. (31)

Dinah's mother is also spoken of as a woman of silences and headaches (30) or 'a lunatic with an antique violin and an eternal case of migraine' (31). Their lives become non lives. This sense of loss permeates the play. Shalome is waiting for her life to start. Dinah feels that she has no life and for her it is 'allas autumn' (29). She has sacrificed all her dreams to protect Sorrel.

Innocence too has been destroyed. Dinah tells Sorrel that she was twelve years old when her mother sent her to her father's bed for the first time. Sorrel is blamed for not being careful after her father rapes her. In Sorrel's decision not to marry Dara Mood she has taken on the guilt of her father. She was the 'one perfect thing in the house' (45) and this has been destroyed. Ded's innocence has also been destroyed by what he has been forced to witness. He is threatened with emasculation if he dares speak. His existence is now marginal to the patriarchal culture. He is not a real man and his music-playing and fearful, timid nature aligns him more with the world of women than men. His girly fiddler hands (44) are reminiscent of Gabriel's high girly voice in *Portia Coughlan*.

While the play deals specifically with sexual abuse, in particular incest, it could also be read as a play about trauma and the loss of soul/ loss of childhood/ loss of innocence. One needs to ask whether the narrator of the play is an individual voice (similar to *Baglady*) or whether it is more a play of multiple voices. Does it function more as a cultural critique when one reads it as a statement of the state of the Irish soul? While it deals very specifically like all Carr's work with a particular midlands' family in contemporary Ireland and its intergenerational inheritances and mythologies, could it also be offering a comment on the experience of trauma in the formation of Irish identity/Irish soul, both at an individual and a communal level? Consequent on trauma an individual experiences dissociation and fragmentation of identity. There is difficulty in sequencing narratives and the disjointed stories that emerge show a degree of enmeshment that is difficult to decipher or interpret. In family systems theory, the whole family plays roles, with one dysfunctional member carrying the trauma in a particular destructive or out-of-control manner. The other family members play different roles that either acknowledge or deny the trauma. Where the basic maternal attachment is absent, patterns of insecure attachment develop which are expressed in avoidant or resistant behaviour often with an ambivalence around attachment.

The absence of the mother or the bad or inadequate mother is characteristic of Carr's work. The absence of Dinah's mother through silences and headaches and her subsequent sacrifice of her daughter to an incestuous relationship constitutes abandonment and results in her children's failure to form healthy and life-giving relationships. Her failure or inability to confront her own reality allows her to sacrifice both her children. Ded is also sacrificed as he is in some way blamed for taking part in the traumatic experience of his sister giving birth. Ded as a consequence of being flooded or overwhelmed by the trauma has become mentally ill and incapable of relationship. Dinah has in turn sacrificed herself by never marrying and spending her whole life protecting and watching out for Sorrel. She avoids the truth of her own traumatic experiences by a combination of entrapment and protection. She also continues to engage in a sexual relationship with her father. While everyone in the family is aware of it, they turn a blind eye, engaging in a denial that allows it to continue. The fact that Sorrel grows up thinking her mother is dead yet suspecting that Dinah is her real mother is another example of the denial and the extent to which the secret is at the heart of the family and yet cannot be named.

The play doesn't allow the secret of the Raftery household to be named. However the theatrical experience does. While Sorrel's wedding will most likely not happen because of the need to protect the family secret, the theatre audience is made aware of it. The unspeakable has been named which breaks the cultural silence. We watch as Sorrel becomes a colluder in her own oppression. She is also asked to apologize to her father. She cannot wash away the sense of defilement. No matter how many baths she takes she will never feel clean again (44). Red, when talking to young Dara Mood, tells him that to be young means your slate is clean (24). Dinah informs Red that 'All the Shannon wouldn't wash you clane, Daddy' (45). In the closing scene where Red cleans his gun with a strip of the wedding dress he blames Shalome for ruining it rather than admit that he was the cause of defilement.

Red's interpretation of what he has done is complex and multi-layered. On the one hand there is a sense that his behaviour is justified at some primal or instinctual level and yet culture has always developed incest taboos. At another he believes that he is putting manners on Sorrel in retaliation for a conversation he overheard when she was critical of him. He swears he hardly touched her and yet Dinah says there are marks on Sorrel that haven't healed for three weeks (44). There is also an underlying sense of men having rights to women's bodies, similar to their rights to land. In one conversation his rape of his daughter is spoken of metaphorically in terms of a plough in another man's field (52). It is interesting to note here the situation in Irish Law in relation to rape. The crime is perceived as a violation against the State and the victim is a witness for the State. The crime is against the property of the State. Similar overtones of land ownership and rights are implicit. Older Irish law had a complex system of honour price, where the value of a woman was interpreted in relation to her being the property of a man whether it was her father or her husband. Violation against a woman was a crime against the man to whom she belonged.

The animal-human relationship is integral to the play. Senseless brutality or wanton destruction of animals questions the perpetrator's capacity for compassionate human relationship. The play's questioning of our understanding of human nature is foregrounded initially by Ded's appearance and his living in a cowshed. Dinah rebukes her brother for not eating his dinner at the table, Sorrel remarks that Dinah is 'only barkin' (15) when she rebukes Ded. Dinah speaks to Sorrel about her fate, as she considers her brother's mental state:

> A'ya blind young wan? He should be puh away. Why should I be the wan to watch him splinter into a thousand pieces? You'll go off and marry Dara Mood and I'll be left wuh thah wan racin round like a march hare in her nightdress and Ded atin his dinner like a dog at the duur and Daddy blusterin and butcherin all the small helpless creatures a tha fields. Even workhorses nades a day off every wance in a moon. (18)

As Shalome enters she strews flowers over the landing, the stairs and the kitchen. In her mad Ophelia-like state she says goodbye to the house and the surrounding countryside, naming the mountains and townlands in their particularity. She threatens to give Dinah as 'asses bite' if she stands in her way (17). Shalome tells a family story of being captured by a gorilla when the family lived in India, and remembers throwing orange blossoms down on her mother from the orange tree (18). Later in the play Dinah remembers people talking of her mother as an angel, but she curses her to 'roast like a boar on a spih in the courtyards a Hell' (30). Recalling Shalome's earlier story she remarks that people are 'gorillas in clothes pretendin to be human' (30). Shalome remarks that Red 'butchered' his wife (31). After her rape Sorrel describes the family as 'a band of gorilla swingin from the trees' (56).

When Ded blinks in terror in front of Red he tells him to stop 'You're not a hare a'ya?' (26). At one point in the play Ded remarks that Sorrel and himself are only cattle (38). In the brutal rape of Sorrel that follows Red's killing of the hares and the senseless destruction of all the baby leverets, (19) he tells her that he will show her how to gut a hare (38). As he cuts the clothes off her Sorrel struggles and gesticulates. Stage directions indicate: '*Her voice has betrayed her. We hear the odd animal moan or shriek*' (35). No one comes to her aid even though they hear her screams. Is there some inevitability here? Are the family ultimately powerless against the father? Or is there a tacit validation of the abuse? The repetitive nature of family misfortunes has been a characteristic of Carr's work. It tends to assume mythic proportions when the individuals are powerless to intervene to effect change, and are caught instead in a cycle of violence, that endlessly repeats itself.

The rule of the father is presented as shapechanging, monstrous, demonic and enduring even beyond death. Red is spoken of as a genie by his son and as a devil by Dinah. The father who is the law-giver, and the one who makes the rules is also the one who thinks that he can live beyond them. Ded is terrified to come into the house because his father made the rules. When Red tries to talk to him about coming into the house, Ded becomes very disturbed and upset:

> Whah're ya sayin Daddy? Just lay down the rules, don't kape changin them. Don't. I don't know whah to do to make ya happy. And I want me mother, I miss her fierce so I do. She'd kape ya away from me, she promised me she would. I'd liefer she'd pulled me into Heaven after her. (27)

The rule of the father may be brutal and oppressive but at least it should be predictable. It is interesting that the absence or failure of the mother to provide the level of safety that the child needed contributes along with a demonic patriarchal order to the state that Ded finds himself in. Shalome wonders what kind of monsters they must have been in a past life to suffer like they are suffering now. Red answers:

> We were big loose monsters, Mother, hurlin through the air wud carnage in our hearts and blood under our nails, and no stupid laws houldin us down or back in. (31-2)

Dinah has internalized a similar way of thinking and talks of her ongoing secretive sexual relationship with her father as something that they do from time to time, that it's no one's business and that they both want it to stop; 'Ud's just like children playin in a field ah some awful game, before rules was made' (56).

There seems to be a sense that being young/naïve/innocent means that one does not really understand human nature. Red

informs Dara that he doesn't know why men and women fall.
There is a suggestion here of a fall from grace, a loss of an original
innocence. Until one experiences this, one does not understand
human nature. While awareness of and integration of the shadow
are essential for conscious human development, the traumatic loss
of innocence explored in this play almost defies integration. While
philosophy urges us to move beyond the original *naiveté* of childhood and to arrive at a second *naiveté* in a world mediated by
meaning, in *Raftery's Hill* there is such a rupture as to inhibit that
movement. The responses to the original loss of innocence which
are the result of trauma and abuse range from denial to accommodation, to entrapment, to madness. Each response comes from
the desire to keep the secret, whether that is chosen or forced on
the individual. The task of soul retrieval in such a culture involves
a journey that requires recognition of the lie on which the culture
is based. It demands that a voice be found that can speak this
trauma, that is not afraid to travel to the depths of the human
being's capacity for darkness and to acknowledge the painful loss
of soul that accompanies it.

Ariel, Marina Carr (2002)

Fermoy Fitzgerald is a contemporary Irish politician who lives out
of an ancient mythology and symbol system. His obsession with
power and his own particular definition of reality leads him to
sacrifice his sixteen-year-old daughter Ariel in the service of his
God for the advancement of his career. Marina Carr's play *Ariel*
was originally to be called *Destiny* (Sihra/Carr, 2001). In Act Three
Elaine (Fermoy's other daughter) recalls a conversation she had
with her father while on a holiday in Venice. It outlines one aspect
from Greek mythology which underlies the play and one that
specifically determines the behaviour of Fermoy Fitzgerald:

> Ariel was the stroke of destiny, he said, woven into him from the
> beginning. Ariel was Necessity udself, the thing thah's decided
> ouhside a time. And he tould me abouh Necessity. How before ya
> come to this world, Necessity and her sisters weaves a carpet for
> ya. And ya watch as they weave so ya know how things will fare
> ouh below. And then ya turn your back and Necessity puts a twist
> in the weave. Thah's the wan thinh ya can't foresee and thah's the

wan thing will define your stay here. And then you're flung to earth
wud this weave and this twist in the weave that some calls fate.
(*Ariel* 61-62)

It is a play about murder, sacrifice, and obsession. It questions
what it means to be human. It foregrounds the difficulties of
family relationships. It is a play that dredges the cultural
unconscious to see what is buried in Cuura lake, what secrets it
holds. It is about the darkness that is at the centre. It is a play
where images of the divine are majestic and terrifying or measured,
and mediocre. Ultimately it is a bleak tragedy about patriarchal
madness that can sacrifice everything in its path, in the name of its
God. While giving specificity to the female unconscious one must
question whether it ultimately validates the patriarchal aesthetic by
not offering anything in its place. The women in the play are bitter,
angry, vindictive and murderous. They are victims of both the
patriarchal imagining and ordering of history. The one innocent
(spotless or uncontaminated) girl/woman is sacrificed as the oath
has demanded. The play pivots on the repressed aspects of a
patriarchal imagining. The relationship with the mother, and
specifically the female body must be negated in order to move into
the cultural symbolic. But the return of the repressed, seeps
through the cracks. The watery fluid space of the female womb
returns to haunt the characters, through the waters of Cuura lake
and through the torrent of repressed emotions that surge to flood
in the course of the play. 'It is no coincidence that water, with its
excessive drive to overflow, to transgress demarcated boundaries,
is a prevalent feature of Carr's theatrical terrain' (Melissa Sihra,
Abbey Programme *Ariel* 2002:4). The female body fluids of milk
and blood are also spilled and uncontained, implying a similar return of the repressed.

The play's protagonist is a middle-aged midlands politician and
megalomaniac. His family find themselves in the whirlpool caused
by his madness and obsession. His ability to sacrifice his daughter
means that he must locate her in the space of eternity, rather than
emerging from the female womb. This erasure of connections with
origins is a double erasure of the female, first, in terms of denial of
the physical reality of birth, and secondly, in the ability to move
the female into the symbolic by giving her life meaning only

through sacrifice. Virgin sacrifices have often been performed, as
retribution for war to restore balance and integrity to a community
– the female having more meaning (in a patriarchal culture) in the
symbolic than the physical. Edith Hall recalls (in her programme
note to *Ariel*) that powerful men have always been willing to
sacrifice their children. Whether we think of Agamemnon and the
sacrifice of his virgin daughter Iphigenia, (and this Euripedean
tragedy is a backdrop to the play) or the call to Abraham to sacrifice his son Isaac (Gen.: 22), or Jephthah's actual sacrifice of his
virgin daughter as a thanksgiving for his victory against the
Ammonites (Judges:11), which feminist biblical scholars have
called a text of terror), an opposition must be set up between
female (biological) interests and male (social/political) interests.
The spilling of a young woman's blood in a controlled ritual
context could prevent:

> the uncontrolled and indiscriminate flow of male blood in war.
> Integrity reduces to order versus disorder, control versus chaos,
> male versus female. (Larrington, 1992:91)

But if culture has forgotten its roots in the earthly, physical and
material (maternal), there is also a sense in which this very forgetting leaves us in a state of dereliction. Having forgotten who we
are (or more specifically where we come from) we find ourselves
without an adequate myth of origins to sustain us in our becoming.
Where a culture fails to offer women a validation of their embodied subjectivity, there is a confusion around identity. This can
result in an inability to be present to one's own self, or to bring
that presence into consciousness and awareness. There is a sense
in which many of Carr's female characters remain disembodied.
Frances lives in a state of soul loss, without a clear sense of her
own centre as she allows herself to be totally defined by her
unhappy relationship with Fermoy, even in her anger, hatred and
blame. His scheming obsessive nature, his inability to understand
her as a woman, his expectation that she should supply sex on
demand, alongside her belief that he was in some way responsible
for the death of her original husband and child, certainly does not
augur well for relationship.

Frances has spent her life in mourning for her dead children, both Ariel and a younger child James from her first marriage, who died while she was on honeymoon with Fermoy. One effect of this is her inability to be present to her surviving children. While ostensibly present – she remains married to Fermoy because of the children, she is unable to provide the level of nurturing that the children require (despite her continuing to breastfeed Stephen until he is ten years of age). Abandonment *by* the mother alongside the cultural abandonment *of* the mother and the symbol systems that validate such forgetting (or such monstrous knowing) provide a framework for interpreting *Ariel*.

The play opens with a birthday celebration for Ariel's sixteenth birthday and introduces the audience to the Fitzgerald family; Fermoy and Frances and their children Ariel, Elaine and Stephen. Also present is Fermoy's brother Boniface who is a monk in a local monastery and Sarah, an aunt who raised Fermoy and Boniface after their mother's death, and who now lives with the family.

Boniface provides a vantage point for interpreting the status of religion in contemporary Ireland and offers a counterpoint to Fermoy's conceptions of God. He describes the monastery and his (maternal) role:

> The last a the Mohicans. I'm the ony wan under sixty. Spind me days changing nappies, ferryin them to hospitals, funeral parlours, checkin they take their medication, givin em glasses a whiskey to shuh em up, breakin up fights over armchairs and toffees. They go ah wan another like three-year-aulds. Caugh Celestius goin for the back of Aquinas' head wud a hammer last wake. (13)

Violence, senility and lack of faith define their lives. Aquinas who calls Boniface Mammy (13) tells him 'thah he's noh a Catholic anymore, thah he never belaved in the first place' and that all he wants is his 'youh and Billie Holida' (*Ariel* 14).

Fermoy, in contrast, believes that he is on direct terms with the divine and that people like Boniface have ruined God. 'The last person ya shoud ever talk to abouh God is wan a the religious. Yees are the most cynical, rational, mathematical shower I ever cem across whin ud comes to God' (15). While there may be some truth in Fermoy's remark in that many attempts to come to terms with the divine tend to domesticate and reduce the mystery to more manageable proportions, his own interpretation of God argues for an utterly transcendent and vengeful God. His arguments against Christianity reject the cosiness of traditional formulae and interpretations:

> I'm sick a ya talkin down to me from the heights a your canon law and the foosterins a the Pope a Rome and your cosy mehaphysics and your charihy. For all your religion ya know natin abouh the nature a God. (15)

Fermoy's God is

> beauhiful. When he throws hees head back hees hair gets tangled in the stars, and in hees hands are seven moons tha he juggles like worry beads. (16)

In contrast to Boniface's image of God – 'an auld fella in a tent, addicted to broccoli' – Fermoy's God is

> young. He's so young. He's on fire for us, heaven reelin wud hees rage at noh bein among us, the eternihy of eternihy hauntin him.

When one's image of God loses touch with history (with embodiment and particularity) and becomes an abstract or remote symbol system it can be used in many destructive ways. The destruction can be viewed along a continuum. At one end it can involve using the symbol system uncritically to bolster up an oppressive *status quo*, at the other it can be used to validate and legitimate all kinds of transgressive, perverted and monstrous behaviour. Boniface and the monks seem to inhabit one end of the continuum and Fermoy the other.

As children, both Boniface and Fermoy had to grow up with the realization that their father had murdered their mother and drowned her in Cuura Lake with a boulder tied to her wrist. Boniface carries a number of mixed feelings around his mother. Along with the shock of her murder, he also carries the guilt of not being there for Fermoy, as he was in the novitiate at the time. His trauma at the nature of her death, his inability to play the maternal role, alongside his realization that their Aunt Sarah was 'replacing' their mother, means that he cannot leave her memory behind. His own recurring alcoholism, triggered again by the death of Ariel, suggests a haunted man, with a deeply troubled unconscious. When Stephen finally manages to separate himself from his own mother towards the end of the play, Boniface reflects:

> Whah I shoulda done forty year ago. Good man, Stephen. How did ya do thah? Mammy's off the menu for ever more. Thah's how ud's done. Like thah big fah cluckin Mammy owl I seen on National Geographic the other nigh. And this Mammy Owl is huntin like Billy–O to fade Owl junior. And she comes back to the nest this nigh, big rah in her mouh, all important like, I'm fadin the young lad, aren't I a model Ma. And Junior's gone, fled when her back was turned, no goodbyes, thah's the way to do ud. Or salmon, sure salmon has ne'er a Ma ah all, and y'ever watch them, lords a the waher, sun shinin for em. Or trees, don't get me started on trees. Seems to me everythin worth lookin ah in this world has ne'er a Ma ah all, ud's just there by udself in a flowerin gorgeous-ness, orphaned and free. (*Ariel* 69)

Boniface abandoned by a mother who never said goodbye, because of her traumatic death, remains haunted by her memory. As he comes to the realization that he has in fact never let her go, he conjures a new story, where *he* leaves the mother, when her back is turned, without saying goodbye. But his ambivalence around the mother remains and he proceeds to imagine a world without mothers altogether, preferring an existential sense of being orphaned and free than one of being mothered and abandoned.

Fermoy, too, has been traumatized by his mother's death. We are told that he witnessed it, and helped his father to hold her down and drown her in the lake. He carries this memory, in all its experienced and repressed dimensions, into adulthood. One wonders whether this is at the basis of all his monstrous behaviour. His own tyrannical father is compared to one of Lucifer's crew and Boniface feels that Fermoy's traumatic experience 'is bound to take uds toll on a person's view a the world' (26). Frances comments that out of this experience 'the size a the nigh in thah man is past measuring'. In contrast to Frances (a mother who never stops (s)mothering her son Stephen by continuing to breastfeed him until he is ten years of age, as a way of getting back at his father), Auntie Sarah as surrogate mother to Fermoy provided a different kind of nurturing: 'a packet of biscuits and a bottle of red lemonade' every night before bed (17).

Fermoy does not want to be nice, does not need to be liked. He is utterly contemptuous and dismissive of every aspect of contemporary social justice and swears that he is going to bring in a new religion with 'no more guilt, no more sorrow, no more good girls and good biys, just the unstoppable blood pah a the soul' (18). He feels that the 'earth is over, paple knows thah in their bones, ozone layer in tahhers, oceans gone to sewer, whole world wan big landfill of dirty nappies. We're goin to lave this place in ashes like the shower on Mars'. He sneers at Boniface's belief in gardening and cornflowers, arguing that the last two thousand years have been a complete farce, that mortal sins are 'back in fashion', that the age of compassion has had its turn and failed and that the earth is ours again. There are echoes here of the monstrous priesthood of Bataille. Richard Kearney writes about Bataille that he was

> proud that he could out-Sade Sade in his lust for degradation and obscenity, that he could out-Nietzsche Nietzsche in his abhorrence of a Christian God of charity and peace, promoting instead a sacred cult of 'infinite sacrificial orgy'.

Kearney writes of Bataille's notions of founding a new religion based on profanity. His inspiration came from what he considered privileged epiphanies which included ritual child sacrifice (*The Irish Times* Nov 9 2002:12).

Mortal sins have a particular meaning for Carr. She takes her ideas from Chekhov (another dramatist influenced by Catholicism) and they tie in closely with her ideas on destiny:

> For him, the mortal sin was the stroke of destiny. It was a necessary sin to commit, and therefore necessary for those all around to accommodate as they could, or not…the big sins – they are almost beyond us, we have to do them, we have to commit them. (Sihra/Carr, 2001:58)

Fermoy believes that he has been called to offer up a blood sacrifice to his God, that this is his destiny and that he cannot avoid it no matter what the cost:

> Whichever road I take is crooked. Thah's the price a God. If I make the sacrifice, then ud's all mine. Buh the cost, the cost.

Impossible. Buh if I refuse this sacrifice I'm facin the grave meself and worse, facin him after refusing me destiny and, worse agin, after refusing him the wan thing he asks as payment for this enchanted life. (19)

Fermoy's misguided belief that he has been 'put on this earth to rule' needs a symbol system to validate it. His God demands sacrifice, requires 'blood and more blood, blood till we're dry as husks, then pound us down, spread us like salt on the land, begin the experiment over, on different terms next time'. There are echoes here of Portia Coughlan's desire never to have been, or her belief that human beings need to be made as nothing in order to be refashioned. Fermoy's belief in this terrifying God is not supported by Boniface who is ready to admit that the world is not Utopia, but is not prepared to discount two thousand years of civilization. He tells Fermoy that if he calls up this God that 'he's a wolf and ud's a wolf you'll be growlin wud if ya dredge him up'. Boniface is worried that Fermoy is talking about some sort of old pagan ritual involving the slaughter of an animal, but he also senses that he might be talking about 'something far older and more sinister' (19).

The mother-daughter relationship features in many of Carr's plays, and it is more than likely to be problematic. With Frances and Elaine we can identify many of the features of Portia's relationship with her mother in *Portia Coughlan*. Even at twelve years of age Elaine's hatred for her mother is obvious and she says that she can't wait to be outside her door forever. She is resentful of the attention Ariel gets as the eldest, and of her mother's decision not to wean Stephen. She is not afraid to speak the family secrets, and likes the sound of talking about her grandmother's death: 'She's ah the bohhom a Cuura Lake where me granddaddy puh her, in a bag wid a boulder, nowan ever found her' (23). Aunt Sarah says she inherited her grandmother's eyes (Frances accuses her of giving her the 'avil eye') and talks of her as the 'babby witch in the cauldron' (24). Frances feels that Elaine's hatred for her is 'not natural' but is not really prepared to see that her own fixation on her dead son James could have provided a very unhealthy atmosphere for Elaine as she grew up. Her preoccupation with the 'beauhiful dead' continues into the present as she still wears a locket with photos of her dead husband and child.

In a conversation with Fermoy, his political rival Hannafin tries to discredit Fermoy by making reference to the lineage he shares with his murdering father. Fermoy prefers to judge a man 'be hees own merit, as if he'd ne'er a smithy bar God heeself' (33), an interesting reference to God as the blacksmith. Hannafin however sneers at this:

> The pipe dreams of the self-med. You were forged in a bloodbah, Fitzgerald, and the son allas carries the father somewhere inside of him. ... And ud's time the paple beyond this parish knew the gruesome blacksmith hommered you to earth and the symmetry can be predicted from there. (*Ariel* 33)

The sense of repetition and fate is a familiar theme in Carr's work. Hannafin attributes the same blacksmith powers to a demonic source. This resonates with Boniface's earlier observation that many people no longer believe that God created the world but that 'ud was Satan and hees fallen armies, thah we were masterminded in hell, only Lucifer's pawns to geh ah God' (15). In his ensuing final conversation with Ariel, Fermoy recalls the night of his mother's death and his father as 'man in a navy raincoat who butchered' her. He recalled him lighting a cigarette and putting him up on his shoulders as they left the lake, and going for drinks in the local bar.

> I was there too. And though I was only seven, an excuse on this earth, I was also seven thousand and seven millin, for the soul is wan age and mine just stood and watched. I'd seen him drown a bag of kittens, blind, tiny pink tongues and fairy teeth. Really this was no different. (36)

In contemporary focus on soul retrieval, such a traumatic memory would be considered a primary cause of soul loss, whether or not one holds to the Platonic notion of an eternal ageless soul. The image of a seven-year-old child observing his mother's death and drowning and feeling nothing more or less than observing the drowning of a bag of kittens, stands out as one of the points of horror in the play. It also represents the violence at the heart of a patriarchal ordering of history, where what is feared or misunderstood or not needed is simply erased, returned to its watery womb/tomb, to emerge later in dreams, nightmares, flashback, hallucination and obsession. The sacrifice of the female (m)other which has ensured the continuation of a particular ordering of history has also contributed to a profound loss of soul, at individual and cultural levels, that is only now being recognized and named.

The second Act is set ten years later. Fermoy Fitzgerald has risen in power and now seems certain to become the next Taoiseach. We learn that Ariel disappeared ten years earlier, that Frances and Fermoy no longer live together, that Boniface has started drinking again, that Stephen is a film producer who barely sees or knows his father and that Elaine is working as PR person for Fermoy. In Acts Two and Three as the cracks begin to show, the obsessions and madness of power are revealed, and the past floods the present, as repressed and buried memories and emotions resurface. The haunting presence of Ariel in the troubled souls of the survivors, breaks up the realist frame. Later the sound of her ghostly voice and cries will haunt Fermoy and his own ghost presence will prowl restlessly through Elaine's unconscious. Boniface has joined the family for the annual Mass for Ariel. His soul is haunted and troubled, as he recalls Ariel's death and Fermoy's ideas on blood sacrifice:

> Listen. I can't stop drinkin. Can't slape, can't ate, garden be moon-ligh, go to bed in the morning. I'm afraid I'll tell me psychiatrist, thah it'll just spill ouha me. They don't know what's wrong a me. Me soul, I tell em, me soul ud's hurtin me fierce, like being flayed from the inside. ... You're the wan should be in Pat's. You're the wan should be bleedin from the eyes. (50)

Boniface seems to feel the soul pain that Fermoy denies. There is always someone in a family who carries and embodies what other family members repress. He asks Fermoy: 'Why didn't ya listen? All we have in this world is the small mercies we can extend to one another. The rest is madness and oblivion' (*Ariel* 50). But Fermoy has learned this lesson too late. It would also appear to be too late for the rest of the family.

As with *On Raftery's Hill*, the play makes many references to human beings using animal imagery. The underlying question is whether we are human at all, and whether we have moved from the caves in our quest for civilization. Fermoy's mother is spoken of as having a dark mane of hair, 'like a beauhiful Egyptian horse' (27) that the father didn't understand or know how to handle. Fermoy insults his wife's intelligence by referring to her as having a 'bantam head' (28). In his dreams, when he sees himself dining with powerful figures from history, Fermoy remarks that 'we all had tiger's feet under the white linen tablecloth' (14). Boniface identifies the God that Fermoy is dealing with as a wolf (19). When Frances worried about Ariel before her birth she imagined her being born deformed like one of 'thim frog babbies' or 'birdy-headed little creatures' (51). Sarah remembers Boniface as a baby being like a greedy little *bonamh* (53). Frances when confronted with the horror of Ariel's death remembers the gentle people she came from, and in particular her own father's gentleness towards animals, in contrast to the 'nest of hooves' in which she now finds herself (59). When she thinks of Elaine she utterly disowns her, believing that '[s]ome zebra stallion grafted you onta me' (74).

Elaine is working for her father. She shares his world views and his vision. She adores him and believes that he is charismatic with crowds and that people love him. She is obsessive and possessive around him. Her continuing rejection and hatred of her mother escalates into a frenzy when she realizes that her mother has killed her father, after his admission that he sacrificed Ariel. When her mother has the father's grave disturbed in order to bury him again with Ariel, Elaine attacks and kills her mother.

Elaine's pain is that of the abandoned child. She feels that her mother never had any time for her or her brother, being so obsessed with her dead children. She has no sympathy for her mother's grief and accuses her of being addicted to sorrow and having 'shrunk to a pip over your two dead children' (52). Elaine's own sorrow is palpable when she speaks about herself as the unlovely daughter, but she expresses it as anger and rejects its underlying grief:

I know wan thing abouh sorrow. I learned ud watchin you. Sorrow's an addiction like no other. You won't be full till you've buried us all. Well, ya won't bury me, Ma. I'm here, thrivin, your unlovely daugher is thrivin' … Ud's just me now, me and Stephen. (52)

Frances is not really prepared to acknowledge her contribution to the failed relationship and prefers to interpret its failure in terms of an ancient ongoing battle between mothers and daughters:

We never goh on, I do't know why I want us to now. This skirmish betwane us is ancient. Y'ever feel thah? Seems to me we been battling a thousand year. (66)

There is no acknowledgement that what may really be dividing them is their self-definition posited by a patriarchal imagining. There is no female-centred myth of origins, either ancient or new, to sustain them. Frances is driven almost to insanity and despair when she realizes what Fermoy has done. As victim of his imagining she is left without anywhere to stand. Fermoy believed that Ariel came from the divine on loan and that he simply returned her.

Fermoy: I tould ya I returned her to where she cem from.
Frances: She cem from here, from you, from me.
Fermoy: She rode ouha God from nowhere and to God she returned.
Frances: You sacrificed her! Aaagh. Why didn't ya sacrifice yourself if he wanted a sacrifice? Why didn't ya refuse?
Fermoy: A cuurse I refused. I fough him till I couldn't figh him anymore.
Frances: That was no God ya med your pact wud. No God demands such things.
Fermoy: My God did.
Frances: Blem God, blem the world, anywan bar yourself. Ud's all comin clear now, clear as a bell. Ya done ud for power, didn't ya, some voodoo swap in the dark for power. You laid my daughter on an altar for power. You've flourished these ten years since Ariel. You've flourished on her white throat. You swapped her in advance. (58)

As the full horror sinks in, Frances stabs him repeatedly, until he reveals that he has left Ariel's body in Cuura Lake. Elaine, who is left with the responsibility of dealing with her father's death and funeral, now holds much more anger towards her mother than she ever did. She interprets Fermoy's behaviour in terms similar to those he used to justify his actions and she accuses her mother of simply acting out of violent revenge:

> **Elaine:** I can tell the difference between a crime of eternihy and a low, blood-spahhered, knife-frenzied revenge. And then your coward's insanihy plea on top of ud. Whah my father done to Ariel had the grandeur a God in ud. Pure sacrifice. Ferocious, aye. Buh pure. Whah you done to him was a puckered, vengeful, self-servin thing wud noh a whiff of the immortal in ud.
>
> **Frances:** So your father spills blood and he's a haroh. I spill ud and I'm a coward. You've spint too long around the min, me girl, too long cavortin the corriduurs a power to understand the first thing abouh justice. (64)

While Frances has partially succeeded in reconnecting with an older ethic based on the significance of birth and the mother-child relationship, the reconnection destabilizes her and drives her to murder. Elaine refuses to see any significance in the ethics and justice that Frances speaks of and refuses any hint of connection with her mother: 'I'm as different to you as the auld world is from the new, sem as my father was' (65). Stephen in turn articulates his reactions to the murder of his father. He accuses his mother of doing it for her dead children and of not thinking of the consequences for Elaine and himself:

> There was ony over two chambers in your heart, Ma, two dusty chambers, me and Elaine tryin to force our way in. Our playground was a graveyard, Ma, we ran among your tombstones like they were swings, we played hop, skip and jump on the bones a your children, your real children, while we whined for ya like ghosts. (68)

Frances's obsession with the dead, pulls her away from connection with the living. Everything is out of joint when a mother loves her dead children more than her living ones. (Echoes here of Mother Ireland endlessly mourning her dead sons, and what Henderson calls the preoccupation with wounds that characterizes Irish drama (Henderson, 1989)). The mother who breastfed the child until he was ten and yet provided no real nurturing now dreams of breastfeeding a snake 'and insteada milk comin ouh it's blood' (68). She finally admits to Elaine that she 'wanted a son to make up for James. And I goh you' (74), but that may be the admission of the defeated in the game of mother-child relationships.

Sarah is a type of kindred spirit to Elaine – they both know the darkness. Elaine accuses Sarah of being the one who 'coaxed the darkness in':

> Addicted to nigh is what y'are, slobberin over ud like the cah wud the crame. But ya won't grab your own piece a nigh, no, ya covet mine from the corner. You ud was watched the first murder in this house, you watched your sister die, ya watched me grandfather tie her wud stones and ya said natin and ya done natin, ony watched in a swoon, black flowers sproutin ouha your chest. Yes, ya whispered, yes, I'll watch anhin, I'm the woman who'll watch anhin. (71)

Sarah replies that:

> To watch a thing is ony to half wish ud. And to half wish a thing is a long way off from doin ud. Buh I'll watch no longer. I'm bowin ouha here. I'm no match for ya anymore. (72)

Sarah tells Elaine that there is a 'divil the size of a whale inside you' as she asks about the source of Elaine's hatred of her mother. Elaine says that when she looks at her mother she feels that something is missing.

> **Sarah:** And whah is ud ya think is missin?
> **Elaine:** I think she has no soul.
> **Sarah:** And since when have you become the decider a souls? A cuurse she has a soul, if she hadn't a soul she wouldn't be alive.
> **Elaine:** They say there's some born wudouh em and I think she's wan a them. She tells me we been slashin wan another since time began. Well, if we have, this here is my turn, this is my opportunity to geh a good go ah her and silence her till Judgement Day. (71)

Elaine wonders whether the part that is missing is in her mother or in herself. The question of soul loss haunts many of Carr's characters and makes living very difficult. It is likely that both women suffer from soul loss because of the culture's tendency to erase links with the maternal in the move into the symbolic. But Elaine continues to live out the script of the woman in a state of dereliction, and finally silences the (m)other by stabbing her to death. In the Abbey production Elaine then lay down and pulled her dead mother's arms around her, suggesting that Elaine finds a final re-union with her life's blood but only in death.

Conclusion

In Carr's garden-shed theatre 'Everyone was capable of redemption except Witches'. But because of her magic and power they could not eliminate the Witch and she would 'escape on the handle of an old spade.' Their childhood dramas, aware instinctively 'that morality is a human invention, fallible and variable as the wind, were strange and free and cruel...We loved the havoc, the badness, the blood spillage, but loved equally restoring some sort of botched order and harmony.' And yet in many of Carr's later plays her characters do not earn or cannot imagine redemption. Carr speculates about the Witch:

> And the Witch? Maybe she was Time. Time we didn't understand or fully inhabit, and yet we respected and feared her. And fell away humbly under her spells and curses. (Carr, 1999:x)

If the Witch is to be thought of as time or mortality, this brings us back to the territory of the female body and a culture's attitude to it. Older earth-centred traditions revered and celebrated the female body, as life-giver, that mirrored the great life-giving womb of the cosmos, and found validation for this in female imagery of the divine. Patriarchal traditions in contrast define themselves in terms of separation from the female body, and privilege in turn culture over nature. We can consider for example the transition in Ireland (Condren, 1989) from a pre-Celtic matricentred culture that valued the female body and the processes of birth, to a Celtic warrior society where the warrior gave birth to culture through death and sacrifice. The female body and its power in turn has been demonized and scapegoated within a patriarchal imagining. The Witch was originally the Wise Woman or healer. Within patriarchy female power is dangerous or suspect. It becomes caricatured, and feared until it emerges in the figure of the Witch in children's fairytales. Perhaps the Witch is the ageing sexual female body – perhaps she evokes the abject:

> Abjection is a supple term: it names the undesirable contents of our being – pain, disease, body waste, and death – as well as our active repudiation of these contents. It names, too, the condition or state of being both downcast and outcast, of being both burdened and outraged by our mortality, and of being rejected or scapegoated as a representative of that which is undesirable. (Caslav Covino, 2000:12)

The female writer, at this point in time, if she is true to the promptings of both her own and the cultural unconscious will find herself writing about the repressed. This remembering may be violent, and unsettling:

> When 'The Repressed' of their culture and their society come back, it is an explosive return, which is *absolutely* shattering, staggering, overturning, with a force never let loose before. (Cixous, 1997:101)

Such may be the language of a Portia Coughlan or Hester Swane. Carr's women destabilize the patriarchal aesthetic, by speaking the unspeakable. But the space of female subjectivity in Carr's plays is fractured and unstable. Her protagonists cannot find their own point of balance, and topple over into despair and suicide. The absence of a maternal genealogy, the lack of a divine horizon and the cultural construction of motherhood create conditions which make it difficult for women to emerge as subjects in their own right. The nature-culture divide that underpins patriarchal imagining creates a level of disembodiment that leads to profound soul loss. What would happen to culture if we were to engage in a new imagining, that started with em-bodiment? Rich is convinced that there are ways of thinking that we don't know yet (Rich, 1976:283). Like Irigaray, she urges women to begin to 'think through the body' (284) and to imagine beyond the nature-culture divide, and imagines a world where

> women will truly create new life, bringing forth not only children (if and as we choose) but the visions, and the thinking, necessary to sustain, console, and alter human existence. (285-86)

It seems to be closer to the territory of Carr's garden-shed theatre, that respected time and embodiment, that believed if not in an original innocence, at least in the possibilities of newness or recreation through play:

If I'm after anything when I'm writing plays, it's the scuts' view of things as they are or were or should be, and perhaps once in a blue moon be given a sideways glance of it all as the first dramatist might see it and how it should be done. (Carr, 1999:ix/x)

4 | Journeys of Transformation

> Don't ask me how exactly I entered here, I was full of dreams at
> the moment I lost the true way. (Dante)

How can theatre become a site for transformation? How can it
function as a container for energies both destructive and creative?
How can it hold and transform these energies into possibility? In
the journey of soul how can it represent the urge towards
transcendence with the need for embodiment? The plays in this
section deal with the contradictions and complexities of the human
journey towards wholeness and integrity. Frank Hardy's need to
still the maddening questions (*Faith Healer*), JPW's desire to
possibilize the possible and to sing like Gigli (*The Gigli Concert*),
Matt Talbot's mystical sense that the darkness is Gawd (*Talbot's
Box*), Carravaggio's struggle with salvation and damnation in his
life and his painting (*Innocence*), present us with characters whose
journeys to wholeness through half-conscious and unconscious
depths are urgent, even relentless. Frank Hardy is an alcoholic
healer whose gift is unpredictable, JPW a failed therapist, Matt
Talbot struggles with the darkness and solitude of both alcoholism
and an outsider's mystical vision, and the artist Caravaggio is a
volatile, self-loathing murderer. Disillusioned architect Jerome
Furlong comes to terms with his own haunting demons, as he
snorts cocaine and experiences the stigmata, (*The Passion of Jerome*),
Lil Sweeney tries to have hope in the midst of madness and death,
(*Mrs Sweeney*) and Father Welsh's suicide in *The Lonesome West*
offers feuding brothers a possible route towards reconciliation.

Self-destruction and self-realization cannot be separated in these plays. Yet the characters are motivated, inspired, and driven by a belief that their lives can be transformed; that their own self-destruction (or others in the case of *Mrs. Sweeney*) may be the very site for transformation, albeit a transformation imagined in very different ways.

I propose to consider the plays in this section in relation to journey – whether that is heroic, mystical or shamanic. If the outcome of the journey is to bring something back for the healing of the individual or community, how does theatre function to facilitate this journey for the audience? The alchemical space of theatre can become the space where the raw material of our lives is changed into gold. The raw material should call us back to particularity, sexuality, embodiment, to our capacities for violence and destruction, alongside our capacities for compassion and forgiveness. Our clay bodies are the same bodies that aspire towards the transcendent. The female body can no longer be assumed to be the sole container for all that is corporeal. The bodies of men and women must be allowed to become containers for both our rage and our compassion. Theatre as sacred container will then become a holy theatre, where through earthy laughter, the excess of carnival, the shock of parable, and the witnessing of new rituals, audiences can experience their lives reframed, and re-imagined, in terms of newness and possibility.

Whether mythological, creative or personal, people have always told stories in order to explain the world and their place in it. In fact it could even be argued that it is only when haphazard events are transformed into story and made memorable over time that we become fully human (Kearney *2002*:3-4). The great primordial narratives were essentially re-creative (8). The community experiences regeneration through return to a time of origins. Through the annual repetition of the cosmogony, (the myth of how the world came to be, recited in a sacred time and sacred place) time began again as a sacred time – the *illud tempus* in which the world first came into existence (Eliade, *1987*).

David Cole in *The Theatrical Event* sees 'theatre as an opportunity to experience imaginative life as physical presence' (Cole:1975:*x),* and everything that happens in theatre as a process of manifestation. He develops Eliade's concept of the *illud tempus* which can be 'made present again at any moment by the performance of a ritual' (Cole:1975:7) or dream.

Cole interprets the actor's role in terms similar to that of the shaman, the psychic voyager to the world of the gods (Cole, 1975:14), or the hungan, 'the human being whose presence becomes, through possession, a god's presence' (Cole: 1975:14). Both of these figures journey on behalf of their community into the realm of the gods or the *illud tempus*, and bring something back for the healing or transformation of the community. Eliade's major work on Shamanism (Eliade, 1964) identifies shamans as 'persons who stand out in their respective societies, by virtue of characteristics, that, in the societies of modern Europe, represent the signs of a vocation or at least of a religious crisis. They are separated from the rest of the community by the intensity of their own religious experience' (Eliade, 1964:8). While one can find certain parallels between shamans and mystics and saints of religious traditions one should not push the comparison too far:

> for it is the shamans who, by their trances, cure them, accompany their dead to the 'Realm of Shades,' and serve as mediators between them and their gods, celestial or infernal, greater or lesser. This small mystical elite not only directs the community's religious life but, as it were, guards its 'soul'. The shaman is the great specialist in the human soul; he alone 'sees' it, for he knows its 'form' and its destiny. (Eliade, 1964:8. Emphasis in original)

Cole suggests that the shamanic journey can function as a metaphor for the actor's journey, and one that can enable audiences to experience the presence of other powers. Cole notes that 'the shaman does not simply make the journey we all dream of making; he makes it on our behalf as our envoy. The shaman goes to the gods 'to present the wishes of the community' (Cole, 1975:18). While Cole pays particular attention to the actor's role, he is interested in the theatrical process as a whole. He interprets the theatrical event as a ritual process (facilitated by everything that makes this event happen) that enables audiences to experience a journey to a time of origins, to reconnect with what is needed or lost, in order to experience healing and renewal. This metaphor for the theatrical event calls to mind many of the plays of Murphy or

Friel, where the artist (or protagonist) like Frank Hardy (*Faith Healer*) and JPW (*Gigli*) fulfils a similar shamanic function on behalf of the community, towards some new imagining. Cole pays particular attention to the inner experience of the shaman in fulfilling his public role: 'Primitive peoples believe the *illud tempus* to be an actual historical period and not merely, as in our view, a constellation of mental archetypes. Nonetheless, for them, too, the *illud tempus* is within – not, as for us, *only* within, but *also* within. Consequently, any voyage there is going to have to be pursued through outer and inner space simultaneously, through the cosmos and through the mind' (Cole, 1975:21. Emphasis in original). In contemporary experience (while one must acknowledge the revival of interest in the practices of shamanism, which Cole does not do) the way of journeying for the majority of people is through the dream space of the unconscious.

Many of the plays in this section access a new knowing through altered states of consciousness whether influenced by drugs, alcohol, incantation, song, fasting or physical punishment. Others access lost knowledge through the language of dreams, visions and dialogues with the ghosts of the dead:

> The actor takes us on this way. With the light of the poet he climbs the unexplored peaks of the human soul, his own soul, in order to transform it secretly there and to return with his hands, eyes and voice full of wonders. (Reinhardt quoted in Cole, 1975:26)

The rich dream sequence in Act Two of *Innocence* enables Caravaggio to access the depths of both his own and the cultural unconscious. This journey enables a reframing (both for Caravaggio and the audience) of inherited understandings of the relationship between salvation and damnation. Cole makes reference to Stanislavski's 'magic if' (Cole, 26) which can lift the actor out of actuality into imagination and suggests that the 'magic if' is seen as making possible a shamanic ascent' (26) in a way similar to that which lifts us from the ordinary to that of the *illud tempus*, or realm of the imagination. Attention to how theatre facilitates access to the realms of imagination is consciously adverted to in *Faith Healer* which raises questions about the meaning of theatre, the possibility of performance, and access to miracles of transformation for both characters and audiences (A similar questioning is to be found in Jim Nolan's *Blackwater Angel, 2001*).

As well as ascent, the shamanic journey also involved descent into the depths of an underworld, where the shaman encountered many levels of blackness and all kinds of terrifying beings. The ambiguity of the shamanic journey as involving both ascent and descent draws attention to how one may either find or lose oneself on the journey. Stanislavski in training actors noted how the levels of the play are like the strata of the earth:

> As the levels go deeper down into one's soul they become in-creasingly unconscious, and down in the very depths, in the core of the earth where you find molten lava and fire, invisible human instincts and passions are raging. (Quoted in Cole, 29)

Many of the plays that we have examined so far in this study (most notably Carr's work) journey into the depths, and into the dark, and bring audiences face to face with the monsters, buried and submerged in both the personal and cultural unconscious. Descent into the dark is also a feature of many of the plays in this section. In whatever way the territory of the dark is negotiated, many of the characters in these plays (unlike Carr's protagonists) complete the journey home, however critical one may be of how and to what degree this is achieved. Audiences are faced with images of integration rather than disintegration, and different interpretations of transformation and renewal in the place of dissolution and death.

Faith Healer, Brian Friel (1979)

Brian Brady in an interview (*Irish Times* Jan 27th 2000) wrote about theatre as a religious experience:

> I believe in theatre as a religious experience. In a post-Christian society it's important that a community of people sit together in the dark, focusing their thoughts and more importantly their goodwill, on a happening, a ritual, and encounter their vicarious lives, their dilemmas and emotions, played out for them on stage. It's a collective experience that celebrates humanity – and this is what everyone in the theatre is trying to do.

This is very close to Friel's own understanding of theatre which he also speaks of in terms of ritual and alternative sacred space (Pine 63). So often in his plays he assumes an artistic quasi-priestly function – becoming, as Pine suggests, a diviner, with a gift 'for being in touch with what is there, hidden and real, a gift for mediating between the latent source and the community' (Heaney quoted in Pine, 35). Friel shares many of Victor Turner's insights on the relationship between drama and ritual (cf. Ch. Two) and the sense that both involve transition (Pine, 16).

Murray suggests that Irish playwrights in the 60s and 70s took a dim view of religion, and 'saw the old bonds loosening, moral and spiritual values collapsing, and the question of identity become more problematic than ever' (Murray, 1997:175). One can interpret many aspects of *Faith Healer* as 'an apparent mockery, parody, and caricature of religion' (Block, 2000:198). However the many religious allusions (in this play and in others like *Wonderful Tennessee* and *Dancing at Lughnasa*) do 'convey a fragmented sense of religion in a post-modern world' and function as 'a kind of impersonal 'memory' of a religious dimension now virtually lost in everyday life' (198). Block interprets Friel's drama in relation to a contemporary inability to sustain a sense of mystery, which he calls an experience of dispossession (also very apt in relation to *Wonderful Tennessee*) (201). He mentions a continuing tension between the immanent and transcendent in Friel's plays and suggests that '[t]hroughout *Faith Healer* are scattered seeds of the Christian myth, distorted or refracted by the postmodern world and *its* fragmentation' (200). He argues that 'just as Frank Hardy is haunted by his gift, postmodern drama itself – and perhaps the playwright – is haunted by the simultaneous appearance and paradoxical hiddenness of religious figuration' (200)

Faith Healer (Friel, 1996: 327-76) is a series of four monologues spoken by three characters, Frank Hardy, Grace and Teddy. The opening and closing monologues are by Frank Hardy, the Faith Healer of the play's title. It is a play that raises questions about the nature of theatre, the possibilities of performance, the narrative voice, the unreliability of memory, truth-telling and telling lies, the relationship between body and spirit, the urge towards self-fulfilment or self-destruction, the inadequacy of law and order or any religious metaphors to offer systems of interpretation, the similar functions shared by the priest/artist/faith healer, and the dependence of the gift of healing/transforming on chance or fate.

The only way that Frank Hardy – Faith Healer, who is drinking himself to death, because of the unpredictability of his gift and the maddening questions that are undermining his life – can gain control of his life is to offer himself as a sacrificial victim. The only possible reconciliation is to be found at a spiritual or artistic level – this alone affords access to a unified vision. It is similar to the artistic vision which underpins *Dancing at Lughnasa* where the work of art remains the only testimony to a disappearing world.

The audience gradually becomes aware that the voices of Frank and Grace are voices from the grave. They are both dead before the curtain goes up. And we are invited to listen to the fictions of their lives, knowing that they are not really alive. Hughes suggests that this is a version of what Yeats called the 'Dreaming Back' where

> the Spirit is compelled to live over and over again the events that had most moved it; there can be nothing new; but the old events stand forth in a light which is dim or bright according to the intensity of the passion that accompanied them. (Quoted in Hughes, 1994:176)

The space of theatre is the space of remembered and imagined fictions where audiences suspend disbelief at least for the duration of the play. Out of the darkness comes Frank's incantation, his recital of the names of the towns and villages through which he has passed, uttered like some kind of prayer, 'the mesmerism, the sedation, of the incantation' (*Faith Healer* 332) evoking a state of shamanic or mystical trance, enabling him to enter the ritual liminal space where the healing might occur, if the healer is ready and the audience arrive.

As the lights come up the stage is set up as one of the many halls in Scotland and Wales where Frank Hardy performed – the large poster, its fabric soiled and abused proclaims: *The Fantastic Francis Hardy, Faith Healer, One Night Only*. The seats are arranged for the audience that will come to meet the wonderful Faith Healer. Friel's sense of theatre as an alternative sacred space with its own rituals and sacraments is put before the audience as Frank describes the towns and the meeting halls with their relicts of abandoned rituals:

> The kirks or meeting houses or schools – all identical, all derelict. Maybe in a corner a withered sheaf of wheat from a harvest thanksgiving of years ago or a fragment of a Christmas decoration across a window – relicts of abandoned rituals. Because the people we moved among were beyond that kind of celebration. (332)

The theatre audience may also have moved beyond such celebrations and now may seek in theatre (as they mirror the audience that Frank awaits) an alternate symbol system to interpret their lives. Throne writes of how the world is beyond human control and how

> those in the little dying villages of the world, who suffer the casual cruelty of disease and despair, have nowhere else to turn except to the magician, the charlatan, the mountebank, who might really be the gifted one with whom the transcendent universe deigns to communicate. (Throne, 1987:23)

Frank describes himself as a faith healer, Grace his wife or mistress describes him as an artist. Whichever way we choose to interpret the play the terms are interchangeable. This faith healing is 'A craft without an apprenticeship, a ministry without responsibility, a vocation without a ministry' (333). As for how Frank got involved, 'As a young man I chanced to flirt with it and it possessed me'. This is the territory of the shaman:

> The shaman does not seek his power; he is chosen by the spirit or transcendent world, and he has no control over the spirits with whom he communicates. (Throne, 1987:22)

Frank recalls his feeling of completeness, his harmony within himself when he allowed himself to become one with his gift and its expression:

> I did it because I could do it. That's accurate enough. And occasionally it worked […] And when it did, when I stood before a man and placed my hands on him and watched him become whole in my presence, those were nights of exultation, of consummation – because the questions that undermined my life then became

meaningless and because I knew that for those few hours I had become whole in myself, and perfect in myself. (*FH* 333)

The play is full of contradictions indicating at one level the unreliability of memory. At another level the contradictions draw attention to the fictional nature of theatre, where the artistic truth is to lie and the audience encouraged to imagine 'what if?' Theatre and history are both the stages of competing fictions. Frank and Grace's versions of events are significantly different. Teddy's voice may perhaps offer a more objective position but there is no reason to believe that he has the truth either. The telling of the story with multiple narrative voices is akin to the evangelists telling the Good News of Jesus Christ: different questions, different starting points, different audiences, different experiences of the one event, the unreliability of eye-witnesses, the subjectivity of experience, the inadequacy of language, the resort to the poetic. Theologian David Tracy writes about the impossibility of truth and speaks instead of highly tentative relative adequacy:

> We can never possess absolute certainty. But we can achieve a good – that is, a relatively adequate – interpretation: relative to the power of disclosure and concealment of the text, relative to the skills and attentiveness of the interpreter, relative to the kind of conversation possible for the interpreter in a particular culture at a particular time. (Tracy, 1987:22-23)

Frank the artist and faith healer consistently recreates the past, including his parents and the person of Grace. In her monologue she even voices the horror that she may be becoming one of his fictions. He calls her his mistress and changes the details of her surname or place of origin, as it suits him. Like Mona in *The Gigli Concert,* Grace looks after the physical needs of the hero in order to free him for his role as shaman or meaning-maker. In fact throughout the play Grace carries the corporeal dimension to Frank's existence. It was she 'who fed me, washed and ironed for me, nursed me, humoured me. Saved me, I'm sure, from drinking myself to death' (335). Frank becomes more and more incapable of producing anything, and Grace has three miscarriages, including a still birth which her story and Teddy's story attest to, but not Frank's. Teddy's perception that Frank felt Grace's pain all the more, even though he walked away as she went into labour in the back of the van, simply allows the artist to free himself from the messiness of ordinary birth and death in order to create the perfect expression of it artistically.

Frank admits to finding Grace's loyalty and devotion to him an irritation rather than an inspiration:

> Because that very virtue of hers – that mulish, unquestioning, indefatigable loyalty – settled on us like a heavy dust. And nothing I did, neither my bitterness nor my deliberate neglect nor my blatant unfaithfulness could disturb it. (335)

Grace as self-sacrificing victim can hardly stand as a role model for women seeking authentic experiences of subjectivity in relationship. Grace's inability to sustain any kind of self-image that was not connected to Frank led to her continual abuse in the relationship and her eventual self-destruction through the choice of suicide.

Frank remembers Grace as 'controlled, correct, methodical, orderly' (335) – everything that his artistic temperament rails against. On nights when he couldn't perform Frank became desperate and Grace tells us:

> then he'd go for me with bared teeth as if I were responsible and he'd scream at me, 'You were at your very best tonight, Miss O'Dwyer, weren't you? A great night for the law, wasn't it? You vengeful spiteful bitch.' And I'd defend myself. And we'd tear one another apart. (350)

The fact that Frank believed that his gift was beyond the scope of both law and church but still essentially unpredictable probably caused such transference. Frank's subsequent abuse of Grace and her retaliation reflects a dynamic within a relationship where both parties are intent on self-destruction. The tyrant will find it easier to function however when others, with low self-esteem or none, allow themselves to be tyrannized. McGuinness writes:

> She is his irritation not his inspiration. Their love acts as spur to goad each other forward. These acts are to Grace sustenance, a source of nourishment for their survival, in her case emotional survival, in his, more desperate case, psychic survival. They are each other's salvation and damnation. And their communion is

through alcohol. Among its many shifting foci, *Faith Healer* is a study of alcoholism, and of suicide. (McGuinness, 1999:61)

Frank the faith healer saw himself as 'always balanced somewhere between the absurd and the momentous' (336), aptly brought home to us by the playing of the Jerome Kern song 'The way you look tonight' as 'the crippled and the blind and the disfigured and the deaf and the barren' came and sat down for the performance. They were a despairing people who came to confirm the hopelessness of their condition. 'Abject. Abased. Tight. Longing to open themselves and at the same time fearfully herding the anguish they contained against disturbance'. Frank believes that they hated him, because in coming to him they exposed their desperation. Their coming to him was almost seeking 'confirmation that they were incurable'; they came not in hope but to eliminate hope (336-37).

Paul Ricoeur writes about the revelatory power of poetic and religious language to nurture and evoke the passion for the possible. In this instance the possible could be termed the impossible. Frank almost implies that these people who come to him have no imagination. The lack of imagination can paralyse and hinder any kind of movement or growth, whereas imagination can offer healing and hope. If the despairing people can genuinely open themselves to imagining differently then newness may emerge. When the miracle happens it results in 'panic' and '[t]heir ripping apart! The explosion of their careful calculations! The sudden flowing of dreadful, hopeless hope!' (337). The activity of the faith healer might issue in this new world, this new way of imagining and being. It can be risky and disorientating. Equally theatre and this performance might enable the same passion for the possible to occur for the audience if they could only surrender their hopelessness.

The ones who come are seen as delegates. 'legati, chosen because of their audacity; and outside, poised, mute, waiting in the half-light, were hundreds of people who held their breath while we were in the locality' (337). This suggests a group peripheral to the liminal space who need the activities of the liminal space to give meaning to their lives. If those who come cannot believe in the power of the imagination and its ability to transform then what hope is left for the culture as a whole?

The community needs the shaman – someone to journey to the *illud tempus* and return with a boon for the community. All the idiosyncrasies of the shamanic personality can be tolerated once he/she can continue to perform. Frank admits that by the time he returns home 'the whiskey wasn't as efficient with the questions as it had been' (338). Frank is feted as a hero when he heals the man with the bent finger. The scene takes on the aura of a pagan fertility festival, then a Dionysian feast – a time of excess where the boundaries are more permeable and the ordinary is suspended, and replaced with the fluid space of carnival and play. 'A frenzied, excessive Irish night when ritual was consciously and relentlessly debauched' (340). A night however where dark forces are released and we find ourselves thrown into the space of dark play and transgressive forces. Ritual may be debauched but it is not forgotten and holds enormous power as the unfolding events of this night will reveal.

The community demands (will demand) the sacrifice of the faith healer/artist/shaman for his inability to perform the miracle – to take the ordinary and transform it, to make the broken whole, to still the questions, to create harmony, to effect a final restoration and homecoming:

> Once the shaman can no longer heal, he must be sacrificed, for he has not only lost his ability to benefit his society, but also his very presence in this society becomes a threat. He is allowed to live only because of his miraculous powers. (Throne 1987:22)

These very powers which often point to the impotence of human law, order or religious rituals, 'mock and threaten the fragile fabric of human consciousness' (Throne 1987:22).

Grace is incidental to the play. She doesn't even exist as the classic muse to the artist. Her monologue reflects her steady decline and disintegration as she spirals from an upper class educated affluence into a seedy, poverty-stricken existence, a broken woman, unmade and destroyed by her obsession, devotion and loyalty to Frank Hardy. As she remembers the last year with Frank she recalls the number of times she encouraged him, convinced him of his gift, offered endless affirmation while he drew sustenance from her and finally drained her completely (342). As she tries to gain access to her memory she too uses the ritual incantations of the place names, to calm and sedate her. She recalls Frank, in the van, before a performance, the whisky bottle between his legs as he recites the place names 'in such complete mastery that everything is harmonized for him, in such complete mastery that anything is possible'. She recalls how he would look past her 'out of his completion' (343) and how 'then, for him, I didn't exist. Many, many, many times I didn't exist for him. But before a performance this exclusion – no, it wasn't an exclusion, it was an erasion – this erasion was absolute: he obliterated me. Me who tended him, humoured him, nursed him, sustained him – who debauched myself for him' (344).

Her story of the still birth of her child on a wet day in Kinlochbervie has many contradictions when compared with Teddy's story of the same event and Frank's exclusion of it altogether. She remembers Frank as a 'twisted man! With such a talent for hurting' (345). He continued to erase her through forgetting or changing her surname and her place of birth, and constantly calling her his mistress which he knew would wound her. She interprets his compulsion to lie as 'some compulsion he had to adjust, to refashion, to re-create everything around him'. So Teddy becomes the devoted servant and acolyte to the holy man rather than the fit-up man constantly in trouble with the police for pilfering. She sees all the people Frank came in contact with as extensions of himself – 'his fictions that came into being only because of him' (345).

Grace's father was a judge, who had a stroke. Her mother 'in her headscarf and wellingtons was a strange woman who went in and out of the mental hospital' (347). The absence of a healthy mother-daughter relationship may in part account for Grace's low self-esteem. Although that was also nurtured by her father's judgement of her. At her last meeting with her father she feels he is passing sentence on her and she has a desire to:

> assault and defile him with obscenities and to articulate them slowly
> and distinctly and brutally into his patrician face; words he never

used; a language he didn't speak; a language never heard in that house. (*FH* 348)

When Grace returns to Frank the only outcome of their reunion is 'a black-faced, macerated baby, that's buried in a field in Kinlochbervie in Sutherland in the north of Scotland' (349).

Grace speaks of faith healing as 'this gift, this craft, this talent, this art, this magic' that she could never understand. She saw it as something that possessed Frank and defined him – his essence, which she could not approach. By mutual agreement she kept her distance, Frank interpreting her desire to rob him of his gift so that he no longer eluded her as the ultimate treachery. In Grace's memory Frank needed to set himself against her as she in some way represented the legal mind that denied the miracle of his craft. A similar polarity between the legal and the marvellous is found in *Wonderful Tennessee* where the marvellous is an offence to reason. In turn Frank would either gloat over or feel humiliated by the legal mind, depending on whether his gift worked or failed to work.

Grace feels that she has become one of Frank's fictions and knows that she cannot go on without his sustenance. Grace's narrative voice indicates how much woman's voice is peripheral to the male journey. The harrowing story told by a woman obviously on the verge of a breakdown (or suicide as we later discover) finds no reconciliation. No spiritual insight is offered to Grace. She gains no access to a world where she is the maker of meaning. She exists as a symbol of how the corporeal cannot be integrated into the spiritual vision. Her erasure takes place on three levels – within her relationship with Frank, within herself as she commits suicide, and culturally as she is incidental to the reconciliation achieved by Frank in his sacrificial death.

Teddy on the other hand is a survivor. The only living voice of the play, he believes that he has received the healing look from his master that gave him (at least temporarily) some feeling of completion. His jaunty air, coupled with his outsider voice (Cockney/London English dialect specified by the stage directions, 354) offer the audience another vantage point, another way of interpreting the events. His accent provides a third narrative voice, but no guarantee of objectivity, given his past and his homo-erotic love for Frank, whom he serves like a devoted acolyte. All his life he has dealt with artists and believes he knows them, listing their ambition, talent and lack of brains as their identifying and uniting characteristics (355). He remembers how Frank 'was never more than a mediocre artist' and 'all those bloody brains ... castrated him' (357).

Teddy recounts the events of the evening in Glamorganshire when Frank cured the ten people. He recalls how 'there was no shouting or cheering or dancing with joy, nothing at all like that. Hardly a word was spoken. It was like as if not only had he taken away whatever it was that was wrong with them, but like he had given them some great content in themselves as well' (359). Perhaps the outer physical symptoms are manifestations of a deeper spiritual or psychic disease that was also cured. Teddy goes on to recount how one of the people, an old farmer who had been lame, made a little speech. 'Mr. Hardy, as long as men live in Glamorganshire, you'll be remembered here' (359). Teddy reflects on the lilting Welsh accent and 'whatever way he said it, you knew it was true, and whatever way he said Glamorganshire, it sounded like the whole world'. The ritual always takes people back to the time of origins. The ritual locates people at the centre of the world. And while it is particular to a time and place (this people in this time) it is also not only a geographical centre, but a mythic centre, where wholeness and integration are possible.

As Teddy recalls the events of a fateful night in Donegal his telling takes on the air of a mythic narrative. The details of the date and the crossing and arrival in Ballybeg now have a familiarity for the audience. He talks about seeing Frank and Grace in the pub as if he were remembering them:

> it was like I was seeing them as they were once, as they might have been all the time – like if there was never none of the bitterness and the fighting and the wettings and the bloody van and the smell of the primus stove and the bills and the booze and the dirty halls and that hassle that we never seemed to be able to rise above. (367)

The myth of the eternal return to the mythic time of origins when everything was perfect – is reminiscent of an Edenic narrative that posits an original harmony and wholeness. Teddy, unlike Grace, receives enough from his relationship with Frank to sustain him. Ballybeg becomes for Teddy the centre of the world, when Frank holds him in his gaze for thirty seconds (as with the gaze of the dancing dolphin in Frank's Ballybeg epiphany, *Wonderful Tennessee*). Teddy tries to explain the nature of this serious yet compassionate look:

> it's a look that says two things. It says. No need to speak – I know exactly what the trouble is. And at the same time it says: I am now going to cure that trouble. That's the look he gave me. He held me in that look for – what? – thirty seconds. And then he turned away from me and looked at her – sort of directed his look towards her so that I had to look at her too. And suddenly she is this terrific woman that of course I love very much, married to this man that I love very much – love maybe even more. But that's all. Nothing more. That's all. And that's enough. (368)

The final evening in the pub in Ballybeg is steeped in ritual. It includes the mythic crossing and journey to the place of origins, the drinking and the homecoming, the expected flowering/full blossoming, the ritual of healing the bent finger and the Dionysian night of excess that followed all, and culminated in the threatening, challenging encounter with otherness in the ritual space of the yard with its arched entrance and the trailer with its implements. Elements of Frank's description in the fourth monologue also have a sense of a dream sequence to them. 'It was a September morning, just after dawn. The sky was orange and everything glowed with a soft radiance – as if each detail of the scene had its own self-awareness and was satisfied with itself' (375). He describes how

> the 'yard was a perfect square' the 'arched entrance', the tractor and the trailer in the back of which were an axe, a crowbar, a mallet and a hay fork. He notes two mature birch trees, and the smooth cobbled ground as he walks across to the the four wedding guests, posed almost symetrically, 'and in front of them, in his wheelchair, McGarvey'. (375)

Frank has been warned about these 'savage bloody men … they'll kill you' (374). He has been told that there is nothing anyone can do for McGarvey and yet Frank walks consciously into this space both of the real and of the unconscious, towards the dark, towards the crippled other:

> McGarvey. More shrunken than I had thought. And younger. His
> hands folded patiently on his knees; his feet turned in, his head
> slightly to the side. A figure of infinite patience, of profound
> resignation, you would imagine. (*FH* 375)

Ruth Neil explores the range of characters in Friel's plays who
display some type of disability whether physically handicapped,
mentally disabled or disturbed. She pays particular attention to the
'disabled soul' which finds expression in characters (usually
women) who suffer nervous breakdown and depression. She
suggests that Frank Hardy (also a disabled soul) willingly chooses
death, and in so doing he accepts the human condition as
incurably broken. Neil argues that

> Disability is part of the system, part of life; above all it cannot be
> redeemed. Friel's drama constantly moves against any striving for
> wholeness, any attempt to promote a simplistic, unified system of
> meaning. (Neil 1999:156)

One must accept the brokenness of the world. However Frank
Hardy's way of acceptance is to offer himself as a sacrificial victim.

The dream-like nature of the final morning continues as the
scene appears to shed its material reality:

> And as I walked I became possessed of a strange and trembling
> intimation: that the whole corporeal world – the cobbles, the trees,
> the sky, those four malign implements – somehow they had shed
> their physical reality and had become mere imaginings, and that in
> all existence there was only myself and the wedding guests. And
> that intimation in turn gave way to a stronger sense: that even we
> had ceased to be physical and existed only in spirit, only in the need
> we had for each other. (375-76)

The reality is that he is walking to his death at the hands of
savage and bloody men, and that he had not listened to the voice
of his wife and her call to relationship. The only reconciliation
possible is at a spiritual or non-corporeal level. Frank has moved
out of history and into the mythic – he is at the centre of the
world/returning to his myth of origins. Jose Lanters suggests that
one interpret the play (along with *The Gigli Concert*) in terms of
myths of gender and identity (Lanters, 1992). If, as Cheryl Herr
has noted, the body 'is the missing link in Irish identity', we can

explore how the male experience in both these plays (in crisis and striving for healing and wholeness) is given a 'female counterpart in parallel terms of sterility and creativity, sickness and healing' (Lanters, 1992:278). If myths of Irish identity have been constructed around a severing of mind and body, then the journey of this play can be perceived as an attempt to enter the territory of this myth, and to discern whether it is liberating or incarcerating. Frank must let his old self-definition die in order for new possibilities to emerge. Grace in turn must die, as her self-definition is equally tied up in a debilitating myth. 'To achieve wholeness in familial and social terms the incarcerating sense of Irishness in which mind dominates matter must be abandoned and a healthy relationship between mind and body restored' (Lanters, 288). Frank Hardy's self-realization (of private despair as a medium of healing) also

> demands the exclusion and negation of the false mirror of the female Other at the same time that it creates the possibility for a future healthy relationship. (Lanters, 288)

The poet Eavan Boland talks about moving out of myth and into history. What kind of reconciliation might have been possible for Frank if he had stayed at the level of the corporeal where it opens out to the spiritual? How might a non-dualistic reconciliation integrate the male and female, body and soul, flesh and spirit? How might a culture place birth not death at the centre of its imagining?

Talbot's Box, Thomas Kilroy (1979)

While Murphy, Kilroy and Friel all seem to write versions of one another's plays there is no doubt that Kilroy is the most experimental with theatrical form. His 1979 play *Talbot's Box*, (Kilroy, 1997) presented in a Brechtian epic type of theatre with many of its techniques of distancing and alienation, explores many religious themes and is an interesting play to study from a feminist point of view. The play's experimental playfulness with set, props, characters and time-frames challenges the audience beyond any simple identification. Realist notions are challenged by the many ways that characters move in and out of roles and different historical periods. The audience becomes more aware of the relationship between person and role both on and off the stage. Anthony Roche notes the 'deep kinship between the stage and the act of dreaming whereby the normal boundaries that separate and define human beings no longer operate and one identity blurs readily into another' (1994:202)

The use of a huge timber box, as the stage directions indicate, '*occupying virtually the whole stage*' should have the effect '*of a primitive, enclosed space, part prison, part sanctuary, part acting space*' (*Talbot's Box* 9). In the course of the play it will evoke a work space, a containing space, a besieged space, a coffin, and a theatrical resource as '*all the actors, costumes and props required in the play are already within the box*' (*Talbot's Box* 9). The constant foregrounding of the artifice of theatre resists the tendency towards any kind of absolute truth either in theatre or outside.

Of the five characters in the play four play multiple parts. Only Matt Talbot remains constant. And he is also a representation, albeit based on a real life character who lived in Dublin from 1856 to 1925. Poverty and alcoholism were an integral part of life in Dublin's slums where he was reared and lived. A profound conversion experience in his life caused him to give up alcohol and devote the next forty years of his life to living a harsh secret life of prayer, penance and fasting. An unskilled worker and mystic his cult was encouraged after his death and the movement towards his canonization began. Matt Talbot was reputed by some to have betrayed his fellow workers during the Great Lock-out of Dublin workers in 1913, but many disagree.

Kilroy's intention in writing the play was to write about

> the mystic and the essentially irreducible division between such extreme individualism and the claim of relationship, of community, society. [...] In the beginning I was possessed by the crude manipulation of an eccentric, inaccessible man by forces which sought a model for the purpose of retaining power over people. What I think I wrote was a play about aloneness, its cost to the person, and the kind of courage required to sustain it. (*Talbot's Box*, Author's Note)

The play raises a series of interesting questions about inter-pretation, and manipulation, about the possibility of sanctity, about otherness and difference, about the individual and community. In its exploration of one ordinary man's mystical journey it opens into the dark. The classical mystical tradition places huge emphasis on the dark and the subsequent apophatic theology questions all facile answers, formulations and solutions. The search for words to articulate this experience pushes language to its limits, and questions the smallness of our categories, and the limitations of the rational as language halts before the ineffable.

The subject of this play is a poor, working-class mystic. His position is one of outsider to the dominant ways of knowing. As other people try to interpret his life and his knowing they will naturally try to 'box' it for their own purposes. Their interpretations will be manipulative and reductionist. The question of whether the knowing of the outsider (in this case Matt Talbot) can remain intact and work in an interruptive way is the problem faced by this play. The fact that Kilroy chose a Brechtian style in his writing and staging may allow for this interruption to occur which will result in a challenge to perceived ways of knowing and being in the world.

The sheer theatricality of the piece is highlighted from the opening moment of the play. A priest figure played by a woman, preaches from a mobile pulpit while another woman stands in a pious pose as the Virgin Mary. Audiences gradually realize that they are in the morgue of Jervis Street Hospital, and that Matt Talbot has been found dead on the streets of Dublin, his body bound with penitential chains and cords. Immediately there is a problem.

> **First Man:** I thought 'twas to be a sorta trial.
> **Second Man:** 'Twas my understanding 'twas to be an entertainment.
> **First Man:** A kind of temptation of the saint.
> **Second Man:** A sorta quiz show but without the hand-outs.
> (*TB* 11)

The audience are in confusion. This isn't *real* – a woman priest, a disgruntled talking statue, disagreement about what is taking place. It is necessary to adopt a new position for meaning-making to occur within this 'play'. What is theatre? What is its relationship to the real? What is representation? What is performance? Within moments the authority figures of Church and Police have been thrown into some kind of disrepute and an existentialist mortician tries to interpret the meaning of death, urging less haste as 'we could be on the brink of an apotheosis' (12)

The excesses of Matt Talbot's spiritual practice can be traced back to the eremetical tradition of the desert fathers and mothers in ancient Egypt. This spirituality came to prominence around the fourth century after Christianity had become more acceptable with the conversion of Constantine. As persecutions ceased many sought a more authentic expression of their Christianity and withdrew to lonely places to practise their spirituality. An excessively dualistic philosophy and theology resulted in a tendency to separate mind from body, spirit from flesh, male from female etc. The goal of the spiritual life was to become pure spirit, leaving behind all traces of bodiliness, and ties to nature. The Celtic monks brought this spirituality to Ireland in the 6th century. The Céilí Dé reform movement of Irish monasticism (8-10th centuries) laid down rules and codes for a very strict penitential form of Christianity which captured the Irish imagination for centuries. The play firmly locates Matt Talbot within this tradition (15)

The Church will be the first to claim Matt Talbot as one of their own, to use him as a model for the working-class of Dublin: 'a model of Christian loyalty and obedience, to fight off the false doctrines, subversive influences, dangerous and foreign practices, that threaten our faith' (17). Ireland tried for so long to remain outside of the influences of secularization and all of the threats of the encroaching modern world. There is a sense that if the Church can claim Matt Talbot he can be used as a bulwark against any kind of change. The extraordinary can be re-appropriated and domesticated, the edge blunted and the vision, if there was any, lost.

Matt Talbot rises from the dead. Kilroy has already experimented with this idea in another play *The Death and Resurrection of Mr Roche* (1969), another outsider. The audience would be familiar with the motif of death/resurrection. Its use as a theatrical device to revisit a life, as the person goes on his last journey into the dark is a re-appropriation of the symbol (It also calls to mind Yeats' idea of 'Dreaming Back', discussed earlier in relation to *Faith Healer*.) When Matt Talbot comes back to life he begins by binding his hands, legs and torso while reciting a prayer. As he flings his arms out cruciform (an ancient practice observed in many monastic and eremetical traditions), stage directions indicate, 'blinding beams of light shoot through the walls of the box, pooling about him and leaving the rest of the stage in darkness' (*TB* 17). This evokes images of transfiguration, the resurrection of Jesus and questions the relationship between this ordinary person's humanity and his/her capacity to incarnate the divine.

The doctor is only interested in the human body as a machine, and wants Matt Talbot's dead heart in formaldehyde – another box. His sister Susan has been trying to keep him going over the previous ten years, trying to keep 'body 'n soul together' for him since their Mother died. (Consider similar roles of Grace in *Faith Healer* and Mona in *The Gigli Concert*.) The call to the life of the hermit is juxtaposed with the call to family life and is almost impossible to understand. Letting go of all ties of relationship was an integral part of the spirituality we have discussed. For Matt Talbot as for many others, it meant leaving family and friends, embracing virginity, and foregoing marriage. All of his life will be a struggle against his nature, against the pull of the body which drags him down. He still remembers with extraordinary pathos Lizzie, a woman in service with whom he used to walk out and who wanted to marry him. And yet there are rewards. 'Having given it all up, it was all given back to me, but different, y'know what I mean. All the world and the people in the world came back to me in me own room. But everything in place. Nothing twisted 'n broken as it is in this world. Everything straight as a piece of good timber, without warp' (23).

As the capitalists and the Church try to appropriate Matt Talbot for their own ends, the workers reject him as a scab. Neither side can understand a stance that is different or that refuses to validate their own. A number of books and pamphlets are piled on top of the dazed Matt as the interpreters try to get him to speak to their cause. They treat him as if he were a race horse that they are backing – 'a short price but a good gamble' (*TB* 33). The possibility of owning him as a saint sets the process of canonization in motion. The juxtaposing of voices allows the audience no single vantage point for interpretation.

Talbot is presented in his box while the uproar of the police charging the crowds of workers is heard outside. There is a sense in these closing moments of the first act that the vantage point of the mystic may offer an alternative position of interpretation. How others interpret him as a tool of the Church against the workers, as a scab, as irrelevant or as a saint does not matter (35). Stage directions tell us that Talbot has thrown himself against the back wall as if holding it with his body. Roche sees the assault (on the box-set)

> as one of the most succinct paradigms of the pressures exerted on the solitary man of vision, be he mystic, artist or homosexual, by the force of external historical events – in this case the Great Strike of 1913. (Roche, 1994:204)

The text indicates that Talbot feels the pain intensely, yet has the compassion to bless and forgive. His speech that closes the first Act is a poignant statement of his outsider status which has simply arisen in response to his own truth. Because he refused to take strike pay for work he didn't do, his co-workers 'turned away' from him, and he from them. His benediction on the people and streets of Dublin is reminiscent of The Breadman's blessing of the people of the Donegal town who have accused and marginalized him (McGuinness, *The Bread Man*, unpublished). It is a prophetic and revolutionary prayer, with echoes of the Magnificat and the radical edge of the Christian Gospel:

> Blessed be the body
> For its pain is the message o' the spirit.
> Blessed be the starvin' peoples of the earth
> For they bring down the castles of the mighty.
> Blessed be the dung o' the world
> For on it is built the City on the Hill! (36)

The Second Act shifts the time-frame again and affords the audience a glimpse of an earlier stage in Talbot's life. The voice of the Catholic Church (through the priest figure) continues to try and claim Matt Talbot as one of their own. Glossing over the harsh economic reality of grinding poverty, alcoholism and violence within which the family lived the church claims Talbot as a model of sanctity 'in his poverty, his obedience, his self-denial, his chastity' (38). The voice of the church reflects the kind of spirituality that is able to separate body and soul. The physical reality is brutal, obscene but the spiritual life is to rise above this rather than transform it:

> As the modern attacks upon the Christian family close in upon you, divorce – contraception – abortion – drugs – delinquency – foreign periodicals – everything against our Irish way of life – cast your thought upon that simple home which nurtured Matthew Talbot. Draw strength from that sanctuary. (38)

The same Christian home is anything but a sanctuary as the father regularly beats the mother in front of the terrorized children.

The endless spiral of poverty, alcoholism and violence is repeated in the next generation and Matt Talbot tries to become free of it. As he lies collapsed in a heap, with alcohol poured down his throat by his family, two gentlemen characters attempt to interpret his behaviour from their perspective. They dismiss him as marginally human, belonging to a lower class (negatively defined), and an addict. Their equation of addiction and religious mania allows them to dismiss Talbot completely and to hold the middle ground securely for themselves as paragons of virtue and moral responsibility (45).

Matt Talbot's conversion scene follows. Kilroy claims a mystical awareness for Talbot, an awareness of the place of the dark in any genuine spirituality. The apophatic theology characteristic of the mystical tradition, found in great mystics like John of the Cross, advocates a darkness as a way into the divine. One cannot ultimately know God, it is only through the *via negativa*, the way that is not, that one can come to know. There must exist some kind of *Cloud of Unknowing* between the human and the divine. All naming of God falls short. The long dark night of the soul when the individual feels unable to find any foothold in experience or language becomes the greatest teacher.

At twenty-eight, Matt approaches the church in order to give up the drink. The priest is unable to understand Matt's motivation and tries to suggest that he is sinful, hates himself or hates his drunkenness. But Talbot claims 'I knows meself', and that 'I knows the darkness' (*TB* 46). He claims that it is inside everyone and he wants to be able to meet the darkness as himself, something he could never do while he is drinking. The priest remains puzzled and tries to pin down this darkness in familiar categories suggesting that Matt's darkness is the absence of God caused by his not practising his religion.

> **Priest Figure:** We'll have to start there, Matthew. Because there's no change unless God be within you. That's your darkness, Matthew, the absence of God.
> **Talbot:** Beggin' your pardon, Father, I think meself the darkness is Gawd. (*TB* 46-47)

Talbot has become aware of the essential aloneness that is integral to the human condition and is prepared to 'be alone with gawd' (*TB* 47). Kilroy portrays the church more sympathetically as the priest figure agrees to 'take a chance' on Matt because 'I've never come across the like of you' before. The church has always (reluctantly at times) accepted its mystics, and sought ways to validate their unique individual experiences of the divine. However it has never been officially suggested that this is the path for all Christians. Karl Rahner the theologian who was so instrumental in shifting contemporary theology towards the focus on experience and historical subjectivity once stated that the Christian of the future would be a mystic or wouldn't be a Christian at all.

While one can critique the essential body/spirit dualism that underpins Matt's spirituality, there is a depth to what he has learned in solitude about the human condition. He sees the fact that people 'have no quietness in themselves' (*TB* 50) as explanation for abusive and inhuman behaviour:

> An' I do think that all the sufferin' in the world comes from that'n all the wars 'n destruction in the world, the terrible hunger for what oders might have, instead of lettin' them be, 'n turnin' to wha's missin' inside hisself. (*TB* 50)

When his girlfriend Lizzie wonders about how he could endure the loneliness of his solitary life he answers simply, 'I've measured it. The length and the breadth of it. I fit into it' (51).

The closing scenes of the play continue to grapple with the question of what is normal or sane behaviour. The supposed sanity of the world is posited against Matt's insanity or the madness of the desert fathers and medieval saints. Withdrawal from the world may enable the person to enter the darkness of the human condition and see it for what it is. Maybe 'there is no demon, only man' (55). Maybe the light discovered in solitude enables the perception of a new beginning of the world. Running from the madness of what the world has become may seem eccentric behaviour. It is like trying to outrun a tidal wave. The darkness of the soul's journey into the truth of the human condition necessitates a descent into the dark, where there are no comforting answers, images or experiences of divine presence to sustain one. 'Talbot's movement towards self-realization is not upward and outward, but inward and down, the fall into a darkness which yields the fortunate consummation' (Roche 199:205). Kilroy's Matt Talbot knows the darkness of his own body, his own soul's journey, and he has no time for church devotions as ' 'tis only people runnin' from themselves' (56) and looking for a 'distraction from misery'. Talbot confounds the Church again by claiming no experience of divine presence 'Nuthin'! Nuthin'! Nuthin'!' (57) The priest figure trots out the formula for prayer that is supposed to guarantee presence. Matt interrupts him with an attempt to put into words the mystic experience of oneness of self with God, which is articulated in terms similar to Jung's concept of self-individuation:

> There be nuthin' to see when Gawd comes 'cause there's nuthin' other than yerself 'cause yerself is wan with what ya see so ya see nuthin' 'cause ya can only see what's separate than yerself, ya can only count what's different, not the same, not the wan, not the only. (58)

Kilroy appropriates a Christ-like function for Matt Talbot in the closing scenes of the play. Matt has always only wanted to work with the timber that he loved, and the image of the father and son in the carpenter's shop in Nazareth closes the play, as the son leaves home with the sounds of crucifixion in the air. The final moments in the morgue address the question of how another human, as human, can assume divinity on our behalf. The odour and stench that comes from the body with its putrefying wounds from the ropes and chains that have bound the flesh is a challenge to the normality of the lives of those watching and attending. The choice of one human being to suffer, in the flesh, for the sins and darkness of himself and others stands as a challenge to other ways of being in the world. It is perhaps the question of incarnation that Kilroy is addressing. 'He threatens our freedom' (62): Talbot who modelled his spirituality on that of a suffering-soul mysticism is another Christ challenging the interpretation of what it means to be human, what it means to be divine.

The Gigli Concert, Tom Murphy (1983)

In the enclosed claustrophobic space of JPW's office an English-man and an Irishman examine the process of soul-making in modern Ireland, facilitated in their doing by the music of Gigli, the myth of Faust, Jungian psychology, and the philosophical idea of the power of the possible (Heidegger/Kierkegaard/Ricoeur). At the heart of *The Gigli Concert* (Murphy, *After Tragedy*, 1-39) is sickness and disease, an unborn child, a non-corporeal spirituality and a rejection of the perceived stasis and light offered by tradi-tional Judaeo-Christian religion in favour of a descent into the dark and a longing to soar in song with a god of the future, who possibilizes the possible.

The seedy office of a displaced Englishman, quack psychiatrist, dynamatologist JPW King is the liminal space within which the action of the play takes place, with the music of Gigli framing and pacing the action. The Irishman who comes to consult King mirrors King throughout the play – in lines like King's opening one 'Christ, how am I going to get through today' (*GC* 3), through depression and mandrax, to imagined life stories and to a desire to sing like Gigli. Whether one interprets this mirroring in terms of *alter ego*, or characters seeking wholeness or fractured and split subjectivities, the two male characters represent the contours of the male hero/shamanic journey which is played out at the expense of women in the play.

At the outset it must be noted that this play achieves what it does primarily through performance. The seedy squalor of the surroundings (Ireland in the eigthies?) may still enable some kind of new imagining/transcendent leap if the conditions are right. There are limitations in approaching the play primarily as text. This applies to all Murphy's work but especially this play. The urge to perform the self *in extremis*, to listen to the sound of a soul in torment, to search for a sound to clothe that longing cannot be appreciated if we treat the play simply as a text. It is the engagement with the audience that defines Murphy's theatre. It is a ritual space where the actors are perfomers/shamans/priests taking the audience with them on a journey to a time of origins, to an *illud tempus*. To limit a play like *Gigli* to a realist frame is to miss the moments when the fissures in the text open the play to another level of meaning, beyond the literal. Interpretation from the perspective of myth, symbol, ritual may be more helpful. Whether one would want to imitate the kind of self-realization of JPW is another question. Perhaps the play is more interested in the possibility of such realization – the possibilizing of the possible, whatever way one moves towards it. From a feminist point of view, however, one must question the patriarchal aesthetic that advocates such a disconnected aspiration towards a transcendent. The play finally validates such an aesthetic, the imagined state of pure perfection is preferable to an engaged wholeness.

The self-made man (the Irishman) is in contrast with the Englishman JPW whose organization is more interested in self-realization (4). The binarisms of madness / sanity (and Irishman / Englishman in a reversed sense) underpin the play, foregrounding the question of what is normal. The Irishman is a builder who has built over a thousand houses, houses which were 'built out of facts: corruption, brutality, back-handing, front-handing, back-stabbing, lump labour and a bit of technology' (6). Now he doesn't want to build any more houses because: 'This – something-cloud has come down on me'. The resultant depression leaves him wondering (like King) 'Christ how am I going to get through today'. The only way to break the silence in his home and relationships is to roar obscenities. Both JPW and the Irish Man have experienced their 'outbursts' taking them by surprise, and leading to increased violence. Both lead imaginary lives. The Irishman tells his life story, as the story of Benjamino Gigli, JPW fictionalizes a wife and two children. The Irishman's aspiration to sing goes beyond talking. 'Singing, d'h know? The only possible way to tell people' (9).

The nurturing corporeal dimension is held by the women in the play, be they mothers, wives or mistresses. The idealization of woman (so-good) or JPW's fantasies about Helen make it impossible for real women to appear in their true embodied subjectivity, either in the play itself or in the male imagination. Equally where there is an idealization of family, both in The Man's and JPW's narratives, there is a failure to deal with the reality that, for many, Irish family life is a sordid, violent, unhappy, uncommunicative space. The confinement of the space to women and children reinforces the nature/culture divide that is endemic to patriarchal imagining, and reinforces the kind of public/private split that allows the sphere of the family to remain outside of the meaning-making of the culture, although not beyond its control.

The Man speaks about the effect that listening to Gigli's singing has on him. He identifies him as 'the devil' (12), perhaps in terms of the hold he has on his soul. He cannot stop listening to him:

> And it's beautiful – But it's screaming! – And it's longing. Longing for what? I don't know whether it's keeping me sane or driving me crazy.

Filling his soul with this restless, impossible longing leaves The Man unable to communicate at all with his wife and child. He has moved from silence to obscenities and in a mad frenzy burned all his child's toys. He confesses that he waited until his wife has left the room before he roared 'Fuck you, fuck you, fuck you' (13) in response to her love and concern for him. One can only ask what kind of restless impossible longing has been kindled. Later in the play when JPW follows through with the longing to sing, he will go through a similar inarticulate longing, filled with cursing and contradictions (37). JPW is also a lost soul, displaced (an Englishman in Ireland), forgotten by his organization, unable to heal himself, never mind his clients. He believes that there are too many facts in the world and is equally dismissive of religious, philosophical and psychotherapeutic paradigms of thought. The Man's equally dismissive attitude to philosophy and education mirrors JPW's (14). The Man has never been beaten in life – an

Irish self-made man who has 'left a few cripples around the place' (echoes of the corruption of Irish social and political life as witnessed today in the many tribunals investigating Ireland in the eighties).

Mona's corporeal reality is vital and yet incidental to the ultimate direction of the play. The sexual choices that women are given in realist plays must be questioned. The supposed freedom of choice (Mona picks JPW up in a supermarket, has insatiable appetites and wants lots of men) is simply freedom to function, to validate the underlying patriarchal aesthetic. The interruptive presence of a real woman in her particular embodied subjectivity, who has moved out of the mythic or the fantastic would perhaps be more threatening or undermining of the same aesthetic. As Ní Dhomnaill puts it:

> My womanness overwhelmed you
> as you admitted after to a friend
> over a mutual drink.
> Fear, certainly of castration
> fear of false teeth in my cunt
> fear my jaws would grind you
> like oats in a mill. (Ní Dhomhnaill, 1986:68)

The paradigms within which Murphy's characters operate are essentially those of the patriarchal symbolic – whether religious or philosophical. Whether one explains the crisis of soul as original sin or existential guilt the paradigm is one which is dualistic, arising out of the universalizing male disembodied *cogito*. While JPW seems to be ranting in a stream of incoherent jibberish he is in fact decrying the loss of original innocence that is the legacy of patri- archal imagining. Simply attempting to notice and redress the obvious imbalances in such a system of thought, by including what has been ignored, repressed, relegated to the dark may not be sufficient. Restoration of the instinctive, feeling function while maintaining the overall dualistic paradigm, does not lead to new ways of thinking and imagining.

Male fantasy and longing underpins much of the narrative of this play. At times this is directed towards women who are either uninterested or unavailable. All the women in this play (real or imagined) are adversely affected by their relationships with the two men. The man's wife ages, Mona develops a life-threatening ill-ness, Ida has a breakdown, Helen is tortured by JPW's stalking and obscene phone calls and JPW's mother attempts suicide. The in-ability to deal with the real world of relationships and the longing and frustration at failed sexual relationships leads JPW to suggest a 'whore-house' to The Man as an outlet for his repressed longing. Women in *The Gigli Concert* occupy this space – projections of the male unconscious, symbols of the repressed, and carriers of very specific meanings. The ease with which both The Man and JPW can transfer their longing to the desire to sing like Gigli illustrates the point. How to give expression to such longing is the important issue.

The scene where JPW parodies Freudian psychoanalysis in tracing everything back to early sexual experiences has a strangely voyeuristic tone to it. And as audience we are the voyeurs to this narrative. The Man in relating his earliest sexual experience shifts the narrative from the fantasy childhood to the real, disclosing a family where the father is sick and dying (the old patriarchal order?) and the eldest brother Mick (new patriarchal order?) rules in a violent and tyrannical manner. The brutal, violent family background obliterates the innocence of childhood, and erases any sensitivity to beauty. The layering of these experiences in the adult psyche leads to the 'impotent hatred' which characterizes The Man as he hisses 'I hate ! I f-f-f.' (29). Stage directions indicate that The Man is trying to speak/sing:

> *A few whimpers escape. Fixed, rooted in his position, he starts to shout, savage, inarticulate roars of impotent hatred at the doorway developing into sobs which he cannot stop. Terrible, dry sobbing, and rhythmic, as if from the bowels of the earth. (The 'performance' is an atonal aria.)*

Impotent hatred, repressed violence, misogyny, the need to articulate and roar obscenities, burning children's toys, emerge in the narrative of the self-made Irish male as he ritually confesses in the sacred space of the therapy room. Coming to this level of frustration and release is something he has done before. It is both tolerated and redeemed within the patriarchal symbolic, enabling The Man to return to his wife, as if nothing had happened. When he returns to JPW the following day he has totally reinvented himself and his past – 'Listen I'd just like you to know for one thing, boy, that I had a very happy childhood' (31). The momentary breakdown will not become a complete breakdown for that would be to question the whole order on which meaning is made. Even JPW, who will follow through The Man's longing and attempt to sing like Gigli, does not radically question the received ways that meaning is made.

Even if we accept the nature/culture divide that underpins this play, Mona is not offered any way to 'possibilize the possible'. The baby she had when she was sixteen, the child she longed for with JPW, her imaginary god-child haunt the play, but offer no site of renewal or hope. The body is barren. Physical barrenness, sterility and life-threatening illness give way to the metaphysical.

The play moves into magic as JPW tells the audience, 'This night I'll conjure' (38). Stage directions indicate that he switches off the record player, consumes a cocktail of mandrax and vodka, calls on the spirits of the dark (underground) as he plunges into the abyss of his own darkness and soars in singing like Gigli. If the magic has worked the audience will have suspended disbelief, allowing theatre to become the space of possibility, or the space where the impossible can appear real. The ritual space of theatre allows the song of soul to come to expression. The reversal of the traditional Christian dynamic where damnation is affirmed over salvation is in fact simply an acknowledgement of the dark, the shadow as integral to human knowing. JPW's final calling on his mother 'Mama! Mama. Don't leave me in this dark' may simply reflect this embrace of the dark (the other as repressed culturally) and its accommodation within the existing male symbolic. This has always been the artistic function. The question a feminist critic must ask is how can this validation of the dark stand as a corrective to the dominant ways of knowing and urge a movement towards a new way of knowing. What kind of song of soul has in fact been sung? Roche interprets JPW's plea not to be left in the dark as an ultimate court of appeal to the female 'a plea that abandons the myth of male sufficiency and creation' (Roche, 1994:188). Lanters goes somewhat further and suggests that the King who emerges still needs completion:

However since King's former, false self-image was largely sustained and reinforced by female characters who themselves existed for King only as imagined projections of his own mind, the realisation of a true self that would be capable of healthy relationships entails not only the destruction of the false self but also of woman as myth. The play implies the duality of the physical void, which is both symptom and cure of King's disease, by stressing the absence and neglect of the body through images of denial, infertility, sickness and death. (1992:281)

Within this play Murphy correctly identifies the crisis as a crisis of soul. However he fails to frame the questions in an appropriate way, whether theologically or philosophically. His play surrenders to the final powerlessness of language, opting instead for the musical score of the opera. The passion and amorality of the opera as a site of resolution for the crisis of soul is inadequate. The bypassing of the whole Christian mystical tradition with its attention to the *via negativa* leads to a very superficial rejection of Christianity. JPW's stress on the sense of future implied in the Hebrew 'I Am Who Am' (YHWH) is not a new insight and the interpretation of revelation as the surging up in existence of the power of the possible has been expressed by many philosophers, most notably Paul Ricoeur. The soul-journey becomes a male hero journey, sacrificing any human connection in its path. The ultimate resolution taps into the dualisms so characteristic of western thought and in fact of Christian asceticism. The failure to confront the patriarchal order sufficiently leads to a superficial resolution. There is ultimately no integration of male and female, body and soul, spirit and flesh. The journey to the spiritual heights, akin to the Shamanic journey to the *illud tempus* fails because it is inadequately grounded in the body, with its needs, feelings, etc. The aspiration of body towards becoming conscious of itself as spirit is not matched by a descending journey of consciousness and spirit becoming embodied.

Innocence: The life and death of Michelangelo Merisi, Caravaggio, Frank McGuinness (1986)

Frank McGuinness's 1986 play *Innocence*, (McGuinness, *Plays 1*:199-289) subtitled 'The life and death of Michelangelo Merisi,

Caravaggio', is a thoroughly modern play. While ostensibly based on the real life 17th century Italian painter (1571-1610), forced into patronage, by the social conditions of his age, it is nonetheless a play with challenging and contemporary themes: themes concerning the artist and culture, his rights and responsibilities regarding the subjects of his painting, the social and political compromises he is forced to make, the integration of his sexuality, and the relationship between patronage and prostitution. Essentially it is a journey play, a journey both inner and outer. The artist is pulled/drawn to the edges of darkness, to the abyss and returns again. It is a play of colour and images that journeys between the real world of waking and the ever more real world of dreaming and unconsciousness.

The lens of carnival and the figure of the fool provide useful interpretive horizons for understanding the play. When we also consider carnival in the context of the medieval world, where it was often closely aligned with parody and rituals of reversal, it can provide an opening for an interpretation of Caravaggio as a lord of misrule, who turns the world upside down by his antics. The play in turn can then be seen as offering the audience a new vantage point for interpretation both of Caravaggio's world and our contemporary one. Jordan writes that McGuinness's comic use of carnival is 'a blending of two types of consciousness in order to offer a leap of faith, a trust in the ridiculous, in the illogical and in the inappropriate. Carnival can deploy parody, irony, mockery or travesties to telling effect' (Jordan, xxiv).

Catherine Belsey (1980) has proposed the idea of theatre offering interrogative texts where the question of subjectivity is more fluid and the play is interpreted and presented in terms of a contest of meanings within culture. It seems appropriate to consider *Innocence* in such terms. It is also important to consider the play in terms that are not confined by the conventions of realism. It is a highly theatrical piece both in its imagery and its foregrounding of a carnivalized world.

The earthiness of humour that reconnects us with bodies, sexuality, hunger, disease and death is the same energy that is associated with the carnivalesque, where travesty and transgression enable transformation and renewal. The medieval experience of carnival had the overall effect of debasing or bringing down to earth. It allowed the sacred and the profane to become enmeshed rather than held apart as separate realms. The pattern of death and renewal in the mock crownings and de-crownings allowed a laughter at exalted objects which was at least ambivalent.

Simon Dentith's work on parody (2000) draws attention to many medieval examples of liturgical parody where the experience of carnival and the mockery of all that was held sacred allowed an experience of release from the crushing authoritarianism, intolerance, and intimidation of a hierarchical church. The Feast of Fools, celebrated on the Feast of the Holy Innocents on 28 December allowed junior clergy to perform an elaborate parody of the church's liturgy, where they elected a bishop or abbot of fools and dressed in women's clothes or vestments worn back to front, and engaged in various rituals of inversion which were often obscene or blasphemous. The feast heralded a space of undisciplined wildness, unrestrained wantonness and irresponsibility. Whether such ritual transgression merely maintained the *status quo* while containing dissent, or whether it enabled genuine renewal, is difficult to ascertain.

Linda Henderson (1986) writes about the world of *Innocence* as a world of darkness, inhabited by creatures of the night. She interprets it as a world moved by primal and Dionysian forces of hunger, disease, lust, drunkenness, avarice, and violence, and sees it as a world dominated by Caravaggio as a lord of misrule. Caravaggio's behaviour seems to speak an alternative, disruptive language that breaks up received patterns of meaning and offers new interpretations. The foregrounding of male homosexuality further questions his society's notion of compulsory heterosexuality. In turn the religious vision of Caravaggio's paintings is scandalous in portraying the poor, the prostitute – those on the margins as manifestations of the divine. McGuinness in conversation drew my attention to Caravaggio's *John the Baptist, The Weeping Magdalen* and *The Death of the Virgin* as direct inspiration for the characters of Lucio, Lena and Anna. The red drape that figures in many of the paintings is a very important theatrical prop throughout the play.

The opening sequence of the play presents a circle of characters, which Caravaggio observes. He is

> *fingering a skull. Lena caresses a red cloak, like a child. Antonio and Lucio caress each other. Whore rocks herself to and fro, weeping. Cardinal recites the Offertory from the Tridentine Mass, holding a host. Servant kneels at Cardinal's feet, with Brother.*

The opening prayer of the play transfers the traditional ritual of the Mass to the new sacred space of theatre where the audience is invited to witness another kind of miracle – where the artist will transform the stuff of everyday into the lasting beauty of art (both as playwright and painter). In the dream space of theatre, readers and audiences encounter in the opening moments of the play the rough yet holy theatre of ritual and symbol and possibility. The culture of 17th century Catholicism and many images from the paintings of Caravaggio are put before us. The raised skull mirrors the raised host and offers a site of ritual transgression. The two men caressing and kissing, juxtaposed with the servant and brother prostrate before the Cardinal foreground an alternative sexuality. The prostitutes call to mind those economically and sexually marginalized. The characters appropriate the Latin for themselves. It spreads in words, becoming noises, becoming animal sounds. In the collapse of the Latin language into the semiotic we are faced with an undermining of the official language of rite and sacrament. The red cloak becomes a horse – symbol of sexual energy, of ritual travelling, of animal instinct, wild and untamed. While Caravaggio tries to tame it with the image of death, it screams and wraps itself around him. Hands which will feature throughout this play (and in many of McGuinness's other works) beat Caravaggio and he falls down roaring.

In the liminal space of Lena's hovel/kip we meet the temporarily blinded Caravaggio and Lena a prostitute, friend and sexual partner. In a scene with two voices sounding different notes/tones we are subject to a mixture of boasting, bawdy play and sparkling riposte. The symbols from the opening sequence become props. The red cloak (a feature of many Caravaggio paintings, as cloak, curtain, mantle) is being repaired by Lena, again. Used to providing healing remedies and physical sustenance to Caravaggio, her words provide a counterpoint to Caravaggio's boastful assertions of who he is and what he tries to achieve in his art:

> In all Rome I stand supremely alone as painter, seer and visionary, great interpreter of man...I paint with my hands as God intended the eyes to see and to see is to be God, for it is to see God....For my art balances the beautiful and the ugly, the saved and the sinning. (*Innocence* 208)

Caravaggio appropriates the priestly actions that are central to the Christian mystery of Eucharist. Where the bread and wine are transformed through the ritual actions of the priest into the body and blood of Christ, Caravaggio believes that he performs a similar mystery of transformation in his painting. 'I take ordinary flesh and blood and bone and with my two hands transform it into eternal light, eternal dark' (208). He continues to appropriate a Christ function for himself and his art in being the revelation of God to the world:

> I paint as I see in light and as I imagine in darkness, for in the light I see the flesh and blood and bone but in the dark I imagine the soul of man for the soul and the soul alone is the sighting of God in man and it is I who reveal God and it is God who reveals my painting to the world. (209)

The appropriation of the Christ/priest function displaces the earlier ritual symbolism of the cardinal with the elevated host. Caravaggio stresses the relationship between seeing and working with his hands – both aspects are essential for revelation. He is the one 'who works with his hands, paints with his hands, and his hands are the hands of God alone'. Lest we get carried away however, with Caravaggio's assertions about himself and his art, Lena offers a counterpoint to this genius: 'I am Michelangelo Merisi and I am a wanker' (210). There is certainly no security of a unified subjectivity.

A street scene introduces the characters of Antonio and Lucio – male prostitutes, waiting to be hired. Their humorous exchange cannot hide the poverty and desperateness of their situation ('A whore for the sake of your belly', 'Hunger drives you mad' (220)). The foregrounding of male homosexual prostitution opens up the received perceptions of prostitution. Antonio recounts his encounter with a ghost the night before. Lucio wonders 'Are you in one of your visions?' Medieval mysticism (particularly amongst women) was very open to vision, as a way of validating one's own experience and thereby gaining access to power within a patriarchal church. When Antonio and Lucio try the last resort (prayer) they speak of how they are so hungry that 'we could eat each other'. Lucio suggests that they should say something religious:

> **Lucio:** This is my body.
> **Antonio:** This is my blood.
> **Lucio:** Turn me into bread, God.
> **Antonio:** Me into wine.
> **Lucio:** Give us a miracle.
> **Antonio:** Give us a man.
> **Lucio:** Not even that. Work a reverse job. Flesh and blood into bread and wine.
> **Antonio:** Give us a feed, Lord, if it's only ourselves. (222-223)

The two men appropriate the ritual words of the Eucharist: This is my body/This is my blood as religious language to frame their desperate prayer, which arises out of their hunger. The parody and ritual reversal implied in the idea that they seek a reverse job, to be turned into bread and wine to feed each other may appear at one level sacrilegious or scandalous. At another it may in fact be a truer understanding of what the symbol of Eucharist implies – being changed or transformed in order to nurture one another in relationship. The men are looking for a man, a saviour, to deliver them now from their hunger. The play on incarnation continues. God has already sent a man/his son/who was God. At this stage Antonio and Lucio don't mind who they are sent – God or man it is one and the same. It is interesting to observe that the one who will appear is Caravaggio who proclaimed 'to see is to be God' (208) and 'it is I who reveal God and it is God who reveals my paintings to the world' (209).

Caravaggio (in his role as pimp, prostitute and servant) brings the two young men to the palace of the Cardinal, which is hung with tapestries and paintings and where food and wine are plentiful. In the palace of the Cardinal, Caravaggio plays the fool and leads a carnival of the animals in a drunken night of frenzy and excess. The energy of carnival with its trust in the ridiculous and the illogical or inappropriate offers a site for transformation and renewal. The laughter of the carnival however is not simple parody. It combines both the comic and the tragic becoming almost serious, as Kristeva notes in her understanding of carnival (Kristeva, 1986, 50). In its seriousness it allows another perspective to emerge that questions all received interpretations. As a place of transgression and play, it allows the exploration of roles and identity while introducing themes of repression and transference.

Animal imagery which emerges early in the play brings an earthiness that combines both the magical and the grotesque. Caravaggio calms the two men calling them his unicorns (Lena called Caravaggio a unicorn and a goat in the earlier part of the scene). Lucio becomes a hound, a wild horse, a dragon breathing fire and a bull. Antonio becomes in turn a hare, an eagle, a fighting bull. Caravaggio becomes a poisonous lizard. 'Creeping on you. Touching you. Kissing you. Poison. Touching. Kissing. Poison. Kissing. Kissing' (an obvious reference to AIDS: *Innocence* 233). The sense that Caravaggio contaminates the two men by his touch will be echoed later in the play when he realizes that he has also contaminated his models by painting them. He couldn't save the people he painted. Whatever beauty he saw in their poverty one by one his models die from diseases, hunger, drowning. The animal imagery continues as Caravaggio and Lucio talk about scars and wounds. Both Caravaggio and Lucio were kicked by a horse and sustained wounds – Lucio on his thigh, Caravaggio a scar on his face. The wound on the thigh is possibly a castration which could also carry a wounding in the generative function – a wounding that runs through the play. Later Caravaggio will name and bless the animals in a chorus of transgression.

Caravaggio's crude, aggressive exchange which follows betrays his increasing feeling of compromise and entrapment. But he has been in this game for some time. He speaks about his relationship with the Cardinal, how he served him himself:

> I know the value of his money. I do as I am told. Painter and pimp. Painter to Cardinal del Monte, pimp to the Papal Curia, whore to the Catholic church. And they need me for I'm a very special whore. (239)

Caravaggio crawls around on all fours, offering the cardinal a wine cup – playing the fool. The Cardinal refers to Caravaggio both as his animal and his fool. But as his fool he is on a leash and has no power in the Cardinal's house. The real transgressive and interruptive power of the fool however runs through the play. The character of Caravaggio embodies many aspects of the fool in his topsy-turvy representation of a world, his liminal status and his ability to journey to the depths of what it means to be human. From the wild trickster spirit to the wise or holy fool, however one imagines, casts or plays Caravaggio, as fool he enables himself, other characters and in turn the audience to celebrate a new wisdom that is embodied and particular, and one that challenges the received orthodoxies about salvation and damnation.

The Cardinal knows Caravaggio, knows that he likes to be punished (240), knows that ultimately he is the one in power. He holds Caravaggio's knife before his face saying 'We know what excites you, Caravaggio? Blood.' He knows Caravaggio's weakness and knows that he wields power over him – a power he could use (if he chose) to put out his eyes, and leave Caravaggio blind and in the dark. But Caravaggio is also dependent on the Cardinal at another level. The Cardinal asks him: 'Why do you fear my hand?' Caravaggio answers. 'Blesses. Yours is the hand that blesses. I fear that blessing and I need it. For I have sinned. And I sin. And I will sin. Forgive me' (242). The Cardinal's speech confirms his knowing of Caravaggio, and also names why he is feared:

> A dangerous man, aren't you, Caravaggio? You believe with a depth that is frightening. And with a vision that is divine. Don't think I am ignorant of your vocation. You believe, and since you believe you are chosen, not commissioned. (*Innocence*, 243)

The Cardinal believes that he knows Caravaggio and that that is why Caravaggio fears him:

> The painter of the poor. Dirty feet, rags, patches, kneeling in homage to their Virgin Mary, another pauper, mother of their God.

The Cardinal tells him:

> You remind us of unpleasant truths, Caravaggio. For that you may be hated. Your sins may be condemned. But you will be forgiven,

for you are needed. Forgiven everything eventually. Dangerous words. A dangerous man. Saving himself by the power of his seeing. And by his need to tell what he sees. Tell me your sins. Confess, Caravaggio. (243)

As Caravaggio recounts his watching and hiring of the two boys he recalls his own anger and jealousy. They were both still young and desired. His violence is real:

> I wanted to smash their laughing skulls together for eternity. I wanted the crack of their killing to be music in my ears. I wanted them dead. I wanted red blood from their brown flesh to stain their white shirts and shout out this is painting, this is colour, these are beautiful and they are dead. (243-44)

The murderous desire out of which he creates is a violent hammering out of life into his art. It is like painting in blood. The violence is mirrored in guilt and repression of his own basic sexuality. Sinful loathing is also directed inwards in self-destruction as well as outwards into his art. His ambivalence about his sexuality is echoed in a conversation with his brother (a priest) who has come to find him, to urge him to return home and continue the family name, as his sister has died. While Caravaggio denies any connections with home his brother touches on Caravaggio's shame and ambivalence about his sexuality. 'So you are what you say you are?' Caravaggio answers, 'Yes, no, yes, no, yes, yes.' His brother offers no affirmation of his painting 'You paint like a drunkard sees. Badly. It's as if you're asleep. All in the dark. A drunk man imagining in his dreams' (254).

In a wild, mad carnivalesque gesture Caravaggio tears the tapestries and paintings from the walls of the palace, as he ransacks the room and slashes the cushions. The others steal a bag of booty which includes a chalice, a gold cross, a silver bowl and a red cloak. The greed, to possess life and literally to have more to eat and drink, motivates the theft which is so often at the heart of comedy. The redistribution of the symbols of the church amongst the poor adds to the sense of the toppling of hierarchies which is so characteristic of medieval parody. It now appears as if Caravaggio's violent outburst, facing his past, his homelessness, and his sexuality has enabled him to come to a point of clarity and awareness where he can say:

> I see clearly. I see this knife. I see the hand that carries it. I curse my hand. I curse my life. I damn my soul. Trust me. (255)

Jordan suggests that it

> is violence that gives all the different strands of the play a considerable cohesion. The spectator witnesses the violence of power, language, families and societies, brutality against homosexuals and the savagery of fear and hunger. We can add to this list the ferocity of dreams and the violence of carnival. (64)

Later in the play Lena has a dream where she imagines herself in a beautiful room with all of Caravaggio's paintings, and she imagines that she can still see him in them even though he has gone. Suddenly she looks up and sees him looking down at her and says:

> I started to laugh because it hit me you were looking at them from above, so you must see them all upside-down, and I knew then somehow we'd won, we turned the world upside-down, the goat and the whore, the queer and the woman. (284)

Turning the world upside-down is the task of the fool. Following Caravaggio's own dream sequence in the second act the audience witnesses a descent into the unconscious (or dream consciousness) and an encounter with the dark. This descent opens to an otherness which foregrounds the interconnected issues of damnation, homosexuality, guilt and transgression. It is the traditional descent into Hell or Hades now represented by the individual's journey to the Self. Here the conscious mind drops into the archaic world of the unconscious as it journeys deeper into the dark.

The second Act entitled Death takes us deeper into the unconscious. Caravaggio enters bloodied and wounded. The Whore continues to taunt him about his sexuality 'In my day men were men and respected women.' Caravaggio's violent reaction leads him to grab her by the neck and force her face into the bowl of bloodied water. His anger is displaced and transferred onto a vulnerable substitute. He has just killed a man who insulted them

(Lucio, Antonio and Caravaggio) by calling them names (girls). Caravaggio says that the dead man 'was beautiful':

> I didn't notice how beautiful until I saw his blood. It became him. Flesh and blood. Beautiful [...] I was following him. Waiting to kill him. All my life. Maybe he was following me. Finally, we touched. (264-65)

Flesh and blood evokes incarnation and also the sacrificial death of Jesus which in turn evokes the bread and wine of the Christian Eucharist. Caravaggio enters into the beauty of the human condition, knows the depths of its darkness in his own murderous intentions and actions. A constellation of images is presented – painting, the blood that is spilled, the sacrifice that makes whole or redeems. Caravaggio's painting will come from this deep dark centre, will paint humanity as if in blood and it will redeem. His touching – his reaching into the dark, enables him to see. McGuinness writes about Caravaggio:

> I took very seriously what I think is in Caravaggio's paintings, which is a desire for death, or desire for oblivion. His religion had a lot to do with that – the Catholic Church with the crucified Christ as its central emblem. That was how he explained himself to himself; that he was born to suffer, to die. And his homosexuality was a burden, another nail in the hand. His painting was the only way to get rid of that burden, his painting took out the nails. [...] But his dilemma is a common one.[...] Catholicism is just an explanation of that universal struggle; the fact that I must love and I must die. This is something that oppresses everyone.
> (McGuinness quoted in Mikami, 2002:56)

But while the darkness is pre-eminent in his work and is much in evidence throughout the play, McGuinness 'enters a dream consciousness in order to deliver a state of reversibility, proliferation and licence, where the main subversive force is taken from the rejection of negativity and by the preparation of a space for creativity and living' (Jordan, 61)

Caravaggio becomes the holy fool, the wise fool, who leads the audience through his own descent into his own darkness. It is a ritual enactment of a shamanic journey towards a retrieval of something that has been lost. The journey of soul-retrieval is done on our behalf. Through this journey he meets with the damned, and those traditionally outside or on the margins of orthodoxy or respectability. In facing the depths of his own negativity, his capacity for self-destruction and annihilation, Caravaggio comes face to face with all who have been negatively defined – all who are other to the dominant naming. In a Christ-like fashion he descends into Hell, and prepares a space for creativity and living. The programme note for the production included the following extract from Dante's *Inferno*:

> Our life's a journey and halfway through mine I found myself in a dark forest when I lost my way forward. Oh, it's a tough job to speak of that forest – wild and rough and thick. Just thinking about it puts the fear of God back in me. Could death be any worse than that bitter place? If I am to talk of the good I found there, well I must also tell of other things I saw there. Don't ask me how exactly I entered here, I was full of dreams at the moment I lost the true way. (Quoted in Mikami, 67)

The long dream sequence of the second act uses images of fluidity, and has a quality of timelessness and evokes a space that is not defined by chronological time. The whole act plays with the shapeshifting of subjectivity. All the characters are Caravaggio – the goat and the whore, his own mother and father. His sister Caterina appears as a ghost and plays many different characters, thus encouraging the audience to resist the identification with fixed roles. Caravaggio's child was born dead, his sister died in childbirth. The death/life, dark/light themes of the play become more focused in a mind/body dichotomy as in the following lines:

> **Sister:** Your hand wants to stop. Your flesh knows what will kill it. Your work will finish you.
> **Caravaggio:** It's wrong. My flesh is wrong. My body's all wrong. My mind knows better.
> **Sister:** What does it know?
> **Caravaggio:** Knows itself. Knows everything. Sees everything. Lets me paint other flesh. Loves it. Hates my own. Hates body. Wants body to die.
> **Sister:** Flesh had a dead son. (272)

The fundamental dualism between body/mind or flesh/spirit is evident in these lines. Whether this simply indicates that Caravaggio has inherited the theological dualisms of his time, or whether the dualism goes deeper is difficult to ascertain. He certainly seems to have a problem integrating his own sexuality. He appears to be able to glory in other human flesh in his paintings but not in his own life. His mind can be allowed to go on seeing but not his body.

The Cardinal and Servant enter the dream – roles reversed, (echoes of the rich man and Lazarus) and a hint of androgyny as the servant nurtures the cardinal from his breasts. (But then the nurturing Jesus would have appeared in medieval iconography.) The cardinal speaks of Bread: 'Bread? Do you remember bread? The smell of it? Fresh and brown, like the boys you loved?' (273). The Cardinal tries to grapple with good and evil and how one might reconcile them with a good God. It leads him to a prayer of blessing that is transgressive and startling:

> Blessed be the hands that anoint me with iron. Blessed be the tongue that spits curses on my head. Blessed be the feet that walk the way to damnation. Blessed be the eyes that see the same damnation, for they have looked on truth and found it lacking. I have looked on God and found him lacking, Caravaggio. There's nothing there. Nobody there [...] (275)

This is a speech that questions the truth of all belief systems, all statements abut God. It promises only emptiness. It validates questioning and criticism of truth systems, but somehow holds open the transcendence or the 'power of God'. The medieval mystic Meister Eckhart prayed to God that he might rid him of God.

The next characters to enter the dream are those of Lucio, Antonio and the Whore – his models whom his painting could not save. They have died from drowning, disease and hunger and cry out for ritual burial. There are echoes here of Anne Le Marquand Hartigan's *La Corbière* (Cf. Ch. One) where Caravaggio tries to offer his models the ritual and burial that he couldn't give them in life. Caravaggio has fed off his models – they have been his bread and cheese but also his genius and his reputation. And while he has brought their lives to light in his paintings, they will still perish in darkness – at least in this historical time.

The theme of home continues to haunt Caravaggio as his sister (in the dream sequence as his mother) urges him to come home and fill their house with sons. Caravaggio cannot go home but has to go home in the dream space in order 'to confront the personalities and perceptions which have locked him into a cycle of violence and damnation' (Jordan, 62). The barrenness of Caravaggio – as outcast and desperate has overtones of a Lorca play, where the barrenness of a character like Yerma has implications for the whole community and calls on the need for attention to deeper powers – outside of the Christian ritual and tradition. (In 1987 The Peacock Theatre in Dublin staged a McGuinness translation of Yerma.) Caravaggio's obsession about the sinfulness of his homosexuality persists: 'I filthy your memory with my sin. You know your son. He knows his sin. It is mortal. Go from me' (278). His inability to father children probably heightens the sense that death is stalking the play. His life will end with his death, there will be no line of succession. In his encounter with his father he develops this theme of death in relation to his painting:

> Watch me, father. (*He paints the air with his knife*) This is how I die. How I kill myself. This is how I paint. Living things. In their life I see my death. I can't stop my hand. I can't stop my dying. But I can bring peace to what I'm painting. (279)

The violence of his painting – with a knife – and the close association with death raises interesting questions. Death is an ever-present, encroaching reality, which cannot be denied. The Tibetans would speak of one growing younger towards death, when this realization occurs. Caravaggio's painting is his daily growing younger towards death. He is compelled to paint 'I cannot stop my hand.' The hand must tell the story as he sees it. Caravaggio's paintings must show how in every living thing, he sees his own death. Darkness permeates so many of Caravaggio's paintings and only bare hints of light escape in the later works. It is only in painting that Caravaggio 'could see and speak for ever without dying' (281). The father has offered a kind of benediction to Caravaggio when he responds. 'Then raise your hand in peace. Paint' (279). The stage directions indicate that as the sister takes the knife from Caravaggio: *Light rises from his raised hands, drawing Whore, Antonio and Lucio from the darkness*' (279). Caravaggio ritually moves to each of the characters, and dries the Whore's hand in his own, wipes the disease away from Antonio's face, kisses Lucio. The words of healing are poetic, ritualistic, incantatory. They call on the spirits in a ritually transgressive way. The drowned whore is asked to 'Pray for us sinners', in place of the Virgin Mary. The god of the grape, Bacchus, is invoked in praise and celebration of Lucio's body. Caravaggio dramatically calls the models from their frames as he stands in the fullness of his power as fiery shapechanging dragon painter that he is. In a final litany calling on all the animals and birds, even the mythical unicorn, he prays for the protection and preservation of the species – another transgressive moment that appropriates the litany in a fashion totally different to how it would normally be used. The prayer has pagan and deeper mythological undertones, as it calls on the dragon, the steed, the bull and the lizard. It continues:

> Hare, lie with the sleeping hound.
> Eagle, see with all seeing eye.
> Hound, play with the wounded lion.
> Lion, roar your lament of love. (280)

And yet there are elements of the prophet Isaiah for whom the reversal of the established order can herald the dawning of a new age.

> The wolf shall dwell with the lamb,
> and the leopard shall lie down with the kid,
> and the calf and the lion and the fatling together,
> and a little child shall lead them. (Is. 11: 6)

Through the dream sequence Caravaggio faces both his mother and his father and his fear of the dark. In going down into the dark, it is resonant of the descent into hell of the Christian story. The path to final transfiguration is through the darkness of death and hell. The religious imagery is particularly appropriate to the journey of Caravaggio who must journey into his own darkness, to the depths of his pain/loss/denial before he can emerge into any kind of light. His expression of the journey will be his painting: 'He called what his hands spoke and saw, he called it painting … Only in painting can the light darken and the dark lighten' (282).

Caravaggio's work is like the prophetic imagining that heralds a new or a messianic age. McGuinness appropriates this messianic

imagery for Caravaggio throughout the play. His appropriation of
the imagery of incarnation/eucharist/divine priesthood culminate
in this scene where a new age is introduced. The symbols are re-
distributed among the poor. The bag of booty from the cardinal's
house contains a chalice, a gold cross, a silver bowl, a red cloak.
They are to be used differently and will carry different symbolic
meanings. Their symbolism is no longer confined to the authority
of a hierarchical church. In the final moments of the play when
Lena realizes that she and Caravaggio have succeeded in turning
the world upside down, she raises the gold cross and orders
Antonio (in a mock exorcism) to take off his clothes: 'I command
you in the name of the Father and of the Son and of the Holy
Ghost to get your clothes off' (288). She proceeds to arrange the
red cloak about his body, posing him and using the props in her
own way. Lena reproduces the creative impulse of Caravaggio. As
she admires the beauty of her composition she calls on Caravaggio:
'Can you see us? It goes on and on'. She laughs – a laugh that the
whole play has moved towards. This is not polite laughter but a
visceral laughter that comes from the bowels of the earth itself.
This is the laughter of the trickster spirit, the spirit of disorder and
enemy of boundaries and definitions. This is the laughter that
recreates the world. The survival of the paintings and the impulse
towards creativity is like the cosmic joke – the final laugh of
something greater that survives.

The Passion of Jerome, Dermot Bolger (1999)

How does one understand, define, categorize or interpret religious
experience? What is the nature of such an experience? Where does
one locate it in relation to other so-called normal experiences?
What is the relationship between a person's psychological well-
being, their unconscious and the way they subsequently interpret
their experiences. These are some of the questions raised by
Dermot Bolger's play *The Passion of Jerome* (1999). Jerome Furlong
is a successful forty-year-old businessman who has lost touch with
his soul and is living out of so many lies that he has forgotten who
he is. In a seedy flat which he is using as a base for an affair, he is
forced through a series of experiences to confront his demons and
to face the truth about himself. Over a number of days, from

Thursday to Sunday, in the traditional Christian Holy Week he undergoes his own Passion as he finds himself dealing with the supernatural manifesting itself to him through the haunting of a poltergeist and the experience of the stigmata. In a state of near mental, physical and emotional breakdown he believes that he has been called by the spirit of a dead child to play Jesus for him. The play deals (in an interesting but ultimately flawed way) with the devastating consequences of such apparent revelation.

Pelletier suggests that the play can be read at different levels:

> It is the story of a haunting, a metaphor for the rescue of a Catholic soul from some kind of living purgatory as well as an allegory about a dysfunctional, materialistic society – but it is ultimately a meditation upon faith, mixing the real and the surreal, as most Bolger plays do. (Pelletier, 2000:254-255)

Dermot Bolger said that when writing this play he was thinking of the affluent Dublin men and women who were benefiting most from the Celtic Tiger. He wondered what could cause the most upset and devastation to their world. He decided that it would either be a tidal wave or the experience of God. He chose to explore the latter and wrote the play *The Passion of Jerome*. However, the image of the tidal wave may have remained with him, for his portrayal of what may or may not be the interruption of the divine has similar effects. It is an overpowering, destructive experience, which is outside of one's control, but at the same time is awesome in its mystery and power.

Jerome Furlong trained as an architect but now works devising jingles for a second rate advertising agency:

> I was too ambitious. The world doesn't need another second rate architect churning out warrens of apartments for tax break investors. It had to be cathedrals or burst for me, and no one builds cathedrals now except to shop in. (*Passion of Jerome* 9)

A successful but disappointed businessman who is an atheist and is having an affair with Clara, his receptionist, rents his brother's flat in Ballymun (where a fourteen-year-old boy had committed suicide), takes some cocaine and wakes up to a haunting and the stigmata. The question of what actually happened and how it might be interpreted is the subject of the play. The doctor's interpretation suggests 'Chronic fatigue? Paranoia? Schizophrenia?' (25). Jerome finds himself back in the same hospital where seven years earlier his infant daughter had died. In conversation with Rita, a Ballymun woman whose granddaughter is dying from cystic fibrosis the question of prayer is raised. Jerome feels that one would be better 'talking to the speaking clock, except at least the speaking clock answers back (29). When asked about what he believes in he responds, 'My own eyes ... logic ... reason. That objects can't move by themselves, wounds that don't keep re-opening' (29). He tells Rita about his experience in the flat and the dead boy leaning over him and saying 'Play Jesus for me' (30). Jerome's world has no room for this kind of miracle where these wounds might be the wounds of Christ. Rita's interpretation is to see the wounds as a sign that he might be gifted as a healer, and to validate Jerome as some type of latter day Matt Talbot ('One of our own who knew suffering.')

Clara's interpretation sees it as the effects of cocaine, perhaps exacerbated by business problems, along with a nervous break-down. Jerome slips in his own interpretation. It is God, The Devil 'or some manifestation' (35). But as he doesn't believe in God this causes a problem:

> God should be like the measles, a short childhood illness we can't get twice. He went out with black and white TV. But can't you feel it around you? Something good or diabolical or both. Something in this flat, watching us. (35)

Having taken a day away from his life he sees things with 'a clarity I haven't know since childhood' (36) and now believes that everything he's done for years is a mockery (37). Clara suggests that the secrecy of their affair and his guilt around it caused him to mutilate himself: 'There's no God, only guilt. There are delusions and drugs to cure them (38) ... That's not stigmata, it's neurosis you can't face up to' (39).

Jerome is haunted by the story of the flat in which he finds himself. He is also haunted by his own childhood, and his dis-appointments and shame around his own alcoholic father. The final demon to haunt him is his daughter Felicity who only lived eight days and for whom he has never grieved properly and which caused such pain that he shut down completely, not feeling anything:

> There was just a monotonous ache that went on until I stopped noticing it. Not even screwing Clara was an escape, only part of the same routine, life by numbers. Fiddle the books, fiddle the taxman, fiddle the wife. Fiddle yourself into believing you're still alive. (43)

In order to return to the flat and speak to the ghost Jerome has been drinking all day to give him courage. As he decides that there is no 'mysterious' explanation for what has happened he seems to agree with Clara:

> It wasn't some ghost I saw here when I was stoned. It was the stupid kid I once was come back to haunt me. Guilt and cocaine did the rest. It's time for home with my tail between my legs. Doctors, rest and another squalid secret to cover up. (43)

But the poltergeist activity continues, followed by a glare of blinding light to which Jerome responds in terror:

> Who's out there? Who's doing this to me? I never gave consent, you understand? I do not believe in you … I refuse … refuse … do you hear? You cannot just barge in on my life … fuck you, blast you, whoever you are. I will not serve…If you want his soul so much then come in for him your bloody self, because how the hell do I know how to bring him to you? It's not my problem, so why have you chosen me, Christ? Why does it have to be me? (43)

The second Act opens with Jerome recounting the events of the previous night to his wife, Penny. The wounds in his hands are intense, more painful. He speaks about the presence that he experienced:

> A radiance pressing against the balcony window, hovering like a sword of light under the door, desperate to reach him…Call it God, the Devil, call it what you will, but it was like a throbbing wave of heat. (45)

Penny suggests a psychiatrist. Jerome continues:

> I've never believed in anything…But all the time that crucified little Jew lurking in his tabernacle. I'm petrified, because he's after breaking loose, like a big brother stalking me… (46)

Penny suggests it is the repressed grief about their daughter coming out in some form of madness. Jerome ignores this interpretation and wants validation of what he believes is the religious dimension of the whole experience. Rita is the only one to offer him an interpretation that suggests it may be from God, when she suggests that he becomes a healer and begin by laying hands on her granddaughter.

Jerome's long speech as he tries to pray over the little girl is a key to an interpretation of the play. The wounds in his hands have made him aware of pain, putting him in touch with his own repressed pain. He sees pain as having no purpose and feels that the child's suffering is simply satisfying God's 'blood-lust.' He has a sense of wanting to atone for his life (quite an old Christian concept). He wants to take on the child's suffering (another Christian theme) in order to find some meaning in his own. His anger at God – 'You're holding all the cards, five bloody aces. You're winning hands down, so how about blinking just once, show one scrap of mercy. You owe me one, you bastard…' (*PJ* 58) reveals a lot about his concept of the divine.

The local priest who is quite realistically and sensitively portrayed advises Jerome that the last thing he and the people of Ballymun need is a miracle-worker with stigmata giving false hope to the hopeless. The priest's own vision is more prophetic, liberating and embodied:

> The last thing I need here are miracles. They're a nuisance, freak show curiosities. I don't need statues weeping blood or apostles' faces in wardrobe doors. And I definitely don't need middle-aged executives meddling with forces they know nothing about, […] I'm sorry, but what I need is a hostel for homeless boys, a stable for stray horses, schools for traveller children. I need a network of bogus addresses outside this area so that school-leavers can get called for job interviews. […] I need people looking up to demand their rights, not down on their knees before some mutilation.
> (69)

Jerome continues to believe that he is being tested by God, that like Jesus he falls and is whipped and crowned with thorns. 'I'm the hermit forced out of hiding in my cave in the mountains to deal with all the shit and the squalor I'd run away from' (72). While he begins to face his own pain he is still unable to hear or face his wife's pain at the loss of their daughter and the death of the relationship that followed it. He is more anxious to cleanse his own soul and admit to his affair with Clara.

The penultimate scene sees Jerome being attacked by three thugs while the spirit of the dead child speaks through him seeking redemption and release. The play ends with Jerome leaving the flat (his wife having left him) to start life again 'as myself'.

What is the author trying to do with this play? The audience is presented with a man in the throes of a mid-life crisis. Aware of his lies and mediocrity he is also haunted by guilt because of his affair, and is carrying years of repressed grief, both in relation to his own lost childhood and the death of his infant daughter. Out of his own environment in a seedy flat, with amounts of drugs and alcohol, he experiences a haunting and the wounds of the stigmata. An atheist, he nonetheless believes that he has had a religious experience. The legacy of a Christian imagining still very much underpins the work. A constellation of Redemption themes in relation to blood/sacrifice/atonement coupled with suffering and pain provide the backdrop for this play. The notion of a big brother God, freed from his lurking in the tabernacle, coupled with anger at a God who has all the best cards indicates both the God he is trying to escape from and the God he believes he has met in the course of the play. This is a punishing, demanding, violent and interruptive God, utterly beyond logic, and completely beyond one's control.

Theologians speak of limit situations where the individual comes to a deeper realization of self in relation to what they perceive to be the ultimate horizon of their lives. Limit situations whether of joy or sorrow push the individual beyond the limits of how they ordinarily interpret their lives. The notion of God as transcendent, ultimate, more, encompassing, transfiguring newness, can appear to come to the person, when at the limits of their human logical way of knowing and being in the world they are offered a horizon of possibility which locates their lives within something greater. The experience is a grounding and deepening of their being in the world, in continuity with their human experience but offering a depth or horizon that may not have been

apparent before. It may be extraordinary in that it appears as
something unmerited or undeserved or even inexplicable. Such are
the moments of grace or epiphany where the divine is made manifest and recognized even fleetingly by human beings. Depending
on the depth or intensity of the experience it may call for radical
life changes or reappraisal of one's values, direction, and priorities.

Bolger's play is flawed in that it tries to deal with too many
themes and is founded on a very narrow interpretation of religious
experience. It confuses the paranormal and the supernatural. Its
dualistic theology and anthropology means that the interpretation
of the religious dimension of human experience will always be seen
as something extraordinary, different to or certainly not in continuity with the rest of human experience. Appeals to others in the
play to interpret what is happening to Jerome give the typical
spectrum of responses. Either it is explicable in modern scientific
and logical terms or in older traditional religious ones. There is no
adequate understanding in the play of the human being as a spiritual being. The modern man or woman simply has no need for a
God reference to their world. When Jerome undergoes his experiences in the haunted flat he falls back on the inherited
mythology of Christian salvation and redemption or finds support
in the suffering soul mysticism of Matt Talbot as interpreted by
Rita, an older grandmother. Interestingly the priest who might be
expected to offer an interpretation of religious experience is re-
luctant to do so. His energy is focused on action for justice and he
has no time for such freak shows or curiosities as the stigmata. On
the opposite end of the continuum he represents the prophetic
approach to religious experience, whereas Jerome represents the
mystical. Pelletier sees Jerome

> travelling the same road as the priest but in the opposite direction:
> from the material to the spiritual; he had silenced his spiritual being
> after the death of his baby daughter, he had abandoned his child-
> hood ideal of building cathedrals. The strange experience that
> befalls him forces him to confront his inner self and hopefully start
> anew. (Pelletier, 2000:255)

The priest appears as a much more credible character. Jerome's
experience is presented in far too tortured and convoluted a man-

ner to make it accessible. Was the experience of the haunting a religious experience? A man in a limit situation in a liminal space finds himself face to face with himself and his demons. In a state of heightened emotional anxiety he experiences a presence that is interruptive, that calls for truth and a return to some kind of original innocence. It is really a question of interpretation.

Mrs. Sweeney, Paula Meehan (1997)

In her author's note to the publication of her play Meehan writes:

> I've always been fascinated by the ancient legend of Sweeney and his exile amongst the birds. It spoke across the centuries to me and, though I identified strongly with the cursed king himself, I wondered what it must have been like to be his woman.
> (Meehan, 1999:463)

While her first inspiration was to write a poem 'Mrs Sweeney' which begins with the lines 'I cast my song on the water./The sky stirs,/clouds are driven under the trailing willow' (Meehan, 1994:63), Meehan adds that

> immediately I'd finished the poem the thought flashed – *get a grip, woman, it wouldn't be songs cast on water at all, at all.* Scraping the shite off the mantelpiece you'd be. The whole shape and smell of the play came immediately into mind. A room came into focus. And Lil Sweeney entered. (1999:463. Emphasis in original.)

Based on the Sweeney myth of the pagan king who was exiled after a clash with a powerful Christian abbot who condemned him to madness and flight, Meehan's play is the story of Lil Sweeney and 'those who survive' (McMullan, 2001:83). Ann Clune in an article on 'Mythologizing Sweeney' (1996) looks to the many ways that different Irish writers have revisited the story of Sweeney, (*Buile Shuibhne* or *Suibhne Geilt*) granting it almost the status of myth (as with Cuchulainn or Finn). Interpreting the original medieval story (based on a historical character) in mythic terms is possible because of the multi-layered nature of the text, as writers try to find resonances and relevances for a contemporary Irish consciousness. Clune suggests that 'the elements of the tale that have proved to be the most important to contemporary writers are Suibhne's origin in Northern Ireland, his conflict with the church, his great anger, his displacement from society, his madness and suffering, and his status as a poet, particularly as a poet of places and of the harsh contrasts that characterize the natural world' (Clune 1996:51-52). Clune cites Nuala Ní Dhomhnaill's poem 'Muirghil castigates Sweeney' which interprets Sweeney as a 'pathetic failure who nevertheless has macho notions of his own heroic stature which are driving Muirghil 'mad' (58).

Ní Dhomhnaill, professed herself to be 'tired of the reworking of all the male militaristic myths and interested in the myths of the mother goddess, one of which she sees as a precursor to Sweeney' (59). While Sweeney was so often used as an image of 'poetic exile and creative inspiration' (McMullan, 2001:83), in Meehan's play he never speaks and dies in a psychiatric hospital, the year after the story ends, his bird-like existence becoming the inspiration for a carnival of costumes and feathers, which enable the women to go on, despite the madness of the world.

Lil Sweeney's story is set in the flats (Maria Goretti Mansions) in inner city Dublin. The place and time are particular, and recognizable. Lil Sweeney's world is late twentieth century Dublin where the issues of poverty, violence and drugs are a daily reality. Having lost her only daughter to AIDS a year before the play begins, she is now faced with the ongoing madness of the world in which she lives. Her husband (Sweeney) has a collection of pigeons. They have served as an object of transference for him since his daughter came home and announced that she was dying. All his attention and care has been lavished on the birds while his wife Lil alone remains connected to the daily reality of her daughter's dying. The play opens with news that his pigeons have been massacred. Subsequently, Sweeney retreats into a world of silence and dissociation, where human language is impossible. As the play progresses his only method of communication is a birdlike existence, which combines instincts of nesting, protection and mating. However, he still manages to adjourn regularly to the local pub for a drink with the lads!

This is a harsh world, but one where tenderness and compassion are also present. This is a community that faces at least one drug-related death a week, that regularly finds homes ransacked and robbed, and that lives with the violent behaviour associated with drugs and alcohol. The play succeeds however in witnessing to an alternative reality. The interruptive space created by humour and carnival allows the play to break free from its realist frame and offers both the characters and the audience another vantage point for the interpretation and celebration of their lives. The Second Act which is set at Halloween involves preparations for a community festival. All the flats are to be decorated with homemade bunting and the masks and costumes of carnival will enable both a naming and transformation of their lives through the space of enacted play. As another teenager dies the women question whether the festival should be cancelled. Mariah answers:

> We can't cancel. You'd end up cancelling everything. Let's cancel the rest of our existence now and save us all the bother.
> (Mrs Sweeney 436)

It is precisely this spirit that is captured in the play, where in the midst of madness and death it is possible to have hope, to believe in life and experience re-birth, resurrection and renewal.

As the play opens, two young thugs are ransacking and robbing Lil Sweeney's flat. She arrives home to the devastation and notices that Sweeney's trophy is missing

> his shaggin' trophy with the golden pigeon on it, Leinster Champion 1989. King of the Fanciers. Ugly fucking yoke. King of the Avoiders would be more like. Head in the Sand Award. Eyes closed and up to the neck in shite award. Creek with no paddle award. (399)

Lil feels that the burglars are preying on her like vampires – sucking away her very life's blood. As neighbours arrive with news of the massacre of Sweeney's pigeons, down at the pramsheds, the senselessness of the crime is beyond understanding, along with many other violent happenings:

> **Mariah:** Who'd do such a thing?
> **Lil:** Who'd beat up old Nedser Casey for his few bob pension? Who'd hang the Doyle's cat from a lamppost until it was dead? And stick darning needles in its eyes? Who'd rape Mary Murtagh's granny? (401-402)

Besides the tensions between people in the new flats and those of the older 'Mansions' there is also tension about what constitutes community development and who should be involved in it. Father Tom, the local priest is presented somewhat sympathetically (but also cynically) as someone with a liberating vision for the poor. The women show a certain respect and formality when in his presence but have no problems speaking very blatantly about him in his absence. There is no naivety here but a genuine realization of the reality of priests in sexual liaisons whether genuine or abusive. A cynical reference to the image of the Holy Family interrupts its function as a traditional icon and is reminiscent of similar questioning in Tom Murphy's *Sanctuary Lamp* and Frank McGuinness's *Innocence*:

> They're all at it. Holy families everywhere. What can you expect? You send those boy priests off and they come back up to their eyes in Christ the Liberator and the next you know they're crawling all over the flats finding us every bit as exotic as the Ballubas. (409)

The sense of the exotic will be echoed in the second act as the characters dress themselves as exotic birds in preparation for the festival. Father Tom feels however that he is burning himself out:

> Meetings, meetings, meetings. I thought I could organize the people. Empower them, you know, Lil, the basic Christian community stuff. Live amongst the people, share their shelter and their lives, release their spirit, direct the anger, fight injustice. I feel more like a politician than a shepherd these days. I may have to channel my energy back into pastoral care. (444)

While Father Tom speaks of the failure of the traditional Christian symbol system to hold the people's lives together (even in a less institutional setting), he is also aware of a depth of love and compassion in the community. However he also has power in the community. He has the veto on who gets the job as co-ordinator of the women's project. Mariah a former junkie and friend of Lil's daughter Chrissie, does not get the position, despite her own efforts to turn her life around and to make a commitment to building up her own community. The women are aware of money that is available for the development of the area but are equally suspicious of how that money is being spent and are critical of how many of the jobs are going to outsiders. They are fearful too of people in their own community whose vigilante attitudes are almost more frightening than the behaviour of the junkies.

Oweny is a friend of Sweeney's. As a counterpoint to Sweeney's silence, Oweny talks all the time. Almost like a magpie he has picked up lots of interesting pieces of information that range from pop psychology to new age religion to conspiracy theories about AIDS. As he has failed to integrate any of this information his interludes provide alternative angles that appear exotic and ungrounded but at least offer another interpretive lens. He remembers Chrissie's death and suggests that she too was like a little pigeon at the end.

> **Oweny:** He hasn't been the same since Chrissie died. It was watching her die like that. Sure she was like a little pigeon herself towards the end. He couldn't handle it all. Amn't I right Sweeney?
> **Lil:** Except he didn't. Watch her die I mean. He was up and out to those shaggin' pigeons first thing every morning. It was like she wasn't there, Oweny. Like she was invisible. He wouldn't even talk about it. (415)

Sweeney's behaviour is similar to denial consequent on trauma. The increased level of dissociation caused by the recent massacre of his pigeons, has pushed him further into a grief that he cannot understand nor bring to any level of conscious awareness. As Oweny contributes whatever happens to be his latest theory on the state of the world or the impulsive behaviour of Sweeney, Lil continues to board up the windows, increasingly fearful for her safety:

> Fucking lovely behaviour. The whole place is gone to the dogs. And everyone is cracked, or half cracked or doing a very good impersonation of a nut. It's no life, Oweny. I should get the whole she-bang cemented over. (418)

Within minutes Lil is offering sanctuary to her neighbour Frano whose husband is on one of his drunken rampages and threatening to kill her. Her inability to leave a violent and abusive relationship (even if she has done a Personal Development course) may come down to the fact that at heart she still cares about her husband, the way Lil cares for Sweeney. Lil is not willing to accept conventional wisdom that recommends either excessive medication or a psychiatric institution and fights to keep him at home – no matter how difficult he may be. Her problems are exacerbated by the fact that no doctor will visit the flats after dark and she sees no value in a solution like Oweny's which offers a bottle of whatever tablets he happens to have come across on the street. Her stance is essentially a critique of the traditional model of medicine which is not sufficiently centred on healing and which treats symptoms rather than the whole person.

Lil's memory tries to hold the past present and future in such a way as to be a container for the events which enfold in her life. Her inability to 'remember ahead to the future' (*Sweeney* 432) suggests a failure of vision. While she can clearly recall her childhood and times that have passed, she does not have a similar clarity around what the future may bring. This is not simply a desire to know what is going to happen but reflects a paralysis of the very capacity to imagine any kind of future at all. A sense of stasis and a com-munity besieged deepens during the first act and as the curtain rises on the second act there is a sense of entombment, from which it is almost impossible to imagine newness. The first act ends with Lil's recital of part of the *Salve Regina*, a traditional Catholic prayer addressed to Mary, that offers hope and con-solation. Can the traditional religious imagery and poetry enable newness as it tried to do in Murphy's *Bailegangaire*? Lil's sister brings her back a gaudy statue of the virgin from a pilgrimage to Lourdes. The cheap gaudy icon is so far removed from the power of the original symbol that it becomes an object of ridicule and is powerless to touch their lives.

The second act which takes place at Halloween evokes associations with the ancient Celtic festival of *Samhain*. One of the four principal feasts in the Celtic calendar, it was believed to be one of the times when the veil between the worlds was thinnest and the spirits of ancestors roamed freely in the everyday waking world. Samhain signalled the beginning of the Celtic New Year. Rituals of disguise ensured protection and the annual celebration gathered the resources of the community for the coming winter. A time of excess, and celebration, juxtaposed with the ordinariness of the everyday could enable transformation and newness.

In Lil Sweeney's flat the windows are almost completely boarded up. Sweeney has become more birdlike and lives much of the time under the table among mounds of shredded newsprint. As her friends sympathize with her plight in humorous banter Mariah remarks:

> You'll be scraping the shite off the mantelpiece morning, noon and night. (437)

which could be interpreted as a metaphor for what Lil does in fact do. In conversation with Father Tom she realizes that Mariah has not been offered the job in the local community and that she is going to be notified today.

> **Lil:** You could have waited until tomorrow. She did so much work for tonight. It's her way of staying clean. To have something to get up in the morning for. Have you any idea what it's like? (440)

Father Tom has been researching the options for Sweeney and wants Lil to consider psychiatric care. She is adamant that this is not the route for her and even manages a joke about prayer: 'I tried the few prayers, Father. I'm developing a particular devotion to the Holy Paraclete' (440). Unfortunately Sweeney attacks and bites the priest, convincing him that Sweeney should be locked away. When the priest leaves, Lil gives vent to her frustration, as Sweeney in playful mood gets in her way:

> Enough is enough. Did you not hear him? The drift of it? You'll be taken from me. Locked up. Do you understand? Will you get that through your skull [...]. Stop messing. You're fucking up me head. I'll sign myself in. Do you not understand, Sweeney? (447)

Her anger gives way to violent sobbing and Sweeney comforts her by encircling her in his 'wings' a gesture which captures the sense of entrapment and tenderness that characterizes Lil Sweeney's existence.

As the women make the final preparations for the Halloween celebration, the colourful bags of decorations contrast with the drabness of their lives. Stage directions indicate that they are '*an extraordinary assortment of colourful buntings*' (452). When Lil produces her own banner it is a magnificent piece, which is put in place and hoisted to the ceiling. Mariah remarks:

Ah look. Ah look. That blue stuff's from Chrissie's kimona. She loved that velvet dress. Do you remember she wore it, there! There! She wore it with that goldy waistcoat! Our docs'n frocks days. These are all Chrissie's things. She wore that the day we were thrun out of school. (453)

The patchwork of memory has become a symbolic way of holding together the lives of those who have died from AIDS. It functions like a container for the many stories that make up a human life and allows the memories to be held in such a way that the brutal disfiguring death need not be the final image that a family have of their loved one.

As the three women begin to transform themselves into their costumes of exotic birds (*Mrs. Sweeney* 457), each of them is transforming aspects of their lives whether it is disappointment, violence or loss. But the transformation is only momentary, and superficial. Lil tries to imagine the future for herself and her friends. It is a bleak outlook. Father Tom will have left for Peru. Frano will be living in one of the new houses, but pregnant again and still being beaten by her increasingly violent husband. Mariah will be back on drugs and Sweeney having been committed to St. Brendan's will die within the year from a broken heart. Her 'own future's a blank to me, a darkness' (461). In spite of this she is ready to celebrate and the play ends with the word 'Magic' (462).

The Lonesome West, Martin McDonagh (1997)

Martin McDonagh's *The Lonesome West*, (1997) at one level a parable for Ireland's North-South conflict, offers a Cain and Abel type exploration of two brothers engaged in deadly conflict amidst a murderous and suicidal community. He offers a model of transformation which shares the excesses and perversity of cartoon. Mick Moroney referred to the play as a 'manic treat'. In a review he described the play as a

visionary *Deliverance*–style hyperdrama of two fratricidal hillbillies, [...] Set in the same demented Connemara of McDonagh's imagination, this was John Millington Synge refracted through roughneck poteen and horse-amphetamines. (Moroney, 2001:6)

With the exaggeration and violence of cartoon McDonagh offers these two brothers the possibility of redemption. Through the suicide of a young disillusioned alcoholic priest he offers the brothers access to transformation. The notion that these two violent, childish, murderous men might be worth redeeming, or that suicide itself be considered redemptive, offers the audience a vantage point for interpretation that is disturbing, and one that upsets preconceived notions of morality and justice.

Two brothers Valene and Coleman live lives of desperation and poverty in the West of Ireland. Adults who have been too long dependent, (their father has only recently died) they are stunted in mind, body and spirit. Each resorts to violence under the slightest provocation for insignificant misdemeanours, and the stage is regularly the site for the kind of thrashing more associated with cartoon. Their emotional illiteracy and inability to communicate has echoes of Murphy's violent, inarticulate characters from *A Whistle in The Dark*. It is essentially an all-male world. Moroney calls it a 'murderous amoral childworld' where Coleman is 'the cowboy-bully who gets cheap thrills from sadism, women's magazines and poteen' and on the other hand 'the dank, unctuous, mean-minded Valene, fussing over' his figurines (Moroney, 2001:6). The one female character Girleen, is almost incidental to the plot. A poteen-selling schoolgirl who can curse as well as any man, she is in love with Father Welsh (or Walsh, no one can remember his correct name) who does not share her feelings, but is kind and friendly towards her.

Father Welsh, the local curate, is a disillusioned alcoholic who becomes maudlin and sentimental as he reflects on his ministry which has turned out to be far worse than he imagined. He laments over local murders and suicides, the endless fraternal fighting, and even the violence of the local girls' football team as he descends deeper into the despair that will lead him to take his own life. A level of repressed or suppressed *eros* haunts the play. The absence of outlets for the development and expression of a passionate life force, results in all kinds of aberrant behaviour. The accompanying loss of soul is evident in lives that have become stunted, petty and mean. Again similar territory to a Murphy or Carr play. Similarly there is the absence of mythic or religious narratives or any containers that can hold their lives together and offer interpretation, healing or hope. Father Welsh's suicide and the letter he leaves for the brothers are his attempt to speak of salvation. The Church cannot contain these lives, nor can he as priest communicate the message of Jesus. There is an unbridgeable gap between their lives and any healing or sustaining ritual. Funerals in the community are simply occasions for drink and *vol au vents*. Father Welsh tries to speak and embody the message through his suicide. His death becomes a performative utterance and perhaps the only way to break the cycle of violence in which the two brothers are embroiled. He dies for them that they might learn to love and forgive one another. Equally he needs them, he is 'betting' on them to love each other and free his soul from Hell. His letter becomes the ritual connection of memory that enables repeated access to transformation, if the brothers can allow it.

The characters in this play are monstrous, their deeds bloody and grotesque. The neighbours are a pack of vultures, Valene would 'steal the shite out of a burning pig' (*The Lonesome West* 2). A girl that Coleman fancied as a teenager 'got a pencil stuck in the back of her gob one day' and a local boy is remembered for hacking 'the ears off of poor Lassie' and letting him fecking bleed to death (4). When Father Welsh tries to suggest that there's enough hate in the world without the brothers adding to it he is completely ignored. Valene comments on the priest's ministry:

> A great parish it is you run, one of them murdered his missus, an axe through her head, the other her mammy, a poker took her brains out … (6)

The priest's inability to speak of God is heightened by the parishioners' refusal to accept responsibility for their actions. 'Two murderers I have on me books, and I can't get either to confess to it.' When Coleman suggests that talk of murders is pure gossip and that accidents could happen to anyone Welsh remarks: 'With the scythe hanging out of her forehead, now, Coleman?' (7) Coleman accidentally shot his 'dad's head off him, point blank range' (8) (because he criticized Coleman's hair). Even the girls' football team are a bunch of foulers (8) who leave the captain of the opposition in a coma in intensive care, before being suspended.

Welsh feels that he is a 'shite' priest, that he cannot get his parishioners to confess to their murderous actions, and that he cannot speak of God when situations demand it. The brothers are familiar with his reflections and hope that he is not having 'another fecking crisis of faith' (8). Coleman suggests that there are a lot worse priests than him:

> The only thing with you is you're a bit too weedy and you're a terror for the drink and you have doubts about Catholicism. Apart from that you're a fine priest. Number one you don't go abusing poor gassers, so sure, doesn't that give you a head-start over half the priests in Ireland? (7)

The horizons of meaning that traditionally sustained people are no longer functioning in the community. At a surface level there are still rituals that mark significant moments in life but they have been emptied of any real meaning. Valene collects figurines of Mary and the saints, like a child would collect a set of models or toys. When he finds them destroyed (Coleman has baked the entire collection in a very hot oven) he takes down the shotgun and threatens to kill Coleman. Father Welsh protests: 'You can't go shooting your brother o'er inanimate objects' (28). Lanters suggests that in McDonagh's plays language and identity are in crisis:

> Because the characters are confused about language, identity and values, they tend to invest their emotional capital in consumer items and in the concrete, unchanging reality of inanimate objects. (2000:218)

Father Welsh tries to offer a different vantage point for interpreting the violence and rivalry between the brothers. On one occasion he plunges his hands into boiling plastic to distract them from their murderous behaviour. His decision to commit suicide, while an expression of his own utter inadequacy among his parishioners, and his inability to fit into the 'murder capital of fecking Europe' (4), is also an attempt to offer the brothers an opportunity for reconciliation. When the brothers attempt to carry out his instructions, a series of apologies for a series of violent and aberrant acts of each towards the other (while taking a step back), it escalates into a competition, with each trying to outdo the other in his confessions. The resultant mayhem where Coleman blows up

Valene's stove and threatens to shoot him too indicates a return to the original state of relationship. But Valene changes his mind about burning Father Welsh's letter, and leaves it pinned beneath the crucifix with a small heart pendant that Girleen had bought for the priest. If, as Lanters argues, McDonagh has shifted the moral centre from the play to the audience

> the plays are effective only because they rely on the audience to perceive and feel what the characters do not. (219)

And while the characters many be largely unaware of the 'difference between the mundane and the meaningful, the trivial and the tragic' (219), the audience is not unaware, and can recognize the symbolism even where Valene does not.

Karen Vandevelde, writing about the 'Gothic Soap' of McDonagh, suggests that

> the imitations and echoes of literary precursors are so apparent throughout the trilogy that the playwright's self-reflexivity becomes ironical, if not subversive, and that this double edge makes it possible to read the trilogy as either a canonical or a radical text. (Vandevelde 2000:293)

She identifies his unique brand of storytelling as innovative and subversive in the way his writing 'constantly switches between reality and imagination':

> The fusion of a grotesque style, inspired by Tarantino and a melodramatic mood reminiscent of many contemporary soap operas brings about an unusual juxtaposition of opposite emotions, actions and temperaments: mercilessness and tenderness, love and hatred, dreams and depression. (296)

'We should not laugh', says Coleman when the brothers discover Father Welsh's Christian name, as they read his suicide note. Yet the audience cannot help but laugh at some of the most intense moments in the plays. It is a laughter that makes the spectators uncomfortable as they realize that there may be more truth than fiction in these plays, that the grotesque images of life in contemporary rural Ireland, (economic deprivation, murder, depression and suicide) are also descriptive of who we are, and were, behind all the closed doors of our past:

McDonagh's Leenane is a grotesque modification of what might be a reality in Irish rural life. The fact that this drama can make people laugh about sacred issues and the romantic myths of the West by no means alters the weight of the dramatic action. The absurd is a necessary detour to invite the spectator to look beyond the sacred and the romantic. (Vandevelde, 299)

Whether the audience will actually make the leap from the exaggerated realism of the cartoon to the perverted notion of transformation that McDonagh offers, is a risk that the play has to take. But parable has always been reduced to allegory or moral fable and the radical edge of disorientation blunted in its domestication. If the audience can genuinely experience the disorienttation, feel the affront to their established notions of right and wrong and what constitutes fair play, then perhaps the play can open to newness, and enable a radical re-appraisal of salvation and redemption.

Conclusion

In their introduction to *Celtic Wisdom: A Celtic Shaman's Sourcebook*, (2001), Caitlin and John Matthews note that

within shamanism certain individuals are chosen, by the spirits or by virtue of their unusual skills, to act as walkers between the worlds, interpreters of the spirit realms. (Matthews, 2001:1)

They also stress that the title 'shaman' was not applied by the Celts to their spiritual practitioners, that they preferred titles like *file*, *taibhsear* and *awenydd*. In the Gaelic, Scots and Welsh traditions respectively, these indigenous names carry meanings of vision-poet, vision-seer and inspired one. Thus the druids and poets were seen as the ones who engaged in soul-journeying and vision-making for the community. The druid was one who was proficient in the interrelation of the worlds of seen and unseen, especially for ordering the political and social patterns of life; he or she may have had the additional abilities of seer, judge, poet, prophet or philosopher.

In ancient Ireland there were many poetic schools, with highly developed teaching techniques and practices, which were only accessible to descendants of the poets. A text from 1722 refers to the House of Memory, which was almost in complete darkness, except for candlelight, within which the trainee poets were given subjects to meditate on as they lay on their beds or reclined. These houses were incubation chambers of inspiration and vision: 'the kindling of vision for both poet and seer derived

> from the inspiration of the otherworld and was fuelled by human need – these are the basic constituents of the quest for all people. (224-25)

For the Celts the otherworld was accessible through imagination, which was the burning glass of the soul. The vision poets were 'vessels of prophecy and inspiration, able to answer questions and transmit knowledge' (238). So it is appropriate to consider the poetic tradition as fulfilling a type of shamanic function in the community. The imagination provides a doorway to the otherworld or to a transformation of consciousness. The imagination provides the doorway to dreams, visions and ideas which are in turn implemented in ordinary reality. It was part of the poetic (and shamanic) function to enchant or to infuse with song. Enchantment is one expression of the move from chaos to cosmos in the establishment of a world. It is almost a search for a primal note by which creation comes into being. 'All societies need their gifted ones, their artists and mystics: without them, the land becomes weary and disenchanted' (225). In the Celtic tradition Brigid as the Triple Goddess was the Goddess of healing, poetry and smiths. One of her symbols was the cauldron and she was seen to bestow the nine gifts of the cauldron which included poetry, reflection, meditation, love, understanding and wisdom. Healing, poetry and the work of the smith can be interpreted along the lines of traditional alchemy – each engaged in a process of radical transformation. Shamanism is also

> an alchemical craft which uses the available ingredients of a situation, illness or problem; it diagnoses the cause and distils the remedy by directly accessing the spiritual world. (237)

Soul-work, soul-journeying, the role of the poet, artist, shaman – these are all considerations of the playwrights we have explored in this section. Whether their songs can re-create the world, for the individual or the culture as a whole, depends on the relationship between transformation, embodiment and performance. Creativity and destruction, salvation and damnation, darkness and light, violence and love, theism and atheism, madness and sanity, heterosexuality and homosexuality, rational and irrational, spirituality and sexuality, spirit and flesh – are some of the more obvious couplings in these plays. While the patriarchal aesthetic tends to think in hierarchies and oppositions and to privilege and value one side over the other, we need to hold open a new space for interpretation where the two aspects of the binarism are not so radically separated, and where they can interpenetrate and mutually interpret one another.

Each of the plays represents a different journey towards wholeness, towards some new consciousness. While ostensibly realist in design, the plays are radical in intention. The particularity of the plays allows us to identify towns and villages in Ireland (or by parallel Rome/Derry in *Innocence*). Whether it is the Ballybeg of *Faith Healer* or the Dublin of Matt Talbot, Jerome Furlong or Mrs. Sweeney, whether it is the squalid Ireland of the eighties in Murphy's *Gigli* or the contemporary gothic horror of McDonagh's *Leenane*, we know these places. And yet they could be anywhere. The soul-journeys are hammered out in the particularity of these embodied lives. Whether the performance is to heal others or to restore oneself, whether it is to enable one to go on believing in possibility, miracles or magic, the plays urge audiences and readers towards transformation. The plays urge us to hear the sound of our own soul's longing and to find a way of becoming one with the expression of it. Whether it is as artist, wounded healer, mystic or holy fool, whether it is expressed through carnival, parable or haunting dreams, the texts of these plays are poetic pointers towards the retrieval of soul. In performance they can become the containers for transformation and renewal.

5 | Journeys and Vision

Any truly revolutionary art is an alchemy through which waste, greed, brutality, frozen indifference, 'blind sorrow,' and anger are transmuted into some drenching recognition of the What if? The possible. (Adrienne Rich)

Journeys like human lives often have a circular or spiralling quality, where one returns to the place from which one started and comes to know it as if for the first time. Like the pattern of great mythic narratives in ritual contexts, the journey often requires returning to a time of origins, in order to recreate the world. Many stories from different wisdom traditions illustrate the paradoxical nature of the quest, implying that what we were in fact searching for we had all along. It seems however that the journey is necessary; the preparation, the setting out and the search, the encounter with helpful or threatening guardians, the befriending of darkness, waiting without knowing, finding what was lost and returning home transformed. Transfiguring the darkness and emerging with vision is also the pattern in the classic mystical journeys where the path is from awakening through purification to illumination or enlightenment. Many of the plays in this section represent aspects of a vision quest or mystical journey. The traditional containers for such transformative journeys have been found in community rituals and traditions. Whether these are the ancient shamanic patterns of tribal communities, great ritual celebrations where the myth is narrated, or the soul journeys of the great mystics (East and West), the human journey towards wholeness is essentially a journey of integration and vision.

What distinguishes the plays in this section is their attention to the realm of the possible, their desire to make 'hope and history rhyme' (Heaney). Theatre as secular ritual space offers audiences sites of transformation. Theatre now becomes the *temenos*, the sacred space within society, and the sacred container (as in traditional alchemy) for the transformation of energies. In these plays we find more light than darkness, more attempts at reconciliation, as the protagonists move from grieving to newness, from the wound to the promise. A number of the plays deal with the reality of war, and dare to face it with an alternative possibility (*After Easter*, *Pentecost*, *Carthaginians*). They re-appropriate traditional Christian rituals and symbols as a language to hint at newness. The traditional Christian Holy Week and the major feasts of the liturgical year provide the backdrop for the passage of time in plays like *After Easter*, *Carthaginians*, and *Pentecost*, or as a reminder of the place of remembering in *Una Pooka*. Many of these plays are not ashamed to seek the resurrection of the dead but equally are not prepared to buy into the traditional dualisms that underpinned much traditional imagining. They seek moreover to bring together human and divine, bodies and spirits, heaven and earth, often using the more ancient symbols of fire, earth, water, and air. Most importantly they invite audiences to look again at the question of difference, and how communities have defined themselves in relation to the other, whether that is in sexual, religious or cultural terms.

The plays here are invitations to audiences and readers to be-friend strangeness, and difference, in real historical time. They offer spaces to re-imagine, as they suggest different ways to deal with the past, often using the interruptive language of vision (represented through ghost (*Pentecost*), angel (*Prayers of Sherkin*) and visiting spirit (*Una Pooka*), to question received assumptions about identity and direction. Many of the plays identify women who have had visions (*After Easter*, *Carthaginians*, *Sherkin*), or represent people who are in borderland states (*Carthaginians*). Equally the borderland of madness (and/or personal disintegration) allows the energy of the margins to question the centre (*After Easter*, *Carthaginians*, *Pentecost*). These interruptive presences include Greta, a woman who steals the communion wafers from the churches to redistribute them in a gesture of reconciliation (*After Easter*), and Dido, a homosexual playwright who writes and performs the play within the play, that allows grief to be transformed (*Carthaginians*). Their presences interrupt in a manner reminiscent of the holy fool. They too are outsiders whose vision demands attention and embodiment. Their language is that of the poet, their territory that of embodied particularity, their invitation to tell stories, and to dream. But their real gift is the invitation to play. To enter the world of 'what if' is to allow an imagining of the future that is not a mere repetition of the past. A truly liberating vision facilitates engagement with the play of possibilities, and invites audiences beyond the paralysis of imagination and the stasis that is the legacy of a patriarchal ordering of history. The possibility of acting differently, comes out of imagining differently. Vision, if one listens carefully and intuitively enough, may invite people to move in unexpected ways (*Prayers of Sherkin*), it may allow one to leave the places of the dead (*Carthaginians*), or allow a new storytelling to emerge, that is connected with bodies and the earth (*After Easter*), or encourage a re-imagining of the relationship between bodies and spirits (*Pentecost*, and *Una Pooka*).

After Easter, Anne Devlin (1994)

Anne Devlin's play *After Easter* (Devlin, 1996) is a humorous, poignant, spiritual play about one woman's journey to repossess her soul and voice and come home to her own heart(h) and the truth of her life. It concerns Greta, a woman in her late thirties, who has left Northern Ireland and who has been married and living in England for the past fifteen years. Devlin in the programme note for the play suggests that it is 'a quest play', where Greta 'allows the ghosts to call her home' (Quoted in Cottreau, 1999:212).

One critic of a London production of the play suggested that it was all tangents and no centre, that it was many plays in one, linked by a character who was herself inscrutable (Nightingale quoted by Cottreau, 1999). Other critics suggest that the journey itself is the plot of the play:

A voyager within, and also beyond, place and time, she seeks the 'place of the heart' and time to relax within this space. All her journeys occur within the paradoxically freeing constraints of theatre. The pliability of stage space and time map the possibilities available to her. (Cousin, 1996:201)

The play uses the space of theatre to map Greta's quest and her journey home.

In *After Easter* we encounter a strong female narrative voice. In the course of the play Greta will re-discover her own voice and move from a dissociated to an integrated space. Her voice will be like a Pentecostal tongue of fire integrating the different aspects of her journey allowing her to enter the inner room of her own self as she shapes the narrative of her life. The voice that emerges tells new stories, and offers hope and inspiration to her child and to the human race. The fragmentation of identity in response to repression or trauma is much in evidence along with states of denial or dissociation. However Greta manages to integrate her personal narrative with others in the community and to return to her place within it. While reclaiming the lost parts of herself she succeeds in maintaining a relationship with the present, both in familial and social terms. As a 'primarily inner drama of quest … *After Easter* elaborates both the need for and the possibility of rebirth through suffering and self-confrontation, orchestrated through confrontation with the ongoing narratives of the patriarchal culture' (Kurdi, 1996:108). Unlike the male protagonists whose personal journey requires the dissociation from family, Greta's quest returns her to her family and her children. Greta finds a way that she can re-enter the community without 'relinquishing the role of the prophet' (Clutterbuck, 1999:118).

The play uses the language of vision and dream to confront the literalness of the age/context in which Greta finds herself. This use of the visionary or mystical allows the character and audience access to a realm that is metaphorical or symbolic and open to many meanings and interpretations. Ricoeur has noted how symbolic language which is polysemic and multivalent opens worlds and nurtures and inspires a passion for the possible. Symbolic and metaphorical language confronts and possibly confounds the literal-minded:

> The terms in which Greta experiences her spiritual journeys are those of her Catholic past. Though she has relinquished her faith, it is this that provides the iconographic reference points that enable her to begin to map the worlds in which she finds herself. (Cousin, 1996:190)

The re-appropriation of traditional religious symbols and images (Virgin Mary, Pentecost, Eucharist) is a useful way of enabling access to a symbol system that validates a personal journey but does not confine its interpretation to traditional categories.

After Easter addresses particular binarisms and dichotomies that confront our protagonist in the shaping of her identity: male/female, personal/political, Irish/English, sacred/secular, Catholic/Protestant, literal/symbolic, sane/insane. In attempting to move beyond the limitations of such binarisms in the quest for personal integration Devlin pushes the parameters of knowledge to include the repressed, the non-said. The woman as other to the dominant discourse (she cannot use the words in the same ways men do) is doubly or multiply colonized when we focus on the question of being an Irish female (Catholic) mystic in Britain. The subsequent journey home to the self through multiple layers of silenced lives is both demanding and rewarding. To have a female protagonist who journeys shaman-like into the depths of her own personal history, using many traditional symbols to guide her, to see her return to an integrated bodily experience of her self, is life-giving both for the character and the audience/community. When the journey taps into what is most repressed culturally – namely the female voice and its journey towards embodied subjectivity – then the community is challenged to re-imagine its ways of knowing.

After Easter offers woman a subject position, a new vantage point as meaning-maker, rather than simply being the surface on which many meanings have been scribbled: 'I'm capturing you with my story', Greta says to her sisters (*AE* 13). The audience is invited to collude with the same meaning-making that Greta engages in. Even though, Greta informs us, 'I'm not – supposed – to – use – the – words!' (3), Greta's story must be told.

While Greta is staying in her sister's apartment (Scene Two) a blood-curdling wail (9) comes from the bedroom where Greta is sleeping. Greta denies that she made this sound and attributes it to a visitation from a banshee. Later in the play, on hearing of her father's death, she will make a similar sound that she acknowledges as her own (58). Greta's journey is towards the embodiment of voice, which she achieves through telling her story. On the one hand, Greta's story involves coming to terms with her childhood experiences of love for her father and many beatings from her screaming, jealous, alcoholic mother that she tolerated because she believed her father loved her more. On the other hand, Greta must come to terms with a series of visions that have occurred over the previous fifteen years, and now urgently demand attention and interpretation.

Greta tells the audience that she always longed 'to be full of light' (20). This theme of light moves through the play and is used specifically in relation to the articulation of visionary experience. Two of Greta's visionary experiences involve fire and both her sisters speak about mystical experiences in terms of light. When the family seeks shelter under the table in their mother's house, Aoife remarks: 'You know this table isn't as solid as it looks. There's light passing through it all the time. Only we can't see it' (69) and Helen later recalls an experience when numb with grief she closes the car door on her thumb and spends the night with an ice-pack on it dulling the pain. She slept badly and she recalls how around five in the morning she observed

> wings and eyes of light were falling through the rooms. Swirling and falling and gathering, passing through the roof and walls. And it's there all the time. Like Aoife said. I believe it's there all the time. (73-74)

This play pushes beyond the literal. Greta questions: 'Is it my fault if people are so literal? (2). It tries to speak a language of possibility. One of the ways it succeeds is in its recourse to the rich symbolic language of dream or vision. Helen speaks about her visionary experiences:

Sometimes when I'm out of my normal environment or someone
takes me by surprise, or I wake up before I've finished dreaming, I
forget for a moment what it is I'm supposed to see and that's when
I achieve it. That's when I come closest, when I grasp the possibilities before the walls or the rooms I'm supposed to see assert
themselves. (74)

This fluid shape-shifting space is the space of vision and one
with which any mystic or shaman would be familiar. Contemporary work within the area of mind/body/spirit draws attention
to energy fields and energy bodies that support both Greta and her
sisters' experiences of the essentially non-solid nature of reality:

> Human embodiment, therefore, is not primarily a physical
> structure, but rather, a relational matrix, for which the physical
> body is a permeable container. [...] Just as the human cell may be
> described as memory with membrane wrapped around it, so all
> embodied forms consist primarily of creative energy that
> materializes in a vast range of psychic, behavioural, and creaturely
> interactions. (Ó Murchú, 2002:134)

At the beginning of the play Greta recalls a near death experience which happened to her two years after her arrival in
England. She and her husband had rented a cottage for a mid-term
break. Greta was feeling depressed, suicidal and very homesick:

> I swear to you I wasn't dreaming when I opened my eyes – I was
> lying out under the stars with the night wind on my face and I was
> so close to the heavens, as if I were lying on top of a mountain,
> that I could see quite clearly the star constellation. I was in such
> despair that I opened my mouth and let out a huge cry until my
> voice filled the whole sky. And I felt it leave my body and go up
> into the stars. I did. And I knew I had died that night. (14)

Greta's level of dissociation sounds at times as if bordering on the
schizophrenic, or psychotic as she hears voices and appears to
hallucinate. This may be similar to the language of the hysteric in a
culture that denies woman access to her capacity as a meaning-
maker (Diamond 1997). After all Greta does say 'I had no self to
give away' (15). As Greta shares the experience (that she has
denied for so long) she is gripped by a series of painful con-
tractions as if something is trying to be born. She believes that the

banshee visitation is a type of Mother Ireland figure, who is full of woe. 'It felt as if the whole of Ireland was crying out to me' (11). Her sisters' initial responses suggest dreaming, anger and guilt as possible interpretations as they have no adequate frameworks for interpreting mystical experience. Whatever the nature of Greta's experience, her sisters do not deny it. The society Greta lives in is quick to categorize her because of her experiences and the play opens with her in a mental hospital, with the question of custody of the children looming on the horizon.

Greta seeks out her cousin Elish (a Catholic nun in Belfast) for help in the interpretation of her visions (Scene Three). 'If I tell a doctor I am having religious visions, he will tell me that I am ill; and that is closure. If I tell a nun I am having religious visions then we can agree we are both ill and at least begin the conversation on an equal footing' (24-25). So much depends on the paradigm of the interpreter and the level of power they have. Greta continues 'You see I don't intend being locked up for what one half of the world regards as an achievement of sanctity. My liberty is very important to me' (25).

Greta relates three experiences of which she is somewhat ashamed as she claims that she is not a religious person (24). She relates the experiences in reverse chronological order (suggesting a kind of circular or spiralling narrative where the space is woman's time). If we consider the experiences in the order they actually occurred, there is one birth narrative and two accounts that involve fire in some way. The first experience had occurred the previous year on Greta's twenty-fourth birthday. At one level it communicates the crushing and stifling confines of a patriarchal religious inheritance. Lying in a sleeping-bag Greta has a sense of being in the womb. She recalls a priest-like figure trying to smother and silence her, and hearing a gentle voice in her ear saying:

> 'Turn round. You have to turn around.' So I did, I turned myself around and found I could breathe again and ahead of me I could see this oh most beautiful globe, a sphere lit up in space far below me, and I found myself floating falling towards it. And the same voice, the one that told me to turn around said: 'Enjoy your fall through space and time.' So I knew I was born that night. Or I was reliving my birth. (25)

Cousin interprets the beauty of the Earth in this vision as 'a symbol for the inner world that Greta gradually constructs' (Cousin, 1996:187) and interprets Greta as a time and space traveller in free fall 'beyond the confines of established spatial and chronological dimensions. It is an image that physicalizes the spiritual and emotional journeys Greta undertakes in the play' (Cousin, 1996:187). Many contemporary feminist spiritualities have recourse to the symbol of Gaia (Primavesi, 2002), as an earth-based Goddess, that stands in contrast to the dominant male images of the divine in patriarchal religions. Gaia as life-principle of creation, offers a horizon of possibility that enables the telling of a new story of embodiment, interrelatedness and inter-dependence, which is specifically connected with women's ways of knowing.

Greta's second mystical experience had occurred on 2 February, traditionally the feast of Candlemas or the Purification of the Virgin Mary:

> As I moved the candle to the fireplace and reached into the fire and then transferred the lit candles to the stand – the flame leapt. It lit up my hair, which at the time was long and I suddenly found myself surrounded by a curtain of flame. (*AE* 24)

When her husband clapped his hands together around her hair to put out the flames a strange cry came out of Greta's mouth. The chanting sound she makes is signalled in the stage directions. She makes a beautiful sound echoing the sound of the nuns as they sang the Office of the Dead (24). Recourse to the symbol of the Virgin – Greta has already claimed that she and others are the Virgin Mary (2) – or to Venus as her mother (2) suggests a search for a female symbol system that will support and validate her in her becoming. (Marina Warner's study on the myth and cult of the Virgin Mary draws attention to how Mary embodies many of the features associated with the ancient mother Goddess and how her representation shows many similarities to the depiction of other female Goddesses like Athena, Isis and Venus.) Later in the play when Greta's behaviour (distributing communion to people in the bus queue) is misinterpreted by the local press as a protest against the Catholic Church's failure to ordain women as priests, Greta remarks:

> So that's it. If a woman can be a priest, God can be female.
> **Helen:** Who cares?
> **Greta:** I care. It means that women might be loved. (57)

The third visionary experience occurred early one morning: 'a flame appeared in the curtain facing my bed' (23). But Greta turns on the light and the flame disappears. Greta later discovers that this experience occurred on Pentecost Sunday, a Christian feast day traditionally associated with tongues of fire and the outpouring of the gift of the spirit on the frightened disciples gathered in the upper room after the death of Jesus.

Cousin interprets Greta's religious experiences and her symbolic death experience in terms of Greta becoming 'a shamanic Christ figure. Like Christ descending into Hell prior to his resurrection, Greta traverses spirit worlds where death and birth co-exist' (Cousin, 190). Re-birthing, which is facilitated in many contemporary therapies, is framed and interpreted in this play through the re-appropriation of traditional religious language. Passion/death/resurrection imagery permeates the play. The actual events occur during Holy Week and the week after Easter Sunday. In the Christian liturgical year Holy Week is celebrated in the week leading up to Easter. It is a time of heightened awareness for the Christian community. It is a time for the community to journey the Way of the Cross with Jesus, to experience his Passion and Death, and to know the joy of Resurrection (to experience a kind of death and re-birth). The visionary experiences that Greta recounts to Elish have taken place as we noted at times associated with the Christian liturgical calendar, with Pentecost being the most noteworthy as it relates to speaking and voice. The spiritual or metaphorical death of the character Greta is counterpointed by the actual deaths of many people in Northern Ireland over the same period.

Elish is unable to offer the kind of interpretation that Greta wants. At one level Elish is jealous of the visions. After her whole life of prayer, self sacrifice and self-denial she has never had any such experience (27). Elish tries to offer protection to Greta, by suggesting that she become reconciled to the Church. This she believes to be a necessary move as Greta will attract evil as well as good and needs the sanctuary of the church for protection (28-29). The path that Elish offers – which incidentally needs a priest or other male mediator (29) – will involve repentance, communion, remarriage in the Catholic church, and having her children baptized. Elish offers a very bleak alternative: 'I warn you if you decline to enter the church it is your own business. You may end up as a fortune-teller in a circus or a fairground' (30). The church which can offer interpretation of the visions, and a certain space to contain them, is also associated with patriarchal authority and obedience. If Greta refuses the sanctuary that is offered (given the cost), Elish implies that she may end up as a freak. The culture cannot offer sanctuary or an adequate interpretation of the experiences. But the space of theatre can be a container that holds these mysterious energies within a secular culture, enabling transformation both for the characters and audiences.

As Greta attempts to come to terms with the impending death of her father and other violent deaths that are happening around her, she tells her sisters about how her visions are sometimes accompanied by religious messages. She tells of how she has been told to 'Take the communion out of the churches and give it to the people in the bus queues' (16). She seems to have no intention of carrying out the vision. However the following day Greta is arrested for stealing a chalice from Clonard Monastery and distributing communion to people at the bus queues. When she is released she tells her family that she felt 'compelled' (49), that she did it because 'I wanted to stop the killings. I thought if I obeyed the Voice it would all stop' (49). Her sister Aoife describes Greta as looking 'radiant' (50). Greta's re-appropriation of the symbol of the Eucharist also allows her to appropriate the Christ/priest function. In distributing communion outside of the different Christian churches she also invites a radical re-appraisal of the meaning of the symbol. Rather than looking on the symbol as a source of division and conflict, Greta speaks in a subsequent interview about the need for integrated schools, which might nurture respect for difference rather than foster divisiveness, intolerance and violence.

Memory is important in the play. Coming home in the literal and metaphorical sense is part of the journey of the play. Home is an ambiguous symbol when the past contains traumatic memories and the present offers no real sense of sanctuary or protection. The journey home demands facing and integrating the shadow. As family members, Greta, Helen and Manus each have to let go of the hold of their father over their lives. Manus and Greta have also to move towards forgiving their mother for the beatings. Their father was a Communist, who reared his children without the con-tamination of money or the bigotry of religion and nationalism. Each reacted differently. Helen became a capitalist, Greta a mystic and Manus searched out his roots in Irish music. All three have to let go of the hold of the past on their lives and also to let go of their hold on it. Helen and Greta, like two dinosaurs who don't get on ('Triceratops and diplodocus don't get on, did you know that?' (71)) must each allow the other to be, must give each other the 'power to create and free' (73). As Helen persuades Greta not to jump from Westminster Bridge where they have come to scatter some of their father's ashes, Greta imagines she hears the sound of a baby laughing.

> The magical place of both Helen's and Greta's is one of the soul, the centre of inner peace and freedom, indicating the real home-coming to the self, which does not depend on specific location because it is not determined by outside sources. (Kurdi 1996:105)

Greta's final scene (75) presents her as storyteller, with her child and the traditional empty chair. Her beautiful tale is like the be-ginning of a new mythology, a re-mything that re-establishes the centrality of the mother-daughter connection. The young woman (the daughter) must tame the hungry frozen stag, by feeding it berries from her hand, until it thaws and assumes human features, and everything begins to flow again. Jung and others often des-cribe access to the unconscious as initially encountering a frozen landscape. Where vital parts of the psyche are unreachable they are often represented as covered in ice. The befriending of these parts and often the taming of a wild animal symbolize the journey to wholeness which is so important for the healthy personality.

McMullan notes that as Greta refuses the 'dominant narratives of place and identity' (2001:86) and as she undergoes her symbolic deaths and rebirths, she 'finds her home, not in walls and a room, but in her own story' (86). This journey takes Greta beyond the limiting confines of realism. Greta's marginality gives her a perspective from which she can critique and re-imagine. The embodied space of Greta's re-imagining allows her to narrate a new story of origins, a new mythology, which focuses on the mother-daughter relationship, and the human relationship with the earth itself.

Pentecost, Stewart Parker (1987)

Stewart Parker's theatre has been considered in terms of a theatre of hope which

> endorses 'play' and builds hope on the fanciful. [...] It reinforces the idea that humour is essential today for the successful dramatization of horror. (Murray, 1997:194)

Murray identifies how Parker's 'whole dramatic aesthetic was bound up with a concept of play' (197): Parker himself believed that

> if ever a time and place cried out for the solace and rigour and passionate rejoinder of great drama, it is here and now. There is a whole culture to be achieved. The politicians, visionless almost to a man, are withdrawing into their sectarian stockades. It falls to the artists to construct a working model of wholeness by means of which this society can begin to hold up its head in the world. (Parker, 1986:19)

Denise Levertov, adverts to a similar function for the artist in a poem entitled 'Making Peace' (Levertov, 1988:41). She suggests that the poets are the ones with the responsibility to 'give us imagination of peace, to oust the intense, familiar / *imagination of disaster*' (emphasis in original). Stewart Parker's *Pentecost* (Parker, 2000:169-245), set in the Belfast parlour house, 'slap bang in the firing line' (*Pentecost* 179) of the late Lily Matthews, a house, 'almost suffocated with the furnishings and bric-a-brac of the first half of the century' (*Pentecost* 171), invites the audience through a type of 'heightened realism' towards such a new imagining:

> When we come to offer the audience an image of wholeness we
> can cease the task of picking over the entrails of the past, and begin
> to hint at a vision of the future. (Parker, 1986:19)

Pentecost draws attention to the power of the imagination to
imagine the as yet unimagined. In turn it looks critically at many
inherited ways of imagining, whether in thought, belief, or action
that hinder and hamper the emergence of the full human being. It
focuses on the dualisms and dichotomies that emerge from such
limited imagining. This play uses the resources of theatre to enable
the audience to suspend disbelief, to imagine 'what if', to face the
roots of conflict, to dialogue with shadows and ghosts, in order to
imagine an end to the endless cycle of retribution, that the Northern Ireland troubles had become.

Pentecost explores many questions around the areas of identity
and belonging, home and exile, relationship and barrenness, feelings and passion (whether accepted or denied) and the ability to
grieve. The inability of any of the characters to sustain healthy or
fruitful relationships, caught as they are in various repetitive
patterns of dependency or destruction, mirrors the warring society
outside the door. The way religious ideology encourages such a
narrow, bigoted and limited way of imagining is contrasted sharply
with the broad mystical vision that is at the heart of Parker's
imagining. In an article in 1985 Parker stated:

> I see no point in writing a plea for unity between prods and taigs.
> What use has piety been? I can only see a point in actually
> embodying that unity, practising that inclusiveness, in an artistic
> image; creating it as an act of the imagination, postulating it before
> an audience. (Quoted in Parker, 2000:xi)

The courageous use of the figure of Lily Matthews as a ghost
throughout the play reflects the same urge to push our imagining
beyond the realist frame, beyond the known into the as yet unknown. The fact that the ghost's story indicates an unhappy or
incomplete spirit, with a history and a life based on denial or
secrets never spoken, can symbolize the ancestral voices that haunt
this new imagining. Dialogue with these ancestral voices is vital for
the community in the now. While the present has to embrace the
shadows of its past, the ancestral voices must equally let go their

hold on the imaginations of the people in the present. When the present connects with its pain – loss, denial, and impossibility – then a new imagining will occur. Parker re-appropriates the traditional Christian symbolism of Pentecost, as a symbol to hold the energies that he is trying to release. The symbol in the hands of a new community (and not necessarily tied to any religious ideology) will pour a benediction on the people as the spirit is released into the community.

Pentecost is a kind of history play. The action takes place before, during and after the Ulster Workers' Council (UWC) strike of 1974, when

> militant Protestant workers managed to topple the power-sharing executive intended to replace direct rule from London with local authority divided between Protestants and Catholics.

Their strike included 'the closing of factories and the shutting off of the power supply and proceeded to threats to the water and sewage systems before the Unionist members of the executive resigned, thus ending the experiment in self-government.' (Richtarik, 2000:269)

The entire play takes place in the house of one Lily Matthews (deceased), to which four younger people are drawn, an estranged married couple Lenny and Marian, Ruth a battered wife, and Peter, a returned emigrant. Stage directions in the first act indicate that Lily Matthews' house '*in spite of being shabby, musty, threadbare*', has all '*clearly been the object of a desperate lifelong struggle for cleanliness, tidiness, orderliness – godliness*' (P 171). All the memories of her life are contained within this house, all her souvenirs, mementoes, secrets – a chronicle of a century, which embraces the personal, the religious and the political. The four younger characters (three who are thirty-three years old and one who is twenty-nine), invade this space, bringing with them their stories, seeking reconciliation or resolution. They, in turn, bring their personal, religious and political imaginings into dialogue with one another and with the ghost of the place. Lenny, a one-time socialist, who plays the trombone, has just inherited Lily's house and is offering the contents of it to Marian (his ex-wife), who has a furniture antiques shop. Lily was a Free Presbyterian, loyal to the crown as her many Coronation mugs attest. Lenny agrees to sell Marian the house if she signs divorce papers which she has not done even though they have been living apart for almost two years. Marian would like her divorce acknowledged by the Catholic Church – 'the one and only place where it actually means something' (178). For Lenny

> the church is beneath my notice, it's beneath contempt, if the church won't recognize my divorce, that's fine, great. Because I don't recognize its existence. (178)

The ghost of Lily Matthews appears for the first time in Scene Two. Marian has made a cup of coffee, into which she has poured a shot of brandy. She proposes a mock toast to the late resident. Marian is convinced that her mind is playing tricks on her when Lily appears, and refuses to be frightened. 'I don't want you in my house … I don't want you in here, breathing strong drink and profanity, and your husband deserted' (181). While Marian assures her that she has not brought with her all the symbols of Catholicism, nonetheless Lily feels that she is an idolater, and her resistance goes very deep – to what is inside the other.

> **Marian:** I've changed nothing. I've brought nothing with me. See? No Sacred Hearts, no holy water, not even a statue of yer woman – everything still in its place the way you left it, the way you wanted it.
> **Lily:** You're here. With all that's in you. (*Entering the kitchen*) This house was my life. (181)

The symbols that define religious traditions have a powerful hold on the imaginations of their devotees. The Catholic/-Presbyterian divide is one of word versus sacrament, where any Catholic attempts to image the divine are interpreted by Lily as idolatrous. The house has been her life, since she moved to it in 1918 with her husband Alfie. It was burnt down in 1921 'by a pack of Fenian savages' (183). Marian, however, identifies with Lily's dislike of her, 'seeing as the place where I'm least welcome of all is the inside of my own skull … so there's something we can agree on at least, Lily. I don't like me either' (183). An initial moment of connection between the two characters although initially denied by Lily, will give way later in the drama to a shared loss, guilt and an inability to grieve.

The second appearance of the ghost sees her still quite dis-gruntled that the four intruders are 'tramping your filth all over my good floors' (209). Lily's sense of insider/outsider is named in terms of filth. And she continues: 'You've been to your mass again, I can smell it off you.' The sense of self-definition is sus-tained by naming the other in terms of dirt/excrement/unclean. This perception of the other as unclean or a defiler enables the perceiver to feel morally superior, cleaner, and hence more godly. Such negative perceptions of the other builds barriers that allow a denial of the other's humanity. It is a short move then to perceive the other as more animal-like, as the next outburst from Lily reveals:

> ... look at this place, you have it like a pigsty ...are there not enough runty litters running the streets, whelped by your kind, reared with a half-brick in their fists, and the backsides hanging out of their trousers. (211)

Marian tries to break through Lily's defences by sharing some-thing of her own human journey, her own loneliness and struggle and desire for privacy, while Lily tries to drown out her request by singing an old hymn ('Oh, God Our Help in Ages Past') – almost as if to exorcise her. But Marian continues to speak:

> You think you're haunting me, don't you. But you see it's me that's actually haunting you. I'm not going to go away. There's no curse or hymn that can exorcise me. So you might as well just give me your blessing and make your peace with me, Lily. (210)

When Marian produces a child's christening robe from Lily's sewing basket we know that we are in the realm of the unspoken, the hidden, dark secrets that underlie a life. The text tells us that Marian found it folded up, 'hidden amongst your underwear' (211). Lily's denial of her connection to this shadow causes her to project her anxiety outwards and to name the one who has uncovered the secret as the 'devil', and 'The Antichrist' (211). The attribution of the title of the demonic to what has been denied or suppressed in oneself ensures that people will continue to persecute each other in order to keep the shadow at bay.

Marian's own shadow haunts her, the death of her child Christopher at five months of age, five years previously. The spectre of barrenness and childlessness also haunts the play. Ruth has lost three children, partly due to the violent beatings of her abusive partner. Lily's story of the child conceived, born and abandoned almost thirty years earlier unfolds in the course of the play. Marian feels that she is at home in the house because it is a childless barren house. She recalls the death of her own child:

> **Marian:** Christopher would have been five in August. Starting school. If he hadn't gone. Left me. Given up the ghost in me. My own soul left for dead. He was our future, you see. Future, at a time like this …what could it possibly mean – a future? In a place like this? (212)

The loss of the child brings about a corresponding loss of soul both personal and political. It also stands as a powerful metaphor for the inability to produce anything new or sustaining in the political situation. Lenny's account of the child's death voices similar feelings. The birth of the child had radically changed their relationship, they had become 'married lovers'.

> It's the one time so far I've ever felt one hundred per cent alive. For five months. That was how long it lasted … that was how long the sprog lasted. At that point he checked out, he'd seen enough. Maybe it was the prospect of having me as a da, you could hardly blame him … (205)

The marriage started to 'go dead too' from that moment on. No new imagining was possible.

Outside on the streets there are sounds of escalating violence as the Loyalist strike continues and the Northern Ireland Agreement is under threat. The outside is now mirrored on the inside of the house where Marian feels increasingly besieged. The house for her was a refuge, where she felt she could withdraw, find some peace, be on her own. She speaks lines reminiscent of Lily's earlier in the play as she asks Lenny and the others to leave:

> I'm sick of your filth and mess and noise and bickering, in every last corner of the house, I've had enough […] You find a refuge, you find a task for your life, and then wholesale panic breaks out, and they all come crowding in the door, her and you and that trend-worshipping narcissist. (224)

The conflict between Marian and Lenny is deep and the wounding repetitive and unrelenting. The lines of argument are familiar to them both. Lenny accuses Marian of avoiding facing her own reality, she accuses him of not being able to face up to emotions (226). Lenny feels that Marian is unhinged, having heard her talking to herself in the middle of the night. Marian urges him to leave her in the house: 'I'm staying here with my tongues – and you're going home with your trombone' (227).

Lily's story begins to unfold. An initial mirroring takes place in relation to Marian and Lily's age. Lily was thirty-three, (the age of Christ and the age Marian is now) when she went to Groomsport with the English airman Alan Ferris. After the affair she was forced to abandon their child in the porch of a Baptist church. She spent her whole life keeping the secret, torn apart with guilt, grief and fear of the wrath of God:

> nobody to help me, only me here in this house, gnawing and tearing away at my own heart and lights, day in day out…until I was consumed by my own wickedness, on the inside, nothing left but the shell of me, for appearances sake. (231)

At all costs she had to preserve the outward façade of respectability as she made her life-long secret atonement for the sins of her flesh. The tension between flesh and spirit is very strong. Marian senses how much Lily loved Alan Ferris, and tells her that he introduced her 'to the body's actual passion' (232) but Lily's religious paradigm will only allow her to interpret the relationship negatively. He was at first like a 'fair-skinned archangel' but in memory and retrospect he becomes 'a dark angel. Angel of death. Agent of Satan' (232).

The telling of Lily's story opens a new space between the characters where a new imagining can begin. Peter recalls a time when the troubles had just started when he, Lenny, and another friend, high on LSD, 'felt a messianic impulse, to slay these ancient monsters, we felt summoned as a holy trinity of the new age, father, son and holy ghost' (235) to take a stash of jars of LSD and put them into the reservoir and into the city's water supply as a solution to the ancient animosities:

> We could turn on the population, comprehensively, with one
> simple transcendental gesture, that would be it, the doors of per-
> ception flung wide, wholesale mind-shift, no more bigotry and
> hatred, a city full of spaced-out contemplatives like the three of us.
> (26)

Fortunately or unfortunately the reservoir had just been blown
up by the UVF and their plan was foiled. His speech echoes
Blake's admonition to those seeking religious experience to cleanse
the doors of perception. As a transcendental gesture it would go
beyond anything previously imagined. (Although there is evidence
that in the 1960s many interested in mystical and psychedelic
experiences considered something similar.) It seems that the ability
to imagine such an action is almost more important than carrying
it out. The parodic use of religious images in the 'messianic
impulse' or the new age 'holy trinity' accompanied by the energy of
'what if?' allows a playful new imagining to take place, at least for
the audience.

Marian recounts her imagined version of the sexual encounter
between Lily and Alan and how Lily's life was interpreted as a
punishment from a wrathful God for the sins of the flesh. Lenny
wonders what it 'was like here before Christianity' (238) implying
that there might have been a healthier attitude to bodiliness and
sexuality than what emerged in the Christian era. Lenny's story
leads further into this imagining and re-visioning the relationship
between body and spirit. He recalls a night when he sat on the
beach with a woman (out of her head on various substances) who
lay beside him naked, singing in a deep throaty voice the words of
'Just a Closer Walk with Thee'. At the same time he observes a
group of nuns going swimming, exulting childlike in the water. His
reflection leads him to see a profound connection between body
and spirit and a new way of imagining how religion before Christianity might have celebrated this connection:

> – and it doesn't take a lot to see that the nuns are experiencing
> their sex and the vocalist her spirit. And for a crazy few seconds I
> all but sprinted down to the nuns to churn my body into theirs, in
> the surf foam, and then bring them all back to the lady vocalist, for
> a session of great spirituals … and maybe that's how it was what it
> was like here. Before Christianity. (239)

Ruth offers a correction to Lenny's interpretation of Christianity, seeing it in more joyful, incarnational and embodied ways:

> You don't even know Christianity. You think it's only denial, but that's wrong. It's meant to be love and celebration.

The day is Pentecost Sunday which leads to a long recital from the Acts of the Apostles about the coming of the Holy Spirit on the apostles who had assembled in the upper room. The passage concludes with the promise from the prophet Joel which deals with the outpouring of the Spirit: 'Your sons and your daughters shall prophesy, and your young men shall see visions, and your old men shall dream dreams. This passage validates the dreaming and the imagining that preceded it and continues to open the space towards further imagining. It is assessed cynically by Peter who says that for a people never done calling on the name of the Lord that the province of Ulster should be the most saved in the world instead of the most 'absolutely godforsaken' (241). He parodies the group of them gathered in the house as a holy family. Inescapably bound up with that which he has tried to escape, Peter appears like a character from a Murphy play as he lashes out in anger and disgust at the iconography and the place called home, hating it and needing it at the same time:

> We're such an Irish little family, the strong saintly suffering ma and the shiftless clown of a da here, no damn use to man or beast. (242)

The only absence is the Prince of Peace himself whom Peter then goes on to imagine

> dandering down Royal Avenue … The Son of Man … in the middle of the marching ranks of the Ulster zealots, watching at the elbow of the holy Catholic Nationalist zealot as he puts a pistol to a man's knee, to a man's brains, to a man's balls, the Son of God in the polling booth, observing the votes being cast in support of that, suffering the little children with murder festering in their hearts, what would Jesus Christ do with us all here, would you say? (243)

The sense of traditional religion (both Catholic and Protestant) as having strayed very far from the peaceful ideals of its founder, and its contemporary expression as zealous, hypocritical and deceitful akin to the biblical Pharisees is also a theme found in Murphy's plays. Lenny takes Peter's imagining further and suggests that Christ would 'close down every church and chapel, temple and tabernacle in the whole island, put them to the torch, burn them into rubble', that he would lead the priests, pastors and people up to the lonely mountains and 'flay them into the rock, until the Christianity was scourged out of the very marrows of their bone'. When traditional religion no longer existed, a new kind of redemption would be offered:

> until the people could discover no mercy except in each other, no belief except to believe in each other, no forgiveness but what the other would forgive, until they cried out in the dark for each other and embraced their own humanity ... that's the only redemption he'd offer them. Never mind believing in Jesus Christ. That's the point at which Jesus Christ might just begin to believe in us. (243)

There is a sense in which Lenny's vision is the essence of the Christian story which traditional religious ideology has obscured. Contemporary theological interpretations of religion make many similar points in their hermeneutics of suspicion. Even within the Christian tradition, contemporary feminist and liberation theologies offer a prophetic critique of how and where religion has sided with the rich and powerful, validating certain experiences and denying or negating others. The call to a radical rereading of the gospel message has also led many theologians to critique the notion of religion *per se*, inviting a new kind of imagining (Cf. Ó Murchú 2000).

Marian urges Peter and Lenny beyond their anger, towards a letting go of church, priest and pastors arguing that '...there is some kind of christ, in every one of us' (244) which we either honour, deny or violate. The other characters are uncomfortable with this language. Marian continues to talk about her child whom she had called Christopher:

> Because he was a kind of Christ to me, he brought love with him ... the truth and the life. He was a future.

Marian's experience of the death of her child has taught her much about what it means to be mortal and human. For years she felt him 'like a raw scar across my own spirit' (244). Her journey through his death, set against the background of Northern Ireland and its conflict pushes her beyond cause-and-effect thinking, beyond blaming the other into a new embrace of a shared humanity. The child's mortality teaches her about her own mortality, and urges her beyond hatred to a space where she can begin to love the Christ both in herself and in others:

> I denied him. The christ in him. Which he had entrusted to my care, the ghost of him that I do still carry, as I carried his little body. The christ in him absorbed into the christ in me. We have got to love that in ourselves. In ourselves first and then in them. That's the only future there is.

There is a sense of indebtedness to the ghosts of the past:

> We owe them at least that – the fullest life for which they could ever have hoped, we carry those ghosts within us, to betray those hopes is the real sin against the christ, and I for one cannot commit it one day longer.

Parker's 'image of wholeness' enables him to move beyond an endless obsession or lamentation over the past into a vision of the future. This sense of re-visioning is also applicable to Parker's search for new forms of theatre that are more inclusive, and transformative. Harris suggests that Parker's expectation

> that Irish theatre might create harmony through shared experience is consistent with theatre's ritual beginnings, with its mythic death-and-rebirth theme. (1991:233)

and suggests that theatre's subtle effect on audiences is 'both cumulative and unquantifiable'. Parker believes that 'the play impulse can mediate and offer an alternative to continual sacrifice' (Harris 235), and in turn offer an opportunity for re-mything:

> The challenge will be to find a belief in the future [...] to inspire rather than instruct, to offer ideas and attitudes in a spirit of critical enquiry…and above all to assert the primacy of the play-impulse over the death-wish. (Parker 1986:19-20, quoted in Harris, 235)

Mary Condren (1989) similarly draws attention to the sacrificial myths that underpin Irish society and also looks at the gender ideologies behind and within such imagining. She proposes alternate symbol systems where birth not death might be at the centre of a culture's imagining and meaning-making. Frank McGuinness also explores the futility of sacrificial mythology through the destabilizing effects of play (*Carthaginians*), and allows theatre to function in a similar mythic way, proposing alternate horizons of possibility. McGuinness (like Parker) also pays attention to the worn-out symbols that cultures use to define and segregate themselves. He playfully explores this through the character of Billy in his unpublished play *Gatherers*. Billy sells religious icons and symbols to both the Catholic and Protestant community in turn, changing his allegiance as it suits his business.

Parker's work witnesses to wholeness and the possibility of redemption – believing that 'a farther shore is reachable from here' (Heaney). As Stephen Rea noted, Parker does not imagine a specific future for this desolate society, rather

> what he did in those particularly dark days was to imagine the possibility of a future at all. (Stewart Parker, *Plays: 2* Methuen 2000 *xii*)

In *Pentecost* one of his final images is that of Pentecostal fire, suggesting that Parker's work glows with images of 'light-fire in opposition to death-fire':

> Torch, burn, turf, drive, flay, scourge, expunge every old view, every old hurt, every old story, every old way of treating each other, until they cry out in the dark and embrace humanity, until they can move from pastness to wholeness. (Harris 1991; 240)

Such a vision is radical, and new. It moves from the wound to the promise in offering a poetics of culture that can begin to sustain a new imagining that finds expression in transformed lives.

Prayers of Sherkin, Sebastian Barry (1990)

Prayers of Sherkin (Barry, 1991) is set on Sherkin Island – Island of Winds, off Baltimore, West Cork in the 1890s. Barry's imagination filled out the scant details of his great-grandmother's life and what emerged was Fanny Hawke's story in *Prayers of Sherkin*. It is a type of historical play, which explores the intersection of time past, present and future, in a lyrical, quasi-mystical fashion, as Barry sketches the parameters of a sustaining vision.

The play centres on the lives of the last remaining family on Sherkin Island, survivors of a Quaker-like sect that arrived there two generations earlier, from Manchester, inspired by the vision of one Matt Purdy. Their lives are sparse and separate. As they await the dawn of the New Jerusalem their work as chandlers introduces the theme of light that runs through the play. As the community dwindles and the winds of change gather and threaten, the play explores in a poetical and at times mystical language, the kind of new visioning that will enable the younger people to find life and fulfilment. What kind of seeing is possible? The vision of the original founder is placed alongside the new scientific seeing with a telescope, and the fading eyesight of Sarah is placed alongside Fanny's own inner vision that calls her to a new way of being that will ensure her own survival. The Hawke family's self-identity and continuity will be challenged in the light of the arrival in Baltimore of a young lithographer with whom Fanny falls in love:

> this is a play about the transition between visions, states of consciousness, views of the world and of human destiny. It is an exploration of what it might mean to try to live within an absolute and self-denying religious vision in the face of the contingencies of the larger, changing secular world, and an exploration of what forces animate and inhibit the transition from one to the other. (FitzGibbon, 2000:228)

The Hawke family, the father John, the Aunts Sarah and Hannah, and the adult children Fanny and Jesse are the only surviving members of the sect. The opening scene in John's workshop introduces the values that underpin this community which include a deep pride in their craft as chandlers, a belief in the importance of cleanliness, simplicity and plainness in clothes and food, and a highly ritualized experience of life.

The original vision that inspired the move to Sherkin is kept before the audience through the appearance on stage of Matt Purdy as an angel. An angel, like a ghost, breaks open the realist text, creates fissures. The angel does not have the same powerful interruptive presence associated with other contemporary artistic and dramatic depictions.

The millennial urge in Barry's plays seems restrained and remote. They lack all the crash and bang of the American ones, the sensational violence, the grandiose emotionalism, the insistent angels, the apocalyptic flair. (Cummings, 2000:299)

But nonetheless there is still something of a millennial urge in Barry's work. Locating *Prayers of Sherkin* at the end of the nineteenth century is almost like a mythic return to origins, before Ireland's present day political struggles began – before Easter 1916, in contrast to Devlin's *After Easter*. Whether one looks backward to imagine a time before conflict or forward through telling a new story there is a similar desire to refuse to engage in endless repetition of the past.

The German poet Rilke writes of every angel as terrifying but also sees angels as 'hinges of light.' And it is this very quality of light that accompanies both Matt Purdy and Fanny Hawke throughout this play. The light is present whenever he appears, whether it is moonlight, sunlight, moving veins of light, or a covering of stars. The light can be seen by similar creatures of light. His opening speech creates the world to which the families set sail:

We embarked from the dark port of England and sailed to Cork in the whitest ship. There were storms in the purple sea and there were fruitful fishes, and the three families clung to the rails and found their haven. (*Sherkin* 6)

The darkness of the port is contrasted with the whitest ship. The vision calls him to Sherkin, where he is promised a space where they can abide and 'wait for the city of light'. John Hawke's nightly ritual prayer around the family table 'Lord, we are not lonely but we are few' (7) evokes their sense of isolation and the fear that the Lord may have forgotten them.

The play, while showing the tolerance of certain individuals towards other traditions, also draws attention to the notions of purity and separateness that define any religious denomination. An us/them or insider/outsider imagining underpins so much of the ideology that is the basis of religious segregation. The existence of sects like the Sherkin Island group is simply a more explicit form of self-definition, which requires greater degrees of separation and purity in order to continue to exist in an uncontaminated state. The importance for this sect to define themselves against the other who is perceived as either dark or strange increases their sense of separateness and superiority. It also increases their isolation and inhibits their continued development. The ability of the group to sustain such an imagining raises questions around the use and abuse of power. Whether a religious tradition can continue to hold its members together in a liberating way is one of the questions faced by the play. If fidelity to one's own journey (voyage) and one's own light calls for radical discontinuity can this in fact be a truer expression of the original vision?

While the Hawke family have a real pride in their tradition as chandlers their contact with the outside world is minimal. The Pearses who own the shop on the mainland and Mr. Moore, the ferryman are outsiders on whom they depend. Moore assumes almost a mythical status. He has a long white wooden rowing boat and is dressed in ancient clothes (18). His sense of wisdom and generosity, we sense, is learned from his work. His silence and knowing are gleaned from close careful observation. His contact with an otherness that is almost exotic is captured in his association with Valparaiso and his role as ferryman of the dead.

The new way of seeing (that of the technical/scientific mind) is very much the antithesis of the vision of the New Jerusalem. As Jesse watches stars, Fanny also engages in an 'irreverent' imagining. She imagines a stage with foreign cancan dancers, kicking up their legs, and revealing that they are wearing nothing underneath. Repressing either the inquiring mind or the instinctual passionate side of human nature suggests a constant struggle with what it means to be human. There is also a struggle with nature itself – represented by the gathering storm. Sarah promises that when they go to town the next day 'I will pass the ribbons. I will not put my hand in the ribbon-box' (15). Yet on entering the shop with Fanny she will exclaim 'Wonders. It is all girlhood here' (23). Instinctive tactile urges are so strong that even for this elderly woman they have not been overcome/sublimated. The aunts protect Fanny from her own sexuality and cover her nakedness with a big sheet when helping her prepare for bed. As Fanny searches for memories of her own mother there is a sense of loss of both the mother and the maternal function. But the night is Fanny's time: 'mine own hour that I cannot fear' (16). As the house and the islands sink into sleep her prayer moves over the waters of the world, invoking peace for the Ganges, the Amazon and The Shannon, and praying for peace for 'the darting fishes and the crushed fishes of the deep'. Her ability to be so at home in the dark and the prayer over the waters evokes a sense of the Hebrew Christian God of Creation hovering over the face of the waters and giving life to its depths. It expands the traditional male metaphor in suggesting a brooding maternal divine function. The darting fishes are similar to the fruitful fishes in Matt Purdy's opening speech. When Fanny awakes abruptly the following morning the first word she says is 'Drowning' which could be descriptive of what is happening in her life. She had dreamt that she 'was fighting in a waterfall of the Orinoco.' (Resonant with modern Ireland in evoking Enya's very successful song *Orinoco Flow*.) Later Fanny will be compared to a number of Greek and Roman Goddesses.

As the aunts and the children settle into the boat for the crossing to Baltimore, Matt Purdy appears again in the sunlight. He now recalls the darker element of his original dream; 'What was to be if ever there were none to marry? That was the dark figure in my dream' (19). Once again no one sees him. Yet moments later Fanny notices; 'Do you see the curtain of light hanging there? It seems to travel along' (20). Jesse's reply is to speak of the Aurora Borealis – the Northern lights that Mr. Moore has seen. Jesse wonders about how 'to measure such a thing' but Moore's answer stresses another way of interpreting the experience:

> You don't care to measure them, Mr. Hawke. You are leaning on the ship's rail. Your coat sticks to it with a glue of pure ice. It is the dark of the night, when the world is a whale and you are Jonah. Overhead, clear through the black spars, the wonderful sheeting of strange light. You think of your God. (21)

The reference to Jonah in the belly of the whale echoes back to Fanny's dream of drowning and also suggests a transitional or liminal space within which anything might happen. The experience of seeing these lights unites the travellers. But their interpretations vary. The scientific imagination reduces the experience to one of empirical verification. The religious imagination remains open to the totality of the experience. In response to Sarah's praise of his rowing, Moore goes into a trance-like state, (*The curtain of light falls around* Mr. Moore, *Sherkin* 21), imagining himself lord of the birds, and fish, grasses and dunes, for which he expresses gratitude.

Entering the lithographer's shop of the outsider Patrick Kirwin, Fanny and Jesse are introduced to a world about which they know nothing. Before he came to Baltimore Patrick worked for a newspaper, reporting on murders and other such events. The mystery and magic of his craft is in evidence as he talks about the lithographer's stone. It is almost as if it were quarried from the centre of the earth. 'A stone like this comes from but the one quarry in the whole world' (29). The fossils are 'little creatures held forever in the stone' which Patrick insists the world misses greatly. The pleasure he derives from smoothing the stone is reminiscent of John Hawke's pleasure in ladling the wax.

Outside the shop a singer begins to sing. Fanny recognizes the tune as a religious dance, which she performs. Stage directions indicate that it is '*a stiff, circular walking dance*'. Patrick feels honoured to have such a religious dance performed, seeing it as 'a blessing for my new life here in this shop' (30). The ritual nature of the dance is now transferred from a religious to a secular world. It becomes more of a courtship dance. As dance it stirs up the instinctual, the animal. Fanny feels 'as damp as a pony.' The bee that has been flying around is 'stirred up'. When Patrick attempts to draw the sting out of Fanny's hand he refers to his own hand as a 'paw'.

In a conversation with her father Fanny wishes that she had the opportunity to meet Matt Purdy, their founder. John remembers knowing him when he was young:

> But he was a man of splendid eyes. His face was as soft as yours all his life, his hair rose up in a pleasant mass of flames. He was a curious seer. Our perfect father. (35)

We note that the description includes fire, seeing, light, vision. It is interesting that so many people also see Fanny as light/-fire/heat or feel her force wash in on them but that she herself feels cold. Fanny recounts how on meeting Patrick Kirwin her 'cold body stirred, I was moved towards him' (35). John acknowledges her desire to be a mother, seeing it as a desire more ancient even than that of the nuns. But his belief system forces him to acknowledge how 'all present cities and towns are dark things, which light cannot alter' (35). While his work as chandler brings some light to Baltimore, he also sees children as light.

Fanny tells of her meeting with Patrick, of his pride in his trade, his buoyancy, his lack of malice. And even though he was 'dressed in the world' she knew him. Her father reminds her of their promise to abide and wait for whoever will be sent to them from Manchester in order for them to build a lasting city. He realizes that what has awakened in Fanny 'is the gazelles of life. It is the spirit of your children'. But for Fanny to marry Patrick

> There would be a tearing in you. To marry such a foreign sort, you would need to embrace more than him, you would need to loosen us from your arms, and embrace his beliefs. (36)

However he does not want to force Fanny to stay there against her will:

> **John:** There is nothing to keep you with us, Fanny Hawke. The four doors of the island are open. Walk away out if you wish or must. Ah, you could not return from such a voyage, but it would be a true voyage and your own.

Her father will only allow his own 'light daughter' to stay in her own freedom.

Patrick undergoes a type of ritual of initiation as he spends the night in the only hotel on Sherkin, where there is such dampness that there are fish swimming in the mortar of the walls, and fleas in the bed. Can he endure such an island night? Even birds that chance to stay there look dishevelled in the morning as if they had spent the night with Daniel in the lions' den. He will spend the night haunted by his vision of Fanny, wondering if he is right to take such a visionary child away from her island. He suffers a hellish night, on fire with love. 'Christ, I am lost for this bright woman'. He imagines the transformation she will bring. 'I'll be greater than I am. I'll be subtle, I'll be a real dancer. No one will know me. I'll get a shock in mirrors' (50).

Central to the movement of the play is Fanny's gradual awakening to an awareness of her own vision. This is facilitated by a vision which occurs on the edge of the strand, where she is walking in the wind and moonlight. '*Matt Purdy shines out across the strand, he is yellow with light and has his heap of wings. He announces himself*:

> I am thy grand old man, Matt Purdy, an artisan of Manchester. This is our strand, yours and mine. I know you, the little fire that walks through the house. (56-57)

He tells Fanny that he has sent her a 'lithographer out of Baltimore', and has also given 'him a dream of thee, that he may come to fetch thee' (57). As Fanny hears her name being called, Matt Purdy tells her:

> They are the voices of thy children. They wait for you up the years and you must go. [...] I saw a vision in time, that will not serve me outside time. I give you back to the coming century, Fanny, and your children are calling you.

The reach of the past into the present is raised throughout the play. The original vision should not hold people captive in time, caught like fossils in stone. The timelessness of the vision is in question here. In order for it to assume mythic dimensions it needs to stand outside time, and is not accountable to changing historical circumstances. If it fails to dialogue with real lives in changing times the vision becomes fossilized – incapable of sustaining life.

In this play Matt Purdy hears the prayers of Fanny Hawke. He returns her to time, (to a changing Ireland in the twentieth century, and to the many new children that will be born amidst the turmoil and Troubles). The time of the original vision has passed. This time needs a new visioning. Going from Sherkin to create a new future with a lithographer is fidelity to one's own vision in this new historical time. Fanny's own insight and vision is validated in her encounter with the angel. It gives her permission to go, but she still must choose. The angel does not simply validate the old: he also appears to a young woman, suggesting how much has in fact changed.

Stage directions for the next section of the play indicate '*the bulk of the town in spring*'. John Hawke sets sail for Baltimore with the

Easter Candle he has made for the nuns. '*The big Easter candle sticks up, pointing forward.*' The ancient symbol of the Easter Candle, symbol of the risen Christ, which will be plunged into the baptismal waters to make them fruitful is a great phallic symbol of regeneration and new life. These waters are both womb and tomb. As John sails to Baltimore, Patrick sails to Sherkin. He stands like the hero on the pier, shouting for a boat, and Meg wishes him well on his journey, advising that 'a city bed' would suit Fanny. Patrick envisages the time ahead when both he and Fanny will have become wilder creatures, when they have moved beyond the town of Baltimore.

> **Meg:** I? Not speak to the hero? I think I will speak to you.
> **Patrick:** Not in this town, I think – I hope she and I will be March hares by then, or April, be deer by then, be wilder creatures all wrapped and sitting up in a rough dogcart. (58)

Patrick unwittingly helps John Hawke out of the boat, takes the candle from the boat and then returns it to John – a symbol of the transition? On the island, Hannah and Sarah are stitching and we become aware that Sarah is losing her sight and is almost blind. The island is full of the sounds and scents of spring. Patrick has his arms full of flowers causing Sarah to question, 'Who is this person with the spring?' The whitethorn is in first flower, after the barrenness of winter. Fanny is out hunting for eggs. When Patrick describes how still the sea was for his crossing, he almost identifies himself with the Christ figure:

> It was terribly still. It is golden water there this morning, but glass-clear. A better man than me might just have walked across. (60)

When Patrick proposes to Fanny he tells her that he has 'dreamt of something' and has purchased a premises in Cork city beside the new theatre hall – echoes of Fanny's thoughts from Act One:

> **Fanny:** The theatre hall?
> **Patrick:** Over the shop are two entire floors, for a house of children. A spring-cleaning. A new start. (62)

He invites her to come with him to Cork city. Stage directions indicate that Fanny *gathers words to speak, opens her mouth, but only gabbles.* Finally '*She makes her leap of faith*' and agrees to come with him, saying 'Yes. I will go from my family like a dreamer, and wake in the new world' (62). The depth of her father's reaction is initially captured in his conversation with Jesse as he touches the wax, saying, 'A work is enough to hold our world' (65).

Sarah's sight fades as Fanny's own sight (vision) improves. Sarah with her girlhood dreams of ribbons and fine material no longer needs anything 'so extravagant as eyes', on the island. She leaves the house in the fading light to collect shells for Fanny, as she had done for her mother, when she had left the island, in death. As the family prepares for their final evening prayer, John talks about the island, and its hopeful farms. While the strand is peaceful a storm is brewing far out to sea, where 'nothing breaks the wild surface of the storm there but dolphins and angels'. He addresses Fanny:

> Do you go easily? You do not at all. You go like our father's dolphins, breaking into the stormy air. You will need all your muscles. (67)

As John prays for peace for the family he also prays for the 'silence and the storm of Sherkin'. But he gets into difficulties, cannot speak with emotion. Hannah prepares Fanny to leave, realizing how old she is herself and how her future expectations involve waiting for the joyful resurrection of all the women who have died. In the case is a mirror that belonged to Fanny's mother, suggesting a new seeing, a mirroring, a way of being where vanity about appearance is not dark or sinful. 'The river of light flows despite many a curiosity.'

John's parting gift to Fanny is the celebratory memory of her birth that he recalls in a most poignant speech:

> There was a singing in the wind and all full of your name, Fanny Hawke, Fanny Hawke, and I that never could dance could dance that day, and I danced, and shook out my legs.[…] Remember these things, Fanny. (68-69)

The beauty of the physical moment of birth and the transformation it brought about in John Hawke is similar to the transformation in Patrick in his love for Fanny. Both men are liberated into the space of dance – a ritual beyond words that perhaps puts them in touch with some otherness. As John urges Fanny to remember these things the depth of his sadness is evident in that he can never call her daughter again, nor see her children, and yet he wants to share this gift with her.

The closing scene between Fanny and Sarah shows both women faithful to their own paths. Sarah wonders if Fanny would take her with her, but instead chooses to stay:

> No. This is my path here. (*Going purposefully forward*) Now I will go along it. (*Turning to her*) May your own journey be as safe and bright, my love. (70)

Fanny walks between the darkening hedges, calls Eoghan, the fisherman to take her over to Baltimore in 'this falling dark.' As she sets sail John's light diminishes and Patrick's light increases with each splash of the oars.

Prayers of Sherkin is a tender, poignant play about change and vision. Its movement is framed and punctuated by different kinds of prayers. It succeeds in affirming and valuing different spiritualities in their historical time and manages to portray individuals with compassion for otherness, despite the negative heritage of religion and ideology. As the characters make their own journeys Barry is aware of the cost of following one's own vision but also aware of knowing when it is time to let go of an old vision that is no longer sustaining. Barry as poet expresses his meaning 'in the imagery as much as in the argument of the play' (FitzGibbon, 2000:226).

> Fanny's step from island to mainland is a step from one view of the world to another, from the transcendent to the contingent, and it is only one stage of a dialectic that shapes and unifies the play. [...] Through his imagery he broadens out the meaning of the play and shifts the focus to different kinds of migration – from one community to another, from one vision to another. (227)

The play can be seen as a metaphor for Irish social culture that has been negotiating similar transitions. In a sense Barry is mapping that transition in his work. 'All of Barry's characters speak a rich, lyrical language that renders their experience with poignancy and grace. This is precisely what makes the millennial urge in Barry's work so palpable as if the form of the play itself was fomenting the peace that the characters yearn for, if not now then in a world to come' (Cummings, 2000:300). And while this play does not deal directly with issues like North-South conflict 'their millennial urge to break free of the past would seem to stem in part from his response to the turbulent times in which he lives'.

For all their separateness and isolation the families who were faithful to the original vision were profoundly connected with the earth, the seasons, family and craft and the ritual celebration of this. John Hawke's wonderful recollection of the day of Fanny's birth, when 'I that never could dance could dance that day', is a grounded spirituality. Rooted in bodies and birth it leads to the bodily expression of joy in dance which is a powerful evocation of the vision of the heavenly Jerusalem where the lame walk and cripples dance and the impossible is possible. This is the vision John Hawke leaves to Fanny, that a future is possible, in this world, where she will be surrounded by her children and her husband too will dance for joy. In theological terms we are speaking of a realized eschatology – the future has begun.

Una Pooka, Michael Harding (1989)

In his author's note for *Una Pooka* Harding wrote about how central memory is to Christian identity. His interest however shifts remembering to the alternate sacred space of theatre and highlights the inability of the traditional vision to sustain any kind of new imagining. Set in 1979, at the time of the Papal visit to Ireland (a time of great religious fervour and hysteria), Harding's play is a strangely haunting psychodrama which explores the legacy of a patriarchal religious sensibility that is misogynist, disconnected from history, and fearful of the body. Incapacity for and violence in intimate relationships, alongside a more ancient and primitive spirituality provide the backdrop for the play. Its fluid sense of time as it shifts and retraces, the doubling of roles, the presence of ghosts, talk of the Pooka Man, possession and changelings, suggest the space of the repressed, the unconscious or dream, a territory developed in Harding's other works. If theatre is a gateway for the unspeakable to reach the community (Harding quoted in Grant, 1991:47), *Una Pooka* certainly plays its part in uncovering hidden or repressed aspects of the Irish cultural unconscious and bringing them into the light. Where the traditional religious remembering that characterizes the Christian Holy Week is situated between the triumphal entry of Jesus into Jerusalem (Palm Sunday) and the stark reality of crucifixion (Good Friday), Harding remarks that:

> In 1979 we in Ireland, I believe, rooted ourselves too firmly in the unfurled banners of Palm Sunday. We cheered and swooned, and in the end, were ill-prepared for the absurd and macabre nightmare that has been an aspect of our being in the world since.
>
> Statues moving – serial hunger strikes – death by ritual – Enniskillen and all its works – the venomous political feuding over private morality and the civil law. (Harding, Author's Note to *Una Pooka*, 1990:164)

Harding's play is a 'journey out beyond the walls of political and religious righteousness, out beyond the fancy painted streets, into the dark solitude of death and silence'. Similar in ways to McGuinness's *Carthaginians* the play leads audiences 'into the terrible unease where faith is measured by despair' and where 'even God … is silent':

> It is the dream in which Palm Sunday meets Good Friday that finds implicit remembrance in *Una Pooka*. Just as the church constantly reaffirms its identity in remembering the Truth of its original Event, so Theatre at certain times can have no higher function than to be faithful, both actors and audience, in remembering the interior truth of specific historical events which bear upon the ground of our being, and touch upon the ground of our anxieties, even in the present.
>
> The play […] attempts to catch in some small way, that interior dream, that moment of human frailty when we look for signs and certainties, only to end up discovering that all the while, we were looking in the wrong direction. (164)

The play opens on the eve of the Papal visit in the Dublin Council home of Aidan and Nuala Kevitt. Aidan's mother, Mrs Kevitt, his brother Liam and sister Una have travelled from the country to stay the night. Father Simeon, a family relative (whom no one seems to have met before) also joins them. Stage directions indicate that 'a naturalistic set is not recommended' (Harding, *First Run 2*, 1990:165). Family tensions, marital problems, the child-ishness and emotional illiteracy of the men, a dominating mother, an all-pervading soul-destroying version of Catholicism and a mysterious otherworldly visitor provide a backdrop for the unfolding events of the play. Very shortly into the first act the first time shift occurs and we find Una and Angelo (The Pooka Man) in conversation (a month later) about what happened on the night. The sense of what happened or what didn't happen brings us into the imaginative or dream space of theatre. A violent death occurred, but we are misled until the closing scenes as to who it was that actually died. Whether Father Simeon did arrive on the night is in question. Is Angelo also Father Simeon or a projection of the unconscious, in particular, the expression of a frustrated, unlived female life? The play takes place in a liminal or threshold space where the conscious and unconscious worlds blur and overlap. In suspending disbelief (or over-dependence on the rational) the audience is invited to make meaning from the hints, wishes, fantasies and desires of the unconscious mind as it becomes a gateway for the unspeakable.

Harding once said in an interview that 'theatre isn't just packaged nostalgia' (Harding in conversation with Grant, 1991:47). In *Una Pooka* he explores the nostalgic longings that accompany the papal visit and the expectations that the visit will make everything different, or bring Irish Catholics back to the sacraments, in some way restoring a lost harmony. These nostalgic desires are matched by the contemporary reality of violence within marriage, inability to communicate, denial and lies, undertones of sexual impropriety and a religious practice that is superficial, or hypocritical, full of platitudes or nonexistent. Harding offers a critique of the debilitating effects of a patriarchal religion. Catholicism as it is practised keeps people in a state of perpetual childishness. Aidan plans to go to the Phoenix park as a Boy Scout Leader, wearing his uniform shorts, which Nuala wears in parody in the first act (*UP* 179). She tells Una about Aidan's obsessive behaviour around the Pope's visit:

> And then he has this big idea that the country is going to be different. Afterwards. When the Pope is gone. Everybody is suddenly going to be good, and perfect, and holy, just like the Boy Scouts. (183)

Nuala suggests that the Pope ('That yeti. That misogynist') is like a 'big Daddy to the lot of them' and that Aidan is more like a child than a man (203). Mrs Kevitt continually tries to influence and oversee the religious practice of her offspring, while subscribing to a traditional conservative (and somewhat miserable) Catholicism, that is not open to change. Her behaviour as mother is also reflective of the cultural crisis adverted to by Irigaray, where failure to symbolize the mother-daughter relationship sufficiently means that women are forever competing for the unique place occupied by the mother (Whitford, 1991:88-89).

Una wants to believe that her

> family are normal, happy, content ordinary people [...] We're not the kind of people who suddenly decide to go into the toilet and commit suicide. We might suffer a bit of stress now and then, but we handle it. We don't go and drown ourselves. (178)

The play pushes beyond simple exposure of small-town hypocrisies to an underlying despair that cannot even be acknowledged let alone spoken. While Harding's later play *Misogynist* (cf. Chapter Two) explores more fully the misogyny that underlies a patriarchal culture, similar themes are to be found in *Una Pooka*. As Aidan and Nuala's marriage crisis deepens and they stop having sex, she is blamed for infertility (despite having had all the tests), and there are indications of physical and emotional violence that push Nuala closer to the edge.

There are many references to Nuala being possessed, interpreted as a witch, or being seen as a slut. The tendency to demonize the female because of her sexuality or growing self-awareness (or dissatisfaction) finds expression in the symbol of 'the witch', that 'free-floating anxiety symbol of diabolic femaleness' (Radford Ruether, 1975:101). Aidan says that his wife has changed since he first met her (he was her teacher), that she has stopped going to Mass and has become a vegetarian, that she reads Astrology books and Tarot cards and has dreams that she takes seriously. He also feels that she doesn't believe that he wasn't guilty of some kind of sexual impropriety when he accidentally entered the women's showers when one of the fifth year students was showering. He says to Father Simeon/Angelo: 'I'm telling you that my wife is a witch. My wife is dead. That is a shell upstairs. Possessed by something that wants to destroy me' (199). There are echoes here of the tragic story of Bridget Cleary, a young financially independent married woman who was burned to death because her husband and relatives believed that the real Bridget Cleary had been taken away by the fairies and someone else left in her place (Bourke, 1999). Aidan blames his wife for things that have been happening in the house – a projection that enables him to evade responsibility and not face up to the reality of the breakdown in relationship, both with Nuala and within his own family.

As Una engages in a lengthy conversation with Angelo in the second act, she remarks that he (Angelo) is evil and he answers:

> No just showing you what you're afraid to look at yourself. Sometimes, when people are afraid of truth, they call it evil – to protect themselves. (226)

Angelo speaks the truth of Una's life, indicating the problems that will arise from marrying a man for whom she has no feeling:

> **Una:** I have no choice.
> **Angelo:** You have.
> **Una:** How?
> **Angelo:** You could be so passionate.
> **Una:** With the right person. With a real man. I could I could I could...
> **Angelo:** Open the floodgates ... burst. Your body is like a dry land. It needs rain. Monsoons. It needs to be washed back to life. (229)

While the conversations with the Pooka Man are placed after Una's death, the chronology seems unimportant. In the fluid space of the unconscious, time is seamless. Una is trying to come to terms with her own death, and her own life. No matter how hard she tried she was unable to escape, to break free, even in conjuring up a love affair with the passionate and dangerous Pooka Man. She could imagine but not effect change, being hampered by her brothers' dismissive and scathing opinions of her, their ultimate power of dispossession (they could throw her out of the family home), and her mother's rejection of her spirit of defiance. The Pooka Man offers her one last chance:

> It's your life, Una. Your one, single, precious life. You could still get out you know. You could still get out that door. (234)

Instead she chooses suicide. Nuala on the other hand manages to escape her brutal marriage and has already left for America:

> As to the 'interior dream' Harding speaks of, that is at the heart of the mystery: a terrain where the Pooka from Irish folklore holds dangerous sway. Decoding, one might say that for Harding the Pope's visit to Ireland [...] was a step in the wrong direction for the Irish who need to listen instead to the Unas of this world, and in Beckett's phrase, 'all the dead voices'. (Murray 1997:235)

When one considers the supernatural in the Irish tradition, the nexus of symbols associated with it are those of the other. The otherworld is the world of the dark, the hidden, what is feared, demonized and other – the world traditionally associated with the female. Harding's foregrounding of these in such an original way challenges audiences to confront their own shadow whether personal or cultural, and dares to suggest an alternate imagining.

Carthaginians, Frank McGuinness (1988)

Reading *Carthaginians* (McGuinness, *Plays 1*:291-379), calls to mind a passage in the novel *Night* by Elie Weisel, a Jewish survivor of the holocaust:

> The SS hung two Jewish men and a boy before the assembled inhabitants of the camp. The men died quickly but the death struggle of the boy lasted half an hour. 'Where is God? Where is he?' a man behind me asked. I heard the man cry again, 'Where is God now?' and I heard a voice within me answer, 'Here he is – he is hanging there on the gallows.' (Weisel, 1981:76-77)

Frank McGuinness's play, *Carthaginians*, could be subtitled 'Where is God?' or more accurately 'Where was God?' when, on Bloody Sunday (1972), thirteen innocent people, marching for Civil Rights, were gunned down and killed. The play is set in 1988 in a graveyard, where a group of people await the resurrection of the dead. Each of them has been touched in different ways by the horror of what happened on that fateful day. Each carries this horror and trauma within them. The play is about suffering and pain, about loss of innocence and hope, about death in all its

guises. The play is about memory – about remembering what has
been repressed or forgotten or denied:

> Pathologies of memory are characteristic features of post-traumatic
> stress disorder (PTSD). These range from amnesia for part, or all,
> of the traumatic events to frank dissociation, in which large realms
> of experience or aspects of one's identity are disowned. Such
> failures of recall can *paradoxically coexist* with the opposite: intruding
> memories and unbidden repetitive images of traumatic events.
> (Greenberg & van der Kolk, quoted in Caruth, 1995:152)

Carthaginians is about a vision of hell that needs and cries out
for a vision of resurrection. It can be read as a contemporary
Passion narrative. The brutal obscenity of death by crucifixion is
mirrored in the obscenity of the murders on Bloody Sunday. If
crucifixion can be interpreted as humanity at the zero point, for-
saken by the divine, so too can the events of Bloody Sunday. How
can such a story be told? How can one forgive oneself for having
survived? What kind of reconciliation is possible between the
warring communities and the warring aspects of the individual
human psyche? What can heal such splitting apart? The hope of
resurrection – of passing from death to life – is the journey of the
play. It unfolds in the liminal or threshold space of a graveyard:

> The graveyard, hiding place in time gone by for outcasts, lepers,
> fugitives, the insane; shunned by the living because of their fear of
> the dead; becomes for McGuinness another borderland. The
> watchers have moved into this borderland under the stress of loss
> or guilt (O'Dwyer, 1991:112)

From the Wednesday to the Sunday morning the characters
'marginalized by their grief' (Hurt, 2000:280), will face the demons
of the past, as they tell their stories. Their city, like Carthage, has
been destroyed, as has each of their lives. The setting of the play
amidst the ruins of history is characteristic of McGuinness' work,
and as is typical of many of his plays, dead bodies haunt the
grieving protagonists of *Carthaginians*. In the womb-tomb space of
the graveyard the characters will play and sing and ritualize their
way towards a new imagining. The alternative sacred space of
theatre will facilitate a coming home, a transformation both for the
characters and the audience, in their transition from death to life.

Hurt claims that there is a remarkably consistent vision throughout the plays of Frank McGuinness, the essence of which is grief:

> McGuinness's protagonists live in a kind of after-life, scarred by traumatic encounters with the death of friends, family or loved ones. Their experiences, though, have not left them numbed or defeated but have rather given them the gift of tongues. Remarkable talkers, they rewrite their world in bravura feats of storytelling and dramatic improvisation. (Hurt, 2000:285)

The consciousness that underlies this play is quite specifically Catholic. 'The characters go to the graveyard prompted by an odd mixture of banishment, voluntary exile, sanctuary, protest and a need to grieve'. As it taps into the Catholic consciousness of pilgrimage and ritual journeying it also leads to

> the ritualization of the space, undertaken first as an act of repentance and secondly, in the expectation of transformation or renewal. (Jordan, 85)

While the ritual space also stresses integration and community 'the solemnity and sensibility of pilgrimage is turned on its head by the dynamic of carnival' (85).

The play can be interpreted as a contemporary passion narrative, and the unfolding days of the play seen as a mirroring of the traditional Holy Week in the Christian calendar, as the community prepared for Easter. Liturgically, in the Catholic tradition the ceremonies of Holy Week set before the participants the events leading up to the crucifixion and resurrection of Jesus. In the sacred space of ritual and story, participants are invited through a state of heightened awareness to journey the way of the Cross with Jesus. Christians are called to feel his suffering and pain, to identify with it and in so doing to experience their own suffering and grief transformed. The journey of Holy Week is a journey towards the glory and joy of resurrection. The play *Carthaginians* places this same journey from death to life in a secular setting, where there is no promise of salvation from outside, and the characters are called to be saviours of themselves and one another and the 'arbitrary moments of blessedness, enabled either by art or individual human compassion' (Hurt, 285) are the tangible signs of hope and redemption. The travesty of carnival and play can also offer moments of unexpected and undeserved grace.

In *Carthaginians*, the 'moment' of Bloody Sunday is refracted and reflected through the lives and stories of the protagonists, many years after the event. As the characters wait in the liminal space of a graveyard for the 'shock' of the resurrection of the dead, the extraordinary nature of their vision presents an angle of interpretation that questions all received interpretations of history which 'opens through moments of spiritual transcendence' towards a new imagining (Hurt, 277). The women, Maela, Greta and Sarah, have had a vision; 'what the three of us have seen, Maela' (*Carthaginians* 298). They believe that the dead will rise. They have come to keep vigil in the graveyard, to wait for the miracle to happen. They have been joined by three men Paul, Seph and Hark. The seventh character Dido is a homosexual who is a type of Mother Courage figure at one level and at another he plays a transgressive role as the transvestite playwright, Fionnuala McGonigle. While the play is ostensibly realist, the question of the women's vision alongside the interruptive presence of Dido pushes against the boundaries of the realist frame. It will be further fractured and questioned by Dido's play *The Burning Balaclava*, where characters play different parts and different genders and Dido himself (playwright Fionnuala) plays two distinct roles as a tormented female martyr figure and a nameless British soldier. The play within the play stretches the realist parameters in its content and performance. Dirty jokes, snatches of song, remembered poetry, nursery rhymes, football chants and talk about the Western genre of cinema suggest an intertextual reality within which the play (as a whole) operates. There is no seamless narrative of events but rather a series of dissociated voices consequent on the experience of trauma:

> The traumatised, we might say, carry an impossible history within them, or they become themselves the symptom of a history that they cannot entirely possess. (Caruth, 1995:5)

The deep wounding that has occurred in the light of such trauma is in the generative or feeling function of the human being. Seph is so wounded (because of his informing) that he does not speak at all for most of the play. Maela's pain at the death of her daughter from cancer has left her locked and frozen in her denial and unable to move forward. Sarah has lived as a junkie and prostitute in Holland for years, and now wants a child. Hark who has been in prison and now works as a gravedigger feels that the person he was nine years ago (Johnnie) no longer exists. Paul retreats into periods of madness as a way of coping, while he builds his pyramid for the dead, out of the rubbish of the town. Greta has had an operation that makes her feel unwomanly and unable to bear children. (A hysterectomy, one presumes.) Their respective wounds make it impossible for them to be life-givers, either to themselves or others. The dirty jokes they share are often about sex and sexuality – where the wound seems deepest. The man whose penis falls off, the different female approaches to the male sex organ, or Maela's failed joke about the woman with the pain in her child, are further manifestations of the wound in the generative or feeling function.

Maela has been putting clothes on her daughter's grave as if dressing her. She is saving for her birthday, believing 'she's not dead, you know' (C 300). Dido enters wheeling a pram, in which he stores the supplies that the others have ordered. His singing of a section from *Danny Boy* which ends with 'kneel and say an Ave there pour moi' (301) alerts us to where he is coming from. The camp performance with the pram and the song, and later in drag, while foregrounding homosexuality, also draws attention to the interpretative frameworks within which one experiences history. Dido's position offers us the vantage point of the outsider and provides 'a useful perspective – a distance from which events, philosophies, social and moral issues may be evaluated' (Lojek, 1990, 58). The outsider position of the homosexual questions perceived assumptions, not simply about compulsory heterosexuality, but about our ways of knowing.

Dido is making money in his transactions, has moved into Maela's home and is selling their story to the newspapers. Greta reads:

> 'The girls may be suffering from illusions,' Mr. Martin added. 'They are simple but sincere souls, and each has endured a great personal

tragedy,' he concluded. We say good luck, Ghostbusters, and if the dead rise, let us know.

Dido: Typical, typical. I'm doing my best. I need to rouse national interest. Nobody believes you in Derry, they think you're lunatics. The Catholics think you're mad, and the prods think you're Martians.

Maela: Who cares what anybody thinks as long as we believe it? (306-7)

Whatever the original vision, it is not validated by those outside who dismiss it according to their own paradigms. However, the three women in this play support one another, thus authenticating what the others have experienced. Dido is making a collection of pressed flowers, believing that 'Flowers are more gentle when they're dead' (308) and adverting to their magical properties. Paul enters, reminiscent of an Old Testament Jeremiah. As seer, he has become slightly unhinged. His greeting, while addressed to the town of Derry, is actually applicable to the characters we have just met ('Pack of whores. Pack of queers. Pack of traitors'). He recalls the Irish Christian Saint Malachy who had a vision of the end of the world, within which Derry was included. Paul believes that he too can see like Malachy, and blames him for not stopping his prophesy (308). Paul's experience of the destruction of Derry and its people on Bloody Sunday leaves him in a similar role as a prophet of doom. He has seen the 'rubbishing' of all that he held sacred and precious and he is building a monument made of rubbish which he hopes will become a fitting testimony. The prophet in the Hebrew tradition was the one who grieved, that a new future might emerge. Through the work of his own hands Paul intends to build a pyramid through which the 'dead will find their way back to this world' (320)

Greta's inability to save the injured bird serves as an object of transference and brings us closer to the pain she is carrying. Throughout the play she will recite snatches of the rhyme, 'Charlie, Charlie, chuck-chuck-chuck.' Her wound is in her inner female self. She cannot sleep, nor can Paul. He talks of having been at a quiz but said nothing. 'I used to run it. Questions and answers' (309). It is almost as if life has become too painful to fit into the categories it once fitted into. Virgil's leading of Dante through the city of hell can no longer be contained within the parameters of the quiz-game. Now the question Paul asks is 'Who will guide me through this city of hell?' (309). Derry has become foreign to him and he likens it to the ancient city of Carthage, a city similar in size to Derry and ruled and destroyed by a great Empire. Paul's myth of origins is to locate himself as a Carthaginian, 'sitting in the ruins, in the graveyard' (310). His sense of belonging to the place and the earth transcends the claims of empires:

> But I'm no slave. I am Carthaginian. This earth is mine, not Britain's, not Rome's. Mine. (311)

Equally his remembering has mythic dimensions:

> Virgil led Dante through the city of hell and Dante said that to remember times of happiness in times of great woe, that's the sorrow beyond enduring.

The sublimation of sexual energy through religion or violence is an important theme in this play and also highlights the wounded feeling function. Hark, while refusing to acknowledge continuity with what he once was ('Johnny is dead' (316)), is also fearful of a relationship with Sarah, having been hurt before. He wants to hurt her through his singing of the song about the whores in Amsterdam. Sighting the dead bird, he feels pity, the 'poor bird' (317). This moment of compassion is the beginning of his journey back to himself.

A question running through the play is whether the characters can continue to hope, and just what kind of hope is possible. Whether hope and history can indeed rhyme is a fundamental question. Each of their lives has been changed radically through death, loss, betrayal, imprisonment. Hark's voice as the realism of the gravedigger promises no hope in the resurrection of the dead. Paul follows the stars as he has to have faith in something while Greta suggests that he 'should have faith in yourself'. Greta feels too tired to have faith, and Hark hearing 'the cry of a lost soul' (321) asks her (parody of the concerned priest) why she has abandoned hope and turned her back on the faith of her childhood. Greta humorously answers that 'I blame it on television myself'.

The 'wit and wisdom' of Derry unite them in their singing of
'We shall overcome' which leads into a parody of Martin Luther
King's famous speech 'I have a dream'. In contrast to his vision of
unity theirs is one of separation:

> **Hark:** Catholics shall stand with Catholics, Protestants with
> Protestants –
> **Maela:** Should it not be 'Catholics will stand with Protestants.'
> **Hark:** I speak of dreams, sister, not of insanity. Let us be like the
> asshole and let us be apart. (*C* 323)

The inversion of the dream and the crudeness of the imagery
work in a subversive way, questioning and overturning all pre-
conceptions of what unity might mean. The subsequent prayer is a
similar inversion alerting us to the definition of self and other
through hatred and bigotry, that is needed to maintain separate
identities:

> **Hark:** Let us wander forth into the wilderness of bigotry and let us
> spread more bigotry. Let us create a nation fit for assholes to live
> in. For as assholes we are known to each other and like the asshole
> let us forever remain apart. (323)

The rituals of war, sado-masochism and sport seem to validate
the one patriarchal aesthetic. Dido relates an encounter with a
Lebanese, who was wandering through Derry:

> He said 'Listen, listen to the earth. The earth can speak. It says,
> Cease your violent hand. I who gave birth to you will bring death
> to you. Cease your violent hand. That is my dream. I pray my
> dream comes true.' (326)

Dido can only translate this into a desire that Derry City will
win the European Cup—a dream that seems just as impossible.
The vision of a cessation of violence cannot be grounded. The only dream that he might have an inkling of how to realize would be
to build up the local football team.

Sarah cannot be stopped from telling her story, even though
people around her might try to stop her. Her journey through
addiction is a story of a journey from death to life. Like the
fairytale of *The Handless Maiden* she eventually saves herself by the
strength of her own hands, rather than those of another:

> I walked by the canals of Amsterdam. I was sinking under the weight of powder. I sank and I sank until I felt hands lift me. I thought they were yours, Hark, but they were my own. I saved myself, Johnny. I saw myself dead in Amsterdam. I've come back from the dead. I'm clean.
>
> [...] if the dead are to rise again, then we must tell each other the truth. For us all to rise again. (328)

Telling the truth rather than colluding with a culture of lies or silence is the way towards redemption. The community gathered in the graveyard can enable each other to hear the truth of their lives.

Scene four introduces Dido's play, *The Burning Balaclava*, written by his alias, Frenchwoman Fionnuala McGonigle who changed her name in sympathy with Derry people whose city also had its name changed. The play is a contribution to the resistance. The text of the play is distributed along with props. All the characters' names are variations on Doherty (Mrs. Doherty, Pádraig Ó Dochartaigh, Mercy Dogherty, Father Docherty, Jimmy Doherty), the British soldier is nameless. Props include stolen balaclavas, a headscarf and apron, a statue of the Sacred Heart, water pistols for everyone, a Tricolour and a large flag pin, a rosary beads and crucifix, a flat cap, two white sheets, a stuffed dog on a lead, a helmet and toy rifle. Most of the characters are tormented in one way or another.

Mikami interprets *The Burning Balaclava* as functioning in a way similar to psychodrama (Mikami, 42). This is a therapeutic method for conflict resolution, which requires participants to act out their fears, dreams, and ambitions, and one that explores the roots of present conflict in the memories and perceptions of the participants. It is an effective method that can enable the individual to move beyond trauma. If the play within the play can function in this therapeutic way for the characters, perhaps it can have a similar effect on the mindsets of those in the audience (George Mitchell once spoke about the decommissioning of mindsets that was the basic decommissioning needed in the Northern Irish situation). Jordan interprets the play within the play in terms of carnival, whose intention is 'to release energy in order to re-shape reality' (79).

Jordan interprets Dido's role(s) in the context of carnival and sees 'his flexibility' as his strongest characteristic. It is 'the mock

Queen Dido who misrules, bringing the play into an ever more threatening space' (81). For McGuinness role-playing is linked with transformation:

> The tension between rehearsed roles and the unrehearsed ones Dido distributes is essential, as the fragmentation becomes both conducive and threatening at once. Do we become what we play? Or is what we play the thing we need to act out most? Ultimately the goal of role-playing in carnival is to insist that imitation and performances are no longer selections but authoritative selections. (Jordan, 81)

While the similarity in the names within Dido's play suggests that very little separates the characters, the play parodies religious bigotry and political ideology. All of the characters end up dead, even the dog, the wee hound of Ulster which firmly knocks the Cuchulainn myth off its pedestal. But ironically as Jordan notes, the only time that the dead rise is at the end of *The Burning Balaclava* (85). The theme of the long-suffering Irish mother who gives up her children to war is also parodied (O'Casey's Juno, for example). The symbols that define the characters in religious and political terms are easily recognized as they are distributed amongst the characters. The ambiguity of symbols is raised for the audience as the excesses and abuses evoked by them lead to more and more violence. It focuses attention on how much of the war in Northern Ireland is in fact a war about symbols and how and what they mean. The easy stereotyping of the other through the use of symbols in the play allows the audience to see the power of symbols at work in a community. The war over symbols suggests a collapse of the symbolic function into literalism. When the real ambiguity and ambivalence of symbols is denied, the resultant literalism ultimately leads to the death of the symbol, at least in its more liberating aspects. When a symbol ceases to function in an open-ended symbolic way and collapses into a banal literalism, it functions in a diabolic way, tearing people apart, and may result in violence and death. Official religion, represented in this play by the silent Catholic priest, who speaks by waving white flags, in the Waterside area of the city (Father Edward Daly?) is ultimately powerless against the community's misappropriation of the symbolic function.

As the characters fall around laughing after the performance of the play, agreeing it was 'shite' (344), Seph speaks and asks for a cigarette. The ritual space of play has permitted all kinds of transgression. Seph, who has been an informer, now feels allowed to speak about what he saw on Bloody Sunday. A space of remembering has been opened up by the play. It facilitates access to a memory repressed or denied through offering another vantage point of interpretation of the events of history. The characters will gradually come to transform their traumatic memory of the events into a narrative one.

Scene Five takes us further into Friday (Good Friday and the memory of the crucifixion is part of the shared memory, however it is interpreted) and deeper into remembering. As Greta and Sarah talk, the question of salvation is raised:

> **Greta:** Do you think he'll save you?
> **Sarah:** What from?
> **Greta:** Yourself.
> **Sarah:** He has to save himself first.
> **Greta:** Does he?
> **Sarah:** We all have.
> **Greta:** Are we worth saving? (347-48)

Where once traditional Christian theology answered this question through offering an interpretation of salvation through the death and resurrection of Jesus on behalf of sinners, these characters are faced with the task of saving themselves and believing themselves worthy of salvation. Where the community was once nourished and sustained by the memory of Jesus, this community gathered in the graveyard must be faithful to their own truth and their own stories.

Greta, now an orphan, searches for a myth of origins. Her parents' inadequate parenting (in what she remembers as a doll's house) and in particular her mother's failure to initiate her into an awareness of her sexuality leaves her feeling lost and wanting herself back, 'to be what I used to be' (350). Maela finally admits that her daughter is dead. She tells her story of her daughter's death from cancer on Bloody Sunday and her subsequent walk through the dead in the streets of Derry. The scene of her meeting with the doctor at the hospital is played/parodied with Dido as the doctor. The painful memory of the day comes back in a moving speech which is like a vision of crucifixion or hell on earth. The sense of disorientation is huge. The devastation of her personal experience is mirrored through the streets as she hears of more and more dead. Her naming of the streets, William Street and Ferryquay Street and the Strand and Rosville Street and Great James Street stresses the particularity of place and makes what is happening almost unbearable. The memories flow into one another, fluid, almost interchangeable, as she allows herself to remember the pain and the horror:

> They opened fire and shot them dead. I'm not dead. Where are there dead in Derry? Let me look on the dead. Jesus, the dead. The innocent dead. There's thirteen dead in Derry. Where am I? What day is it? Sunday. Why is the sun bleeding? It's pouring blood. I want a priest. Give me a priest. Where am I? In Great James Street. It's full of chemists. I need a tonic for my nerves. For my head. For my heart. Pain in my heart. Breaking heart. I've lost one. I've lost them all. They had no hair. She had fire. She opened fire on herself. When I wasn't looking she caught cancer. It burned her. She was thirteen. It was Sunday. I have to go to Mass. I have to go to Mass. I have to go to Mass. Dido, take me to Mass Dido. (352)

As Dido questions Maela, like a quiz-master, there is a sense of an old order returning. The parameters of their world are being redefined and they may be able to inhabit it fully once more.

Scene six is set on Saturday evening and finds the characters in party mood, singing football songs and remembering the old days. Teams are decided for a quiz which is a complete farce. The humour, banter and camaraderie between the players are in evidence as they enter into a new space of relationship. The transgressive space of play opens the characters to new possibilities within themselves. The truths of their lives begin to emerge. Sarah wants to have a child. Greta questions Paul about his madness and his pyramid building. He associates it with The Last Judgement and the dead rising. He feels that if they do not rise tonight that he will go and join them. He carries the war within his head, in particular the horror of Bloody Sunday. When Greta begins to rip apart his black plastic bag he stops her:

Stop it. Stop it. (*Grabs the plastic bag off Greta*) The plastic bags. They threw them over the dead. Bury them decently. Put them in the ground. Carrying the dead like a pile of rubbish through Derry on Bloody Sunday. Don't tear the plastic bags. Don't defile their coffin. Don't, please, don't. Don't let them die. Don't let me go mad. If they die, I'll go mad. I have to keep carrying them. That's where I keep them. Give them back to me. (368)

Seph says that Greta hates being herself. Seph talks about being a traitor, repeating the ritual action of tearing down the tricolour. He dissociated himself from those who wanted to avenge the dead by informing on the living. Seph, like Paul, still carries the war in his head. Hark in a similar way chose to live by not going on hunger strike. There is a sense of failed manhood about Hark (or at least failed in relation to a particular definition of manhood).

I can't. Can't fire, can't kill, can't eat. Coward. I'm a coward. Want to eat. Want to live, I want to live. And I can't face the dead. Will the dead go away and stop haunting me? I cannot kill to avenge you. All I could have killed was myself. And I couldn't. I can't. Come back to me, Sarah, I'm dead. Come back and raise the dead. (372)

The play repudiates the notion of sacrifice that underpins the ideology of war. Whereas an ideology of sacrifice celebrates and glorifies death, Hark and Seph choose life instead.

Within *Carthaginians* the sense of death continues to haunt the living. Greta carries it within her, intimately within her female self. Her dirty joke is the story of her life – the dirty trick that life has played on her. When she learns that she cannot conceive she goes to her parents' grave: 'She said, Mammy, Daddy, I'm afraid. And she saw the dead. She saw herself. She saw nothing, for she is nothing. She is not a woman anymore. She's a joke. A dirty joke' (373). Having told her story, Greta confirms that the dead will rise tonight.

The intertextuality of their lives is stressed as the narratives of their broken, fractured lives give way to a shared remembering of films and poetry, from the Indians in the Western who had 'the best words…like poetry' (375) to the verses of *The Traveller*. The sense of 'phantom listeners' is heightened by the recitation of the poem in a graveyard. The poetry opens the space of ritual and deeper remembering, where forgiveness might be possible.

Paul recites the names, ages and addresses of the thirteen who were killed on Bloody Sunday. The characters' responses show a personal appropriation of traditional imagery, prayer and ritual, associated with the dead. Taken outside of the churches, it is nonetheless located in the liminal, sacred space of a graveyard. Christian imagery of death and resurrection continues to permeate their prayer. The theme of forgiveness, while not exclusively a Christian one, is still present, although equally removed from its religious setting.

> **Hark:** Sunday.
> **Dido**: Do you see the dead?
> **Greta:** The dead beside you.
> **Maela:** The dead behind you.
> **Sarah:** The dead before you.
> **Greta:** Forgive the dead.
> **Maela:** Forgive the dying.
> **Sarah:** Forgive the living.
> **Paul:** Forgive yourself. (378-79)

The ritual rhythm of this prayer with its repetition and call to forgiveness and hope expresses the heightened state of awareness of the characters. It echoes the ancient Christian prayer—*The Lorica*, more commonly known as *St. Patrick's Breastplate*. It offers protection in a similar manner and sees the continuity of life and death, in the enduring presence of the dead in the memories of those who survive them. Having gathered and told their stories, having faced their terrible pain, having healed their fractured memories, having shared food and drink and song and laughter they have been enabled to move through their darkness into light.

Stage directions indicate that:

> *Light breaks through the graveyard. Birdsong begins. Light illumines them all. They listen, looking at each other, in the light. They lie down and sleep. It is now morning. Dido alone is awake in the graveyard.* (379)

The final speech is Dido's:

> What happened? Everything happened, nothing happened, whatever you want to believe, I suppose. (379)

Was there a resurrection of the dead? Some scholars would say that Christ rose in the hearts of the believers. Through the ritual space of theatre a group of people enacted the transformation of their lives and were witnessed by others. Dido assumes almost a mythical status, world wanderer, between times, and places. The totality of the world for the duration of this play has been the city of Derry, its streets, and its graveyard. As he drops flowers on the sleepers his words are like a blessing, invoking protection, as he urges the characters to watch themselves and to remember him. His final word is 'Play' (379) an invitation to a space of freedom, to which the newly-risen ones are now called.

Conclusion

Grieving was one of the tasks of the Hebrew prophet. The ability to grieve that things were not as they should be also allowed the imagining of newness. Such imagining that came from deep griev-ing allowed the future to emerge as possibility rather than an endless repetition of the past. In this sense the plays explored in this section are prophetic for our time. The journeys of the prot-agonists, while sometimes sharing qualities of visionary or mystical quests, are essentially journeys into the realm of the unimagined, the possible. They lead us to the places where it may be possible to love once the story is told. Adrienne Rich captures something similar in her poem written in memory of Elvira Shatayev and the other women climbers who perished in a storm on Lenin Peak in August 1974:

> When you have buried us, told our story
> ours does not end, we stream
> into the unfinished, the unbegun
> the possible. (Rich, 1984, 226-27)

The particularity of the stories told is important. Their location in a particular time and place calls audiences to an appreciation of embodiment in the now. Many of the journeys are complex and spiral back to an original place, where new awareness transfigures the ordinary, and makes it shimmer. Where many of the plays deal with the reality of war, peace is imagined that is not simply the absence of war but a way of handling the complexity of difference and dialoguing with strangeness, and incompleteness. They are invitations to imagine a culture without scapegoats or victims, to reconnect with the body or the earth and its natural rhythms to ground a new awareness. The wounds no longer determine the identity of the storytellers but become sites for transformation, the belief in healing without scars an imagined space of new life. The raw material becomes the *prima materia,* the philosopher's stone of traditional alchemy that must be found and ground down in order to transfigure one's life.

Such new imagining takes us into the place of ritual, symbol and story, where the invitation may simultaneously involve de-mythologizing and remything. The invitation into the ritual space asks that we pay attention to the symbols and narratives that have shaped identity and also try to find a new way of speaking our name to ourselves and to one another. The space of ritual involves both memory and transformation. When a playwright like Mc-Guinness takes audiences over and over into the new ritual space of theatre, he is essentially shaping a new world, a whole new imagining.

The imagining that takes place in the empty space of theatre is an invitation to move beyond individual and cultural certainties, to move beyond the roles and masks of identity and subjectivity, of religion and gender. It is an invitation to play.

Conclusion:
Sacred Play and the Imagination of the Possible

In the introduction to this work I proposed that Irish dramatists
are attempting to reconnect with, to retrieve or to rediscover soul.
Throughout this study I have been interested in the relationship
between body, soul and spirit, and have suggested that the aspiration towards spirit must be matched by a corresponding desire
for embodiment for the search to be considered in any way
complete. Through a thematic analysis of selected plays, using a
feminist hermeneutic informed by philosophy, theology,
anthropology, psychology and literary theory, I have explored
twenty-eight Irish soul-journeys written and performed within
Ireland's poetic dramatic tradition over the past three decades. The
journeys have taken us through memory, and ritual, into the dark,
towards transformation and vision. Throughout this work I have
considered theatre as an alternative sacred space for the performance of identity and interpreted its function within culture as
a *temenos* – a sacred space and/or container for transformation. I
have also proposed that all theatrical playing takes place within the
context of the play of creation itself and that reflection on the
nature of this play can contribute to the development of a poetics
of Irish culture. Keeping in mind the interpretive lenses of sacred
play, theatre, culture and the plays themselves, I now propose to
map the contours of a new poetics.

I want to compare such a project to how Rosa Braidotti
described the feminist project in philosophy. She used the meta-

phor of a tightrope stretched above the void (Braidotti, 1991:15) and argued that the feminist project cannot yet be systematized, or even represented as a continuous series of clearly elaborated theoretical points. Consequently she argues for a discontinuous line, attention to dissonance and 'a constantly evolving creative drifting' (15).

The new maps that will emerge from this thinking will in turn map new territories both within culture and within the human psyche. It is the territory of the poet – who knows that the maps they gave us were out of date by years (Adrienne Rich) or who dares to dream what ought to be (Maeve McGuckian). Eavan Boland's poem 'That the science of cartography is limited' (Boland, 1994:5) addresses a similar theme. As the poet looks down at an old famine road that ends abruptly, at the borders of Connacht, she recalls how in 1847, after the second failure of the potato crop, 'Relief Committees gave/the starving Irish such roads to build./Where they died, there the road ended' (5). Her awareness that the map of the country will never tell the stories of these people leads her to inscribe them in her poem in an attempt at a new cartography. In similar ways a poetic theatre can contribute towards a more inclusive remembering and imagining and map identity in new ways. In charting the trajectory of the poetics that emerges from such reflections we engage in a similar creative drifting that will lead us towards new ways of thinking where the aesthetic and the ethical unite.

Post-colonial feminist theory adverts to the way we now think about issues like language and experience, the influence of ideologies, the formation of human subjectivity, what we understand by culture and also attends to the issues of race, class, and gender. It urges us to be aware of the hegemony of any one discourse over others and to pay attention to difference (Loomba, 1998:20, 29 and 133f). Attention is drawn to the experience of marginalized groups, whether they are women, non-whites, non-European, lower classes, oppressed castes (231) and the question of access to speech is an important issue. How do the colonized or the subaltern speak? 'In order to listen for subaltern voices we need to uncover the multiplicity of narratives that were hidden by the grand narratives, but we still need to think about how the former are woven together' (241). One cannot stand outside of one's culture, its symbol systems, its language. The history of Western civilization is undeniably a patriarchal history, that privileged (particular) male experience, expression and representation. But as already noted, intervening in symbol systems, and assuming even a tentative subject position, allows one to question representation.

In Irish theatre one must ask whose stories have been heard or represented? In an almost exclusively male canon there is a definite marginalization of women's voices. But equally access to production, direction and selection of plays for performance is controlled by male interests. The colonization of the female body either as site for male meaning or carrier of repressed aspects of the cultural unconscious must be addressed by theatre audiences and practitioners. Plays that seem not to be political because they don't deal with obvious political issues are in fact very political, especially where they draw attention to the colonized female body, within patriarchal systems of representation.

A post-colonial reading of Frank McGuinness's *Baglady* would draw attention to how a colonized body tries to speak what is written on the female body. Traumatic memory that seeks narrative form and cultural recognition is also foregrounded in Mommo's narrative in *Bailegangaire*. Broken and fragmented subjectivities that seek expression and representation and shifting time-frames that weave and backtrack (associated with a female way of knowing) are evident in the women's stories of Anne Le Marquand Hartigan's *La Corbière*, Patricia Burke Brogan's *Eclipsed*, Christina Reid's *Tea in a China Cup* and Paula Meehan's *Cell*. Marina Carr's protagonists cannot be contained within the parameters of a patriarchal imagining and their journeys foreground the limitations of language, symbols and all systems of meaning to contain their searching. Frank McGuinness's *Caravaggio* (*Innocence*) evokes the unstable place of subjectivity in relation to the homosexual artist within a Christian culture. Anne Devlin's *After Easter* tries to deal with cultural binarisms that define and confine the protagonist Greta in her quest for integration.

Addressing cultural symbol systems and their frameworks for meaning-making is a very political act. It goes to the roots of a society's self-definition and interrupts the hegemony of its overarching discourse. Arguing for a multiplicity of experience and expression is important. This applies equally to how women's experience is represented. There is no point in universalizing women's experience as men have already done in relation to particular male experiences. We must keep in mind Braidotti's presentation of a radically different vision of subjectivity that is sexually differentiated, multiple and relational (Braidotti, 276).

Sue Ellen Case suggests that the theoretical project of feminism for theatre could be termed a 'new poetics' (*Feminism and Theatre*). Such new theory would abandon the traditional patriarchal values 'embedded in prior notions of form, practice and audience response' (114) in order to construct new critical models and methodologies. Case identifies the 'constructing woman as subject' as the future liberating work of a feminist poetics (121). In her analysis of what might constitute a new form she suggests that 'It can be elliptical rather than illustrative, fragmentary rather than whole, ambiguous rather than clear, and interrupted rather than complete' (129). With the deconstruction of traditional patriarchal forms of representation the stage can be prepared for the emergence of the female subject 'whose voice, sexuality and image have yet to be dramatized within the dominant culture' (132). One may wonder what kinds of text might open up this space of new imagining. One writer calls such texts subversive, in that they do not provide 'an illusion of seamlessness' or the 'narrative closure' that characterizes realism. She argues for texts that 'open up the negotiation of meaning to contradictions, circularity, multiple viewpoints' and that also provide an 'alternative articulation of female subjectivity' (Forte, 1989:117).

Many of the plays in this study can be interpreted as 'subversive'. Marina Carr may resist the label of feminist, but her plays do allow women's voices to be heard and facilitate access to the female unconscious through her protagonists' searching. Paula Meehan's representation of women in *Cell* challenges the traditional nurturing, maternal stereotyping of women and the character of Lil Sweeney in *Mrs Sweeney* inserts the history of a real Dublin woman into the heroic mythic tale of Sweeney. Anne Devlin's work consciously uses a feminist framework that allows her protagonist Greta (*After Easter*) to question inherited narratives of identity whether patriarchal, nationalist or religious. It is also characteristic of many of Frank McGuinness's plays that they open up the theatrical space to alternative performances of identity. In a play like *Carthaginians* he questions inherited symbol systems that relate to gender, national and religious identity. Parker's *Pentecost* also pays attention to how a people's sense of their own identity can be structured through a demonizing of the other, that keeps them locked in an endless cycle of violence and recrimination. Michael Harding's play *Misogynist* is a brave naming of how misogyny is at the heart of a patriarchal culture's imagining and the interruptive presence of the Pooka Man pushes audiences to acknowledge the kind of forgetting and repression that can underpin and characterize an Irish Catholic imagining. Many of these plays provide examples of the kind of subversive texts that Forte identifies in that they 'open up the negotiation of meaning' both for audiences and culture as a whole.

Theatre allows audiences to imagine what may be in nurturing a passion for the possible and sustaining what Ricoeur has called the mytho-poetic core. Essentially this mytho-poetic core is like an opaque kernel that constitutes the imaginary nucleus of a culture (Kearney, 1982). The mytho-poetic core is what carries the identity of a people over time, in symbols, myths, narratives, rituals etc. But the mythos of any community is also the 'bearer of something which exceeds its own frontiers; it is the bearer of possible worlds' (Kearney: 1982:264). Where theatrical texts enter the area of soul making and soul-journeying, when they exploit the possibilities of a poetic theatre through attention to language, images, symbols and rituals, they are shaping the mytho-poetic nucleus of a culture. Most specifically these plays can become the bearers 'of possible worlds'.

The language of soul is the language of symbol, image and dream. It is the language of the poet, the lover, the artist. It is the language of the visionary, the mythmaker and the shaman. Sometimes it aspires towards a sound so pure it becomes music. At others it cannot be contained within speech and tumbles into the language of the dance, seeking fuller embodiment. It is the language of the mystic who longs for and melts in the gaze of the Beloved. It is a language that includes the non-said, the unsayable,

the unspoken. It is the language of silence, of stillness and emptiness. It is a language of invitation and surrender. It is the language
of the dark. It is terrifying and transforming. It takes us to edges
and chasms where we could plunge to our deaths. It both conceals
and reveals. It is the language of otherness, the language of
mystery. It invites new imagining, new dreaming. It invites expans-
iveness. It is the language of liminal spaces. It is the language of
ritual and play. It is the language of journey. It is the language of
imagination. The plays in this study are part of the Irish dramatic
poetic tradition. While they are primarily text-based plays they
nonetheless come into their fullness in performance. The playwrights present audiences with characters pushed to the limits of
language, pushed beyond the rational into half-conscious and
unconscious depths. Their journeys speak the polysemic, multivalent, paradoxical, haunting and terrifying language of soul. Their
journeys invite both characters and audiences into the liminal
space of play.

Throughout this study, play has been considered in different
ways: the theatrical space of play; the individual plays; the use of
play within the plays and the overall frame of sacred play which
grounds and sustains all playing. Reflecting on the nature of play
can contribute to the development of a poetics of Irish culture.
Huizinga's classic work on Play suggests that ideas of ritual, magic,
liturgy, sacrament and mystery all 'fall within the play concept'
(18), that there is no formal difference between play and ritual.
One cannot formally distinguish the consecrated, or hallowed spot
of sacred performance from that of the playground – and we
might add – theatre. In enquiring into the nature of poetic creation
he suggests that 'poiesis' is in fact 'a playful function' (119), when
poetry moves into the realms of 'dream, enchantment, ecstasy and
laughter' (119). He suggests that 'All antique poetry is at one and
the same time ritual, entertainment, artistry, riddle-making, doc-
trine, persuasion, sorcery, soothsaying, prophecy, and completion'
(120). A poetic theatre embodies many of the features of the
archaic poet and has a similar social function, where holiness and
play overlap, in offering a mytho-poesis.

One of my central ideas has been that all playing takes place
within the context of the play of creation, or within the frame of

sacred play, what the Hindu tradition has named *lila*. Schechner has used the same idea (of *maya-lila* from the Sanskrit words for illusion and play) in an attempt to define and expand the concept of play for western readers. He argues that:

> from the Indian perspective, playing is what the universe consists of. To be 'at play' is to recognize that all relationships are provisional. Ultimate reality, if there is such, is *neti*, literally, 'not that'. (Schechner, 1993:34)

Victor Turner suggests that play contains the possibility of changing our goals and restructuring what our culture states to be reality (Quoted by Schechner, 1993:25). Eamonn Jordan pays particular attention to the play element in the work of Frank McGuinness. He identifies one of play's functions as the establishment of 'a space of transition' (Jordan, 2000:208). He argues that 'play gives rise to liminal consciousness' (197) that it 'confronts rigidity, unsettles lazy thinking and mobilizes possibility' especially where role-play provides 'access to an alternative temporary reality' (197). Richard Schechner identifies the similar functions of art and religion in developing 'systems of transformation from one reality to another' (Schechner, 1993:28), which can function at times like a leap or a shock, and at others with a smooth and imperceptible flow (28).

Theatre as alternative sacred space can nurture and inspire a counter-cultural imagination. On 3 March 2003, in protest at the American Administration's decision to unilaterally attack Iraq, world-wide readings of Aristophanes's ancient Greek anti-war comedy *Lysistrata* highlighted the potential of theatre to embody an ethics of resistance and to inspire hope in a future where war does not have the final word. The space of play can counter fear and powerlessness by locating one's human efforts within a more fluid and versatile space, where stasis and paralysis give way to possibility. Play always takes place in the now of the present moment. It is concrete and embodied and immediate. Like the child's world it is ever shifting and changing, make-believe but deadly serious. When a play ends one may wonder with Dido in *Carthaginians* about what has actually happened:

What happened? Everything happened, nothing happened, whatever you want to believe, I suppose. (*Carthaginians* 379)

Barbara Myerhoff identifies the 'ludic element' as 'the playframe that embraces all performances'. She argues that the ludic is 'neither true nor false', nor does it suggest a 'specific emotional state' but simply points us to the power of our imaginative activities:

> ritual performances are testaments to our capacity to endlessly bring new possibilities into being without entirely relinquishing the old, prior understandings that have given rise to them.
> (Myerhoff, 1990:249)

For a period of time an audience must suspend belief (and disbelief), and in the fluid shape-shifting space of theatre, allow anything to happen. Identities, roles, subjectivities, sacred stories may all have been melted down in the crucible of play. Audiences may emerge from the theatre, less sure of their certainties, and wonder 'what if?' They may dare to imagine a new world.

In contrast to authors who argue for a more conservative function for theatre, in seeing it ultimately as a replication of the politics of society (Pilkington, 2001) throughout this study I have suggested that theatre is a space or site of possibility, where meanings can be contested and explored. This is especially significant when one considers the relationship between theatre and ritual. Ritual, whether cultural or religious, can also be seen as either conservative or innovative. It can tend towards preservation of the *status quo* but also has the potential to be radically subversive. Ritual moments transferred to the new sacred space of theatre have the potential to disclose new worlds. However they can also be reduced to spectacle or entertainment, limited in their efficacy by where we locate theatres and calculate admission charges, become just another object for consumption, no matter how esoteric or mystical their origins may be, and generally provide sanction and sustenance for a patriarchal ordering of history and society.

These are some of the risks that face theatre as a container for transformation. Theatre both interprets and is in turn interpreted by the culture within which it finds itself. A tendency towards entropy and stasis must be challenged by invitations to audiences to think and imagine differently. A framework of interpretation that offers a religious or spiritual interpretive horizon may inspire a passion for the possible in facilitating an encounter with an otherness or mystery that urges audiences beyond limited ways of imagining and dreaming.

In a recent article in *The Irish Journal of Feminist Studies* which is devoted to the theme of Women's Wisdom, Ann-Louise Gilligan turns to the faculty of imagination. She sees imagination holding the 'is' and the 'is not' in tensive balance:

> Imagination opens up new meaning, through the differences, without dissolving them. Imagination feels no need to cast difference in dualistic opposites; it facilitates living with the strange, with the contradiction and allows truth to be revealed in unexpected ways. (Gilligan, 2002:37)

While specific attention is given to the feminist imagination that 'will allow us to lisp new metaphors for our own being and becoming' (37), many of Gilligan's insights are applicable to the potentially transformative work that theatre can accomplish within culture. In its similar play with the 'is' and 'is not', theatre can open audiences to new ways of being and becoming in the world. As Michael Coady so brilliantly captured it in his programme note to Jim Nolan's *Blackwater Angel*:

> Is theatre itself, or perhaps all art, an attempted process of healing and redemption through transfiguration? [...] It is not through reason, but through faith in the imagination that redemption may happen. (Coady, 2001)

The journey towards transformation needs the sustenance of vision, ways of seeing and dreaming that break open old ways of behaving and suggest new ways of being. Even where being has been interrupted by destructive patterns of behaviour, whether personal, familial, historical or cultural, new ways of seeing can offer new starting points or horizons, that enable one to move beyond hurt and anger into relationship. Learning to live creatively in the midst of conflict, to sit in the fire (Mindell,1995), to inhabit edges, to express and understand difference, whether sexual, cultural or religious, is the way to transformation. Artists and playwrights who are not afraid to go to their own edge, to face their own madness, confusion, desire for revenge, alongside their desire for transformation and renewal, can present us with very important characters, whom we recognize as ourselves. McGuinness's characters in liminal spaces, Murphy's outsiders, Friel's broken and lost women and men, Carr's driven protagonists, are all searching for a way of coming home, of being heard and seen. In the empty space of theatre their stories can be told, their suffering given voice, their often neglected, over-shadowed or shamed and belittled lives embodied in performance. In the space of theatre, audiences can experience themselves in a crucible of transformation. The long journey towards integration, whether coming to terms with our own strangeness or the difference of the other can be inspired by an instant of recognition, a moment of insight, or a shift in focus. When the playwright does not resist 'sitting in the fire' and can create characters who inhabit similar places then the seeds of a paradigm shift are sown.

Throughout this book I have explored how different plays can become the bearers of possible worlds. The twenty-eight plays I have studied portray the Irish soul as it journeys through trauma and dissociation, through memory and fragmentation, as it seeks out liminal spaces in search of *communitas*, as it plunges into the dark in search of a myth of origins, as it seeks transformation in shamanic descent and soaring moments of healing and forgiveness, as it journeys to new visions in shared meals, laughter, and tears, in haunting conversations with ghosts and angels, and in subversive moments of carnival and play.

Theatre is the empty space of possibility, an alternative sacred space that can catch audiences off-guard and open like a trapdoor into the mystery. Plays spin golden threads that may lead us into the labyrinth of the self, that may disclose us to ourselves, and may reveal the pure light of reality itself. As a space that opens to the immensity and the silence, theatre can invite us to develop the kind of witness consciousness, that participates without judgement, that can inhabit spaces that are neither right nor wrong, but simply are.

Theatre can invite audiences to reconsider the relationship between body and spirit. In the space of embodied performance audiences can be invited to become aware of the withinness of things, where the ordinary shimmers before our eyes, and an otherness is manifest. Whether it is the traumatic memory becoming narrative for Frank McGuinness's *Baglady* or Tom Murphy's Mommo in *Bailegangaire*; whether it is the dancing Mundy sisters in Brian Friel's *Dancing at Lughnasa*, whether it is the re-membering and ritual burial of the drowned women in Le Marquand Hartigan's *La Corbière*, whether we recall the desperate longing that drives Marina Carr's protagonists or Tom Murphy's JPW, or Frank's account of the Ballybeg epiphany of the dancing dolphins, in Brian Friel's *Wonderful Tennessee*, the space of per-formance can become a place for the embodiment of spirit. In the many ritual moments of sharing, blessing and creating that charac-terize Frank McGuinness's work, audiences are invited within the new sacred space of theatre to travel through wounds and grief to imagine a new world.

Many of the plays I have studied shimmer with light, allow a glimpse of gold as the fine vein is brought to the surface. Within the cauldron of transformation, within the space of performance, the miracle can happen. Theatre as *temenos*, is the sacred container for the transmutation of energies. Through the poetic language of symbol, narrative, ritual and play, playwrights as soul-smiths par-ticipate in an ancient alchemical art. In the empty space of theatre playwrights bring the raw material of their texts into the crucible of performance, where actors and audiences work to transform their daring and dreaming into gold.

Bibliography

Adams Leeming, D., 'Quests'. *Encyclopaedia of Religion*, vol 12, ed. Mircea Eliade (New York: Macmillan, 1987), pp.146-52.

Aston, E., *An Introduction to Feminism and Theatre* (London: Routledge, 1995).

Barry, S., *Prayers of Sherkin. Boss Grady's Boys* (London: Methuen, 1991).

Belsey, C. & Moore, J., eds, *The Feminist Reader* (2ⁿᵈ edition) (USA: Blackwell, 1997).

Belsey, C., 'Constructing the Subject: deconstructing the text.' *Feminist Criticism and Social Change*, eds J. Newton & D. Rosenfelt (New York, London: Methuen, 1985), pp. 45-64.

--- *Critical Practice* (London: Routledge, 1980).

Bertha, C., ' 'Island of Otherness': Images of Irishness in Brian Friel's *Wonderful Tennessee.' Hungarian Journal of English and American Studies*, 2: 2, (1996): pp.129-142.

--- 'Six Characters in Search of a Faith: The Mythic and the Mundane in Wonderful Tennessee.' *Irish University Review*, 29: 1 (1999): pp.119-135.

Block Jr, E., 'Brian Friel's Faith Healer as Post-Christian Christian Drama.' *Literature and Theology*, 14: 2 June (2000): pp.189-207.

Boland, E., *In a Time of Violence* (Manchester: Carcanet, 1994).

Bolger, D., ed., *Druids, Dudes and Beauty Queens: The Changing Face of Irish Theatre* (Dublin: New Island Books, 2001).

--- *The Passion of Jerome* (London: Methuen, 1999).

Boroson, M., 'The Cosmic Playpen.' *The Irish Times Magazine*, 18 May 2002: p.66.

Bourke, A., *The Burning of Bridget Cleary: A True Story* (London: Pimlico, 1999).

Bourke, S., ed., *Rough Magic: First Plays* (Dublin: New Island Books, 1999).

Braidotti, R., *Patterns of Dissonance* (Oxford: Polity Press, 1991).

Brook, P., *The Empty Space* (London: Penguin, 1968).

Burke Brogan, P., *Eclipsed* (Clare: Salmon Publishing, 2001).

Burkman, K., ed., *Myth and Ritual in the Plays of Samuel Beckett* (London: Associated University Press, 1987).

Campbell, J., *The Hero With a Thousand Faces* (London: Fontana, 1993).

Carr, M., 'Dealing With The Dead.' *Irish University Review*, 28 (1998), pp.190-196.

--- *Ariel* (Co. Meath, Ireland: Gallery Books, 2002).

--- *By The Bog of Cats* (Co. Meath, Ireland: Gallery Books, 1998).

--- *On Raftery's Hill* (Co. Meath, Ireland: Gallery Books, 2000).

--- *Plays: One: Low in the Dark, The Mai, Portia Coughlan, By the Bog of Cats* (London: Faber & Faber, 1999).

--- *The Mai* (Co. Meath, Ireland: Gallery Books, 2000).

Caruth, C., ed., *Trauma: Explorations in Memory* (Baltimore: Johns Hopkins University Press, 1995).

Case, S. E., *Feminism and Theatre* (London: Macmillan, 1988).

Caslav Covino, D. 'Abject Criticism.' *Genders Online Journal*, 32 (2000), pp. 1-14.

Cave, R. A. 'Questing for Ritual and Ceremony in a Godforsaken World: *Dancing at Lughnasa* and *Wonderful Tennessee.*' *Hungarian Journal of English and American Studies*, 5: 1 (1999), pp.109-126.

Cixous, H., 'Aller à la mer.' *Modern Drama*, 27: 4, (1984), pp.546-48.

--- 'Sorties: Out and Out: Attacks/Ways Out/Forays.' *The Feminist Reader*, eds C. Belsey & J. Moore (London: Blackwell, 1989, 1997), pp.91-103.

--- 'The Laugh of the Medusa.' *Signs*. Summer (1976), pp.874-893.

Cixous, H. and Calle-Gruber, M., *Rootprints: Memory and Life Writing* (London: Routledge, 1997).

Clancy, P., ed., *Celtic Threads: Exploring the Wisdom of our Celtic Heritage* (Dublin: Veritas, 1999).

Clune, A., 'Mythologising Sweeney.' *Irish University Review*, 26 (1996), pp.48-60.

Clutterbuck, C., 'Lughnasa after Easter: Treatments of Narrative Imperialism in Friel and Devlin.' *Irish University Review*, 29:1 (1999), pp. 101-118.

Coady, M., 'Lost and Found in the Forest.' Programme Note for Jim Nolan's *Blackwater Angel.* The Abbey Theatre, (2001).

Sacred Play

Cole, D., *The Theatrical Event: A Mythos, a Vocabulary, a Perspective* (Connecticut: Wesleyan University Press, 1975).

Condren, M., *The Serpent and the Goddess: Women, Religion and Power in Celtic Ireland* (San Francisco: Harper and Row, 1989).

Costello, S.J., *The Irish Soul: in Dialogue* (Dublin: The Liffey Press, 2001).

Cottreau, D., 'Matriarchy Ascending: The Feminist Mytho-Poetics of Anne Devlin's *After Easter.*' *Hungarian Journal of English and American Studies*, 5: 1 (1999), pp.199-223.

Cousin, G., *Women in Dramatic Place and Time* (London: Routledge, 1996).

Cummings, S. T., 'The End of History: The Millennial Urge in the Plays of Sebastian Barry.' *A Century of Irish Drama: Widening the Stage*, eds Stephen Watt, Eileen Morgan and Shakir Mustafa (2000), pp.291-302.

Dentith, S., *Parody: The New Critical Idiom* (London: Routledge, 2000).

Devlin, A., *After Easter* (London: Faber & Faber, 1996).

Diamond, E., 'Mimesis, Mimicry, and the "True-Real".' *Modern Drama* 32, (1989), pp.58-72.

--- *Unmaking Mimesis* (London: Routledge, 1997).

Edwards, B., *The New Drawing on the Right Side of the Brain* (London: Harper Collins, 2001, 1979).

Egan, H. (S.J.), *An Anthology of Christian Mysticism* (Minnesota: Liturgical Press, 1991).

Eliade, M., *Shamanism: Archaic Techniques of Ecstasy* (Princeton, US: Princeton University Press, 1964).

--- *The Sacred and the Profane: The Nature of Religion*, trans. from the French W. Trask (London: Harvest, 1987).

Eliot, T. S., *Collected Poems 1909 – 1962* (London: Faber & Faber, 1963).

Epstein, M., *Going on Being: Buddhism and the Way of Change* (London: Continuum, 2001).

Feral, J., *The Powers of Difference. The Future of Difference*, eds Hester Eisenstein and Alice Jardine (New Brunswick, & London: Rutgers University Press, 1980).

FitzGibbon, G. 'The Poetic Theatre of Sebastian Barry.' *Theatre Stuff: Critical Essays on Contemporary Irish Theatre*, ed. Eamonn Jordan (Dublin: Carysfort Press, 2000), pp.224-35.

Forte, J., 'Realism, Narrative and the Feminist Playwright – A Problem of Reception.' *Modern Drama* 32, (1989), pp.115-127.

Friel, B., *Dancing at Lughnasa* (London: Faber & Faber, 1990).

--- *Faith Healer* (London: Faber & Faber, 1980).

--- *Plays: One: Philadelphia, Here I Come, The Freedom of the City, Living Quarters, Aristocrats, Faith Healer, Translations* (London: Faber & Faber, 1996).

--- *Plays: Two* (London: Faber & Faber, 1999).

--- *Wonderful Tennessee* (Co. Meath, Ireland: Gallery Books, 1993).

Gelpi, B. C. and Gelpi, A., eds, *Adriennne Rich's Poetry* (New York: W. & W. Norton & Co. 1975), pp.90-98.

Gilbert, H. and Tompkins, J. *Post-Colonial Drama: Theory, Practice, Politics* (London: Routledge, 1996).

Gilligan, A.-L., 'The Wisdom of Imagination: A Feminist Perspective.' *Irish Journal of Feminist Studies*, 4: 2 (2002), pp.31-38.

--- 'Feminist Theology and Imagination.' (1991) *The Field Day Anthology of Irish Writing*, vol. 4: *Irish Women's Writings and Traditions*, eds Angela Bourke et al. (Cork: Cork University Press, 2002), pp.702-705.

Gilsenan Nordin, I., ' "And/A Green Leaf of Language Comes Twisting Out of Her Mouth": Eilean Ni Chuilleanain and the Quest Theme.' *Irish University Review*, 31:2 (2001), pp.420-430.

Grant, D., 'Interview with Michael Harding.' *Theatre Ireland*, (1991), pp.46-47.

--- ed., *The Crack in the Emerald: New Irish Plays* (London: Nick Hern Books, 1990).

Grene, N., 'Talking it Through: *The Gigli Concert* and *Bailegangaire.*' *Talking about Tom Murphy*, ed. N. Grene (Dublin: Carysfort Press, 2002), pp.67-81.

--- *The Politics of Irish Drama: Plays in Context From Boucicault to Friel* (Cambridge: University Press, 1999).

Grimes, R. L., *Beginnings in Ritual Studies.* (Revised Edition) (University of South Carolina Press: 1995).

Hall, E., 'Dead Daughters in Carr and Euripides.' Programme Note for Marina Carr's *Ariel*, The Abbey Theatre, 2002.

Harding, M. '*Misogynist.*' *The Crack in the Emerald: New Irish Plays* (London: Nick Hern Books, 1990), pp.141-188.

--- 'Una Pooka' First Run 2: New Plays by Irish Writers (London: Nick Hern Books, 1990).

Harner, M., *The Way of the Shaman.* 3rd edition (USA: Harper San Francisco, 1990).

Harris, C., 'From Pastness to Wholeness: Stewart Parker's Reinventing Theatre.' *Colby Quarterly*, 27, 4 (1991), pp.233-41.

Hart-Davis, R. *The Plays of Ibsen: When We Dead Awaken* (London: Soho Square, 1960).

Hederman, M. P., 'Musings on Ariel.' Programme Note for Marina Carr's *Ariel*, The Abbey Theatre, 2002.

--- *Manikon Eros: Mad, Crazy Love* (Dublin: Veritas, 2000).

Henderson, L. 'A Fondness for Lament.' *Theatre Ireland* 17 (Dec.1988-Mar 1989), pp.18-20.

--- 'Innocence and Experience.' *Fortnight* CCXLV, Nov. 1986, p.26.

--- ' Men, Women and the Life of the Spirit in Tom Murphy's Plays.' *Irish Writers and Their Creative Process*, eds Jacqueline Genet and Wynne Hellegouarc'h. *Irish Literary Studies 48* (Gerards Cross, Buckinghamshire: Colin Smythe, 1996), pp.87-99.

Herr, C., 'The Erotics of Irishness.' *Critical Inquiry*, 17: 1 (1990), pp.1-34.

Horwitz, J., 'Coming Home: The Shaman's Work With Soul Loss.' http://www.shamanism.dk-articles

Houston, J. 'Living in One's and Future Myths.' *The Fabric of The Future*, ed. M.J. Ryan (Berkeley: Conari Press, 1998), pp.23-35.

Huizinga, J., *Homo Ludens: A Study of the Play-Element in Culture* (London: Routledge, 1949).

Hurt, J. 'Frank McGuinness and the Ruins of Irish History.' *A Century of Irish Drama: Widening the Stage*, eds Stephen Watt, Eileen Morgan and Shakir Mustafa (Indiana: University Press, 2000), pp.275-291.

Ingerman, S., *Soul Retrieval: Mending the Fragmented Self* (USA: Harper San Francisco, 1991).

Irigaray, L., 'When Our Lips Speak Together.' *Feminisms: A Reader*, ed. Maggie Humm (New York, London: Harvester Wheatsheaf, 1992), pp.207-210.

--- *Sexes and Genealogies* (New York: Columbia University Press, 1993).

Jackson, J., ' "Making the Words Sing": Interview with Tom Murphy.' *Hot Press*, Issue 4, (1991), pp.18-19.

Jordan, E., 'From Playground to Battleground: Metatheatricality in the Plays of Frank McGuinness.' *Theatre Stuff: Critical essays on Contemporary Irish Theatre*, ed. Eamonn Jordan (Dublin: Carysfort Press, 2000), pp.194-208.

--- The *Feast of Famine: The Plays of Frank McGuinness* (Bern: Peter Lang, 1997).

Judith, A., *Eastern Body Western Mind* (Berkeley: Celestial Arts, 1996).

Kearney, R., 'Myth as the Bearer of Possible Worlds: Interview with Paul Ricoeur.' *Crane Bag Book of Irish Studies* 1977-1981, eds M.P. Henderson and R. Kearney (Dublin: Blackwater Press, 1982), pp.260-66.

--- *On Stories* (London: Routledge, 2002).

--- *Strangers, Gods and Monsters* (London: Routledge, 2003).

--- *The God Who May Be: A Hermeneutics of Religion* (Indiana: University Press, 2001).

Keenan, B., *An Evil Cradling* (London: Vintage, 1992).

Kelleher, M., *The Feminization of Famine: Expressions of the Inexpressible* (Cork: Cork University Press, 1997).

Kilroy, T., *Talbot's Box* (Co. Meath, Ireland: Gallery Books, 1997).

Kornfield, J., *After the Ecstasy, the Laundry* (London: Rider, 2000).

Kristeva, J., 'Word, Dialogue and Novel.' *The Kristeva Reader*, ed. Toril Moi (Oxford: Basil Blackwell, 1986), pp.34-61.

Kurdi, M., 'Female Self Cure Through Revisioning and Refashioning Male/Master Narratives in Anne Devlin's *After Easter.*' *Hungarian Journal of English and American Studies*, 2: 2 (1996), pp.97-110.

--- *Codes and Masks: Aspects of Identity in Contemporary Irish Plays in an Intercultural Context* (Frankfurt: Peter Lang, 2000).

Lanters, J., 'Gender and Identity in Brian Friel's *Faith Healer* and Thomas Murphy's *The Gigli Concert.*' *Irish University Review*, 22: 2 (1992), pp.278-90.

--- 'Brian Friel's Uncertainty Principle.' *Irish University Review*, 29: 1 (1999), pp.162-75.

--- 'Playwrights of the Western World: Synge, Murphy, McDonagh.' *A Century of Irish Drama: Widening the Stage*, eds Stephen Watt, Eileen Morgan & Shakir Mustafa (Indiana: University Press, 2000), pp.204-222.

---'Violence and Sacrifice in Brian Friel's *The Gentle Island* and *Wonderful Tennessee.*' *Irish University Review*, 36 (1996), pp.163-76.

Larrington, C., ed. *The Feminist Companion to Mythology* (London: Pandora, 1992).

Le Marquand Hartigan, A., *La Corbière* in *Seen and Heard: Six New Plays by Irish Women* ed. Cathy Leeney (Dublin: Carysfort Press, 2001), pp.161-93.

--- *Immortal Sins* (Dublin: Salmon Poetry, 1993).

Leeney, C., *Dancing at Lughnasa*, Programme Note for Brian Friel's *Dancing at Lughnasa*, The Abbey Theatre: 1999.

--- ed., *Seen and Heard: Six New Plays by Irish Women* (Dublin: Carysfort Press, 2001).

Levertov, D., *Breathing the Water* (Newcastle upon Tyne: Bloodaxe Books, 1988).

Llewellyn-Jones, M., *Contemporary Irish Drama and Cultural Identity* (Bristol: Intellect Books, 2002).

Lojek, H., 'Difference Without Indifference: The Drama of Frank McGuinness and Anne Devlin.' *Eire-Ireland*, Vol.25 (1990), pp.56-68.

Loomba, A., *Colonialism/Postcolonialism* (London: Routledge,1998).

Lorde, A., *Sister Outsider* (New York: The Crossing Press, 1984).

Luft, J., 'Brechtian *Gestus* and The Politics of Tea in Christina Reid's *Tea in a China Cup*.' *Modern Drama*, 42 (1999), pp.214-22.

Mac Intyre, T., 'Programme Note to *Portia Coughlan*. Peacock Theatre 1996.' *The Theatre of Marina Carr: 'before rules was made'*, eds Cathy Leeney and Anna McMullan (Dublin: Carysfort Press, 2003), pp.80-2.

Matthews, C. and J., *The Encyclopaedia of Celtic Wisdom: A Celtic Shaman's Sourcebook* (London: Rider, 2001).

McCabe. P., 'Interview with Tony Clayton-Lea'. *Aer Lingus CARA Magazine*: (10/11/2003), p.35.

McDonagh, M., *The Lonesome West* (London: Royal Court Theatre, 1997).

--- 'Classics as Celtic Firebrand: Greek Tragedy, Irish Playwrights, and Colonialism.' *Theatre Stuff: Critical Essays on Contemporary Irish Theatre*, ed. Eamonn Jordan (Dublin: Carysfort Press, 2000), pp.16-26.

McGuinness, F., '*Faith Healer: All The Dead Voices*.' *Irish University Review*, 29: 1 (1999), pp.60-3.

--- 'Writing in Greek.' Programme Note for Marina Carr's *By The Bog of Cats*, The Abbey Theatre (1998).

--- ed., *The Dazzling Dark: New Irish Plays* (London: Faber & Faber, 1996).

--- *Gatherers*, unpublished play text courtesy of the author.

--- *Plays: One: The Factory Girls, Observe the Sons of Ulster Marching Towards the Somme, Innocence, Carthaginians, Baglady* (London: Faber & Faber, 1996).

--- *Plays: Two* (London: Faber & Faber, 2002).

--- *Someone Who'll Watch Over Me* (London: Faber & Faber, 1992).

McMullan, A., ' "In touch with some otherness" ': Gender, Authority and the Body in *Dancing at Lughnasa*.' *Irish University Review*, 29: 1 (1999), pp.90-100.

--- 'Gender, Authorship and Performance in Selected Plays by Contemporary Irish Women Playwrights: Mary Elizabeth Burke-Kennedy, Marie Jones, Marina Carr, Emma Donoghue.' *Theatre Stuff: Critical Essays on Contemporary Irish Theatre*, ed. Eamonn Jordan (Dublin: Carysfort Press, 2000), pp.34-46.

--- 'Unhomely Stages: Women Taking (a) Place in Irish Theatre.' *Druids, Dudes and Beauty Queens*, ed. Dermot Bolger (Dublin: New Island, 2001), pp.72-90.

Meehan, P., *Cell* (Dublin: New Island, 2000).

--- *Pillow Talk* (Co. Meath, Ireland: Gallery Books, 1994).

--- *The Man Who Was Marked by Winter* (Co. Meath, Ireland: Gallery Books, 1991).

--- 'Mrs. Sweeney' in *Rough Magic First Plays*, ed. Siobhan Bourke (Dublin: New Island Books, 1999), pp.393-464.

Mercier, P., *Pilgrims* Unpublished play text courtesy of The Passion Machine, 1993.

Merriman, V., 'Songs of Possible Worlds: Nation, Representation and Citizenship in the Work of Calypso Productions.' *Theatre Stuff*, ed. Eamonn Jordan (Dublin: Carysfort Press, 2000), pp.281-91.

Mikami, H., *Frank McGuinness and his Theatre of Paradox* (Buckinghamshire: Colin Smythe, 2002).

Mindell, A., *Sitting in the Fire: Large group transformation using conflict and diversity* (Portland OR: Lao Tse Press, 1995).

Monaghan, P., ed., *Irish Spirit: Pagan, Celtic, Christian, Global* (Dublin: Wolfhound Press, 2001).

Moore, T., *The Soul's Religion: Cultivating a Profoundly Spiritual Way of Life* (New York: Harper, 2002).

Morash, C., *A History of Irish Theatre 1601-2000* (Cambridge: University Press, 2002).

Moroney, M., 'Our Cousin Martin'. Programme Note for Martin McDonagh's *The Lonesome West*, The Gaiety Theatre, 2001.

Morrison, T., *Beloved* (London: Chatto & Windus, 1987).

Morse, D.E., ' "Sleepwalkers Along a Precipice": Staging Memory in Marina Carr's *The Mai.*' *Hungarian Journal of English and American Studies*, 2: 2 (1996), pp.112-121.

Murphy, T., 'The Creative Process.' *Irish Writers and Their Creative Process.* eds Jacqueline Genet and Wynne Hellegouarc'h. *Irish Literary Studies 48* (Buckinghamshire: Colin Smythe, 1996), pp.78-86.

--- *After Tragedy: Three Irish Plays by Thomas Murphy* (*The Gigli Concert, Bailegangaire, Conversations on a Homecoming*) (London: Methuen, 1988).

--- *Plays: One* (Dublin: Methuen, 1992).

--- *The Sanctuary Lamp* (Dublin: Co. Meath, Ireland: Gallery Books, 1984).

Murray, C., *Twentieth-Century Irish Drama: Mirror to Nation* (Manchester: University Press), pp.1997.

Myerhoff, B., 'The transformation of consciousness in ritual performances: some thoughts and questions.' *By Means of Performance: Intercultural Studies of Theatre and Ritual*, eds Richard Schechner, Willa Appel (Cambridge: University Press, 1990), pp.245-9.

Neil, R., 'Disability as Motif and Meaning in Friel's Drama.' *Hungarian Journal of English and American Studies*, 5.1. (1999), pp.143-59.

Ní Dhomhnaill, N., *Selected Poems.* trans. Michael Hartnett (Dublin: Raven Arts Press, 1986).

Nolan, J., *Blackwater Angel* (Co Meath, Ireland: Gallery Books, 2001).

O'Donohue, J., *Anam Chara: Spiritual Wisdom from the Celtic World* (London: Bantam Press, 1997).

---*Divine Beauty: The Invisible Embrace* (London: Bantam Press, 2003).

O'Dwyer, R. 'Dancing in the Borderlands: The Plays of Frank McGuinness.' *The Crows Behind the Plough: History and Violence in Anglo-Irish Poetry and Drama*, ed. Geert Lernout. Costerus, New Series, Vol. 79 (Amsterdam-Atlant: Rodopi, 1991), pp.99-115.

--- 'The Imagination of Women's Reality: Christina Reid and Marina Carr.' *Theatre Stuff: Critical Essays on Contemporary Irish Theatre*, ed. Eamonn Jordan (Dublin: Carysfort Press, 2000), pp.236-48.

Ó Murchú, D., *Evolutionary Faith* (New York: Orbis Books, 2002).

--- *Religion in Exile: A Spiritual Vision for the Homeward Bound* (Dublin: Gateway, 2000).

O'Toole, F., 'Irish Theatre: The State of the Art.' *Theatre Stuff: Critical essays on Contemporary Irish Theatre*, ed. Eamonn Jordan (Dublin: Carysfort Press, 2000), pp.47-58.

--- *Tom Murphy: The Politics of Magic* (updated and expanded edition) (Dublin: New Island Books, 1994).

Parker, S., 'State of Play.' *Canadian Journal of Irish Studies* 7: 1 (1981), pp.5-11.

--- *Dramatis Personae:* A John Malone Memorial Lecture, Belfast, Queen's University, 1986.

--- *Plays: Two: Northern Star, Heavenly Bodies, Pentecost* (UK: Methuen, 2000).

Pelletier, M., 'Dermot Bolger's Drama.' *Theatre Stuff: Critical Essays on Contemporary Irish Theatre*, ed. Eamonn Jordan (Dublin: Carysfort Press, 2000), pp.249-56.

Pilkington, L., *Theatre and the State in Twentieth Century Ireland: Cultivating the People* (London: Routledge, 2001).

Pine, R., *The Diviner: The Art of Brian Friel* (Dublin: University Press, 1999).

Primavesi, A., 'The Wisdom of Gaia.' *Irish Journal of Feminist Studies*, 4:2 (2002), pp.16-30.

Radford-Ruether, R., *New Woman, New Earth: Sexist Ideologies and Human Liberation* (San Francisco: Harper & Row, 1975).

Reid, C., *Plays: One: Tea in a China Cup, Did You Hear the One About the Irishman?, Joyriders, The Belle of Belfast City, My Name, Shall I Tell You My Name?, Clowns* (London: Methuen, 1997).

Reinelt, J., 'Feminist Theory and the Problem of Performance.' *Modern Drama*, 32, (1989), pp.48-57.

Rich, A., *Of Woman Born: Motherhood as Experience and Institution.* (New introduction by the Author) (London: Virago 1976, 1992).

--- *The Fact of A Doorframe: Poems Selected and New 1950 – 1984* (New York: W. W. Norton & Co. 1984).

--- *What is Found There: Notebooks on Poetry and Politics* (New York: W. W. Norton & Co. 1993).

Richards, S., 'Response to Fable and Vision: *The Morning After Optimism* and *The Sanctuary Lamp*, by Alexandra Poulain.' *Talking About Tom Murphy*, ed. Nicholas Grene (Dublin: Carysfort Press, 2002), pp.57-65.

Richtarik, M., ' "Ireland, the Continuous Past": Stewart Parker's Belfast History Plays.' *A Century of Irish Drama: Widening the Stage*, eds Stephen Watt, Eileen Morgan and Shakir Mustafa (Indiana: University Press, 2000): pp.256-74.

Roche, A., *Contemporary Irish Drama: From Beckett to McGuinness* (Dublin: Gill & Macmillan, 1994).

Rogers, A. G., 'Exiled Voices: Dissociation and repression in Women's Narratives of Trauma.' *Working paper 1*, Centre for Women's Studies, Trinity College Dublin, 1995.

Rooney, P., 'The 'Maleness' of Reason' (1994). *The Field Day Anthology Of Irish Writing*, vol. 4: *Irish Women's Writings and Traditions*, eds Angela Bourke et al. (Cork: Cork University Press, 2002), pp.708-712.

Rumi, *The Essential Rumi*, trans. Coleman Barks with John Moyne, (London: Penguin, 1999).

Ryan. M. J., ed., *The Fabric of the Future: Women Visionaries Illuminate the Path to Tomorrow* (Berkeley: Conari Press 1998).

Schechner, R. and Appel, W. eds, *By Means of Performance: Intercultural Studies of Theatre and Ritual* (Cambridge: University Press,1990).

Schechner, R., *The Future of Ritual: Writings on Culture and Performance* (London: Routledge, 1993).

Schussler-Fiorenza, E., *In Memory of Her: A Feminist Theological Reconstruction of Christian Origins* (New York; Crossroad, 1983).

Sihra, M., 'A Cautionary Tale: Marina Carr's *By The Bog of Cats*.' *Theatre Stuff: Critical Essays on Contemporary Irish Theatre*, ed. Eamonn Jordan (Dublin: Carysfort Press, 2000), pp.257-68.

--- 'Marina Carr in Conversation with Melissa Sihra.' *Theatre Talk*, eds L. Chambers et al. (Dublin: Carysfort Press, 2001), pp.55-63.

--- 'Writing in Blood'. Programme Note for Marina Carr's *Ariel*, The Abbey Theatre, 2002.

Throne, M., 'Brian Friel's *Faith Healer*. Portrait of a Shaman.' *Journal of Irish Literature*, 16, (1987): pp.18-24.

Tóibín, C., 'The Talk of the Town: The Plays of Billy Roche.' *Druids, Dudes and Beauty Queens*, ed. Dermot Bolger (Dublin: New Island, 2001), pp.18-29.

Tracy, D., *Plurality and Ambiguity: Hermeneutics, Religion, Hope* (London: SCM Press, 1988, 1987).

Turner, V., *Dramas, Fields and Metaphors* (Cornell: Ithaca, 1974).

--- *From Ritual to Theatre: The Human Seriousness of Play* (New York: Performing Arts Journal Publications, 1982).

--- *The Anthropology of Performance* (New York: PAJ Publications, 1986). `

--- 'Are there universals of performance in myth, ritual and drama?' *By Means of Performance: Intercultural Studies of Theatre and Ritual*, eds Richard Schechner and Willa Appel (Cambridge: University Press, 1990), pp.8-18.

--- *The Ritual Process* (New York: Gruyter, 1995).

Vandevelde, K. 'The Gothic Soap of Martin McDonagh.' *Theatre Stuff: Critical Essays on Contemporary Irish Theatre*, ed. Eamonn Jordan. (Dublin: Carysfort Press, 2000), pp. 292-302.

Vice, S., *Introducing Bakhtin* (Manchester: University Press, 1997).

Walker Bynum C., 'Introduction: The Complexity of Symbols.' *Gender and Religion: On the Complexity of Symbols*, eds Caroline Walker Bynum, Stevan Harrell, Paula Richman (Boston: Beacon Press, 1986), pp.1-20.

Wallace, C., 'Tragic Destiny and Abjection in Marina Carr's *The Mai, Portia Coughlan* and *By the Bog of Cats.*' *Irish University Review*, 31:2 (2001), pp.431-449.

Weisel, E., *Night* (London: Penguin Books, 1981).

White, V., 'Review of Michael Harding's *Misogynist.*' *Theatre Ireland*, 24, (Winter 1990/1991): p.41.

Whitford, M., *Luce Irigaray: Philosophy in the Feminine* (London & New York: Routledge, 1991).

Zappone, K., *The Hope for Wholeness: A Spirituality for Feminists* (Connecticut: Twenty-Third Publications, 1991).

Index

CARYSFORT PRESS

The Press aims to produce high quality publications which, though written and/or edited by academics, will be made accessible to a general readership. The organisation would also like to provide a forum for critical thinking in the Arts in Ireland, again keeping the needs and interests of the general public in view.

The company publishes contemporary Irish writing for and about the theatre.

Carysfort Press was formed in the summer of 1998. It receives annual funding from the Arts Council.

The directors believe that drama is playing an ever-increasing role in today's society and that enjoyment of the theatre, both professional and amateur, currently plays a central part in Irish culture.

Editorial and publishing inquiries to:

CARYSFORT PRESS Ltd

58 Woodfield, Scholarstown Road,
Rathfarnham, Dublin 16,
Republic of Ireland

T (353 1) 493 7383   F (353 1) 406 9815
e: info@carysfortpress.com
www.carysfortpress.com

NEW TITLES

GOETHE AND SCHUBERT

ACROSS THE DIVIDE
EDITED BY LORRAINE BYRNE & DAN FARRELLY

Proceedings of the International Conference, 'Goethe and Schubert in Perspective and Performance', Trinity College Dublin, 2003. This volume includes essays by leading scholars – Barkhoff, Boyle, Byrne, Canisius, Dürr, Fischer, Hill, Kramer, Lamport, Lund, Meikle, Newbould, Norman McKay, White, Whitton, Wright, Youens – on Goethe's musicality and his relationship to Schubert; Schubert's contribution to sacred music and the Lied and his setting of Goethe's Singspiel, Claudine. A companion volume of this Singspiel (with piano reduction and English translation) is also available.

ISBN 1-904505-04-X
Goethe and Schubert: Across the Divide. €25

ISBN 0-9544290-0-1
Goethe and Schubert: 'Claudine von Villa Bella'. €14

PLAYBOYS OF THE WESTERN WORLD

PRODUCTION HISTORIES
EDITED BY ADRIAN FRAZIER

'Playboys of the Western World is a model of contemporary performance studies.'

'The book is remarkably well-focused: half is a series of production histories of Playboy performances through the twentieth century in the UK, Northern Ireland, the USA, and Ireland. The remainder focuses on one contemporary performance, that of Druid Theatre, as directed by Garry Hynes. The various contemporary social issues that are addressed in relation to Synge's play and this performance of it give the volume an additional interest: it shows how the arts matter.' – Kevin Barry

ISBN 1-904505-06-6
€20

CRITICAL MOMENTS
FINTAN O'TOOLE ON MODERN IRISH THEATRE
EDITED BY JULIA FURAY & REDMOND O'HANLON

This new book on the work of Fintan O'Toole, the internationally acclaimed theatre critic and cultural commentator, offers percussive analyses and assessments of the major plays and playwrights in the canon of modern Irish theatre. Fearless and provocative in his judgements, O'Toole is essential reading for anyone interested in criticism or in the current state of Irish theatre.

ISBN 1-904505-03-1
€20

GEORG BÜCHNER: WOYZECK
A NEW TRANSLATION BY DAN FARRELLY

The most up-to-date German scholarship of Thomas Michael Mayer and Burghard Dedner has finally made it possible to establish an authentic sequence of scenes. The widespread view that this play is a prime example of loose, open theatre is no longer sustainable. Directors and teachers are challenged to "read it again".

ISBN 1-904505-02-3
€10

THE POWER OF LAUGHTER
EDITED BY ERIC WEITZ

The collection draws on a wide range of perspectives and voices including critics, playwrights, directors and performers. The result is a series of fascinating and provocative debates about the myriad functions of comedy in contemporary Irish theatre. Anna McMullan

As Stan Laurel said, it takes only an onion to cry. Peel it and weep. Comedy is harder. These essays listen to the power of laughter. They hear the tough heart of Irish theatre – hard and wicked and funny. Frank McGuinness

ISBN 1-904505-05-8
€20

SACRED PLAY
SOUL JOURNEYS IN CONTEMPORARY IRISH THEATRE BY ANNE F. O'REILLY

'Theatre as a space or container for sacred play allows audiences to glimpse mystery and to experience transformation. This book charts how Irish playwrights negotiate the labyrinth of the Irish soul and shows how their plays contribute to a poetics of Irish culture that enables a new imagining. Playwrights discussed are: McGuinness, Murphy, Friel, Le Marquand Hartigan, Burke Brogan, Harding, Meehan, Carr, Parker, Devlin, and Barry.'

ISBN 1-904505-07-4
€25

THE THEATRE OF FRANK MCGUINNESS
STAGES OF MUTABILITY
EDITED BY HELEN LOJEK

The first edited collection of essays about internationally renowned Irish playwright Frank McGuinness focuses on both performance and text. Interpreters come to diverse conclusions, creating a vigorous dialogue that enriches understanding and reflects a strong consensus about the value of McGuinness's complex work.

ISBN 1-904505-01-5
€20

THE THEATRE OF MARINA CARR
"BEFORE RULES WAS MADE" – EDITED BY
ANNA MCMULLAN & CATHY LEENEY

As the first published collection of articles on the theatre of Marina Carr, this volume explores the world of Carr's theatrical imagination, the place of her plays in contemporary theatre in Ireland and abroad and the significance of her highly individual voice.

ISBN 0-9534-2577-0
€20

THEATRE OF SOUND
RADIO AND THE DRAMATIC IMAGINATION
BY DERMOT RATTIGAN

An innovative study of the challenges that radio drama poses to the creative imagination of the writer, the production team, and the listener.

"A remarkably fine study of radio drama – everywhere informed by the writer's professional experience of such drama in the making…A new theoretical and analytical approach – informative, illuminating and at all times readable." *Richard Allen Cave*

ISBN 0-9534-2575-4
€20

HAMLET
THE SHAKESPEAREAN DIRECTOR
BY MIKE WILCOCK

"This study of the Shakespearean director as viewed through various interpretations of HAMLET is a welcome addition to our understanding of how essential it is for a director to have a clear vision of a great play. It is an important study from which all of us who love Shakespeare and who understand the importance of continuing contemporary exploration may gain new insights."

From the Foreword, by Joe Dowling, Artistic Director, The Guthrie Theater, Minneapolis, MN

ISBN 1-904505-00-7
€20

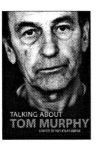

TALKING ABOUT TOM MURPHY

EDITED BY NICHOLAS GRENE

Talking About Tom Murphy is shaped around the six plays in the landmark Abbey Theatre Murphy Season of 2001, assembling some of the best-known commentators on his work: Fintan O'Toole, Chris Morash, Lionel Pilkington, Alexandra Poulain, Shaun Richards, Nicholas Grene and Declan Kiberd.

ISBN 0-9534-2579-7
€15

IN SEARCH OF THE SOUTH AFRICAN IPHIGENIE

BY ERIKA VON WIETERSHEIM AND DAN FARRELLY

Discussions of Goethe's "Iphigenie auf Tauris" (Under the Curse) as relevant to women's issues in modern South Africa: women in family and public life; the force of women's spirituality; experience of personal relationships; attitudes to parents and ancestors; involvement with religion.

ISBN 0-9534-2578-9
€10

THEATRE TALK

VOICES OF IRISH THEATRE PRACTITIONERS EDITED BY LILIAN CHAMBERS & GER FITZGIBBON

"This book is the right approach - asking practitioners what they feel."
Sebastian Barry, Playwright

"... an invaluable and informative collection of interviews with those who make and shape the landscape of Irish Theatre."
Ben Barnes, Artistic Director of the Abbey Theatre

ISBN 0-9534-2576-2
€20

THE STARVING AND OCTOBER SONG

TWO CONTEMPORARY IRISH PLAYS BY ANDREW HINDS

The Starving, set during and after the siege of Derry in 1689, is a moving and engrossing drama of the emotional journey of two men.

October Song, a superbly written family drama set in real time in pre-ceasefire Derry.

ISBN 0-9534-2574-6
€10

SEEN AND HEARD (REPRINT)

SIX NEW PLAYS BY IRISH WOMEN
EDITED WITH AN INTRODUCTION
BY CATHY LEENEY

A rich and funny, moving and theatrically exciting collection of plays by Mary Elizabeth Burke-Kennedy, Síofra Campbell, Emma Donoghue, Anne Le Marquand Hartigan, Michelle Read and Dolores Walshe.

ISBN 0-9534-2573-8
€20

UNDER THE CURSE

GOETHE'S "IPHIGENIE AUF TAURIS",
IN A NEW VERSION BY DAN FARRELLY

The Greek myth of Iphigenie grappling with the curse on the house of Atreus is brought vividly to life. This version is currently being used in Johannesburg to explore problems of ancestry, religion, and Black African women's spirituality.

ISBN 0-9534-2572-X
€10

THEATRE STUFF (REPRINT)

CRITICAL ESSAYS ON
CONTEMPORARY IRISH THEATRE
EDITED BY EAMONN JORDAN

Best selling essays on the successes and debates of contemporary Irish theatre at home and abroad.

Contributors include: Thomas Kilroy, Declan Hughes, Anna McMullan, Declan Kiberd, Deirdre Mulrooney, Fintan O'Toole, Christopher Murray, Caoimhe McAvinchey and Terry Eagleton.

ISBN 0-9534-2571-1
€20

URFAUST

A NEW VERSION OF GOETHE'S
EARLY "FAUST" IN BRECHTIAN MODE
BY DAN FARRELLY

This version is based on Brecht's irreverent and daring re-interpretation of the German classic.

"Urfaust is a kind of well-spring for German theatre… The love-story is the most daring and the most profound in German dramatic literature." Brecht

ISBN 0-9534257-0-3
€10

HOW TO ORDER
TRADE ORDERS DIRECTLY TO

CMD
Columba Mercier Distribution,
55A Spruce Avenue,
Stillorgan Industrial Park,
Blackrock,
Co. Dublin

T: (353 1) 294 2560
F: (353 1) 294 2564
E: cmd@columba.ie

or contact
SALES@BROOKSIDE.IE

*FOR SALES IN NORTH AMERICA
AND CANADA*

Dufour Editions Inc.,
124 Byers Road,
PO Box 7,
Chester Springs, PA 19425,
USA

T: 1-610-458-5005
F: 1-610-458-7103

FORTHCOMING

THE DRUNKARD,
A PLAY BY TOM MURPHY

GOETHE: MUSICAL POET, MUSICAL
CATALYST, ED. LORRAINE BYRNE